SCIENCE FICTION CINEMA

For my parents – Joyce and Peter

SCIENCE FICTION CINEMA
BETWEEN FANTASY AND REALITY

Christine Cornea

EDINBURGH UNIVERSITY PRESS

Edinburgh University Press Ltd
22 George Square, Edinburgh

Typeset in 10/12.5 Adobe Sabon
by Servis Filmsetting Ltd, Manchester, and
printed and bound in Great Britain by
Antony Rowe Ltd, Chippenham, Wilts

A CIP record for this book is available from the British Library

ISBN 978 0 7486 2465 2 (hardback)
ISBN 978 0 7486 1642 8 (paperback)

CONTENTS

ACKNOWLEDGEMENTS AND THANKS

As many academics will know, researching and writing a book like this can feel like a very solitary task, with many hours spent trawling through library catalogues, repeatedly reviewing films and, in the later stages, locked behind an office door, hunched over the keyboard of a computer. However, in looking back over this process it is possible to see how much is owed to family, friends and colleagues for their patience and support. I certainly owe a great debt of thanks to my parents, my sister, brother-in-law, niece and a number of friends, who have not seen me very much over the last couple of years. Gratitude is also long overdue to colleagues, especially those who have given up time in their busy schedules to offer feedback on various chapter drafts. Among those colleagues I would especially like to thank are Mark Jancovich for reading no less than four draft chapters, as well as Sue Harper and Dave Allen who both read early drafts of one or two chapters. I would also like to thank both Linda Ruth Williams and my colleagues at the University of East Anglia for their support and encouragement. In addition, thanks are due to Sarah Edwards, Sarah Hall, and James Dale from Edinburgh University Press, Leslie Mitchner and the editorial staff from Rutgers University Press, and Cheryl Thomas from the Kobal Picture Desk.

This book would not have been completed without the research leave grant awarded to me by the Arts and Humanities Research Council in 2004. Their financial support gave me the time away from teaching that I needed to carry out further research and writing. I am also indebted to The British Academy for awarding me a conference travel grant in 2004 that enabled my attendance at the Society for Cinema and Media Studies conference in Atlanta, USA. This gave me the opportunity to present a paper which represented an early draft of the second part of Chapter 6 of this book. Further, thanks are due to the Centre for European and International Studies Research group at the University of Portsmouth for funding my accommodation expenses for this conference. I must also thank the School of Film and Television at the University of East Anglia for providing further funds in the completion of this book. In addition, I would like to acknowledge the academic journal, *The Velvet Light Trap*, who published my article 'David Cronenberg's *Crash* and Performing Cyborgs' in 2003. I have further extended and revised some of my earlier ideas in this article for Chapter 7.

Finally, my gratitude goes to my interviewees, who gave very generously of their valuable time and provided me with important information and viewpoints in answer to my questions. Without exception I was inspired by all of the practitioners that I was privileged to speak with in my research for this book: Brian Aldiss, William Gibson, Billy Gray, Roland Emmerich, Joe Morton, Dean Norris, Ken Russell, Paul Verhoeven, Stan Winston – thanks to you all.

PREFACE

I must have been about ten years old when my parents proudly demonstrated their new tape recording machine. They had recorded a conversation with friends that had taken place a few days earlier. Of course they were primarily showing off the wonders of this technology to their children, but I distinctly recall that the discussion I heard revolved around their confusion over what was meant by the closing sequence in *2001: A Space Odyssey* (dir. Stanley Kubrick, 1968), a film that they had recently seen. This may have been the event that sparked my interest in the science fiction genre as I remember wishing I had seen the images that had caused so much debate. In my teenage years, without really knowing what I was looking for, I was drawn to the science fiction novels of John Wyndham, Doris Lessing and Arthur C. Clark. In retrospect I think that a form of quiet teenage rebellion had much to do with my interest in the genre at this time. Escaping from the 'girly fantasies' offered by the likes of *Jackie* magazine or the BBC television series *Ballet Shoes*, science fiction seemed to offer me a far more exciting and thought provoking landscape of opportunity. This quiet rebellion was further compounded when I managed to slip in to see my first 'X' film, *Zardoz* (dir. John Boorman, 1974), at barely fifteen years of age. Less interested in the sex scenes than the kaleidoscope of colourful and surreal imagery set before me, this illicit viewing left me with the feeling that I had acquired some kind of sneak preview to the future. It was not until years later that I would come to examine and question the attractions of science fiction. So, in some part, this book is the result of a reflective process that was set in motion when I returned to higher education in the early 1990s.

While I retain a subjective fascination with the science fiction film genre, my aim with this book was to place the thematic and formal concerns raised by science fiction films within wider cultural and historical contexts. The book therefore follows the history and development of the film genre by situating the films under discussion. It seemed to me that this was what was missing in the few broad based academic accounts of the genre. For instance, Vivian Sobchack's *Screening Space: The American Science Fiction Film* (1993) was largely concerned with mapping out the genre's visual and narrative conventions. To do this each chapter drew upon an eclectic range of examples from a variety of historical periods. Sobchack's skilful account of the formal elements of the science fiction film certainly paved the way for its serious, academic consideration, but I was keen to trace some of the historical influences and pressures that informed the development of this genre. Furthermore, although J. P. Telotte's more recent publication, *Science Fiction Film* (2001), is a usefully concise introduction for students, its brief report on the historical trajectory of the American film genre does not engage with the interplay between different national and transnational cinemas. This is an important area given the genre's centrality in an increasingly globalised film market. In understanding the genre as existing beyond the American limits imposed by earlier academics, my own book offers analysis of this kind of interplay by looking at British, Australian, French, Russian and Japanese cinema's engagement with science fiction as part of an overall aim to place films within the cultural context from which they emerged.

Although my study follows a chronological line from early film through to contemporary science fiction, each chapter also focuses upon a specific topic. From the outset I knew that it would not be possible to write an exhaustive account of this hugely prolific genre, so I elected to concentrate on what I felt were dominant or important issues in dealing with a specific period. That is not to say that each of the chapters are somehow divorced from one another, aside from my making references back and forth, it is my hope that readers will relate some of my propositions and ideas to a broader range of examples than those I have chosen.

In the act of locating the films under discussion I have drawn upon a variety of approaches. In my efforts to provide both a breadth and depth of analysis, this study makes free use of a range of popular texts and reviews, as well as previous academic work in the area. I also apply pertinent academic theory in scrutinising the principles and aesthetic conventions of the films, as set within the historical and cultural context from they emerged. In addition, I have included a number of original interviews with practitioners, which I carried out as part of my research for this book. Although I do make reference to the interviews in my analysis of the films, after much consideration I decided to include these as separate from the main body of each chapter. There were several reasons for this decision. First, I was struck by the amount of information imparted by my interviewees and appreciated their thoughtful comments in answer to my questions. The material gathered seemed valuable to me and while I approached the transcripts in a critical manner, I was reluctant to simply take quotes out of context in compiling my own ideas about the genre. This book has therefore given me the opportunity to present my interview material as a further resource for study, as well as a kind of parallel story in looking at the historical development of the genre. The interviews shed further light on the production processes involved in making specific films as well as offering some insight into how these practitioners view their own work within the field. It was necessary to edit some of the interviews, but I have kept this to a minimum. In this way I hope that I have done some justice to this material and have conveyed as accurately as possible the discussions that took place.

Finally, I would like to point out that in dealing with such a wide range of examples it was not always possible to provide synopses of the films. However, I have endeavoured to provide an outline of a film's narrative or of specific visual sequences where I have felt that it was especially appropriate and also where I was dealing with less well known films. To some extent, I have assumed that readers are familiar with many of the mainstream films I discuss or that they might supplement their reading by seeking out films that they have not previously seen.

LIST OF ILLUSTRATIONS

1. INTRODUCTION: THE FORMATION OF THE GENRE

Figure 1.1   Fritz Lang's future city in *Metropolis* (1927). UFA / The Kobal Collection.

Definitions and Approaches

There are almost as many definitions of science fiction as there are critics who have attempted to define it as a genre. Debate and argument has raged for several decades as to exactly what constitutes the essential structures and characteristics of science fiction and over which texts should or should not be included within this generic category.[1] This is most apparent in studies of science fiction novels, where definitions have been bound up with efforts to valorise popular works previously thought of as unworthy or frivolous. For instance, the practitioner and critic Isaac Asimov suggested:

> We can define science fiction as that branch of literature that deals with the human response to changes in the level of science and technology – it being understood that the changes involved would be rational ones in keeping with what was known about science, technology and people.[2]

A broader definition came from the writer and critic Judith Merril, who understood science fiction as 'speculative fiction' and as a literature that 'makes use of the traditional 'scientific method' to examine some postulated approximation of reality.'[3] This suggests that over and above the possible subject matter or focus of the narrative, there is a particular attitude, approach or style of thought inherent within the genre. In addition, Merril's description links the genre with an earlier tradition of utopian fiction, at least as far back as Edward

Bellamy's *Looking Backward: 2000–1887* (first published 1888) and William Morris's *News from Nowhere* (first published 1890). Both of these novels had distinct political agendas and described alternative worlds, which implicitly criticised the values of contemporary society.

A more 'weighty' definition comes from the academic Darko Suvin, who reads science fiction as a literature of 'cognitive estrangement'; a literature that defamiliarises reality and encourages the reader to contemplate upon the known world from a distanced perspective. For Suvin, 'SF is distinguished by the narrative dominance or hegemony of a fictional "novum" (novelty, innovation) validated by cognitive logic.'[4] On a simple level then, the fictional inventions or non-human characters that colonise the genre (e.g. the rockets, spacecrafts, robots, aliens etc.) are logically justified within the world of the genre at the same time as these objects/characters remain outside of a known reality.

The above definitions emphasise conscious, rational and intellectual engagement (on behalf of the writer and reader), thereby separating the genre from the irrational or unconscious meanderings of the human mind. While all of these definitions are illuminating, I do not think that they fully account for the astonishing and sometimes bizarre worlds created in the name of science fiction. Surely we cannot deny the more absurd and incredible elements at play in even the most 'serious' examples of the genre? In my view, Tzvetan Todorov's account of 'the fantastic' as a literary genre offers a path for science fiction that more readily accepts its relationship to that which stands outside of the rational or the realistic.[5] In his study of 'the fantastic', Todorov describes a form that sits in between two other narrative forms: the marvellous and the uncanny. According to Todorov, the marvellous focuses upon the supernatural, upon that which stands outside of the known world, while the uncanny narrative is concerned with the inner workings of the unconscious mind. Just as both of these narrative forms might present the reader with seemingly unfamiliar or irrational events, their worlds can be approached as either originating from a supernatural place that lies outside our understanding or springing from the unconscious mind. In relation to these otherwise incompatible forms, the fantastic vacillates between that which remains beyond comprehension or rational explanation and that which emanates from the deeper recesses of the human mind. Todorov tracks a historical shift toward the uncanny as opposed to the marvellous in recent fiction, which, aside from the influence of the work of Sigmund Freud, I would suggest can be accounted for by the increasing cultural dominance of scientific rationalism. Although Todorov's examples are largely drawn from established literary works (by the likes of Edgar Allan Poe and Henry James) he does make several references to science fiction. For Todorov:

> The best science fiction texts are organized analogously. The initial data are supernatural: robots, extraterrestrial beings, the whole interplanetary

context. The narrative movement consists in obliging us to see how close these apparently marvelous elements are to us, to what degree they are present in our life.[6]

So, the reader of science fiction is caught between that which exists outside of the laws of a known world and that which might be read as a logical extension of the known world.

Picking up on Todorov's work, Rosemary Jackson prefers to see the fantastic as a mode, rather than a genre. Jackson also modifies Todorov's model by replacing the uncanny with what she terms as the mimetic and thereby locating the fantastic in between the marvellous and the mimetic. According to Jackson, the marvellous is exhibited in forms like the fairy tale and science fiction; forms that present the reader with worlds which stand outside of a known world. In opposition to the marvellous, the mimetic is to be found in 'narratives which claim to imitate an external reality.'[7] For Jackson: 'Unlike the marvelous or the mimetic, the fantastic is a mode of writing which enters a dialogue with the 'real' and incorporates that dialogue as part of its essential structure.'[8] Taking my cue from both Todorov and Jackson, I believe that science fiction is most usefully understood as a genre that relies upon the fantastic. I would also offer a further reformation of these two models, which I think is perhaps more useful in terms of the science fiction film: I would suggest that science fiction is a genre that is demonstrably located in between fantasy and reality. My usage of the term fantasy rather than the fantastic is meant to open up this model to further connotations beyond the stricter usages in literary theory. For Jackson, the fantastic is essentially subversive, and while I think this is useful to bear in mind, I would certainly not like to claim all science fiction films as subversive. As will become apparent, there are many film examples that readily support conventional viewpoints and that appear devoid of the kind of revolutionary impulse that Jackson describes in relation to the fantastic. Rather than evoking the fantastic, in that strict sense, the veneer of invention often conceals a reactionary, as opposed to a progressive or alternative, vision of a possible world. I should also explain that when I refer to 'reality' here, I mean the perceived model of the known world as constructed through narratives and through media. So, unlike Jackson's mimetic narrative, my use of the term 'reality' is meant to suggest the ways in which 'realistic' narratives might be seen as part of the world we know, as feeding into that world, rather than as a separate form that simply duplicates the known world.

Writing in the early 1990s, Brooks Landon presented a strong argument for seeing science fiction film as very different from written science fiction. In dispute with those critics who have long found science fiction films to be pitifully lacking in comparison to science fiction novels, Landon was keen to separate film from the written form, stating: 'the two media are frequently, if not always, driven by very different concepts in pursuit of very different goals.'[9] He continued his argument by stressing the sovereignty of the *image* in film as opposed to the *idea* in science fiction literature and although he admitted to the influences that science fiction film has had upon the written novel, he did not believe that the traffic had travelled in the other direction. The cyberpunk writer, William Gibson, largely agrees with Landon's position (see interview on pp. 26–8), although he does admit to a recent shift apparent in cyberpunk's interaction with popular culture. I think that in formulating his argument Landon overstated the differences between science fiction literature and film at the expense of their affiliations. However, this was a point that needed to be stressed if science fiction films were to be taken seriously by academia. I can also see how, as a writer, Gibson would judge film as having had a more powerful impact upon popular culture, but I do think this underestimates the level of influence that science fiction novels have had upon the film genre. I believe there is much that can be learned from the debates surrounding the written form and from paying attention to the interplay between various media. Since at least the 1930s, science fiction has established itself across a variety of media and fans have not necessarily confined themselves to one area in seeking out the genre. So, even though my primary subject of study concerns the specificities of science fiction film, this book will regularly refer to examples of the genre that can found on television, in books, comics, video games and even fine art, as part of my project to locate the films within a wider cultural context.

Unlike much literary theory, film theorists have tended to see generic categories as the product of industrial and commercial practices. So, from this perspective film genres are constructed by an industry that seeks to identify consumer markets, control efficient production and marketing, and maximise profit. Within this context, the formation of a successful and long-lasting film genre then relies upon both creating and satisfying consumer demand. Classically, film academics have therefore set about unpacking a particular genre in terms of its structures, themes, narrative strategies and repeated visual iconography in order to offer up informed criticism and exposure of a genre's underlying conventions and codes. Alongside this, film academics have also studied the response of spectators to particular genres in order to understand the specific relationship between a film text and its audience. The problem with science fiction has been that it does not readily submit to the methods of analysis that have flourished in approaching other film genres. It would be churlish to suggest that this means there is no such thing as science fiction film, after all both popular and academic publications have long used the term 'science fiction' to describe certain films and in this sense the genre has been spoken into existence by the discourses that surround the film industry. Nevertheless, it has proved hard to pin down using film genre theory and the supposed boundaries of the genre remain less than easy to distinguish. There are many reasons for this, one being an ever broadening definition of what counts as science and the way in which a scientific approach is now harnessed in areas of study that would not have previously been defined as science. At a basic level then this fictional form now has a wider variety of topics to choose from and can engage with an extensive number of scientific disciplines. Furthermore, the relevance of this fictional form has also grown alongside the hasty expansion of science and technology since the beginnings of the industrial revolution. But also important in this regard is science fiction's simultaneous reliance upon fantasy and upon reality. This makes it a particularly malleable genre that can deal with a far wider variety of themes and concerns than most recognised genres. Moreover, it means that it can stand both within and outside of the conventions of classical realism (certainly as a style associated with classical narrative Hollywood cinema). So, for instance, even when a science fiction film clearly adopts the conventions of Hollywood realism, or, as in some cases, goes so far as present itself in a kind of pseudo-documentary style, its relationship to fantasy can work to undermine those same conventions.

In discussing the difficulties of definition associated with science fiction, J. P. Telotte suggests that the genre falls under a more general category of fantasy film, which includes the musical and horror film. He then goes on to point to their shared concerns and, drawing upon Todorov's model, maps the marvellous/fantastic/uncanny onto a variety of science fiction films.[10] Telotte's attempt to blur the boundaries between these fantasy genres certainly works to set science fiction within a wider framework of films, but this approach does not always account for the ways in which the genre operates in the larger context of the film industry. For instance, where classical genres like the musical and the horror film have long been segregated from the strict codes and conventions associated with realism, science fiction has been harder to ghettoise in this way. This is partly due to the increasing self-reflexivity in film form that came with the post-classical age and with the emergence of science fiction film into the mainstream at this time, but it is also due to the genre's unusual relationship with reality. I would therefore contend that rather than drawing science fiction under the heading of 'fantasy film' it is more accurately situated between 'fantasy genres' like the musical and the horror film and those genres that more fully conform to whatever style of realism is current and most dominant at the time of their release. As much as I am claiming a special place for science fiction, I agree with Telotte that it is informative to track science fiction's relationship with the 'fantasy genres'. Of course, it has much in common with both the horror and musical film. All three genres are known for employing moments of spectacle that seem to address the audience directly, and each has built up a repertoire of conventions that are rarely found in genres more closely aligned with classical realism. However, even though both the musical and horror film have the potential to disrupt realism and by extension the way in which we might view reality, they are more usually regarded as separate from those genres that purport to imitate or replicate a known reality. Where the musical and the horror film have largely been considered in isolation of standard realist films, science fiction has forged a relationship with realism that makes it a far more indeterminate genre.

Science fiction has certainly borrowed from both the musical and horror film. For instance, the numerous moments in science fiction films when the narrative flow is stalled to make way for visual spectacle resembles the way in which song and/or dance numbers are commonly structured into the narrative of a musical film. Also the repeated use of the diegetic audience in science fiction overlaps with the diegetic audience of the musical as a device that guides the film spectator's response. Although a few hybrid science fiction/musicals certainly exist (e.g. *Just Imagine* [dir. David Butler, 1930]), it is generally easy to distinguish between these two genres, even given their structural similarities. But, as is frequently remarked upon, it can be more difficult to distinguish between science fiction and the horror genre in the case of a number of films. One answer is to look to audience response in establishing generic boundaries. In film theory, part of what defines the horror film lies in its mode of address and its ability to induce a particular response. Indeed, a focus upon audience response is what Vivian Sobchack comes to rely upon when she states: 'ultimately, the horror film evokes fear, the SF film interest'.[11] Sobchack notably goes on to look at the figure of the monster in the so called 'creature features' of the 1950s. These films have proved problematic for theorists and fans alike because they do not fit snugly into either the science fiction or horror genres. Following two world wars, the distinctly dystopian turn in science fiction films of the 1950s led to the genre borrowing from horror in its depiction of science in a less than positive light. But, almost equally, you could say that horror films often sought to diminish the distance between science and magic, thereby updating their subject matter as well as questioning the moral implications of playing with 'God's mysterious design'. Rather than attempting to separate these genres, I remain content that certain films might always oscillate between being seen as one genre or the other. Indeed, the blurring of boundaries between these genres is the strength of some of these films rather than their weakness. The clashing of genres here allows for comment upon the kind of world views that each has to offer, as well as allowing for a degree of audience participation in deciding how to view the film. Having said that, I am well aware that commercial concerns affect the way in which a film is classified and how it might then be approached by audiences.

Both Steve Neale and Rick Altman have recently reassessed film genre theory and overturned many of the received assumptions of the discipline. Neale has achieved this by paying particular attention to the history of generic categories and concludes by calling for an expanded and more flexible conception of genres within film studies.[12] Altman has also urged academics to reassess their approach to genre and especially to reconsider the relationships between audiences, critics and the film industry. In looking specifically at how genres form and transform over time, he refers to *The Creature from the Black Lagoon* (dir. Jack Arnold, 1954) as a prime example of what he calls 'regenrification'. An analysis of the iconography and mode of address of this film would suggest that it falls firmly under the 'creature feature' category. However, as Altman points out, science fiction was proving to be more popular with audiences at this time, so in marketing the film Universal Studios simply redefined it as a science fiction.[13] As has already been pointed out, the boundaries between those genres which blatantly draw upon fantasy in one form of another (musical, horror, science fiction) tend to be less fixed. Therefore these films make ideal candidates in discussing marketing strategies, critical categorisation, or in highlighting some of the weaknesses of an academic theory of genre that fails to take into consideration the conflicting forces and pressures that work to formulate and reformulate genres. In this respect, I am not trying to deny that this study might play a part in that categorisation and assessment process. On the contrary, this book represents an eagerness to join in with the debates that surround science fiction, even as I take up a more academic and objective viewpoint. If one thing is clear about this genre, it is that it has long served as focus for debate. Indeed, writers and critics of science fiction novels have often characterised their own pursuits in terms of a kind dialogue. Samuel R. Delany has called science fiction writing 'a vast and sprawling debate, a great and often exciting dialogue',[14] and this 'dialogue' is also clear in Brian Aldiss's comments (see interview on pp. 22–6). Here he freely admits to answering to other science fiction novels in his own work. As a film genre, perhaps this debate continues on some level in the way that the images and narratives of each film might answer to each other. Throughout my interviews you will find an unusual willingness to admit to previous influences, as well as the creative efforts of the 'team' in making particular films. Admittedly, intertextuality is necessary to the formation of genres, but I would argue that it becomes especially apparent in science fiction. This is foregrounded because the genre deals in the visualisation of imagined images; images that are in turn highlighted by their curious relationship with reality. But aside from the need for genre films to repeat and/or alter familiar terrain and iconography, science fiction also allows for, in fact requires, new imagery and new ideas. In this way, perhaps science fiction film also permits the kind of debate witnessed among critics, writers and aficionados of the written novels.

More than any other genre, science fiction has inspired the creation of vast networks of fans drawn from an extraordinarily wide variety of social backgrounds. These fans have avidly and openly communicated their thoughts and ideas through fanzines, conventions and more recently through internet sites. While there can be little doubt that this fan culture is now encouraged as a component of the film franchises built up around the post-classical, science fiction blockbuster series', fans are also known for intervening and even subverting the narratives and visual components of particular films or series. The *Star Trek* television series and films provide the most obvious example of this phenomenon, in particular those instances of 'textual poaching' when stories and characters are rewritten to bring out an assumed subtext or to alter the sexuality of a character.[15] At the least, this signals a very active science fiction audience, whether their activities are understood as engaging in enlightening debate or seen as an escapist isolation from reality. Also, just as science fictions have drawn upon the latest speculations in science, many scientists are no longer ashamed to admit that they are fans of the genre: Stephen Hawking's liking for the genre is well known and NASA's close associations with *Star Trek* have been well documented by Constance Penley.[16] The tropes and icons of science fiction have also entered into popular culture and even political rhetoric: who can forget President Reagan's announcement concerning the proposed 'Star Wars' project. There is much evidence to suggest that science fiction has become a significant and widely accepted element of cultural reality.

Part of the reason why I find science fiction attractive as a focus for study is because of its inherent uncertainties. For instance, Altman states that 'most genre critics prefer to deal with films that are clearly and ineluctably tied to the genre in question'.[17] This has certainly not been my approach to science fiction. For instance, I have included discussion of films that are less than clear examples of the genre and have chosen to read films like *Crash* (dir. David Cronenberg, 1996) and *The Terminal Man* (dir. Michael Hodges, 1974) as science fictions. I am not sure that it is possible to consider science fiction in the kind of vacuum that Altman suggests is prevalent among genre theorists. I am not sure that science fiction can be successfully removed from at least some discussion of other genres or from the ways in which these films have been categorised within specific historical, cultural and production contexts. At the opening of his study of science fiction writing in the twentieth century, Edward James stated: 'sf today is certainly very different from sf in 1970, let along 1930. To understand sf, therefore, one is forced to become a historian.'[18] I think this also holds true for science fiction film, and while I pay close attention to the formal elements of the film genre, I am also interested in how and why intra-generic cycles of films emerged at particular times and how/why certain thematic concerns come to the fore or are introduced within particular historical contexts. Therefore this book follows a chronological line from early film through to recent examples of the genre. In the second half of this introductory chapter I will be taking a brief look at what might be called proto-science fiction films. That is those films that came before the science fiction film boom of the 1950s. The second chapter then looks in some depth at the American films of the 1950s and focuses upon the social concerns of the period as played out in science fiction. I specifically look at the figuration of the boy in these films as well as the apparent anxieties surrounding the changing role of women in society. At the close of this chapter I make some mention of overseas influences upon the American films and undertake a comparative analysis with British-made science fiction films. Chapter 3 then moves on to discuss a range of films that appeared in the 1960s, before concentrating my analysis on a specific cycle of films that appeared in the late 1960s through to the 1970s. I call this cycle the 'new art' films and look at the ways in which they appropriated and utilised psychedelic imagery, as associated with the counter-cultural movements of the time. While most of the film examples in this chapter were produced in America, I also discuss the influence of European art and art-house film and finish by looking at a number of films produced in the UK. Chapter 4 then concentrates on the advent of the blockbuster science fiction film series. In association with this I look at the depiction of the masculine subject in mainstream American science fiction films from the 1980s into the 1990s. The final section then sets my chosen films within a wider discussion concerning science fiction and the global film market. This also allows for a brief discussion of French, Australian and Japanese science fiction films. Following the focus upon masculinity in Chapter 4 my Chapter 5 looks at the representation of the feminine subject in science fiction. Leading up to my main discussion concerning the central female in science fiction films that appeared in the 1990s, context is provided by referring back to earlier examples of films that featured active female protagonists. Chapter 6 is in some ways broader in scope than some of the other chapters. Here I look at how issues of race are played out in science fiction films. Beginning with an outline of some of the theoretical approaches to racial difference, the chapter is basically split into three main sections. The beginning of the first section sketches out a historical trajectory of the way that the African or Afro-Caribbean American has been represented within the genre from the 1960s onwards, and the second section begins with a look at how the 'oriental' has been featured in science fiction from early film onwards. These openings are intended as backdrops to the main focus in each section, which concentrates on the black and oriental subject in the 'virtual reality' films of the 1990s. The closing section of Chapter 6 takes a comparative look at Euro-American films in this regard, noting marked differences as well as similarities between their representations of racial issues as compared to the American-produced films. Having reached the turn of the millennium, Chapter 7 concentrates on the performance strategies associated with the genre and the special significance of generic performance in contemporary science fiction film. Using David Cronenberg's films *Crash* (1996) and *eXistenZ* (1999) as my primary examples I explore the role of performance within these films as well as discussing the wider implications of performance as encouraged by video and computer games. Chapter 8 concentrates on the technology of science fiction films, both as an intra- and extra-diegetic component of the genre. The main discussion looks at the introduction of computer-generated imagery in science fiction films and includes some speculation as to how the genre might be seen as complicit with its own demise, as we move into a post-celluloid era. Finally I contemplate how the events of 11 September 2001 have impacted upon the genre.

This chapter outline indicates that I am not approaching the genre as though it were somehow beyond history or transhistorical in nature. On the contrary, my efforts are compelled by an eagerness to understand the formation and reformation of this widely recognised genre over time and the specific ways in which science fiction has engaged with the reality of a contemporaneous world.

TRADITIONS, FORERUNNERS AND SCIENCE FICTION FILMS

Any attempt to trace the antecedents of an established genre is fraught with difficulty. In an account of early science fiction writing, Edward James warns:

> It is clear that if we apply the term 'science fiction' to a type of literature produced in the nineteenth and early twentieth centuries, we are applying our own late twentieth-century preconceptions and trying to impose the idea of a genre onto what would in the nineteenth century have been perceived as a disparate and almost random grouping of several different types of story.[19]

Set against the backdrop of an industrial 'machine age' and a period of colonial imperialism, there are numerous European examples of popular stories that tell of strange and wonderful journeys to previously uncharted territories and stories about scientific invention and future worlds. While these may not have been grouped together under the generic label 'science fiction' it is possible to detect both formal and thematic elements that appear to have made their way into later science fiction writing and into films. Well known examples include the stories of Jules Verne, which were published under the collective label of 'voyages extraordinaires' in France. The fantastical journeys undertaken in Verne's *From the Earth to the Moon* (first published 1864) and *Twenty Thousand Leagues Under the Sea* (1869) required that he invent futuristic space rockets and submarines to transport his characters. So, these stories clearly combined the contemporary zest for exploration with a passion for machines and scientific invention. On the other side of the Channel, H. G. Wells' *The Time Machine* (1895), *The Island of Doctor Moreau* (1896), *The Invisible Man* (1897) and *The War of the Worlds* (1898) were generally regarded as 'scientific romances'; a term that was also applied to Verne's work when it was translated and published in Britain. Wells was a political and social commentator and his novels are often taken as critiques of Britain's colonial actions abroad or commentary upon the social implications of scientific discovery and endeavour. Certainly not the only writers of this kind of fiction, both Verne and Wells were later celebrated as science fiction pioneers and their work claimed in the formation of respected canons of the genre.

When it comes to tracing the history of science fiction film, the name Georges Méliès stands out as an early 'originator' of the genre. Méliès created well over 500 short films between 1896 and 1914, many of which have come to be regarded as early science fiction films. Originally a stage magician, Méliès became interested in manipulating film to create 'tricks' and to reveal seemingly impossible events. The story of how he discovered the 'stop trick' has entered into film folklore. During the filming of a simple street scene, the story goes, Méliès' camera jammed and after fixing the problem, he simply continued filming. Once he had developed and projected his efforts, he was apparently struck by the disappearances and substitutions of objects in the film, caused by the camera stopping and the time that had elapsed before he began filming again. While many other early filmmakers were also experimenting with the optical illusions made possible by film, Méliès' efforts in this area were both prolific and astounding. Designed around camera and film effects like multiple exposure, substitution, dissolves, stop-motion photography, colour tinting and so on, his 'trick films' frequently featured conjurors, wizards and illusionists performing directly for the film audience. In this way the effects that he developed could be seen as an extension of the stage illusions that Méliès had mastered prior to making films. In 1902 he released *Le Voyage dans la lune*, which is often cited as the first 'science fiction' film. This fourteen-minute film (at sixteen frames per second, as opposed to eight-minute running time at twenty-five frames per second) reveals the influence of stories like Jules Verne's *From the Earth to the Moon* and H. G. Wells' *The First Men in the Moon* (1901): in particular the film features a large cannon that fires the men to the moon, which was the mode of transport as described in Verne's story, and the Selenite aliens that populate the moon in the film are given the same name as the aliens in Wells' novel.

Méliès, film opens on a meeting of astronomers discussing the possibilities of travelling to the moon. The astronomers file into the meeting hall and are presented with large telescopes. In an obvious example of Méliès' penchant for substitution, the telescopes suddenly transform into chairs and the astronomers sit ready for the meeting to begin. A speaker proposes that they travel to the moon and draws a primitive sketch of how this could be achieved upon a blackboard. After some dissent and disagreement, the astronomers settle upon a design involving a huge cannon in which they propose to insert a space capsule big enough to house a small delegation from their ranks. The next scene takes place in what looks like a large factory workshop, where several comical altercations arise as the astronomers watch the construction of their design. They are then guided to the roof so that they can view the molten metal as it poured into a vast mould for the cannon. The background vista is industrial, tall chimneys are spewing smoke in the distance and fire and steam rises up in the foreground as the metal is poured. When all is prepared, the cannon shoots the capsule out into space toward the moon. The following scene shows the face of the moon set against the night sky; as the moon grows in size within the frame its human face becomes visible and reacts to the approaching strangers. Having established this, we are treated to the now famous stop-motion animation sequence as the capsule crash lands, piercing the eye of the moon in the process. The astronomers disembark and after briefly surveying the landscape decide to set up camp for the night. While they sleep, seven stars are seen on the horizon and the faces of women appear at their centre. Then various 'celestial bodies' hover in the night sky and look on as the men sleep. The astronomers are rudely awakened by a sudden snow storm and decide to take shelter in an underground cave. Here they find oversized mushrooms and also discover the unfriendly inhabitants of the cave: the Selenites. Frightened and dismayed, the astronomers hit the Selenites with sticks and umbrellas only to find that they conveniently disappear in a puff of smoke. However, overwhelmed by their sheer number, the astronomers are captured and taken to the King of the Selenites. Yet another skirmish occurs and the astronomers make a dash for their capsule in order to return to earth. While most of the cohort leaps safely inside their makeshift vessel, one astronomer is left dangling from a rope attached to the tip of the capsule. His weight causes the capsule to simply drop off the edge of the moon. After a speedy descent back down to the earth, the capsule finally splashes haphazardly into the sea. It sinks to the bottom of the sea before floating upward toward the surface. The capsule is then picked up by a passing steamer boat and towed safely back to harbour.

This brief synopsis plainly reveals a narrative line, but the film is really constructed around moments of theatrical spectacle and optical novelty. The visual depiction of outlandish machines and the bumbling escapades of the astronomer scientists suggest that Méliès is gently satirising the reveries of Verne and Wells. Even though the emphasis is placed upon spectacle and visual trickery, this does not mean that the film is necessarily devoid of social commentary. After all, Méliès did not confine himself to 'trick films', he also made fictional re-enactments of actual events that took on a style and gravitas later associated with the documentary film or newsreel. This suggests a filmmaker that was not only interested in fantasy and fun, but fully aware of the major events of his time. Moreover, even his 'trick films' exhibit the anxieties brought about by the fast changing landscape of an increasingly industrialised society. For Elizabeth Ezra the inevitable crash landings of trains, rocket ships, air balloons and so on in these proto-science fiction films, reveals an 'old world . . . in confrontation with the new' and represents 'the collision of different cultural traditions and collective identities'.[20]

Although *Le Voyage dans la lune* has become Méliès' most famous film, two further films also deserve a mention: *Le Voyage à travers l'impossible* (1904) and *L'Éclipse du soleil en pleine lune* (1907). The former film is in many respects a more ambitious version of *Le Voyage dans la lune,* only here our explorers head for the sun. Approximately twenty minutes in length, the film follows the intrepid members of a geographical society who plan a trip around the world using every conceivable means of transport at their disposal: train, automobile, balloon, submarine, boat and so on. Loading a train with the weird and wonderful vehicles they have constructed for the trip, along with a large icebox, they begin their journey. Following several comic capers and a disastrous crash in an auto-carriage, the unperturbed travellers continue their journey by high-speed train, which promptly flies off a mountain slope and into space. At this point the face of an anthropomorphised sun rises in the sky. The train is then caught up in the yawning mouth of the sun, causing the sun much distress and some indigestion. The travellers explore their new environment, but find it is far too hot. The icebox provides some shelter, but here the travellers freeze. Making their escape from the obviously inclement surroundings they all pile into the submarine, which is propelled off the edge of the sun. As the submarine descends back down to earth, large parachutes open to soften their fall. Landing in the sea, the passengers of the submarine begin to explore once again. However, a fire breaks out and the submarine explodes. The tip of the submarine crash-lands on shore and the passengers climb out, apparently unharmed. They disembark clutching large telescopes that resemble those seen at the beginning of *Le Voyage dans la lune.* Given a lack of narrative reasoning behind the reappearance of the telescopes it is tempting to see this as a recurring motif, deliberately placed to signal the idiocy of male conceit.

While sexual symbolism can be read into these two films, sexuality becomes central in his later *L'Éclipse du soleil en pleine lune.* This is a cheeky little film (its running time is approximately nine minutes) featuring what appears as a homosexual encounter between an effeminate moon and devilishly masculine sun. Again, the film opens on an astronomy lecture during which the assembled audience are instructed on an impending eclipse. As they all rush to the observation tower to see the eclipse through enormous telescopes, the second act of the film begins. In this section we see a lascivious sun and expectant moon licking their lips in anticipation as they slowly move closer together. During the 'eclipse' the moon covers the face of the sun. The expressions on the face of moon indicate that they are having a sexual encounter and as they part the sun is exposed. Now looking somewhat exhausted the sun goes to sleep. The third section of the film basically consists of series of heavenly bodies hanging precariously in a night sky. Here the performers are draped over representations of stars and moons and the section culminates in a battle between two male bodies over the body of a female moon. This is followed by an orgasmic meteor shower that has been double exposed to reveal the ghostly figures of girls falling from the sky. Finally, the film returns to earth. Apparently overcome by what he has witnessed, the lecturing astronomer staggers and topples from his tower in shock and dismay. The sexual symbolism is undeniable in this later film, in which sexual desire is elided with the supposedly reasoned exploits of the scientist. The aspirations of the male technocrat in these films are therefore undercut in the suggestion that it is sexual desire rather than rational science that fuels their ambition. Of course the apparatus of this early cinema was itself a product of the machine age, so the film could equally be read as self-conscious parody of the filmmaker's art. Indeed, the clashing of scientific logic with a less than logical sexual desire was to return as a central theme in numerous science fiction films.

Many of Méliès' films were pirated and plagiarised before the motion picture copyright law was passed in 1912, but this does not account for the sheer number of silent shorts of the period that made pseudo-scientific endeavour and exploration their main theme. So, having concentrated on Méliès' work I do not mean to suggest that he was the only creator of proto-science fiction films. These kinds of films appeared from all over Europe and America and covered a great range of scientific subjects in a seemingly frenzied attempt to come to terms with a fast changing world. For instance, the shock wave caused by Charles Darwin's revolutionary book, *The Origin of Species by Means of Natural Selection, or The Preservation of Favoured Races in the Struggle for Life* (first published 1859), was felt throughout the late nineteenth and early twentieth century and many early films showed a concern with human evolution and the biological sciences. British-Gaumont's *The Doctor's Experiment: or, Reversing Darwin's Theory* (1908) featured a mad scientist who turned several men into apes, and many later films contained a similarly Darwinian perspective married with narratives resembling Robert Louis Stevenson's novella, *The Strange Case of Dr. Jekyll and Mr. Hyde* (1886): examples include, the British-made *The Duality of Man* (1910) and a Danish film called *Den Skaebnesvangre* (1910). One of the first film adaptations of Mary Shelley's *Frankenstein* (1818) also appeared in 1910. This was produced in America by Thomas Edison and directed by J. Searle Dawley. What is notable is that once the biological sciences are invoked in these films the majority move closer to what we might now regard as horror. Although I will be discussing this as an ongoing issue in later chapters, perhaps it is not surprising that the years leading up to World War II should witness films that expressed a greater level of fear and sheer horror in the face of modern man's scientific achievements.

As war became reality, the production of early 'science fiction' films went into decline. However, the interwar years did see the release of a number of landmark films from Europe. The most famous of these being the Soviet film, *Aelita* (dir. Yacov Protazanov, 1924), based upon a 1922 novel of the same name by Alexei

Tolstoy, Germany's *Metropolis* (dir. Fritz Lang, 1927), and Britain's adaptation of H. G. Wells' *The Shape of Things to Come* (1933), simply entitled *Things to Come* (dir. William Cameron Menzies, 1936). All of these films are epic in their construction of detailed and futuristic urban settings as well as in their narrative scope and ideals. *Aelita* is primarily remembered for the constructivist sets (designed by Isaac Rabinowitch) and costumes (designed by Aleksandra Ekster), which mark the Martian world as separate from the earthly world of our male protagonist, Los. However, the ideas associated with constructivism as an architectural and artistic movement at this time indicate that it was used to convey more than just a futuristic or other-worldly environment. The setting worked to communicate a particular ideological system: a socialist system.

Through the romantic entanglements of Los with the Martian Queen, Aelita, the narrative of this film follows the protagonist's psychological and political shift from individualist to socialist activist. The beginning sets up the apparent devotion felt by Los for his wife Natasha. However, as the film continues Los becomes jealous of Natasha's involvement with the community that surrounds her and believes she is having an affair. In a fit of rage he kills her and takes on the identity of a rocket scientist in order to escape prosecution for his actions. All the while, Los imagines that he is being watched and dreams of a perfect and beautiful woman living on Mars. The Martian Queen is indeed watching him through an enormous telescope and they become the object of each others fantasy. In the guise of the scientist, Los builds a rocket and together with a disillusioned soldier he heads for Mars. At this point, Los is unaware that he is also being pursued by an amateur sleuth called Igor who has stowed away in the spaceship. When the three reach their destination they discover a totalitarian state in which the Queen is simply a figurehead and holds no power. Along with Aelita, they are imprisoned by the prime minister of Mars and led away by robot-like slaves. In order to gain their freedom they start a socialist revolution. Once the totalitarian state has been toppled they are freed, but Los is shocked to discover that Aelita now wants to rule this new world and she tempts him with her body and with the promise of power. Finally Los sees her as selfish and unworthy of his attentions. He pushes Aelita from the high staircase upon which they stand and then awakens to find he is back in Moscow. Relieved to discover that this has all been a dream, he makes peace with his wife.

The female object of desire in this film therefore stands for the temptation of selfish and individualist ambition, as well as the guiding light for socialist reform. The Martian city not only represents the prospect of a kind of idealised vision of urban living, but also becomes the setting against which human desire is played out and ultimately tamed. Although this film proved hugely popular it was later criticised for its anti-socialist undercurrents and was withdrawn from circulation. Aelita's manipulation of Los as set against this ideally constructed environment can well be read as a critique of this perfect world. The

New Economic Policy that was set in place by the Communist Party in 1921 relaxed earlier Communist dictates and brought about a brief period that shifted closer to capitalism than earlier ideals of socialist reform. The greed and corruption of the pre-revolution years has crept back into the Soviet society depicted in the film, which is set off against the socialist programme for recon-struction and rebuilding as also depicted in the film. So, Los is caught up in very confusing times, which in part justifies the ambiguities at the heart of the film's 'message'. Before Los makes his escape to Mars, the vast building site where he works is displayed and compared with the constructivist setting of his dream. So, there is a sense in which the Martian city represents a utopian future that this society is building toward. However, it is implied that the revolution that has occurred on Mars will simply result in the emergence of another dictator. In the end, the hope for the future lies in Los's acceptance of his domestic life with Natasha. On the surface the film appears to promote socialist ideals, but its melodramatic style also places emphasis upon the individual and upon Los's personal fulfilment.

As the title suggest, the city also plays a crucial role in *Metropolis,* working to suggest the literal construction of a utopian world. *Metropolis* was a hugely ambitious undertaking for the German studio, Universum Film AG, and much of the vast budget was spent on the detailed miniatures of the city and the epic sets, against which the film's lengthy narrative was played out (several edited versions exist, ranging from approximately 210 minutes to 80 minutes). Indeed, the players in this film are frequently dwarfed by the sheer scale and grandeur of their surroundings. Partly inspired by a view of the New York skyline that Lang experienced as he was travelling from postwar Berlin, the high-rise architecture in *Metropolis* could loosely be called Modernist in design, although it also displays expressionist, Art Deco and Gothic influences. The lifestyle of the wealthy elite who populate the imposing skyscrapers relies upon the continued oppression of the proletariat, who live and work in a squalid, industrial environment underneath the city. So, this utopian urban vision is lit-erally built upon the pain and servitude of the working classes. The main sto-ryline follows the growing romance between the spoilt son of a rich industrialist and a working-class activist called Maria. Freder's attraction toward Maria causes him to question the divide between their classes. Unable to gain a satis-factory explanation from his father, Freder dresses in worker's overalls and trudges down into the underground tunnels of the city. Here he witnesses the hellish conditions which the workers are forced to endure, as vast machines, spewing steam and fire feed and power the city above.

Standing for the desires of the workers, Maria's high-minded call for change is seen as a threat by the ruling classes. However, Freder is impressed with Maria's call for mediation between workers and management and unaware that his father has enlisted the assistance of Rotwang, a 'mad scientist', to stop the action of the dissidents. Rotwang's plan involves kidnapping Maria and replacing her with a robot double. He literally rebuilds Maria and reintroduces her to the masses as an exotic dancer in a seedy nightclub. Here the robot Maria dances half-naked in such a seductive fashion that a riot breaks out and during the chaos the local waterworks is all but destroyed and the lower levels of the city become flooded. The human Maria manages to escape and fighting against the rising water level saves several trapped children. A rather hurried conclusion sees Freder's father agreeing to a new deal with the workers and Freder and Maria reunited.

Like *Aelita, Metropolis* emerged at a time of political and economic uncertainty during the Weimar period in Germany (1919–33). After the nation's defeat in World War I, a new constitution and Republic were formed, calling itself Deusches Reich. This attempt to set up a liberal democracy basically failed with the rise of Adolf Hitler and the Nazi Party in 1933. The Weimar period was marred by civil unrest, hyperinflation, economic depression and workers' strikes. Lang's answer to the problems of the period was concentrated upon the relations between working and ruling classes. Rather than depicting an entirely alternative world, the city of Metropolis can therefore be seen as an exaggeration of a known world. The conflict that arises in the film between the workers and the ruling elite is resolved in Lang's film through the union of our central romantic couple. What is also notable is that, once again, the alluring female represents both dangerous threat and remedy in this film. Maria is the catalyst for change, which is played out in her dual role as sexual provocateur and nurturing mother figure. The fears and desires of the male characters in the film are therefore written onto the body of Maria.

Metropolis had a huge impact on science fiction that followed and my final example, *Things to Come,* was inevitably compared to this earlier German film. However, *Things to Come* was released after popular cinema had moved into the 'sound period', following the introduction of synchronous sound in the late 1920s. Making full use of this relatively new cinematic technology, *Things to Come* included a musical score by Arthur Bliss and several of the characters were given long, rhetorical speeches. The characters are undeniably stereotypes, intended to stand for ideas and sectors of society. Wells had himself written the screenplay, so one can assume that the speeches given these characters worked to play out his known political views (he was an outspoken socialist). While the film is largely remembered for 'predicting' World War II, the novel was an unashamedly utopian and political fiction that depicted Wells' idea for a 'world state' as a necessary goal to ending war and conflict. As Wells makes clear in the novel, he sees no future for either capitalism or communism and believes that this 'world state' would best be run by a benevolent dictator. Wells placed great faith in the intellectual elite in society, especially scientists, believing that they were best equipped to design and run his 'world state'.

The film is set in Everytown, covering its history from 1940 through to 2106. After war breaks out and the town is ravaged by air raids, it becomes a desolate wasteland. As the war continues, the population are seen at various stages in history. The ongoing devastation brings about a kind of feudal system, although the majority of the population have contracted the so called 'wandering sickness' and are dying. The sudden arrival in Everytown of an airman, John Cabal, changes everything. He represents an organisation called 'Wings over the World', which is based in the Middle Eastern city of Basra. In an effort to bring peace and civilisation back to Everytown, this organisation drop 'Peace Gas' bombs. Society is saved and a reconstruction programme begins. The montage sequence that follows is cinematically spectacular, revealing the labours of workers and vast industrial machines forging ahead in the rebuilding of a safe and harmonious future. When the future city is finally revealed in all its glory, we see a modernist dream of towers and flyovers, connecting pathways and communal activity. But unlike *Aelita* and *Metropolis*, this city has been built underground, leaving the rolling green planes of the land above relatively untouched. Somewhat resembling the shopping precincts of today, this is a dome world; protected from the outside by glass, metal and white concrete, the city uses artificial air and light. Large, flat television screens display news and make community announcements and the technocratic leaders of this society live on the upper levels of the city. Conflict has not disappeared from this utopian vision, only now it takes place between the 'Luddite' artists of the town and the ruling technocrats. The technocrats have constructed a 'space gun' with which they plan to launch a craft into space. The artists in the community want to end all this 'progress' and the firing of the space gun, but their protestations fail to stop the launch of the craft. Science and technology wins the day and 'progress' continues unabated.

These interwar films obviously speak to the political and social unrest of their times. The future city in all three films not only denotes the fruits of a literal programme of rebuilding, but also symbolises social construction and reconstruction. Even though each of these cities is in many ways remarkably similar in design, each represents rather different versions of a socialist ideal. This is hardly surprising given the differences between the national and cultural contexts within which they were made. Although there are certainly dystopian elements in all three films, each in its own way promotes a technocratic society, governed by science or a scientific world view and organised around the model of the modern city. In this way these films look forward to the future with some optimism, an optimism that became extraordinarily rare in this film genre after World War II.

The blatant politicisation of the genre at this time signals the serious intent of these European films. To some extent, both *Aelita* and *Things to Come* also relied upon the kudos conferred by pre-existing novels. While these films were certainly entertaining for their moments of spectacle, they were also didactic. They were not what a contemporary audience might associate with the fast-paced and exciting Hollywood science fiction films of today. The 'special relationship' between novel and film that, to some extent, underpinned the emergence of the genre in Europe, continued with Hollywood's later adaptations (this is particularly evident in the number of Hollywood films based upon the novels of H. G. Wells), but the 'roots' of the American film genre can be traced back to a far wider variety of sources. Following the popular and inexpensive 'dime novels' of the nineteenth century, came what were known as the 'pulps'. These were cheaply produced magazines aimed at a mass market. By the 1920s the pulps were largely specialised magazines, each concentrating on a particular genre (i.e. detective, war, adventure and western fiction). From these emerged the science fiction pulps, although the term was not in regular use until later in the decade. The pulp *Amazing Stories* (first published in 1926) is generally regarded as the first science fiction magazine, although its creator, Hugo Gernsback, originally called it a 'scientification' magazine. *Amazing Stories* was followed by *Astounding* in 1930. Originally published under the name *Astounding Stories of Super-Science,* its stories were largely taken up with wondrous machines and the 'hard' science fiction gadgetry of an exciting future world. The magazine was later taken over by John W. Campbell in 1937. Campbell instituted a new title, *Astounding Science-Fiction,* and a fresh approach. He basically set up a kind of manifesto for his contributors, insisting that they think seriously about how technologies might develop into the future and about how this would affect the lives of human beings.

In addition to the pulps, there is an American tradition of science fiction comic strips and comic books, which can be traced back to roughly the same period. The character Buck Rogers made his first appearance in two science fiction stories published in *Amazing Stories* and later featured in one of the first science fiction newspaper comic strips in the late 1920s. The *Flash Gordon* comic strip followed soon after in 1934. Both of these comic strips followed the adventures of an athletic, all-American hero who fights against strange alien forces. Usually surrounded by amazing technological 'toys' and a bevy of beautiful women, Buck and Flash projected a mixture of potency and technological savvy. While Buck and Flash performed extraordinary feats, they were no match for the numerous superheroes who were to follow. Seen as a sub-genre of the science fiction comic strip, enduring superheroes like Superman and Batman emerged in the late 1930s. Their powers were beyond those of a human hero and their skin-tight costumes emphasised their super-masculine prowess. It was comic strip heroes and superheroes like these that crossed over into science fiction radio serials (e.g. Buck Rogers in 1932 and Flash Gordon in 1935) and later into the cinema serials. The cinema serials were low-budget films aimed at a young audience. Episodes numbered between twelve and fifteen and individual episodes were usually between fifteen to twenty minutes in length. Cinema serials like *The Shadow of the Eagle* (dir. Ford Beebe, 1932), *The Phantom of the Air* (dir. Ray Taylor, 1933) *The Lost City* (dir. Harry Revier, 1935) featured robust central heroes doing battle with evil adversaries. Technological innovation was also a central feature of these serials, but it was not until *Flash Gordon: Space Soldiers* (dir. Frederick Stephani, 1936) that the science fiction genre really came into its own within this medium. Flash was followed by *Buck Rogers Conquers the Universe* (dir. Ford Beebe and Saul A. Goodkind, 1939) and the later superhero serials, *The Batman* (dir. Lambort Hillyer, 1943) and *The Adventures of Superman* (dir. Spencer Gordon Bennett and Thomas Carr 1948). There were very few science fiction feature films produced in America during the 1930s and 1940s, so in terms of numbers the serials remain the most prominent example of the American film genre before the 1950s. The serial was plotted to a set formula that required a fast pace, easily recognisable and colourful characters and regular 'cliff hangers' to tempt children back to the cinemas to see the next episode. Many of these features found their way into later feature films and the American science fiction film genre therefore became inextricably linked with sensation, commercialism and a juvenile market.

Possible examples of a more adult strand in American science fiction film can be traced through the remakes, adaptations and films based on the characters of both Shelley's *Frankenstein* and Stevenson's *Dr Jekyll and Mr Hyde* that appeared throughout the 1930s and 1940. However, these are usually seen as part of the cycle of horror films that proved so popular from the Depression years through to World War II. In addition, while the science fiction radio and cinema serials were primarily aimed at a juvenile audience, an exception can found in the Mercury Theatre's radio adaptation of H. G. Wells' *The War of the Worlds,* which aired in 1938. Shifting the location of Wells' novel to New Jersey, Orson Welles and his troupe of players deliberately imitated a series of newscasts for the radio version. With the announcement that aliens had invaded, widespread panic ensued. Tensions were high at this time with regular news coming from Europe in the lead up to World War II. Also, as set against the more usual style associated with the children's science fiction radio serials, the Mercury's novel approach was certainly unfamiliar to many. This, along with the more adult fare offered by Wells' science fiction narrative, mixed with the stylistic realism of the performance was not a combination that American audiences were used to in their popular science fiction.

It was not until the 1950s that the science fiction feature film genre really took off in America. This 'cold war' period saw the production of numerous science fiction and science fiction/horror films. Traces of both the American and European traditions in science fiction can be seen in many of the films that I will be discussing in the next chapter. What I hope has become apparent in this brief history is the variety of traditions and influences that can be witnessed in what has come to be known as science fiction film. Although I will on occasion refer back to some of the texts mentioned here, this history is certainly relevant in understanding the characteristics of the film genre as it entered its 'golden years'.

INTERVIEW: WRITER BRIAN ALDISS

A: I remember writing my first science fiction story at the age of eight. I became extremely devoted science fiction and read it, not exclusively, but most avidly. Never in my life have I so much enjoyed reading as when I was reading those magazines and those books. Now I seem to have cooled on the habit because if I open a science fiction novel, within the first page or two, I can see the stage being set and I think . . . yes, I see . . . and so I don't go on.

C: You've become too familiar with the codes?

A: Yes, that's right. I've read William Gibson, but I'm not as engaged as I was – as you would expect – as I was in my youth. When I wrote my first novel, *Non-Stop* [1958], I clearly had read a short story – no, a novella – that much captivated me, but that I thought was mistaken. That was by Robert A. Heinlein and was called *Universe* [1941].[21] His universe was a ship going to another star, which travels well under the speed of light. So many generations live on this ship. Something has gone wrong. They've lost their sense of direction and the ship proceeds automatically. They've even lost the knowledge that they're on a ship. This is their universe. So, as a metaphor it's wonderful, but what goes on in the ship I thought was so pulpy and silly and there was no real emotion in it. And I thought . . . to be caged in such a ship, to be caught in a technology that you hadn't invented, forty generations on, what would that feel like? How would they get to understand their situation? So the story of *Non-Stop*, I suppose you might say, was derivative – the way much science fiction is. It takes up ideas and it develops them.

C: So, unlike what we could call 'hard' science fiction, would you say there was an interest in psychology that runs throughout your work?

A: Yes. Oh, yes, absolutely so. Only gradually did I become interested in the various sciences themselves because I wanted to understand better what I was doing. Although I still regard myself as a just a storyteller, the stories that I tell have got to have some connection with the truth. I believe that this is what has happened to science fiction – not to H. G. Wells or that kind of story – but the popular science fiction of the magazines. When they started up in the 1920s and 1930s they were purely out for sensationalism and they had no feeling for what they were actually doing. It was only when this marvellous American editor, John W. Campbell, came along and said, look guys we're talking about something really serious and important, that the understanding dawned that, in a way, one was speaking up for science, one was the poor man's intellectual.

C: Your work has been read in alliance with the British 'new wave' science fiction writers, who developed a particular interest in the psychological under-pinnings of the genre.

A: Yes, I have to give you a rather dodgy answer to that . . . although I regard myself as a very conscious 'artist' I don't know where a lot of what I do comes from. When I start a novel, when I've got an idea and I think here comes another novel, it's because there's a problem to be solved. I don't know how it's going to end. So, I think that in this way you release a lot of unconscious thoughts, or sub-conscious or whatever you call it. Something that H. G. Wells said is impor-tant . . . he gave a lecture called 'Inventing the Future' in 1901, which was very perceptive. He said that there are two sorts of humanity. There are those whose thoughts are always directed to the past and those who are, on the whole, rather governed by what's happened in the past – in the family, or the country, the nation, in history and so on. But he also said there are another, smaller group of people who think that their actions now are going to influence the future and that the future doesn't just arrive, like a bus, but comes from what we're doing now. I do believe this and I think this is where science fiction is vitally important. I mean, I don't want to crack it up. I'm fed up with people who crack it up and say that it's the only literature. Nevertheless, it does have an important function. For instance, it's brought NASA and the space project – I mean that's an obvious example.

C: Some have said that science fiction is about the present as much as it is about the future. Would you agree with that?

A: Shakespeare said that the players hold a mirror up to nature and I think that this is one of the things science fiction does. There is a diversity of things that science fiction does, but one thing it can do is to write a metaphor for the present. For instance, that's what I thought I was doing in my novel *Barefoot in the Head* [1969].

C: Were you doing that with 'Supertoys Last All Summer Long' [1969], the short story that the film *Artificial Intelligence: AI:* [dir. Steven Spielberg, 2001] is based upon?

A: I've been forced of course by the unexpected event of the film to reconsider the story.

C: How do you feel about the film?

A: Let me give you two of several responses that I have to that. One is simply this . . . if a short story is taken to be blown up into a blockbuster film then it's not very likely to be faithful to the story. Why should it be? In any case there is always the difficulty of the translation from the written medium into film. It's no good expecting that they're just going to film your story. They use it as a basis and that's fine. When I wrote the story in 1969, at that time computers were fairly new and there were theories propagated by many people that our dreams were like a computer downloading the day's events. It all sounded at the time much more plausible than it does now. So it was easy for me to think of David as a child who has been programmed and to believe he was a real child programmed to love his adopted mother Monica. I mean it was written for *Harper's Bazaar,* so you can't actually go into heavy science. But I had no notion of the science of artificial intelligence. It didn't exist. But now things have got much more complicated, we can see now that there are people in America and Japan who are working on the idea of creating androids with intelligence. Why on earth would we want to create artificial beings? Is it so these creatures should be happy? No, it's so they should like us. I have to say that I am now referring to an article that I've just written for the *New Scientist* . . . I've figured out what human consciousness is for: it's for pleasure. It's not for getting ahead in business or anything like that. It's for the pleasure that you get in being able to concentrate, to understand, to wonder at the world. So I believe that extended consciousness is there purely for pleasure.

When I was working with Stanley Kubrick he had the idea of getting someone to make him an android to represent David and another one to represent Teddy. His thinking was that, on the whole, the American's didn't like or were scared of robots and androids. But he thought that the Japanese were in love with the idea of androids. So he thought he could get someone out there to manufacture an android. There was one occasion when he called his sidekick and said 'will you get me Mitsubishi on the phone' – it wasn't Mitsubishi, but I can't remember which corporation it was . . . so let's say it was Mitsubishi. So the sidekick said, 'OK Stanley, who would you like to speak to there?' And Stanley said, 'Well, Mr Mitsubishi of course'. Well, twenty minutes later the phone rings and he picks it up and a voice says, 'Ah, Mr Stanley Kubrick, it's Mr Mitsubishi speaking. What can I do for you?' It's mind-blowing, everyone on the planet knew the name Stanley Kubrick. I mean he was that powerful, that renowned. Nothing came of it, but I can see what a great first it would have been. Now of course that's sidestepped in *AI* because David is played by a boy. Perhaps there are scenes where they use computer simulations, but in any case you can computerise anything . . . so Stanley's question has become irrelevant really.

C: Can you tell me a little bit about your recent collaboration with the mathematical physicist, Roger Penrose?

A: I became very friendly with Roger and one night we dined with Roger and Vanessa and got home late – staggered home at about one o'clock – and at four o'clock I woke up and I'd had a wonderful dream. I had dreamt *White Mars* [published in 2000] – the overall picture of it really. And I thought it came not only from my conversation with him, but from my thinking on how we could make a better world. So, I came down and wrote a synopsis of the dream in five or six pages and then I thought, oh, I'll send it to Roger and see what he thinks. He wanted to join in. This was an obvious case of a book that could never have been written without computers, because we sent each other chunks of text and messed around with them, moved them around and eventually created this story.

C: So it was a very fruitful collaboration.

A: Yes, I've never written a novel in conjunction with anyone before. But in a way that was where my mind was taking me to. I mean science fiction itself is doing very well, but so is the popularisation of science. There's so many good books around – some of them quite technical. So, I've turned really to this kind of thing. I've got three books in the publishing pipeline now and the last one, called *Super-State* [published 2002]. This is about the European Union forty years on.

C: So lots more projects to come . . . any more films in the pipeline?

A: No. I'm waiting for offers . . .

C: Do you think you've been influenced by the films you've seen?

A: Oh yes, I'm a great film buff. Last night I was actually watching *The Cabinet of Dr. Caligari* [dir. Robert Wiene, 1920]. There have been some very fine science fiction films. When I wrote *Super State* I deliberately took an idea that Stanley Kubrick had. Stanley said, look forget about the narrative Brian, you don't want narrative, just concentrate on various scenes. He then expounded his theory of non-submersible units. It's slightly revolutionary, but you can see it working out in particular in *2001: A Space Odyssey* (1968), where there are these chunks of narrative. This, I believe, is one of the attractions of *2001* – not only the music, not only the extraordinary silences and the beauty of the pho-tography, but the fact that they don't quite fit together. This gives the film a sense of mystery, so the intelligent viewer has to construct their own narrative. So, actually *Super State* is full of what I hope are non-submersible units. There's no narrative, but you can figure it out for yourself.

C: There seems to be a way in which science fiction encourages dialogue . . . do you think there is a sort of dialogue going on between texts and between people?

A: Well, earlier this month I was at a meeting at the University of Liverpool; a very good meeting – three days of intensive discussion. I believe science fiction has benefited from being an outsider literature. But now I think that's fading slightly – so what do you quarrel with now – with your fellow writer at least – in print at least you can disagree with them. When I said 'quarrel' I was speaking loosely. I would think it was more 'yes . . . but', you know. I think I've lived by 'yes . . . but'.

INTERVIEW: WRITER WILLIAM GIBSON

C: I would like to know about your experiences in writing for film and television . . . *Johnny Mnemonic* [dir. Robert Longo, 1995], *X-Files* [episodes in 1998, 2000] and so on.

G: I've actually written enough screenplays to contract to qualify for a pension from WGA West, yet have never written even one on spec. All of them, aside from *Alien 3* [dir. David Fincher, 1992], were adaptations of my own short fiction, with *Johnny Mnemonic* being the only one to have been produced. I don't regard un-produced contract screenplays as part of my body of work – to the point that I don't even keep copies. They feel more like collaborative design projects than works of fiction. Actually I don't regard un-produced screenplays as 'screenplays'. They are more like the initial step toward something, with the actual screenplay emerging further into production. The screenplay should ideally dry up and blow away as the film is shot, but absolutely has to have been there in the first place.

In Hollywood, scripts serve any number of different, crucial, basically 'ritual' purposes, at different times during the process, and necessarily change to serve these purposes. Screenplays and narrative fiction are utterly different activities. The ease and depth with which fiction conveys specific imagined interiority in a character has no equivalent in film, where everything must either be depicted, or described after the fact. Actors help us forget this, but it remains true.

Episodic television in America is the single most structurally constrained form I know of. The commercial breaks simply don't move. Writing for 'episodic' is a much more immediate experience; you write, they prepare, they shoot. In this sort of television, the players with the most power, today, often began as writers. This is not often true in Hollywood.

When I write narrative fiction, there are no external pressures (other than deadline, should it be a contract piece). The pressures are internal, and I am in effect freelancing. I suppose that this is as true of a spec. script. When I write a script to contract, I am a temporary employee, a member of a large and very powerful union; I can be fired; the amount of my pay, at the end of the project, will depend on the number of drafts requested and completed. Those are not even remotely equivalent situations.

C: Brooks Landon [an academic who has written books and articles about the science fiction genre] has said that cyberpunk writing has been strongly influenced by science fiction film. What is your response to this statement?

G: Quite right.

C: What is your thinking on the 'traffic' between science fiction film/television and written novels or short stories?

G: It's still strongest in Landon's direction: film influencing fiction. Narrative sf prose has historically had remarkably little influence on sf film. Though this began to change when 'cyberpunk' emerged as the first determindedly pop-literate prose sf. Through copious quotation of film, music and video games, cyberpunk made prose sf 'visible' to filmmakers in a new way.

C: There has been some critical acknowledgement of late that your own novels have greatly influenced films – in particular *The Matrix* [dir. Larry and Andy Wachowski, 1999) – not only in terms of concepts, but also in terms of narrative construction. I read recently on the internet somewhere that in formulating a way of 'translating' your seminal cyberpunk novel, *Neuromancer* (1984) to film you are thinking about 'reinventing' certain aspects because so much had been cribbed/visually represented by filmmakers already – is this true?

G: It would be interesting to hear more on this. I have to look at that purely as opportunity. Whatever a film of *Neuromancer* might be, it no longer needs to be anything *The Matrix* franchise has already been.

C: Unlike a lot of science fiction writing your own novels and stories often provide dense and interesting characterisation. Do you think that this makes them more or less 'film friendly'?

G: It's that capacity to directly depict interiority that I mentioned earlier. A lot of sf prose narrative has traditionally been rather light on that, so probably transitions more readily to film. In my fiction, it seems to me, some of the most memorable central characters are environments rather than people. The bridge in *Virtual Light* [1994], for instance. We managed to build something very like that for *Johnny Mnemonic*, but it wound up being tragically underlit, and most of it was lost in the Sony Pictures cut.

The thing that's most difficult to convey about making a forty-million-dollar film is how awkward the entities whose forty million is being spent can be about letting you do whatever you feel you need to do in order to satisfy your sense of what the film should be. They can bridle at that. It's something that those who haven't actually found themselves in that position can't really imagine.

C: You recently completed a feature length documentary – it would be interesting to know how you felt about being on the other end of the camera, as it were, and any other comments about this experience and the making of the film that you feel might be appropriate.

G: It's nothing like acting, so it wasn't 'the other end of the camera' in any 'film' sense. It was like giving a seemingly endless multi-part interview, while being taped through fixed pencil cameras. I dislike the sound of my own recorded voice, and find it unnerving to watch myself on videotape, so I've mostly avoided it. I did watch it once, carefully, end to end, at a film festival, was very pleased, and likely never will again. If you pay close attention, it's in some ways as frank a source of autobiography as I'm ever likely to provide.

NOTES

1. In using the term 'texts' I do not mean to limit this discussion to literary or printed narratives, but also mean narratives as produced in a variety of media.
2. *Asimov* 1983, p. 10.
3. See Merril 1971, pp. 53–95.
4. Suvin 1979, p. 63.
5. See Todorov 1975.
6. Ibid., p. 56.
7. Jackson 1981, p. 33.
8. Ibid., p. 36.
9. Landon 1992, p. 14.
10. See Telotte 2001, pp. 10–16.
11. Sobchack 1993, p. 43.
12. See Neale 2000.
13. See Altman 1999, pp. 77–82.
14. Delany 1989, p. 9.
15. For academic accounts of these kinds of activities see Jenkins 1992. Also Tullock and Jenkins 1995.
16. See Penley 1997.
17. Altman 1999, p. 17.
18. James 1994, p. 2.
19. Edward James, 'Science Fiction by Gaslight: An Introduction to English-Language Science Fiction in the Nineteenth Century', in Seed 1995, p. 29.
20. Ezra 2000, p. 119.
21. Ing and Heinlein 1997.

2. SCIENCE FICTION FILMS IN THE 1950s

Figure 2.1   The titular spacecraft arrives to save the world in *The Day the Earth Stood Still* (1951). 20th Century Fox / The Kobal Collection.

The 1950s marks a turning point in the history of the science fiction film genre. This is a period that is commonly referred to as the 'golden age' of the science fiction film, partly due to the unprecedented number of feature films produced[1] and partly due to a group of highly influential, American-made 'classics' released over the course of the decade. Although the period is frequently associated with low budget, 'trashy' B features, landmark films like *Destination Moon* (dir. Irving Pichel, 1950), *The Day the Earth Stood Still* (dir. Robert Wise, 1951), *The War of the Worlds* (dir. Byron Haskin, 1953) and *Forbidden Planet* (dir. Fred M. Wilcox, 1956) were produced by major Hollywood studios on relatively respectable budgets.[2] In addition, a number of lower budget features are regularly listed amongst the canon of 'classic' films of the era. For instance, *Invasion of the Body Snatchers* (dir. Don Siegel, 1956) has become a central text in discussion of the genre, even though it was produced by Walter Wanger in association with the low-budget studio, Allied Artists, at approximately a quarter of the cost of *The War of the Worlds* and *Forbidden Planet* and half of the budget afforded to Paramount's *The Day the Earth Stood Still*.[3] At the other end of the scale, director Ed Wood's infamous *Plan 9 from Outer Space* (1959) heads up a group of 1950s B-films that have attracted a kind of cult following (i.e. *It Conquered the World* [dir. Roger Corman, 1956], *The Brain Eaters* [dir. Bruno VeSota, 1958], *Attack of the Puppet People* [dir. Bert I. Gordon, 1958], *Earth Versus the Spider* [dir. Bert I. Gordan, 1958] etc.). Made on shoestring budgets, among fan circles these films are celebrated for what are considered to be the wooden acting, clumsy plot lines and laughable special effects.

The 1950s was the decade that marked the beginning of the end for the Hollywood studio system when, following the Paramount decrees of 1949 and the separation of the studios from the major theatrical exhibition outlets, the oligopoly of the major studios began to break down. This was a period that saw film attendance drop significantly, due in large part to adjustments in lifestyle for an increasingly affluent and suburbanised sector of the American populace. Large numbers were literally 'moving away' from the key theatrical outlets and staying home to watch television.

The industry was changing and the majors shifted away from the kind of 'B-movie' production that had grown out of the depression era's demand for double features. In the early 1950s, smaller companies that had previously specialised in the supply of B films struggled to survive in a shrinking market in which their films were now obliged to compete alongside the bigger-budget spectacles that the majors were producing. Especially popular were musicals and biblical epics, in which high production values were flaunted in the large casts, lavish sets and use of Technicolor, in an effort to attract audiences and differentiate the Hollywood product from television's small screen, black and white output. But, as the decade wore on new outlets for films and a growing teenage market encouraged the further production of low-budget 'quickies' to supply, for example, the increasing numbers of 'drive-ins' springing up around the country. With the demise of the classical-style, B film, the 'new B film' generally sought to attract an audience with the promise of novel and shocking special effects and thrilling themes. Science fiction was well placed to take advantage of this new market, as the 'new B films' could tap into a pre-existing fan base built up around the pulps and comics of the 1940s and early 1950s as well as exploiting the success of bigger-budget films. Although the hybrid science fiction/horror films (the so-called 'monster movies' or 'creature features') dominated the 'drive-in' market, independent producers also took advantage of themes played out in some of the more prestigious, higher-budget films, in the creation of what could be taken as low-budget remakes of earlier space travel (e.g. George Pal's epic production, [*Destination Moon*] and alien invasion films (e.g. *The Day the Earth Stood Still*, *The War of the Worlds*). Indeed, the sheer number of science fiction films produced not only established the film genre in the popular imagination but supported the recognition of a variety of sub-genres.

Until recently, the vast majority of the lower-budget features were considered qualitatively poor and therefore unworthy of serious critical attention. For instance, in his relatively early reviewing of the genre John Brosnan splits the period into two halves. While he pays special attention to films that appeared in the first half of the decade, he states that the genre 'took for the most part a major nose-dive in quality' after 1956 and blames exploitation/independent producers like Roger Corman and Bert I. Gordon for the 'bad reputation' that science fiction films accrued in the latter part of the 1950s.[4] However, although academic writing concerning the genre remained sparse throughout the 1960s and 1970s, Susan Sontag's influential article, 'The Imagination of Disaster',[5] certainly took a broad range of the 1950s films seriously enough to use them as a basis upon which to attempt a mapping out of the genre's formal conventions. Denouncing, the genre as 'about disaster' rather than 'about science', Sontag's reductive approach highlighted the dystopian leanings of the 1950s American science fiction film. It was not until the early 1980s that academics began to understand these films as more sophisticated than both Sontag's and Brosnan's earlier appraisals had suggested. For instance, Peter Biskind's study of Hollywood in the 1950s recognised both high- and low-budget science fiction films of the period as culturally significant; as intimately connected with the historical and political context from which they arose.[6] Reading these films as made in the shadow of the 'red scare', the anti-communist witch-hunts carried out by Joseph McCarthy, and the constraints brought about by the House Committee on Un-American Activities, Biskind classified them according to what he understood as their often covert political/ideological affiliations. Backing up his arguments through detailed comparative analyses, he divides the films into 'centrist' and 'radical', seeing 'centrist' films as those that supported the status quo and the dominant powers of the period and 'radical' films as those of either far right or far left persuasion that were critical of the status quo. In paying attention to the differences as well as similarities in a variety of 1950s science fiction films, Biskind's approach provided a more complex picture through his exploration of the political and cultural undercurrents conveniently masked by the genre's lowly status as juvenile, escapist fantasy.

For over a decade, Biskind's assessment of the 1950's films remained practically the last word among academic circles, but recent years have seen a rash of important books that have revisited the era and re-evaluated the science fiction or science fiction/horror films of the period. To an extent, this recent interest can be explained by an understanding that we might be witnessing the demise of cinema as such a dominant and powerful cultural form, sparking an interest in looking back and revising its history. In this light, a return to what Vivian Sobchack regards as the true beginnings of the science fiction film genre[7] can be understood as part of a wider project within film studies as an academic discipline. Alternatively, the last two decades have seen science fiction take centre stage within a global, cultural market place, which has further promoted a serious reconsideration of the film genre. Hollywood has also repeatedly returned to the 1950s science fiction films. For instance, I will be discussing what I call 'the family science fiction films' that appeared in the 1980s and how these engaged with the period in a later chapter. Further, the 1990s also saw a cycle of science fiction parodies revisit the era (e.g. *Mars Attacks!* [dir. Tim Burton, 1996], *Men in Black* [dir. Barry Sonnenfeld, 1997], *Independence Day* [dir. Roland Emmerich, 1996], *Armageddon* [dir. Michael Bay, 1998] etc.), followed in the last few years by earnest remakes of films like *The Time Machine* (dir. George Pal, 1960) and *The War of the Worlds* (dir. Byron Haskin, 1953), released in 2002 and 2005 respectively. Aside from the self-reflexive nature of the Hollywood industry, built in references to the films of the 1950s speaks to the contemporary political climate in the West and encourages comparison with the earlier, 'cold war', period. So, in the context of the triumphalist mood that accompanied the USA's liberation of Kuwait in the Gulf War of 1990 and against the backdrop of the Clinton Administration's moderate, democratic leadership, a confident nation could apparently sustain the ironic swipes at defensive 'cold war' mentality. Whereas, paranoia and political undercurrent might be seen to return in the serious remakes of recent years, as set against the political protectionism marked by the so-called 'war on terror' and the threat from a somewhat nebulous al-Qaeda. I believe that these are some of the factors that have fostered academic interest and the need to interrogate past assessments of the 1950s films from a contemporary viewpoint. Thus, recent studies have expanded upon the work of Sontag and Biskind, offering a more comprehensive picture of the films' formal structures, sub-generic categorisations, and cultural, political and aesthetic meanings.

Picking up on Sontag's evaluation of the genre's preoccupation with destruction, Cyndy Hendershot seeks to resolve what she sees as a kind of 'cultural paranoia largely triggered by the discovery and use of nuclear weapons during World War II.'[8] For Hendershot, the destructive potential of science and technology, demonstrated by the atom bombs dropped on the Japanese cities of Hiroshima and Nagasaki in 1945, fuelled a variety of anxieties that pervaded an otherwise peaceful and stable postwar era. Hendershot backs up her claim by applying a psychoanalytic understanding of paranoia to her readings of the science fiction films of 1950s. As a clinical disorder characterised by totalising delusion, Hendershot explores the ways in which these science fiction films exhibit a kind of collective paranoia, evidenced in the genre's propensity for the creation of seemingly rational yet totally fantastical worlds. This account is fascinating and, at the least, adds depth to an understanding of a 'paranoia' that is not only regarded as symptomatic of this period in American history, but, often understood as a continuing national trait. Given her focus upon what could loosely be called atomic-age science, Hendershot therefore sub-divides the films according to the particularities of their representational strategies in connection with an all-embracing fear of nuclear annihilation.

Jerome F. Shapiro also focuses upon what he calls the 'bomb films' of the 1950s through to the early 1960s.[9] However, contrary to Hendershot, he generally understands 'the bomb' and a playing out of an impending or post-apocalyptic scenario as simply a plot device that obscures the main issues dealt with in many of these films. Likewise, where Biskind had commented that 'the little green men from Mars stood in the popular imagination for the clever red men from Moscow,[10] Mark Jancovich points out: 'The concerns with the Soviet Union were often merely a displacement or a code which different sections of American society used in order to criticise those aspects of American life which they feared or opposed.'[11] Turning the tables, Jancovich suggests that 'if the alien was at times identified with Soviet communism, it was also implied that this was only the logical conclusion of certain developments within American society itself.'[12] In this way, as I understand it, the alien/communist Other comes to represent a displaced fear of the kind of conformity that 1950s American society increasingly required of its subjects.

M. Keith Booker takes a rather different tack in his approach to the cold war science fiction films. Like Jancovich, Booker goes to some lengths to outline what he considers to be the most significant social and cultural shifts that occurred in postwar America, concentrating especially upon increasing standardisation in consumption, the routinisation associated with an emerging corporatisation and America's new role as a global power. In tracing out what he sees as the beginnings of late capitalism, he proceeds to argue for 1950s science fiction as key in locating the rise of a postmodernist cultural logic, stating that 'the consistent doubleness of the science fiction novels and films of the long 1950s can be taken as a sign of the beginnings of late capitalism and of an incipient postmodernism.'[13] Booker's definition of 'doubleness' is at times a little vague, in part because he refers to this in connection with a broad range of approaches to the genre. His use of this term is most convincing when applied to the themes and representational practices within the genre. At its simplest, the 'doubleness' he refers to can be seen in the genre's propensity to reflect upon the nature of being human in the featuring of non-human counterparts. In addition to this, he sees a 'doubleness' in how connotation operates within science fiction films to enable a reading that opposes or contradicts what is apparently denoted, as well as applying this term to how the genre is able to simultaneously reassure and challenge its audience. This leads to a later and more persuasive discussion concerning the ways in which monsters and aliens can be taken to embody a variety of threats. Here he moves on to suggest that: 'The science fiction films of the 1950s are *particularly* multiple and ambivalent in their production of meaning, perhaps due to the fundamental (early postmodern) ambivalence of American society toward so many issues in that decade.'[14]

Booker therefore points out how the genre anticipated the kinds of open or writerly texts that have come to be associated with a postmodern aesthetic. In part, I would say this openness can be put down to the film genre's attempts to give shape and form to fantasy figures, and the concomitant play between the familiar and unfamiliar that this brings about. Also, while Booker often sees individual films as conflicted in their apparent meaning, I believe that this becomes especially clear through comparison between films. Although repetition is inherent within any genre, it is particularly apparent in a genre that has the potential to be less restricted than many other genres. In other words, audiences may well have been made aware of the multivalent symbolism possible within the genre because of the sheer number of films that dealt with remarkably similar themes and situations, and the subtle (or not so subtle) differences between their treatments of, at times, nearly identical narrative material.

My summary of recent approaches to the 1950s science fiction and science fiction/horror film is intended to serve a double purpose: first it gives some indication of the importance of the genre to academic film studies, and second it provides an, albeit brief, overview of the complex political and cultural climate within which the genre managed to flourish. However, one further feature of the era remains unmentioned and has more than a passing relevance to the films I will be discussing. What I am, of course, referring to is the flurry of interest in unidentified flying objects (UFOs) and the vast number of reported sightings over the course of the late 1940s and 1950s. In 1947 an American businessman and pilot called Kenneth Arnold claimed to have seen nine fast-moving objects fly past him, while he was piloting a plane near the Cascade Mountains in Washington State. He reported this sighting to the Civil Aeronautics Administration and, in an informal discussion with a newspaper reporter, described the objects' motion in the air as like 'a saucer' thrown across water. Due to what Arnold later maintained was misquotation, the published story declared that he had seen 'flying saucers'; [15] a phrase that was quickly and widely adopted in the media and by the public at large. The national press also carried further stories about Arnold's experience, which was followed with the reporting of many more sightings. The US Air Force duly set up what became known as 'Project Blue Book' to investigate these sightings and debate raged over the origins of the, so called, 'flying saucers'. If not connected to the US military, it was surmised, the saucers might be Russian in origin, extra-terrestrial machines, or simply the product of an overactive imagination.

The film industry embraced the 'flying saucer' and, in parallel to the continued reports of UFO sightings in the media, a cycle of 'alien invasion' films were produced. Reported descriptions and what became the archetypal image of the 'flying saucer' in films were often almost indistinguishable. In this sense there was a relationship between sightings and saucer films, and along with the lack of conclusive proof as to their existence and provenance, it was hard to detect the divisions between fact and fantasy. Indeed, the uncertain relationship between reality and fantasy was outwardly explored in many of the alien invasion films, which commonly portrayed a person, or group of people, unable to persuade an incredulous public that they had actually witnessed the arrival of an alien vessel (e.g. *It Came From Outer Space* [dir. Jack Arnold, 1953], *Invasion of the Saucer Men* [dir. Edward Cahn, 1957]). Whether the films therefore fostered alarm or worked to reassure an increasingly nervous public is open to interpretation. For instance, many of these films literally represented the reactions of a cynical and complacent public refusing to act upon the warnings they had been given. Alternatively, other alien invasion films emphasised a blurring of the line between reality and fantasy in the adoption of newsreel-style footage and media reports that broadcast the arrival of an alien vessel to an informed and expectant public (e.g. *Earth vs. the Flying Saucers* [dir. Fred F. Sears, 1956], *The Angry Red Planet* [dir. Ib Melchior, 1960]), who frequently looked to the US military or other governing forces to secure their future in a changing world. So, the so-called flying saucer became a central part of 1950s culture and fed into the fears and anxieties of the period.

In the space of one chapter it is obviously not possible to cover the broad range of issues that consideration of 1950s science fiction film raises. Aside from limiting my discussion to what I recognise as two distinct sub-genres (the alien invasion films and the science fiction/horror films or monster movies), my main focus will be upon the way in which these films engaged with social changes during this period. To this end, the chapter is split into sub-sections looking at the repeated figuring of the boy child and father/son relations, heterosexual romance within the genre, and the representation of father/daughter relations in the American films. This is followed by a closing sub-section looking at the influence on the American film of films from Japan and Britain.

My examination of the ways in which intimate social relationships are represented in these films is underpinned with some reference to the cultural influence of psychoanalysis at this time, as well as drawing upon the psychoanalytic paradigm as a critical tool in understanding the films. Psychoanalysis was very fashionable in the US in the 1950s and alongside its growth as a therapeutic and academic discipline a popularised version permeated the cultural currents of the day. The interpretation of interpersonal relations and the importance of family dynamics as central to an understanding of human psychology and behaviour are especially evident in the science fiction films of this period. Although psychoanalysis had previously been linked with the more radical surrealist movement in Europe, in America it was largely co-opted to advocate traditional social arrangements. For instance, in its application as a therapeutic tool it appeared to promote a conservative adjustment of the individual to the cultural, political and social norms of American society, as opposed to supporting a surrealist emphasis upon release of the individual from social and political convention. In large part, psychoanalysis became part of a dominant doctrine in the US that worked to discourage individuals from taking a stand against the ongoing trend toward corporate conformism, through the pathologisation of behaviours and even ideas that were deemed inappropriate. However, it is my contention that the tensions between the conservative uses of psychoanalysis and the revolutionary potential that the surrealists found in Freud's notion of the unconscious are played up in many of the science fiction films of the 1950s. Although the genre is, in some respects, uniquely placed in its ability to provide seemingly rational explanations for irrational events, the less than rational aspects of human nature and belief are frequently emphasised. In some films the irrational is featured as a foil in the ascendance of science as a dominant doctrine and in other films the irrational is used to mark the human apart from an inhuman Other. For instance, as the following analyses will demonstrate, religious belief and ritual is often set up in opposition to scientific rationality. But while a number of films might attempt to resolve a religion/science opposition, a significant number foreground a recurring tension between irrational and rational forces in interesting ways. In these films, rather than presenting the audience with a clear distinction between religion and science, the exploitation of the psychoanalytic paradigm allows for an oscillation between rational and irrational worlds. In fact, it is possible to see psychoanalysis as forming a kind of cultural bridge between religion and science, between the irrational and rational, between emotion and scientific reason, between morality and immorality, and between fiction and reality. In this respect, psychoanalysis becomes an ideal instrument with which to explore the frictions between old and new worlds. On the one hand, the libidinous desires revealed in the Freudian subconscious can be all too easily allied with an old testament account of 'original sin' and the apparent need for a guiding and vengeful God to keep the innately depraved and wanton human being in their place. On the other hand, psychoanalysis offers a secular alternative to the confessional in the 'talking cure': the Godly powers of the priest are seemingly co-opted by the psychoanalyst, marking the ascendance of science as a replacement for religious authority.

FATHERS, SONS AND ALIEN VISITATIONS

The majority of alien invasion films ostensibly represented the alien as a malignant force, intent on destroying or controlling the earth and its inhabitants. Certainly, early films like *The Flying Saucer* (dir. Mikel Conrad, 1950), *Red Planet Mars* (dir. Harry Horner, 1952) and *Invasion USA* (dir. Alfred E. Green, 1952) drew a direct connection between a Soviet threat and the arrival of an alien force, but other films were far more ambiguous in the rendering of the alien Other. Amongst the first flush of alien invasion films, *The Day the Earth Stood Still* (dir. Robert Wise, 1951) is prominent for featuring a visitation from an apparently benign, humanoid alien (Klaatu) and his accompanying robot (Gort). From the outset, the imminent arrival of the flying saucer is communicated across the world as the opening montage reveals various national radio and television stations warning of a UFO circling the earth and eventually heading in to land in Washington DC. The police and military, accompanied by a large group of civilian sightseers, surround the saucer and witness Klaatu

(Michael Rennie) emerge and present a small but unfamiliar technological device to the assembly. Assuming this to be a weapon, a military gunman opens fire and Klaatu is injured. As the crowd rush toward the alien, the more imposing figure of the robot, Gort, exits the saucer. The robot bears down on the crowd that now surround Klaatu and eliminates the surrounding military weaponry with a powerful beam that emanates from under his lifted visor. Klaatu apparently orders Gort to stop and then announces that the device was merely an educational tool meant as a gift for the president. So, the parameters of the film's debate are set up very neatly in the first few minutes. The defensive strategy exercised by the military is ridiculed; not only is their technology insufficient but seemingly unnecessary. In contrast, advanced technology and expertise are associated with the alien's peaceful mission and attempts to enlighten the fearful earthlings.

Sent to warn the earth that their warring ways will lead to their destruction, Klaatu suggests a meeting with the heads of state from around the world in order to deliver his message to a global audience. Various politicians and world leaders are contacted, but they are unable to agree upon a suitable location. Conveniently deflecting the suggestion of antagonisms between the Soviet Union and the US, it seems that it is the British and Soviet representatives who refuse to agree upon a suitable setting, while representatives from the US are even willing to go to Moscow in order to keep the peace. *The Day the Earth Stood Still* was released the same year as the opening of the United Nations official headquarters in New York and Klaatu's request must surely have resonated with the aspirations of this postwar organisation for a contemporary audience, even though the UN is deemed unable to facilitate a meeting in the film because its membership is as yet too limited. Aligned with the alien emissary, the US government is portrayed as beyond what the alien describes as the 'petty squabbles' and 'childish jealousies and suspicions' of the Earth, but, equally, as powerless in this situation. Thwarted in his attempts to meet world leaders, Klaatu decides to break free from the confines of the hospital room in which he has been placed and, masquerading as a human being, wanders among the people of the city in order to 'become familiar with the basis of (their) strange unreasoning attitudes'. Calling himself Mr Carpenter, he books into a boarding house and quickly befriends a young boy, Bobby Benson (Billy Gray), and his widowed mother, Helen Benson (Patricia Neal). A close bond forms between boy and alien and Carpenter/Klaatu eagerly offers to assume responsibility for Bobby while his mother goes out for the day with her boyfriend. The family unit and domestic sphere is therefore quickly identified as the starting point in Klaatu's quest to understand the irrational aspects of human nature.

In the subsequent series of scenes Bobby shows Carpenter/Klaatu around some of Washington's official monuments, beginning at Arlington National Cemetery, where the boy's father is buried. Bobby explains that his father died in service during World War II and is bemused by Klaatu's lack of knowledge regarding these events. Klaatu therefore makes it clear that he comes from a place where 'they don't have any wars'. From the cemetery they visit the Lincoln Memorial, with the tall shaft of the Washington Monument clearly visible in the background. A high-angle shot shows the pair dwarfed by the memorial and Klaatu expresses great admiration for the Gettysburg Address inscribed below the statue. After this the boy excitedly requests that they go to see the flying saucer, which still sits in its landing place in a park in the city. Having taken on the role of substitute father to the boy, Klaatu comes to represent a new kind of masculine authority and his flying saucer takes up its place alongside other Washington landmarks as a sort of monument to a 'new order'.

While this 'new order' is aligned with American values and governance, Klaatu eventually turns to a famous scientist, Professor Barnhardt (who strongly resembles the familiar image of Albert Einstein), in a last-ditch attempt to communicate his message to the world. The inference here is that scientific reasoning remains unsullied by either political allegiance or irrational, human fears and that the hope for a 'new order' rests with the scientific community. The science behind the destructive powers of the atom bomb is certainly recalled when Klaatu tells the Einstein look-alike that 'by threatening danger, your planet faces danger'. However, in the next breath, they talk about a 'demonstration of force' to bring the world to its senses. At the behest of Barnhardt, this demonstration is relatively benign, neutralising non-essential technological power and effectively bringing the earth to a standstill.[16] Having earned the respect of the scientific community, a meeting is finally set up with 'the finest minds' from around the world. Throughout the film, Klaatu is able to traverse normal boundaries, at times literally opening locked doors and, with the help of Gort, passing through stone walls. This ability is apparently echoed in Klaatu's unlimited mental capacity. Similarly, Barnhardt is figured as open to new ideas and as able to think outside of normal social strictures and the boundaries brought about by national and political differences. Science is redeemed and becomes the route toward the unification of the world.

Klaatu's conversation with Barnhardt is a decisive moment in the film for a number of reasons. Not only has a meeting finally been agreed upon, but a synthesis of science and Christianity interestingly begins to surface. In the build-up to their encounter, Klaatu's affinity with rational, scientific reasoning has been stressed, making Barnhardt his most suitable earthly counterpart. It is therefore quite surprising when Klaatu says: 'you have faith, Professor Barnhardt'. Barnhardt dismisses this suggestion in replying: 'it isn't faith that makes good science, Mr Klaatu, it's curiosity'. This is effectively the first time that it has been suggested that Klaatu is ruled by anything other than pure logic. Later in the film his high regard for Christian values is further indicated when, following his resurrection from the dead, he tells Helen that the power of life and death 'is reserved for the almighty spirit'; explaining his revival as a technological technique that can only 'restore life for a limited period'. Also, at the close of the film, when Klaatu delivers his 'do or die' ultimatum to the world, it is notable that it is not only scientists who have been gathered together to hear his message. After Klaatu has spoken the camera lingers on the listening crowd and a series of medium close-ups pick out men in military uniforms and, finally, a black priest among the assembly. 'Primitive' Christian values are undeniably evoked in this film and these values are sutured to an ideology of global, free market, capitalism and white, paternal authority (I will be discussing science fiction's treatment of race in Chapter 6). Klaatu becomes a messiah figure, who, like the men buried at Arlington, is prepared to sacrifice himself for the greater good. Helen's boyfriend, Tom (Hugh Marlowe), takes up the Judas role in this story, having sold his soul in his quest for fame and fortune. Unlike the all-powerful and respectful Klaatu, Tom is exposed as an unworthy hero and unsuitable future father figure. Although Tom's actions could be read as critical of commerce and the American dream, Klaatu's announcement that 'free from aggression and war' the people of his planet 'pursue more profitable enterprises', suggests that free market capitalism reigns supreme in his world. After all, as Tom points out, Klaatu is a rich man and the diamonds he carries around are priceless. What makes Klaatu different from Tom is his willingness to share his wealth and knowledge, or, interpreted another way, his insistence that the world adopt his values and teachings.

Biskind claims *The Day the Earth Stood Still* as a film that 'skated close to the edge of permissible dissent', believing that 'its worst crime was not taking sides, was lumping the United States together with the Soviet Union in its indictment of world politics.'[17] This view is also partly backed up Billy Gray's comments in the interview attached to this chapter, as he recalls the obstacles that the filmmakers were forced to overcome in the production of *The Day the Earth Stood Still,* as well as the apparent risks they took in the subject matter and casting of this film. However, as my analysis has revealed, the film may not be as politically impartial as Biskind suggests. Certainly the existing political machine, as depicted in the film, is not able to offer a suitable framework within which to bring about world peace, but the US government is consistently figured as supportive of Klaatu's ambitions. In this sense government officials are actually distanced from the actions of the military in this film. While Klaatu's long soliloquies might advocate that the world put aside its differences, his evident admiration for President Lincoln allies him with the political aspirations of the United States. Even though Klaatu's display of power is not destructive, his scientific superiority threatens destruction; a threat that is further articulated in his final speech. While the film implies that the politicians' hands are tied or perhaps that they are unwilling to access the ultimate controls offered by science and technology, it simultaneously suggests that backed up by the threat of a superior scientific force, the US government is only too willing to demand world peace. So, although *The Day the Earth Stood Still* appears disparaging of certain aspects of cold-war ideology and was, according to Gray, intended as an 'anti-nuclear weaponry movie', this is not an anti-American film. With God and science on their side, this film sees the United States as the nation prepared to lead the world to a peaceful and lucrative future.

The relationship between Bobby and Carpenter/Klaatu is vital in *The Day the Earth Stood Still*. Although Bobby's centrality may well signal the American film genre's associations with juvenile pulp magazines and comics, he also functions to emphasise Klaatu's authority and the emergence of a new generation of men with respect for the wonders of science. Without the social strictures of adulthood, Bobby is free to exercise his imagination and possesses the kind of insatiable curiosity that Barnhardt exhibits. However, as much as Bobby likes and trusts Carpenter he also comes to fear him. Having surreptitiously witnessed Carpenter return to the saucer late one night, Bobby discovers the true identity of his new-found friend and mentor. In order to enter the saucer, Klaatu instructs the robot to render the military guards unconscious. So, Bobby also sees a display of the alien's aggressive superiority and power and runs back home to tell his mother. After relaying his experience to Helen and her boyfriend, Bobby says: 'I like Mr Carpenter mum I'm kinda scared'. At this point, Bobby articulates the mixture of affection and fear that the ideal figure of paternal authority is required to engender. The paternal interest that Klaatu shows towards Bobby is therefore an expression of his leadership qualities within the microcosm of a family and his function as a controlling influence in the face of an otherwise unrestrained and immature enthusiasm for both scientific and commercial enterprise.

Questions concerning paternal authority are also raised in a later film, *Invaders from Mars* (dir. William Cameron Menzies, 1953). At the opening of this film, a young boy and keen amateur astronomer, David MacLean (Jimmy Hunt), wakes up during a storm and witnesses a flying saucer landing in a field behind his home. The saucer sinks below the earth and disappears from sight. David hurriedly rouses his father, George MacLean (Leif Erickson), who walks out into the night to check the field for evidence of this visitation. The next day David wakes up to find that his father has been transformed from the loving and attentive parent of the previous evening to a cold and aggressive dictator. Gradually the once familiar people that surround David begin to change and the film follows his frantic attempts to alert the authorities to the threat introduced by the alien force. The film portrays the boy's view of a changed world and, contrary to the 'realistic world' of *The Day the Earth Stood Still*, the use of impressionistic sets, forced perspectives and lavish musical score creates an obviously artificial environment within which the events unfold.[18] Indeed, the closing moments of the film reveal that the boy has simply had a dream, although the final twist of the alien craft hovering on the horizon suggests that his nightmare may not be over.

As in *The Day the Earth Stood Still*, the family romance lies at the heart of the film's events. However, *Invaders from Mars* remains more ambivalent about the new man of science as societal patriarch. A useful starting point in understanding the dynamics of this film is to read it in conjunction with Sigmund Freud's ideas concerning childhood fantasies and parental authority. In a short paper first published in 1909, Freud outlined the dynamics at play in childhood daydreams about parentage and family origins. Briefly, at an early age the child exalts his parent, but as he comes to develop his own independence he begins to question his earlier assessment. Freud sees this questioning as a necessary but painful part in the process of the 'liberation of an individual [. . .] from the authority of his parents.'[19] According to Freud, a common childhood Fantasy associated with this process involves a growing awareness that his parents are not the ideal figures of his earlier years, frequently imagining them 'replaced by others of better birth.'[20] However, Freud is also careful to point out that in replacing parental figures with 'grander people';

> We find that these new and aristocratic parents are equipped with attributes that are derived entirely from real recollections of the actual and humble ones; so that in fact the child is not getting rid of his father but exalting him. Indeed the whole effort at replacing the real father by a superior one is only an expression of the child's longing for the happy, vanished days when his father seemed to him the noblest and strongest of men and his mother the dearest and loveliest of women.[21]

So, it is possible to see the entire film as bound up with David's personal growth and the insecurities brought about as part of his own developmental process into adulthood. For example, under the control of alien forces, David's parents become emotionally distanced from him and are later described by a friendly police sergeant as 'the coldest pair I ever saw'. This change causes David to turn to idealised substitutes in the caring and maternal, female medical doctor, Dr Pat Blake, MD, (Helena Carter) and her close friend, Dr Stuart Kelston (Arthur Franz). David's own father is an engineer, replaced now by the young and eager Kelston, representing a fully developed David in his role as the local astronomer and scientific expert. At the same time as the cold and detached demeanour of David's father and his mother, Mary MacLean (Hillary Brooke), calls into question their identities as suitable parents and, indeed, their very humanity, Dr Blake chooses to act upon David's story about alien abduction because Dr Kelston has informed her that the child is 'the cold, scientific type, not given to flights of fancy'. So, the film both dismisses and sanctions scientific reasoning, played out as David's conflicted feelings about his father. Throughout the film, David is surrounded by male figures of authority: all the men in the film are either policemen, members of the armed forces or scientific experts. Although David appears to elevate his mother's social standing in the person of Dr Blake, like so many of the invasion film, she is confined to a supportive role as the men take charge of the situation. Having said that, it is significant that both the high ranking Chief of Police (Bert Freed) and General Mayberry (William Forrest) are not to be trusted and authority is passed to the lower ranking Police Sergeant (Max Wagner) and Colonel Fielding (Morris Ankrum). Once again, ambivalence toward paternal authority is apparent in the simultaneous desire to denigrate and extol traditional masculine virtues, to both pull apart and build up the patriarchal structures of leadership and control.

A similar ambivalence is evident in *Invasion of the Body Snatchers* (dir. Don Siegel, 1956), only here the focal point of the drama is a fully grown man, Dr Miles J. Bennell (Kevin McCarthy). Returning from a medical conference to his small town, suburban home, he is alarmed to discover that a wave of mass hysteria appears to have taken hold of the town. His first encounter with this phenomenon takes place when, on the way back from the station, a small boy runs out in front of his car with the boy's mother in hot pursuit. The mother explains that her son, Jimmy Grimaldi (Bobby Clark), is simply frightened to go to school. However, it later emerges that Jimmy is actually frightened to return home: exclaiming 'don't let her get me', Jimmy tells Bennell that his mother, Anne Grimaldi (Eileen Stevens), is no longer his mother. Sympathetic, but lacking the insight to fully understand the situation, Bennell simply gives the boy a pill and requests that he stay with his grandmother for a while. Unlike the menacing father figure of *Invaders from Mars*, in *Invasion of the Body Snatchers* it is maternal control and authority that most threatens the world of this film. The alarming prevalence of a discourse commonly known as 'Momism' in 1950s America has been well documented and a number of academics have traced its association with the fictional representation of sinister female characters.[22] In the wake of influential publications like David Levy's 1943 book, *Maternal Overprotection,* and Philip Wylie's 1942 book, *Generation of the Vipers* (in which the term 'Momism' was first coined), it seems that mothers were being blamed for all the world's evils. In particular, there was a lot of anxiety circulating around the mother–son relationship, in which the 'smothering mother' was held responsible for the inability of the male child to successfully mature as a properly masculine subject in American society. So, looking at the film in the light of these contemporary concerns, it seems that the nurturing and civilising role undertaken by the traditional mother figure within the family is configured here as the root cause of Jimmy's fears and his later conformity with his mother's wishes as evidence of a threateningly feminising force. This is compounded by the conspicuous absence of the boy's father and his failing as the family's resident patriarch, noted at the beginning of the film by the 'littered, closed up vegetable stand' that he used to manage. But, rather than offering up a substitute father figure, as was the case with *The Day the Earth Stood Still* and *Invaders from Mars,* in *Invasion of the Body Snatchers,* our central hero, Bennell, is unable and unwilling to take up the role of father figure.

It is my contention that the boy in *Invasion of the Body Snatchers* serves to introduce Bennell's own underlying fears and anxieties; Jimmy's fear of his mother and compliant return to the bosom of the family, mirroring Bennell's mixed feelings concerning women and the domestic environment. Right from the start the doctor is regarded as the man who got away. The flirting that occurs between Bennell and his nurse at the opening of the film assures viewers of his heterosexuality, but it is also made clear that she is already married and therefore safely unavailable. Divorced and childless, Bennell seems reluctant to take up his paternal duties and his association with the medical/biological sciences places him in a role more usually reserved for female characters in the invasion films. Also, whatever respect he commanded as a medical expert in the town is gradually eroded as the townspeople are rapidly replaced by alien replicas and are, therefore, no longer in need of his services. In fact, it is with the arrival of the newly divorced Becky Driscoll (Dana Wynter) that the trouble really begins for Bennell. At once attracted by her feminine charms, but fearful of where this will lead him, Becky becomes the site of Bennell's unresolved masculine identity and place in the world. At the close of the film, when he finally kisses her, he recognises that she too has been replaced with an alien replica. She tries to persuade him to stay, but he flees from her and the small town of Santa Mira in horror, while his voice-over narration explains: 'I ran like little Jimmy Grimaldi had run the other day'.

Looking closely at this film's production history, Al LaValley traces out the conflicting authorial influences evident in *Invasion of the Body Snatchers* and describes how the studio (Allied Artists) later insisted on the framing, flashback story and voice-over narration. According to LaValley, the addition of the ending in which Bennell is vindicated and the police and FBI are mobilised in response to the alien force, was largely due to what was perceived by the studio as the 'bleakness' of the film. LaValley further suggests that 'bleakness, of course, implies an ideological position. One cannot be negative about America; one must show that Miles got through.'[23] My own interpretation sees this as bound up with Bennell's masculine identity. Having told a fellow doctor about the events that occurred in Santa Mira, the doctor replicates Bennell's response at the beginning of the film and is unsure about how to interpret this story. Discussing Bennell's case with another colleague, the doctor then overhears that strange giant pods have been found after an accident on the highway. This sighting confirms Bennell's story and the doctor immediately commands that the relevant authorities be contacted. As Bennell's counterpart, the doctor is therefore seen to take control of the situation and order the immediate containment of the threat. So, by proxy, Bennell's masculine identity and his patriarchal rights to authority are rather hastily reinstated in the film's closing postscript.

ROMANTIC ENCOUNTERS

In all three films discussed above, the figure of the young boy operates to bring about a questioning of patriarchal power and the role of the father, or father figure, both within the family and within a wider community. The literal father/father figure, in these films, is a scientist of one sort of another; scientific reasoning and endeavour are therefore being offered as a new route to masculine power and paternal authority. At the same time, anxieties concerning masculine identity in a postwar and affluent America are played out on an epic scale and become a matter of national security. Interestingly, where the figure of the boy is absent in the invasion film, the successful union of the young, heterosexual couple becomes the focus of attention. That is not to say that the father/father figure disappears. On the contrary, the female protagonists' father/father figure is usually present, only to be replaced in many of these films by the 'new man' of science. So, in alien invasion films like *The War of the Worlds* (dir. Byron Haskin, 1953), *This Island Earth* (dir. Joseph Newman, 1955) and *Earth vs. the Flying Saucers* (dir. Fred F. Sears, 1956), a fundamental patriarchal order is not in question; rather, these films mark and/or question the ascendance of science and its role in the supervision of a patriarchal order. For example, as Klaatu embodied a union of scientific and Christian values in *The Day the Earth Stood Still*, the central romance of the young couple in *The War of the Worlds* is used as a vehicle to closely examine a 'marriage' of new and old orders. *The War of the Worlds'* opening montage offers a brief visual account of the devastating technologies used in the fighting of World Wars I and II, leading up to contemporary advances in rocket science. The accompanying voice-over presents an urgent, documentary-style report concerning the expansion of scientific enterprise as 'menacing' to all forms of life on earth. So, from the outset, the film clearly announces itself as standing against scientific endeavour, linking this with mankind's apparent predisposition toward aggression and self-destruction. However, as the film's Technicolor credits take over from the black-and-white, documentary-style prelude, a more traditional, fictional format is initiated by a further prologue sequence, heralding the impending invasion of an alien force. Against the backdrop of a succession of visual renditions of the solar system, the narrator describes a Martian quest to find a new and more fertile planet to inhabit. This sequence is immediately followed by the spectacle of the Martian space ship streaking across the night sky as it crash lands into the earth. Attention then turns to a small town and a crowd of people witnessing this sight while standing outside a cinema showing Cecil B. DeMille's religious epic, *Samson and Delilah* (1949). This playful, reflexive device at once aligns and opposes the biblical epic with the science fiction film genre and also establishes the film's forthcoming evaluation of a traditional Christian order versus an escalating scientific rationalism. Among the crowd of spectators is our leading heroine, Sylvia (Ann Robinson), together with her Uncle (father figure), Pastor Matthew Collins (Lewis Martin). The handsome hero is later introduced as the young, astro-nuclear physicist, Dr Clayton Forrester (Gene Barry), whose expert advice is enlisted by the local townspeople. Gathered around what they initially assume to be a meteorite, the locals plan their commercial exploitation of the event, while Clayton carries out a preliminary examination of the site. It is at this point that Clayton and Sylvia first encounter each other and a sexual attraction between the couple is quickly established. Although Sylvia proclaims that her master's thesis concerned modern scientists, her fascination with the subject seems fuelled by romantic desire rather than a thirst for knowledge and throughout the film she is characterised as the naïve and alluring companion to the informed and logical Forrester.

Having measured unusually high radiation readings emanating from the meteorite it is Forrester who judges it as potentially dangerous. His fears are soon realised when the crew of the alien vessel begin their planned destruction of life on earth, swiftly eliminating anything that stands in their path. The military are promptly called into action, but Sylvia's uncle is determined to attempt communication and to make peace with the alien beings. Against the scientist's better judgement, the Pastor believes that if, as Forrester attests, the aliens are more technologically advanced than mankind then 'they should be closer to the creator for that reason'. However, their technological and intellectual development is obviously not matched by a recognisable spiritual development and the Pastor's assumptions are proved dramatically incorrect when he is quickly eliminated by aliens. In effect, custody of Sylvia is then passed from her uncle to Clayton and the rest of the film focuses upon their fight to survive the alien onslaught and upon their blossoming relationship.

Of particular note is a scene which sees Clayton and Sylvia take refuge in a deserted farmhouse. Surrounded by the devastation that the aliens have wrought the couple attempt to construct a cosy kind of normality. While Sylvia cooks breakfast they talk about old times and the respective differences between their childhood backgrounds. During the conversation it emerges that Sylvia has come from a large family, while Forrester's parents died when he was a child. The strong bond between Sylvia and her now deceased uncle is also elaborated upon when she tells Forrester how, as a child, she sought refuge in a church and prayed 'for the one who loved (her) best to come and find (her)'. Given that her prayer was answered with the arrival of Pastor Collins, Sylvia's religious faith is obviously rooted in her childhood affection and trust for her uncle as paternal protector. With family life and domestic security linked with Christian faith, Sylvia therefore represents those facets that are missing in Forrester's life. While Sylvia stands for a traditional, societal organisation based upon family values and religious convictions, Forrester represents a more contemporary order based upon a scientific rationalism and a kind of disconnected autonomy.

As the struggle for survival continues, it soon becomes apparent that the most sophisticated weaponry that human science has to offer is ineffective against the Martians. Despite all his best efforts, by the close of the film, Forrester is eventually stripped of his cool rationality as he frantically searches for the missing Sylvia during what he assumes to be his last hours. Successfully reunited in a local church, the couple join the rest of the congregation in prayer and it is at this point that the Martian invasion is halted. Forrester's devotion to scientific rationalism is thereby replaced by his devotion to Sylvia. Faith in science is shown to be misplaced; instead human salvation is apparently brought about by a regeneration of reverence for the powers of an 'almighty spirit' and a respect for human relations as sanctioned by the church. While religious faith is most certainly feminised in this film, in the time-honoured tradition of the romance, the hero's attitudes and behaviour are necessarily moderated in the eventual alliance with the heroine. Although it is made clear in the closing, voice-over narration that mankind's miraculous deliverance was due to the Martians' lack of immunity to earthly bacteria, understood as God's creation, these natural defences are here linked with a divine order. So, the film's final message seems to be that science can safely be used as an analytical tool as long as it does not challenge what is understood as a natural and divine order.

In a similar fashion to *The War of the Worlds, Earth vs. the Flying Saucers* also features a central couple fighting for survival in a world thrown into trauma and chaos by the arrival of an alien force. Beginning with the now customary, documentary-style prologue, a voice-over statement refers back to 'biblical times' and man's long-held fascination with 'strange manifestations in the sky'. Set against a montage of shots showing both military and commercial aircraft alongside flying saucers, edited together with witnesses' reaction shots, the voice-over continues to report on the significant numbers of reported UFO sightings across the world. In response to these contemporary 'visitations', we are informed that 'all military installations are to fire on sight at any flying objects not identifiable'. The narration therefore indicates that the sight of unearthly phenomena no longer elicits the reverence and wonder of 'biblical times', but suspicion and fear. Unlike both *The Day the Earth Stood Still* and *The War of the Worlds*, religious belief and Christian faith are therefore set firmly in the past. As becomes apparent, in *Earth vs. the Flying Saucers* masculine aggression, along with a show of technological muscle, is the chief requirement if humanity is to survive and defend itself against the alien threat.

The prologue provides an instant backdrop for the film's narrative and is followed by the credits and the immediate introduction of our central couple. The audience quickly learns that our young hero is a rocket scientist, Dr Russell A. Marvin (Hugh Marlowe), who has just married his secretary, Carol (Joan Taylor). Returning by car to the military base where they both work, Carol is seen in the driving seat, while her new husband sits beside her and dictates a scientific report into a tape recorder. As if to justify the visual dynamic in the scene, the ensuing dialogue makes it abundantly clear that Carol functions as a capable helpmate in support of her husband's important scientific work. However, this intimate scene is disrupted by the arrival of a flying saucer, forcing Carol to stop the vehicle. Dr Marvin gets out of the car to consider what he has seen and, after a brief period, heads back to join Carol. At this point he is reinstated in the driving seat for the remainder of the journey. So, a traditional order is restored with the spectre of the alien force.[24]

When they finally arrive back at work, our young scientist faces further challenges, in his repeated attempts to launch a rocket into space. Each of the previous rockets having apparently failed, the pressure is piled on when Brig. Gen. Hanley turns up to witness the latest launch. The General is also his new father-in-law and is only informed of Dr Marvin's marriage to his daughter upon his arrival at the base. Just before the imminent launch of a twelfth rocket, the flying saucer that the couple had earlier encountered appears. Led by the General, the attending military embark on a pre-emptive attack, but are decimated in the ensuing battle. The aliens then kidnap the General, steal his mind, and turn him into a compliant slave who is under their control. It was the violent action of the General that brought about the retaliatory destruction of the base and Dr Marvin's more reasoning and less aggressive approach to the situation initially appears validated by comparison. Nevertheless, later in the film the General's response is vindicated when the doctor learns that the aliens wish to rule over the Earth and its human inhabitants. Following this discovery, Dr Marvin's scientific expertise is turned toward the development of a new and effective weapon to counter this take-over bid and he gathers together a team of fellow scientists to help him complete the project.

The subsequent battle with the aliens takes place over the city of Washington and sees the saucers destroy some of the same landmarks and monuments featured so reverently in *The Day the Earth Stood Still*. By comparison, this visual display of destruction in *Earth vs. the Flying Saucers* makes it clear that the invading force is distinctly opposed to American values or governance. In the absence of Carol's father, it is up to Dr Marvin not only to assume authority, but to take up where the General left off. As Carol's new husband, Dr Marvin is required to prove himself worthy of her affections and to undertake the aggressively protective, paternal role once performed by her father. As was the case when the couple were first introduced in the car scene, when Dr Marvin's masculine authority is threatened he transforms from the inertly thoughtful man of science to proactive action man. Although a comparison can be drawn between the hierarchical structure of the military and the more equitable and cooperative approach exercised by the scientists in the film, in the person of Dr Marvin, the male scientist certainly picks up the mantel of power, but only once he has demonstrated that he can fight like a man and assure the survival of this world.

Likewise, while the dashing young scientist, Dr Cal Meacham (Rex Reason), in *This Island Earth*, does not have to face a literal father, he is required to win the respect of the self-appointed, father figure to an elite group of scientists before he can secure the admiration of his love interest, Dr Ruth Adams (Faith Domergue). After undergoing a series of trials, the mysterious Exeter (Jeff Morrow) invites Meacham to his headquarters. Scientific pursuit is unabashedly sexed-up in this film and Meacham is immediately drawn as the spontaneous and masterful action hero. For example, the opening of the film introduces Meacham as a well known scientist and glamorous celebrity, hounded by the press before he leaps into a borrowed jet plane in order to pilot himself back to his laboratory in the desert. However, his youthful arrogance and self reliance are quickly challenged with the appearance of an alien force (later revealed to be the work of the alien interloper, Exeter), which literally takes control of the plane. To add insult to injury, Meacham is later obliged to become the passive passenger in a futuristic, remotely controlled plane that is sent to transport him to Exeter's secret location.

Upon his arrival at Exeter's headquarters, Meacham is greeted by an unresponsive and nervous Adams, who drives him to a meeting with Exeter. Here he learns that Exeter has gathered together an eminent team of scientific experts from around the globe in pursuit of an overarching goal to end all wars. However, Meacham remains cynical and is determined to learn more from both Adams and her close friend, Steve Carlson. It is hard to hold a confidential conversation within this environment as Exeter is able to observe their every move via futuristic security cameras scattered throughout the premises. Finally securing a brief period of privacy in an underground laboratory, Adams and Carlson express their fears at being taken over by the mysterious stranger and his unusually advanced technology. As was the case in so many of the alien invasion films, as much as *This Island Earth* stresses independence and a sort of social (also literal) mobility available in the person of the scientist, a loss of personal autonomy is also presented as the inevitable outcome of unchecked scientific advancement. In the competition for Adam's attention, Carlson's politic approach to the situation has obviously not yielded results; it is Meacham who has come to release Adam's from Exeter's controlling gaze. Indeed, Carlson is conveniently killed off by the aliens as the trio attempt escape; leaving Adams sandwiched between Meacham and Exeter in the second half of the film. Once

Carlson is out of the picture, Meacham and Adams are forcibly transported to Exeter's home planet, where they witness the destruction caused by an ongoing, interplanetary war. Their visit is short-lived as the planet is about to be destroyed and Exeter, Meacham and Adams are forced to flee. However, the escape is hampered by one of the monstrous mutants that the aliens have been breeding to carry out menial tasks. The mutant disobeys Exeter's orders and tries to attack Adams, then is finally destroyed by the pressure building up in the spacecraft as they leave the planets atmosphere. As the last surviving member of his alien race, Exeter sacrifices himself and returns the couple back to Earth.

Having made a case that this film is similarly patterned upon the patriarchal, family structure evidenced in my previous examples, it is notable that our heroine is rather more self-sufficient than is usual in the alien invasion films. Initially at least, as an established member of the team of scientists, Adams is figured as more than Meacham's equal. It is only after she has allied herself with Meacham that her role seems to diminish. It is also notable that Meacham's attempts to protect Adams are not altogether successful. For instance, if he were the true hero of the piece, rather than seeing the Mutant's timely disappearance due to pressure in the spacecraft, surely Meacham would have been seen to rescue Adams from the attack? Rather, it is advanced technology that almost incidentally rescues Adams from the Mutant's onslaught. Jancovich has commented that many of these films presented 'women's active involvement in the struggle as absolutely essential to the victory over the menace, and it is the men who fail to appreciate their contribution who are usually portrayed as a "problem" '.[25] It is true that unlike much of Hollywood's output during this period (e.g. westerns like *High Noon* [dir. Fred Zinnemar, 1952], *The Far Country* [dir. Anthony Mann, 1954] or biblical epics like *The Ten Commandments* [dir. Cecil B. DeMille, 1956], *Ben Hur* [dir. William Wylor, 1959] etc.) or even the numerous, family-based, situation comedies that appeared on television in the 1950s (e.g. see following interview with Billy Gray, who briefly describes his experiences as a young actor in the series *Father Knows Best* [1954–60]), women in science fiction films were usually featured as taking up a place in the public sphere, as actively supporting the men of science or as scientists in their own right. However, I would amend Jancovich's statement by pointing out that the more dissociated a central female character in a science fiction film became from a traditionally feminine role, the more the film drew upon elements commonly associated with the horror genre.[26] In other words, the degree of power assigned to a central female character was usually matched by the identifiably horrific nature of the alien menace. It would be hard to argue that Klaatu, or even the formidable Gort, in *The Day the Earth Stood Still,* were presented as recognisably horrific, whereas the unsightly mutant in *This Island Earth,* sporting threateningly large claws and bleeding profusely from its injuries, is more consistent with the visceral imagery common to the horror film. So, to clarify, it is my contention that the introduction of these elements was often intimately connected to the degree of authority allotted to the central female character. In this respect, *This Island Earth* can be viewed a kind cross-over film; clearly it comes under the category of the alien invasion film, but borrows from the science fiction/horror films or monster movies with the presentation of the Mutant. To illustrate my point, we only have to look to science fiction/monster movies like *Them!* (dir. Gordon Douglas, 1954) and *It Came from beneath the Sea* (dir. Robert Gordon, 1955) to find female scientists who play a more crucial and authoritative role.

In *Them!* the FBI, along with the scientific team of Dr Harold Medford (Edmund Gwenn) and his daughter Dr Patricia Medford (Joan Weldon) are brought in to investigate a series of strange murders and disappearances in the New Mexico desert. The scientists soon discover that nearby nuclear testing has resulted in a mutated colony of giant ants. Although there is the hint of romance developing between the FBI representative, Robert Graham (James Arness) and Patricia Medford, her role does not diminish during the course of the film. Instead, her assessment of the situation becomes particularly crucial in the latter part of the film. Because her father is elderly it is Patricia Medford who takes over at this point, bravely leading a combined team of military, FBI and state troopers into the bowels of the earth to investigate the giant ants' nests. Evidently, a growing respect for Patricia Medford's expertise and active involvement is matched by the growing horror of the situation.

It Came from beneath the Sea provides an even clearer example. This film also sports a mutated beast affected by nuclear radiation and the questionable honour of representing the independent and skilled female scientist is again awarded to Faith Domergue. Here Domergue plays Professor Lesley Joyce, proclaimed by her colleague, Professor John Carter (Donald Curtiss), as the 'outstanding authority on marine biology'. Upon the appearance of a giant sea creature that has developed a taste for the 'higher forms of life' (namely man), the reluctant Joyce is drafted in to help the Navy in their fight against this unnatural menace. As was the case with *This Island Earth,* the female scientist finds herself embroiled in a love triangle and faced with a choice between the utterly reasonable and rather staid Carter and the forceful and dominant, submarine commander, Pete Mathews (Kenneth Tobey). Laura Mulvey's famous psychoanalytic reading of the western/melodrama, *Duel in the Sun* (dir. King Vidor, 1946), argues that the love triangle serves to illustrate the female protagonist's inability 'to settle or find a "femininity" in which she and the male world can meet'. In the film, Pearl (Jennifer Jones) finds herself caught between the lustful, Lewt McCanles (Gregory Peck), and his older brother, the respectable lawyer, Jesse (Joseph Cotton), who vie for our heroine's attention. For Mulvey, the feuding brothers come to represent an internal conflict between the passive (feminine) and active (masculine) sides of Pearl's nature: Lewt revealing the sexually active and 'sinful' side of her character, while Jesse draws out the acceptably passive, 'nice girl' in Pearl. However, Mulvey is careful to point out that 'although the male characters personify Pearl's dilemma, it is their terms that make and finally break her.'[27] In reference to Freud's understanding of female sexuality, Mulvey notes that 'the development of femininity remains exposed to disturbances by the residual phenomena of the early masculine period.'[28] So, according to the Freudian paradigm, the active side of Pearl's nature is viewed as a regressive trait.

Unable to find a peaceful resolution, passions run high and *Duel in the Sun* ends in a violent shoot out resulting in Pearl's demise. In applying Mulvey's ideas to *It Came from beneath the Sea,* like the McCanles brothers , Matthews and Carter are similarly opposed in character, each offering Joyce a very different future. The lustful commander certainly succeeds in exciting the passions of the otherwise logical Professor Joyce, but it is also made clear that his domineering attitude irritates her on occasion and interferes unduly with her scientific research. Their ensuing affair is calmly witnessed by a confident Professor Carter, who later enlightens the confused Matthews on the nature of the 'new breed' of womanhood that Joyce represents. Speaking for Joyce, he explains: 'They feel that they're just as smart and just as courageous as man. And they are. They don't like to over-protected, they don't like to have their initiate taken away from them.'

Once the monster has been dispatched, the final scene sees the trio triumphantly celebrating over dinner in a local restaurant. Joyce announces that she will now be able to continue her research in Cairo and Matthews asks if she will 'change, move away, get married, have a family'. Not discounting this as an option, Joyce states that her immediate concern is with her work. Then she asks if Matthews would be willing to collaborate with her on a new book, which she playfully entitles: 'How to Catch a Sea Beast'. Without waiting for a reply, she reaches across the table and gives Matthews a kiss goodbye.

Although it is possible to read the love triangle in *It Came from beneath the Sea,* as functioning to reveal the protagonist's unresolved femininity, compared to *Duel in the Sun,* Joyce's 'dilemma' remains amicably unresolved. In the context of this science fiction/monster movie, Joyce's standing within the scientific community appears to offer her a greater range of legitimate choices. Furthermore, the new world of scientific reason and egalitarianism in *It Came from beneath Sea* embraces those very characteristics that proved to be Pearl's undoing in *Duel in the Sun*. In contrast, the supposedly regressive traits that Pearl exhibited, in Joyce, ostensibly function to expose a progressively scientific world view. Although I remain astonished by the unusual level of autonomy allowed in the characterisation of Professor Joyce, it is all too easy to read this 'new breed' of woman in alliance with the mutated monster. However, Joyce seems acutely aware of the problems stirred up by her presence, as evidenced when she mockingly delivers the title of the book. So, on the one hand, it is possible to see this 1950s film as radically progressive in its attitudes toward women. But, on the other hand, this film also belongs to a science fiction/horror sub-genre in which a manifestly progressive attitude toward women's role in society is offset by the less than repressed horror generated in the arrival of a commanding female figure.

DADDY'S GIRL

While careful attention to the closing scene of *It Came from beneath the Sea* reveals a knowing link between beast and woman, this is further explored in one of the most famous science fiction films from this period: *Forbidden Planet* (dir. Fred M. Wilcox, 1956). Often remembered for its striking and convincing special effects and avant-garde, electronic score (composed by Louis and Bebe Barron), *Forbidden Planet* is also an important film within the genre because of its deliberate and foregrounded references to psychoanalysis. Indeed, if we were in any doubt as to the influence that psychoanalysis had upon the genre at this time, then *Forbidden Planet* makes this abundantly clear in its use of the Freudian, tri-partite structuring of human personality as id, ego and superego. Briefly, for Freud, the id represented the most primitive aspects of human personality from which the ego and superego developed and was understood as the source of all basic human drives. These drives not only included biological impulses like the need to eat or the need to drink, but sexual and aggressive impulses, which, according to Freud, were also instinctive constituents of human psychology. Where the id seeks instant gratification of these instinctive, inner impulses, the development of the ego involves awareness and acknowledgment of an outer reality that has to be negotiated with in order to satisfy the urges of the id. Finally, the superego represented an internalising of the learned values and morals of society and the acceptance of what actions were deemed right and wrong. To summarise, under the influence of a well developed superego, it is part of the ego's function to repress forbidden thoughts or actions that might be deemed wrong or threatening, to push these away from the conscious mind so that they remain hidden in the unconscious mind and only vaguely perceived through the complex symbolism of a remembered dream. In *Forbidden Planet* it is the literal manifestation of the id's most primitive sexual and aggressive drives that threatens the all male crew of the rescue mission sent to the distant planet of Altair IV. Having lost contact with the colony of settlers sent from earth to Altair, the intrepid Commander John J. Adams (Leslie Nielsen) and his crew are sent in a relief saucer to investigate. Upon their arrival they discover that Dr Morbius (Walter Pidgeon) and his nymph-like daughter, Altaira (Anne Francis), are the only two surviving colonists. Although Morbius' wife (Altaira's mother) reportedly died of natural causes, the crew are told that the rest of the colonists were viciously murdered by a mysterious monster, which has since disappeared from the planet.

In the mean time, Morbius has created an Eden-like sanctuary in the wastelands of Altair. As he busies himself with his scientific creations, his daughter is kept company by an assortment of wild animals that populate their garden and her every whim is provided for by a mechanical robot called Robbie. Built and programmed by Morbius, it is Robbie who supervises and protects Altaira and who instantly synthesises whatever she wants or needs. Robbie is certainly meant to possess superhuman strength and intelligence, but, unlike the imposing Gort in *The Day the Earth Stood Still,* he/it is presented as utterly controllable and incapable of harming a human being. In comparison to Gort, Robbie's smaller scale and rotund appearance makes him look almost cuddly and he is also seen to undertake those tasks more normally associated with a mother rather than a father figure (e.g. making dresses, cooking meals, cleaning house etc.). In fact, at one point a member of the crew describes him as 'a housewife's dream'. Even as Robbie stands for an unthreatening and feminised technological tool, the crew soon learn that the same advanced technology that facilitated Robbie's development has also unleashed a far more hostile force. It seems that the colonists were not the first to populate this planet, as evidenced by the technological legacy left behind by the highly civilised and advanced, Krell.

Later in the film, Morbius explains to the crew how his thirst for knowledge led him to tap into the power of the Krell and undergo a dangerous, brain-enhancing procedure. Since then, he has spent practically every waking moment unlocking the secrets of the Krell technology. Morbius goes on to display his degree of mastery over Krell technology by conjuring up a 3-D image of Altaira: the Krell technology allows him to literally project his thoughts and fantasies for the amusement of the crew. Although this display hints at Morbius' preoccupation with his daughter, he is initially represented as the archetypal scientist, as ultra-rational and dogged in his studies, while his daughter lives in a state of protected innocence, at one with nature. Having had little social contact, Altaira is naive and unaware of the effect she is having on the young men around her. Thus follows a sequence of scenes in which members of the crew unsuccessfully attempt to ignite her passions, which are finally awakened with the commander's kiss. From this moment on, there is trouble in paradise and the unseen force that destroyed the Krell and the human colonists is once more unleashed upon this world.

Although the father (father figure)/daughter relationship was an important element in a number of the 1950s science fiction/horror films, as previously discussed this relationship was usually quickly displaced by the heterosexual romance between a central couple. In films like *The War of the Worlds, Them!, This Island Earth* and *Earth vs. the Flying Saucers* the removal of the literal father/father figure from the centre of the action, often through their untimely death, could well indicate a certain anxiety surrounding the father/daughter relationship. In comparison, *Forbidden Planet* stands out as a film in which this relationship takes centre stage, offering an overt working-through of elements that remained more covert in existing films within this hybrid sub-genre. In a recent publication, Rachel Devlin looks at the ways in which the father/daughter relationship was reconfigured during the post-World War II era in America. At a time when paternal authority was seen to be diminishing, the popularisation of the psychoanalytic paradigm allowed for a reformulation of paternal power, as based upon the more 'subtle, psychological power of erotic attraction.'[29] For Devlin:

> The eroticisation of the father-adolescent daughter relationship reformulated paternal power by several means: by establishing that girls' psychological health was *inescapably* dependent upon a good – and most certainly unrebellious – relationship with their fathers; by maintaining that girls' sexual acts were not autonomously undertaken but always reflected prior, Oedipal feelings for their fathers; and, finally, by establishing social conventions that instilled the idea that girls should (and inevitably would) look to their fathers, before anyone else, for sexual approval.[30]

Although much has been said about the so called 'Momism' of the period and how an 'unnaturally' close bond between mother/son was seen as a threat to the sexual maturity and 'correct' development of the boy child, the eroticised nature of the father/daughter relationship has attracted far less comment from academics and critics alike. So, Devlin's study highlights the typically overlooked reformulation of the father/daughter bond, conspicuous in a broad range of cultural artefacts (i.e. novels, television programmes, magazines, films etc.) from that period. Devlin does not extend her analysis to science fiction films, but I would suggest that *Forbidden Planet* not only engages with the kind of reformulation that she refers to, but actually works as a kind of meta-text within this cultural and historical context. For instance, where the absence of a mother/mother figure usually passed without comment in science fiction/horror films, in *Forbidden Planet* this is highlighted when Morbius is obliged to tell the crew about his wife's demise. The absence of the mother figure here obviously focuses attention upon the bond between Altaira and her father. Although this bond is initially underplayed in the characterisation of Morbius as distant and aloof, this simply makes his later unveiling as jealous and possessive father all the more shocking.

As the film progresses the attacks upon the crew of the rescue mission, brought about by the return of the mysterious monster, become increasingly severe, until an outline of this previously unseen enemy is captured in the electronic forcefield that surrounds their spaceship. Eventually, in an effort to understand what is occurring, the ship's doctor undergoes the same brain enhancing process that has affected Morbius. Although the process proves fatal in this instance, with his new-found insight he is able to offer a superior analysis of their circumstances before his death. Following the clues left by the doctor, the commander deduces that what the Krell had overlooked in the development of their technology was 'their own subconscious hate and lust for destruction'. In inventing a technology that serviced their conscious needs and desires, the Krell had forgotten that, without the kind of failsafe that Robbie exhibited, this machine could also play out the less savoury needs and desires of their unconscious minds. Like the Krell, Morbius is also unaware of the extent of the machine's power and is in denial about the more primitive aspects of his own psychological make-up. Morbius has successfully repressed the unacceptable desires and aggression of his primitive self from his conscious mind and remains unaware that the monster that is killing the crew is, after all, a manifestation of his own unconscious drives and desires; drives and desires that are clearly related to his relationship with this daughter. For most of the film Morbius seems outwardly unconcerned by the growing affection between the commander and his daughter, but his innermost feelings are expressed in his repeated warnings that the crew should leave the planet and the increasing threat that his id monster represents. In the closing moments, the situation reaches a critical point when, pursued by the monster, Altaira announces her allegiance to the commander. Shaken by this news, Morbius is now visibly upset and, just as the monster is breaking through the walls of their home, he turns to Altaira and demands: 'tell it you don't love this man'. Altaira refuses, putting her own life at risk in the face of her father's mounting anger. Trapped behind the strong doors of the Krell laboratory, the protagonists can only watch while the monster begins to burn its way through in order to wreak its revenge. No longer able to repress or control his primal urges Morbius is forced to literally face up to himself. This experience proves too much for him and, in an effort to defend his daughter, he is finally destroyed by his own monster.

In the light of many science fiction films of this period, what is unusual about *Forbidden Planet* is the fact that the threatening alien force, the monster, is seen to emanate from the mind of the male scientist. Undoubtedly, Altaira's sexually charged presence appears to trigger these events, but the guilt for the destruction that follows lies with her father. It is, after all, Morbius' overprotective nature and close to incestuous desire that is brought to the surface in *Forbidden Planet*. In a further article, Devlin challenges the assumed influence of psychoanalysis in America during this period by suggesting that it put the acting out of incestuous desire onto the agenda. Backing up her claims with reported case studies from the period, instead of writing off accusations of incest, psychoanalysts began interpreting girls' claims of sex with their fathers 'as proof of the strength of female adolescent Oedipal desire – and therefore its potential enactment – rather than as evidence of the pervasiveness of incestuous fantasy among children.'[31] Of course, in taking her argument further, even though the reality of incest might not have been denied, it seems that the female victim became the object of attention and, you could say, took the blame for incestuous thoughts and even acts. In accepting Devlin's assessment, what is clear is that *Forbidden Planet* took a rather different standpoint on the issue. Even as the film suggests that Altaira's sexuality is heavily informed by the claustrophobic relationship with her father (Morbius has created Altaira as surely as he projected the 3-D image of his daughter in his earlier display to the crew), it is *his* desire and *his* psychopathology which is in question.

In summary, both what I have called the alien invasion films and the science fiction/horror films displayed an overwhelming concern with the family, whether this was outwardly articulated as an alien threat to the future of the traditional family or as a threat emanating from within the family unit. Heavily informed by a pervasive, popular psychoanalytic discourse, the 1950s American science fiction films looked to the family in an examination of societal changes brought about by the rising dominance of scientific reason, technology and corporate capitalism. Indeed, the films' central characters often straddled both domestic and public spheres in the playing out of shifting social mores and values. Overall, scrutiny of these films reveals a highly ambivalent attitude to change. For example, as my analysis bears out, the focus upon the boy child in films like *The Day the Earth Stood Still* and *Invaders from Mars* exposes an unresolved attachment to an earlier state of being associated with wonder, curiosity and an unsullied vision of the world. At the same time as these traits are valued in both films and may well signal an emergent social mind-set, they are nonetheless literally denoted as regressive human qualities. Things become ever more complicated when the focus is placed upon the 'new woman of science'. Even as some of the invasion films featured capable, professional women, their place within the public sphere was usually overshadowed by their superior male counterparts or suppressed in the course of their romantic involvement with a male hero. Alternatively, as witnessed in the science fiction/horror films, their very appearance activated the arrival of the monstrous mutant. Where the female took on a more traditional role, either as alluring sexual object or, less frequently, as powerful mother figure, she was often linked with the arrival and spread of a degenerative force. Although many of these films acknowledged the threat of unbridled scientific ambition, in its association with masculine prowess, restraint was frequently figured as feminine and equally as threatening. So, while the 1950s American science fiction films certainly engaged with changes in American society and often presented a challenge to traditional social order, they were also largely unable to imagine happy or viable alternative social structures.

OUTSIDE INFLUENCES

As much as American science fiction films of this period were limited in their perspective and overwhelming concerned with the survival of an American way of life, they were undoubtedly influenced by science fiction or science fiction/horror films from abroad. Traffic between America and Europe (especially Britain) had certainly been acknowledged in a number of higher budget 'prestige' features based upon well known science fiction novels from abroad. In this respect, the figure of H. G. Wells had loomed large over American science fiction ever since Orson Welles' notorious radio adaptation of *The War of the Worlds* in 1938. This was followed in 1953 by Paramount's reworked film version of the novel, with the close of the decade seeing MGM's rendition of *The Time Machine* (dir. George Pal, 1960). Aside from these literary sources, the popular American science fiction films of the day owed much to the visual aesthetics and narrative strategies of films that emanated from outside of the Hollywood machine. However, in moving away from the juvenile adventures of the Saturday cinema serials (e.g. *Flash Gordon* [1936–40]) and the lively audaciousness of the science fiction/musical, *Just Imagine* (dir. David Butler, 1930), the 1950s, American features did not take up the utopian aspirations of earlier films from Europe (e.g. *Metropolis* [Germany, 1927], *Things to Come* [UK, 1936]). Instead, in keeping with a more pessimistic, postwar attitude toward science and technology, inspiration was drawn from the British, Gothic horror tradition, as revamped in the low budget films of the British Hammer studios, and also from the science fiction/horror films, or kaiju films, produced in Japan by the Toho studios in the 1940s and 1950s.[32] The Toho studio was responsible for creating giant, screen monsters like Mothru, Ghidrah, Rodan and for introducing Gojira (Godzilla) onto the international film scene. *Gojira* (dir. Ishirô Honda, 1954) was first released in America in 1955 to a niche, Japanese-American market, but was quickly followed by a USA/Japanese adaptation, called *Godzilla, King of the Monsters!* (dir. Ishirô Honda, Terry O. Morse, 1956), which was specifically designed for a wider American film market (although later released in Japan as *Kaijû no Gojira* in 1957). The original version had contained direct references to the bombing of Hiroshima and Nagasaki at the end of World War II and to nuclear testing in the South Pacific, thereby linking the destruction wreaked upon Tokyo by the sea monster with Japan's first-hand experiences of atomic devastation and the after effects of radiation. These references were cut from the American print and principle scenes featuring an American reporter (played by Raymond Burr) were added, with remaining scenes dubbed for the English speaking audience. The changes therefore re-focalised the narrative, as seen through the eyes of the American reporter, and dampened the critical aspects of the original film. The success of *Godzilla, King of the Monsters!* in America marked the beginning of a series of films featuring the giant, prehistoric, amphibian that continue to this day. Of course, Hollywood had its own history of giant screen monsters going back to *King Kong* (1933). Nevertheless, the influence of *Godzilla, King of the Monsters!* is unmistakable in the mid- to late 1950s, American science fiction/horror films. For example, parallels between *Godzilla, King of the Monsters!* and the previously discussed, *It Came from beneath the Sea,* are not simply identifiable in the featuring of giant sea creatures, but are also instantly recognisable in the narratives and plots. Like Godzilla, the appearance of the six-limbed, giant octopus in *It Came from beneath the Sea* is reportedly the result of radiation fallout and the scenes that show the final demise of the creature in both films are remarkably similar. While the meanings behind the monster metaphor appear to be differently skewed in each film, the impact of Godzilla is indisputable.

Like so many of the American and Japanese films, the British science fiction/horror films of the time ostensibly dealt with the destructive potential of atomic weaponry and concerns surrounding the development and future use of nuclear power. Anxieties about the changing role of women and female sexuality in general were also prevalent in the British films and often dealt with in more explicit terms. Some British films very obviously exploited the popularity of American science fiction films; a clear example being *Stranger from Venus* (dir. Burt Balaban, 1954). Riding on the success of *The Day the Earth Stood Still, Stranger from Venus* imitated its American counterpart to the point of casting the same actress, Patricia Neal, in the leading role. Likewise, *Devil Girl from Mars* (dir. David McDonald, 1954), also took from *The Day the Earth Stood Still,* but the comic overtones and sexual sauciness of this British film mocked the seriousness of its American predecessor. Instead of Klaatu's dramatic arrival in Washington DC, audiences were introduced to a leather-clad dominatrix, called Nyah (Patricia Laffan), who proceeded to terrorise the inhabitants and guests gathered at a remote Scottish boarding house. In the place of Gort, Nyah is accompanied by her mechanical Johnny and an array of outlandish atomic devices, which she uses to exert control over the isolated group of earthlings. After much deliberation, Nyah informs the assembled group of her intention to take a suitable male specimen from their ranks for breeding purposes, before making tracks for the city of London. While the men outwardly state their contempt for her demands, each, in turn, expresses a suspicious willingness to sacrifice himself to her wishes for the good of the rest of the group. Eventually, a suitable match is arrived at in the person of the robust and surly Robert (alias Albert Simpson). An escaped convict, Robert was jailed for killing his wife and is seeking refuge with his former girlfriend at the boarding house. Bringing Nyah and Robert together proves to be a literally explosive combination as, in the closing stages of the film, the remaining occupants of the boarding house watch as they take off together, only to be blown to pieces as the saucer makes its ascent into the night sky. London is therefore spared the alien onslaught and both the dangerously depraved Nyah and the wife-killing convict get their just deserts.

Unlike the majority of the monster movies that flooded the American drive-in, British horror films were traditionally intended for the adult market, which was further compounded with the scrapping of the 'H' certificate (applied to horror films) and the introduction of the 'X' certificate (as applied to a wider selection of films deemed unsuitable for young audiences) in 1951. So, the targeting of an adult audience often differentiated the British science fiction/horror films from the American films and might go part-way to explaining the overt sexual playfulness exhibited by some of the British films. In contrast, the later run of science fiction/horror films from the Hammer studios did not display the lascivious quality of its immediate, British predecessors. In fact, any hint of romance or sexual activity was driven underground in these films, even as the inevitable associations of an 'X' certification were emphasised in the marketing of the films. Also, where *Stranger from Venus* and *Devil Girl from Mars* were predominantly intended for a home market, Hammer's run of 'Quatermass' films and *X the Unknown* (dir. Leslie Norman, 1956) were specifically made with the American market in mind. Due to some canny manoeuvring, the studio had secured co-production and distribution deals in America, which opened up this market for a succession of their films.

The 'Quatermass' films were adapted from the popular, BBC television series, with the key role of Professor Quatermass now occupied by an ageing American actor, Brian Donlevy, in both *The Quatermass Experiment* (dir. Val Guest, 1955) and *Quatermass 2* (dir. Val Guest, 1957). On a simple level the casting of Donlevy was intended as a point of identification for the American audience, but his performance of the role sits rather uncomfortably with the surrounding British cast of characters. At times it is as though Quatermass is the real alien presence in these films. Taken as the lone representative of his nation's values and ideals, Donlevy's Quatermass appears to be drowning in a sea of British bureaucracy and parochial posturing. Although Quatermass compels the action, in the context of these films and depending upon the point of view of the audience, he can either be read as a dynamic force for change and modernisation or as an agent of unrest and disorder. The character's obsessive ambitions are illustrated in his repeated attempts to set up a successful rocket programme and the first film begins with one of his manned missions returning to earth with a bump. Two of the three astronauts have inexplicably disappeared and the one remaining is struck down with a mysterious illness. Taken to a secret laboratory for study, the peculiar features of the astronaut's disease are made evident when he literally absorbs the characteristics of a cactus plant in his room. Still, it takes the scientists a while to catch up with what the audience already know and although he manages to hide his cactus-like arm, his behaviour and general appearance indicate a dramatic transformation has occurred on the space flight. All of this does not deter his wife from breaking him out of his confinement and remaining strangely oblivious to the threat he poses. Once freed, the action of the film escalates when he is let loose in London, where he continues to kill and absorb whatever he touches. However, among all the mayhem, the pace slows when he meets a young girl by an otherwise deserted canal. The girl attempts to befriend him and is shocked when he angrily destroys her toy dolly and staggers off. In an obvious reference to Mary Shelley's *Frankenstein* (1818), this film makes plain its associations with a British Gothic tradition. In fact, I would go as far as to say that the film uses these associations to critique the 'gung ho' mind-set of the American Quatermass and, by extension, the more zealous approach toward scientific experimentation exhibited by popular American science fiction films of the time.

Eventually the astronaut is transformed into a formless mass and finally cornered and destroyed in Westminster Abbey. Although the filmmakers were forbidden to shoot on location, they went to some effort to construct a convincing mock-up. This setting was especially significant at the time of the film's release, due to the coronation of Queen Elizabeth II in 1953 and the unprecedented media coverage of the ceremony at the Abbey. For Christine Geraghty the coronation was not only a crowning moment for Elizabeth, but for the new woman of the 1950s era. As Geraghty explains, Elizabeth's image was scrutinised by the press and special attention was given to her adoption of the fashionable and commercial New Look in her clothing and appearance. In examining the meanings available in the spectacle of the coronation, Geraghty then maintains that the ceremony was unusual because 'it challenged, in a way more radical than the supposedly medieval trappings indicated, the idea that women should be confined to the domestic spaces of the home.'[33] In backing up this claim, she goes on to argue:

> As her husband and the men of the establishment knelt before her, it was clear that a woman was taking on the highest symbolic role of the state; she was the most troublesome of creatures, a woman who went out to work.[34]

For Geraghty, 'the ideal of the new woman was constructed in four key areas – motherhood, sexuality, work and consumption', all of which were brought together in the image of Elizabeth's coronation. Given this backdrop, the implications of the closing scenes in *The Quatermass Experiment* in terms of the gender politics of the period seem clear. But there are other levels of meaning that need to be explored. In looking at the 1950s Hammer films, Sue Harper discusses textual changes that came, in the first half of the decade, with the studio's British/American thrillers. Aside from the casting of American actors, Harper notes a number of important differences between the home-grown products of the studio and later co-productions. Apart from a preoccupation with gender difference in the co-productions, one of the most important shifts she demonstrates is a transfer of focus from class issues to a concern with consumerism. As Harper describes it: 'These co-productions were unconcerned with class; in a meritocratic manner, they displayed an interest in the status provided by goods which had been earned, rather than in the status of inherited rank.'[35]

Extrapolating from Harper's argument here, I would say that this very shift is also played out in the closing scenes of the first 'Quatermass' film. Yes, the destruction of the alien entity can convey a fear of a female or feminine power, but, unlike the earlier thrillers, class issues have not vanished in this film. As linked to the coronation, this scene surely displays an attack upon the British class system. While Britain sought to strengthen its relationship with the United States after World War II, the period saw a surge in the number of American companies and corporations setting up European headquarters in Britain and fears abounded about an encroaching Americanisation of British culture. So, remembering that it was Quatermass who brought this alien force to Earth, and more specifically to Britain, the amorphous mass can equally be read as an all absorbing and American threat to British tradition.

The idea that alien and Quatermass are somehow linked becomes even more apparent in *Quatermass 2*. In this film, Quatermass is shocked to discover a secret factory built in a remote part of the British countryside. He is especially bewildered because the factory strongly resembles his own design for a moon project. The model for the moon project sits in Quatermass's office and, like the factory, features futuristic dome structures linked by large lengths of overground piping. In answer to his queries, government officials deny any connection with his own plans for the moon project and tell Quatermass that the site is a state of the art facility designed to produce synthetic food. Quatermass remains sceptical and also connects the site with the sudden arrival of strange meteor showers in the same vicinity. Upon further investigation, he finds a number of meteor pods that have landed just outside of the factory. His colleague picks one up and it bursts open, leaving a strange scar on his face. It seems that, once scarred, the unwitting victim of a pod becomes enslaved and apparently controlled by the alien force that inhabits the factory. His fears are confirmed when he uncovers the factory's true purpose is to grow giant alien beings who intend to take over the earth. As was the case with the first film of the series, the alien beings are dark, sludgy masses, which threaten to engulf the world. He rushes to London to warn them of the danger and to enlist the help of his friend, Lomax (John Longden), from Scotland Yard. Lomax puts him touch with an equally irate MP, Vincent Broadhead (Tom Chatto), who Quatermass joins in an official tour of the plant. Ignoring the commands of the factory officials, both Broadhead and Quatermass elude their tour guide to take a look behind the scenes. Refusing to follow in the footsteps of their guide, they are attacked and Quatermass escapes within an inch of his life. However, the visit proves fatal for Broadhead, who becomes covered in a dark, slimy, disintegrating liquid. His dying words exclaim that this liquid is the food the factory is actually making and 'it burns'. Given all these clues and the fact that the factory scenes were shot on location at the Shell Haven Refinery in Essex, surely it is not too difficult to see that the black liquid that overcame the MP is actually oil.

During World War II, an oil-rich America had provided its allies in Europe with the fuel needed to power the armoured ground and air forces, but, after the war, there were fears that America's supply was running dry and US attention was turned to oil fields in the Middle East. *Quatermass 2* was released in 1957, just after the Suez Crisis,[36] which led to the resignation of the British Prime Minister, Anthony Eden. Hostilities between Egypt and both Britain and France began with the threatened closure of the Suez Canal, affecting access to oil supplies in the Middle East. Fearful they might be dragged into a third world war, the Eisenhower administration forced Britain and France into a ceasefire when the Soviet Union threatened to support the opposing side and launch attacks on London and Paris. Although the British Empire was already in decline and Britain's status as a world power had severely diminished, the Suez Crisis made clear that the world was now divided between the two new superpowers of the Soviet Union and the United States. To add insult to injury, Britain's remaining foothold in the area came under increasing pressure as American interests in this oil-rich area grew. So, on one level, oil retained a symbolic association with the wealth and power of the United States in Europe. Thus, the engulfing, alien mass of this second film still represents an overwhelming threat to British sovereignty from an ongoing Americanisation. However, the meanings associated with the first 'Quatermass' film are expanded upon in *Quatermass 2*. Here, the eruption of the sludgy alien from the domes of the factory and the black liquid death dished out to the MP can be seen as a rather obvious reference to the Suez Crisis, which you might say literally blows up in Britain's face in the film. Whether Donlevy's Quatermass is then read as a British ally or as associated with a continuing threat of Americanisation remains unclear, as both meanings appear to be available in this film.

In this second film, there is a notable attempt to distance Quatermass from what can viewed as an American threat. For instance, he rather unwittingly becomes a kind of saviour for the working classes in this film, when he tries to galvanise the workers from the factory into action against the alien invasion. Quatermass leads Lomax and a rather drunken newspaper reporter, Jimmy (Sid James), to the social club frequented by the factory workers and their families. Here, Lomax pleads with the crowd that they listen to Quatermass, but they seem more interested in the dancing of the attractive local barmaid. Representing a more 'down home' version of Geraghty's new woman, the barmaid is distinguished from the crowd by her fashionable attire and wilful ways. Having captivated the clientele at the club, the woman draws them away from the traditional jig they were previously performing and proceeds to flood the hall with the sound of a big band, American Jazz tune selected from the jukebox. Like an earlier stereotype of the British land girl who fraternised with the American fly-boy and eagerly accepted nylons and Hershey bars in many a war film, the barmaid has embraced aspects of American culture. Fears concerning an ongoing 'American invasion' are therefore displaced onto the barmaid, so that Quatermass can be more easily aligned with the struggles of the working men at this point. The barmaid is suitably punished for her indiscretions when further meteor pods reign down upon the hall and the crowd witness as one of these explodes in her face. Following this incident Quatermass ignites a worker's revolt and after a rather weak attempt from Lomax to keep law and order, the men march upon the plant, attacking the management as well as the very fabric of the factory that they helped to build. This all occurs toward the close of the film, but it is not the workers who ultimately destroy the alien threat. In a rather tacked-on ending, it is, after all, the actions of one man, one scientist, one hero, who saves the day; namely Quatermass when he launches his rocket at the alien mother ship circling the earth. In this rather sudden return to the familiar formula of the American science fiction film, this ending avoids any suggestion that Quatermass is attacking British authority. Like the American films, the threat is seen to originate from another world, but also like the American films, the threat reflects back upon what is happening within national boundaries.

So, class, gender and nationality all come into play in the fears wrought by the alien presence in *The Quatermass Experiment* and *Quatermass 2*, and a clever layering of meanings opens the films to a variety of readings that speak to both a British and American audience. Finally, sandwiched between these two films, is Hammer's *X the Unknown,* which bears a striking resemblance to the 'Quatermass' films in the featuring of a slimy amorphous mass; a mass that is even likened to oil at one point in the film. However, this film seems less concerned with issues of class and nationality than it is with gender and sexuality. Indeed, *X the Unknown* picks up on aspects exhibited in the earlier *Devil Girl from Mars* and even draws upon similar plot devices. For instance, both films include young boys in their casts of characters; boys who are innocently drawn to the deadly threat.

X the Unknown opens on a military training exercise in a remote part of Scotland. The soldiers are being taught how to operate Geiger counters and, during this exercise, they unearth a mysterious pocket of radioactivity buried deep in a fissure that suddenly opens up beneath them. Until further investigations can be carried out, the military place a rather ineffective, overnight guard upon the area. The threat surfaces when two young local boys take off to explore a tower in the marshes nearby. One of the boys (the appropriately named Willy) runs off on his own, but quickly returns when he sees something frightful. Following this incident Willy is struck down by a mysterious illness, later diagnosed as radiation sickness, and the doctors at the local hospital are unable to save him. If we were in any doubt of the sexual metaphors at play in the film, a further, otherwise redundant, scene makes this abundantly clear. After the death of the boy, one of the doctors from the hospital arranges a tryst with an attractive nurse. They meet in the Radiation Room of the hospital and, just as things are heating up between the couple, the sludgy monster from the deep oozes into the room. The nurse stays safely behind a radiation shield, but the doctor certainly gets his fingers burned, and a lot more besides, when he approaches the intruder.

In the face of this enigmatic threat, the authorities enlist the help of a scientific expert, Dr Royston. Unlike the outwardly dynamic and driven Quatermass, Royston appears rather more bumbling and pedantic. However, like Quatermass, he is portrayed as a scientific maverick, preoccupied with his private experimentation into radioactivity and with the building of a machine that can neutralise radioactive particles. After Royston's workshop is broken into things get personal and he deduces that the organism is drawn toward atomic radiation, which it feeds upon in order to grow and expand. The attacks increase and the situation escalates as the sludgy creature edges closer to populated areas in its search for radioactive food. Royston's experimentation in the workshop had been on a small scale, but he decides to adapt his equipment to deal with this large-scale threat and sets a trap for the creature. The close of the film sees the monster driven back underground and successfully neutralised. So, while references to Suez and the imminent danger of atomic war are most certainly built into *X the Unknown,* a sexual subtext is also apparent in this film as disease and potential alien conquest become sutured to the feminine/female. Also, what is, of course, particularly noticeable in all three films is the relative absence of female characters from the centre of the action. Where the American science fiction/horror films usually featured a pivotal, central female character who was skilled and respected within their professional field, in these Hammer films the female characters are very marginal. So, whereas the American films tended to match the literally powerful female with an equally powerful monster, these British films largely replace the female with the monster in their fight to retain an orderly, masculine realm.

INTERVIEW: ACTOR BILLY GRAY

C: Firstly, I'd just like to ask a couple of general questions about your career as a child actor in Hollywood . . . could you perhaps say a little about how you got into the field?

B: Well, yes, my mother was an actress, Beatrice Gray, and her agent saw me running around in a theatre. I was five years old I guess. The agent asked me to take her to my mother. It turned out that it was mother's agent and she said that I could get some work. So, she started sending me out on interviews and I usually got most of the jobs that I went for.

C: Were you what they call a bit of 'natural'?

B: Yeah, I think you could say that. I think a brat is more like it.

C: You appeared in so many films during your childhood, how did you feel about acting at this time and, looking back, how do you feel about it now?

B: Except for a very few occasions, I enjoyed it all. The last years of *Father Knows Best* were a bit of a strain.[37] I had been doing that character for so long and being so much older than the character I was playing, it wasn't an easy job. But other than that . . . when I first got started I did mainly 'bit parts' for four or five years and that was just fun. You go in for a day and say your couple of words, or whatever it was, and then you move on to the next one. It was just kind of 'quick and dirty' and it was just a fun thing. There wasn't any long involvement or entanglements with anybody or anything.

C: I've read an interview with you concerning that television series, *Father Knows Best* [1954–60]. In the interview you talked about the sort of idealised image, if you like, of the family dynamics on display in the show . . .

B: An interesting side line is that the show was originally on the radio for four or five years, I think, before it went to television. In the radio version it was *Father Knows Best?* . . . with a question mark.

C: That's interesting.

B: Yeah and when they went to television they figured that they would just keep on going – do the same thing. The only top slot that they could get was owned by P. Lorillard Company, which was the maker of Kent cigarettes. They had a ten o'clock spot and being as the series-makers were desperate to get the thing on and going, they felt like they had to take this, even though it wasn't the right time slot. The other thing that was problematic about it was that the P. Lorillard Company insisted that the question mark be dropped. It was a deal breaker. They didn't want the show otherwise. Robert Young and Eugene B. Rodney, who were partners and owners of the show, were troubled by it, but there was nothing much they could do. It just goes to show you that the original sponsors of the show had something quite different in mind and the title *Father Knows Best* – declared as a statement – is a very dangerous one.

C: Well, that certainly speaks to the gender politics of the time.

B: That and totalitarianism. I mean, that's how Hitler got strong – people just deferred to their Führer and whatever he said as being right. That's how horrible things happen. The other aspect that was unhelpful, I think, was the male chauvinism in the series. There were several scripts that I recall when the girl characters were encouraged to use their 'feminine wiles' and to be duplicitous in their involvement with people – to manipulate them.

C: If I can come now to *The Day the Earth Stood Still,* as far as I am aware, this was your first role in a science fiction film. How did your experiences of working within this particular genre differ, or how were they the same, from say the westerns or comedy films that you had previously worked on?

B: Actually, there really wasn't any difference. It was approached as if it were . . . I guess you'd call it 'cinéma vérité' almost – something that was actually happening. It wasn't a campy kind of thing, like a lot of science fiction. They tried to make it as real as possible, in the hope that they could suspend peoples' disbelief. I think to a large degree they were successful. It wasn't a 'shocker' kind of thing. They weren't going for the gasp.

However, they did run into some trouble with the subject matter. It was not approved by the US government, army department. They were asked to contribute – which was not uncommon if you were doing something that has army involved in it at some level – but they read the script and said, no thanks, we don't want to be involved. So, all the army stuff that's there is National Guard, who had no problem with it.

C: Why do you think that was?

B: It was an anti-nuclear weaponry movie and in 1951 we were in the throes of a manufactured scare tactic to turn us against the Russians. The Russians were known to have the hydrogen bomb. As far as our government was concerned we were in a race to see who could get the most weapons and MAD ('Mutually Assured Destruction') was formulated at about that time. The idea was that if you hit the US with something, the US would guarantee to respond and the whole world would go up in a big conflagration. That was our brilliant plan! Anything that questioned that plan was persona non grata at the State Department or the halls of government or whatever.

C: You had a very central role in *The Day the Earth Stood Still,* I was wondering whether you could recall the kind of direction you received and how you saw the character of Bobby at the time?

B: Fortunately Robert Wise is an incredibly good director and a wonderful person on top of that. I know we say that about people in Hollywood all the time, but in this case it's actually true. I never felt any kind of pressure to do anything other than just be a normal kid. One of the advantages that I had as a child actor was that I was generally about three years older than the character I was playing. For instance, I was playing about ten in *The Day the Earth Stood Still* and I was actually about thirteen. So, that means I can be more objective about it because I'm not portraying myself. That liberates you to do whatever you think the part requires. So, I didn't have any problem with that character at all. I played him just like he was a normal kid and that seemed to go down well with Robert Wise.

C: You had a lot of dialogue to handle in that film.

B: I discovered later in life that I had dyslexia. I had always wondered why I didn't care for reading all that much. My system to learn the lines was that my mum would say them and I would hear them and then I would remember them. That was the way I learned the parts when I was starting out.

C: It seems to me that most of film revolves around Bobby's growing relationship with Carpenter, with Klaatu . . . as a boy, how did you understand that relationship? What did you see it as?

B: I wasn't thinking this at the time, but it was a normal kind of thing. Here is a kid without a father and here is this kind of interesting father-figure type, coming into his world. So it seemed like the most natural thing in the world to gravitate toward him – feel the warmth and all that. It wasn't extraordinary at all. I think that's what made it so effective was that it seemed to be perfectly natural.

C: You obviously worked particularly closely with Michael Rennie – what was that working relationship like?

B: He's English you know and such a gentleman. He carried that kind of air about him. There was a certain reserve in his manner. He wasn't cold at all; he just wasn't getting in your face and was sufficient in himself. It was very comforting to be around him, he was so self-assured and so generous with the whole business of being an actor. There are people who are kind of full of themselves and don't have much time for you. But that was not him at all. In fact he was very interested in my mother. Maybe that's why. He would be getting her coffee and making sure she had everything.

C: The scene in which you discover Carpenter's true identity in the film seems particularly crucial to me – when you secretly witness him entering the flying saucer. Whereas other scenes rely more heavily on dialogue, this scene largely requires that you react to what you are seeing. Can you recall how your performance in that scene was elicited?

B: It's interesting . . . I've done several Q and As after screenings of the movie, with Robert Wise in attendance – honouring him for something. So, at one of those occasions, I recalled his direction about that particular scene and I remembered some direction about that particular scene. 'With eyes as big as saucers', was the phase that I remembered for the reaction to what I was seeing. I asked Robert Wise if he had given me that direction, because I remembered it, and he said that he hadn't. Then somebody gave me a script a while back and I found that it was in the script directions – 'his eyes are as big as saucers'. I didn't think that Robert Wise would give me a piece of direction like that, but I did ask him and he agreed that he hadn't. I guess it came from the script – from Ed North, the screenplay writer of the film. I didn't think that I opened my eyes especially large, but it did seem to work. I've got a website and I use a still picture from that scene on the opening page. It's my favourite picture of myself that somebody snapped off as a still image from the movie.

Something else that I am particularly proud of in that the scene . . . the exit, as I run away from the scene, I fall down. People have remarked about what a realistic fall it was – it looked like it actually happened. It didn't actually happen, it was rehearsed.

C: Following *The Day the Earth Stood Still* there were a number of other films which featured young boys in 'close encounters' with alien beings. Two films that spring to mind are *Invaders from Mars* (1953), which also featured a boy (David MacLean – played by Jimmy Hunt) and *Invasion of the Body Snatchers*, with Jimmy Grimaldi, played by Bobby Clark? Have you any thoughts about how these boy characters function within the genre? I mean, why do you think that the figure of the boy was so important in these alien films?

B: Well, you know, it hasn't been a particularly interesting area for me. I don't go out of my way to see movies generally and didn't at the time either. So, I'm kind of out of the loop as far as being aware of anything other than what I was involved in.

C: So, you weren't a sci-fi fanatic at the time or anything like that . . .

B: No and I didn't become one either. In fact, I didn't look at the movie as if it was science fiction; I just thought it was a regular movie that had some strange characters in it.

C: I also want to ask if you have any recollections about the general reception of the film. For instance, what was your impression of how audiences and critics responded at the time?

B: As I recall, it didn't do all that well. It wasn't like it was a blockbuster or had any particular effect on the population in general. I'm sure the producers would have liked for it to have been a little more effective, but it didn't do anything. As a country we were definitely going full speed ahead in the other direction.

C: So, it didn't have the required effect?

B: No, it didn't – it hardly made a dent.

C: Looking back, what are your views on the film now?

B: Oh, I think it's the best sci-fi movie that I've ever seen – hands down. I've been really surprised at how well it holds up after all these years. I've seen it probably at least four of five times in the last ten years or so and every time I see it there's only one scene that seems a little dated. But I'm not even so sure about that one as a matter of fact . . .

C: Which scene is that?

B: It's where Klaatu is in the hospital recovering and there are two doctors in an anteroom. The doctors are both talking about how quickly he is recovering from his wounds, as they are lighting up a cigarette. I thought well that's just because times are different now and that wouldn't have been a joke back then. But now I think it was intended as a joke, even then. Looking back on it, I think that was intentional on Robert Wise's part. So, the joke was anticipated and a laugh was planned for and hoped for.

C: The 1950s is often called the first 'Golden Age' of the science fiction film. I mean, following earlier films like *The Day the Earth Stood Still* the cinema was swamped with both higher-budget and low-budget science fiction films. You've partly spoken of this, but what do you think was the appeal of the genre at this time?

B: I'm almost positive that it correlated with reports of UFOs. At the time it was just rampant – every other person had seen something mysterious in the sky. I think that's what made science fiction popular at this time.

There's one other thing you should know about the film that is interesting. The actor who was to play the Professor Barnhardt character was chosen by the director and producer – they told the casting people to sign him up. The casting people said, no you can't do it because he's in *Red Channels*.[38] Zanuck, who was the head of studio, said, well we're just going to ignore that and we're going to use him anyway. That showed some real courage. I mean, they already had a problem with the subject and the government, so to thumb their nose at the House Un-American Activities Committee was a dangerous thing to do.

C: Particularly with him in that role as well . . .

B: Yeah. He was for peace and he was ostensibly the Einstein character. Right around that general time, Einstein had advised against the use of the bomb.

C: My last question, again, you've partly answered, but critics and academics have recently reassessed the science fiction films of this period and frequently understand them as intimately connected to 'cold war' politics and life in 1950s America. I was wondering whether you could comment further on this view. What were these films saying about life in America at this time, do you think?

B: Well, I'm just sad that they didn't go an awful lot further. I mean, I think they were very tepid attempts at criticism of something that was so absolutely, horrendously insane, that they didn't do any service to the advancement of sanity at all. I think they dropped the ball. Much as reporters and journalists are dropping the ball on a regular basis nowadays. A courageous and sane person would have spotted this Mutually Assured Destruction for the idiocy that it was and would have said something about it. I don't think anybody really did, everybody was so afraid that their social position would be damaged. Cowardice, big time.

C: The feeling of fear and paranoia must have been incredibly intense.

B: I think it was. I certainly didn't understand it all at the time, but, in retrospect, I'm sure everybody was terrified. It wasn't accidental. I forget who, but the secretary of war or something, at one point, either under the Eisenhower or Truman administration, said that the only way they could pull this off is to scare the hell out of the American public. I mean all of this incredible spending on atomic weaponry. Twenty, thirty, forty thousand bombs – I mean what the hell was going on? I'm embarrassed to be a human being. Iran was a very good case in point . . . don't get me started . . . I think the only film that really tried to do something and was effective to a degree, was *Dr Strangelove*. That was much later of course.

NOTES

1. IMDb lists 193 American-made, science fiction films, produced from 1950 through to 1959, as compared to the 57 produced from 1940 through to 1949.
2. *Destination Moon* cost around $600,000 to make and, released the following year, *The Day the Earth Stood Still* cost 20th Century Fox approximately $960,000. Paramount's *The War of the Worlds* had the highest budget of approximately $2,000,000, while MGM's *Forbidden Planet* came in at around $1,900,000. To put these budgets into context, Paramount's cycle of biblical epics and spectacle dramas were generally made on much higher budgets. For instance, *The Greatest Show on Earth* (1952) had a budget of approximately $4,000,000 and *The Ten Commandments* (1956) an astounding $13,500,000. However, in comparison with Paramount's *Stalag 17* and *Roman Holiday* (both released in 1953), which received budgets of $1,315,000 and $1,500,000 respectively, it would be hard to argue that *The War of the Worlds* was made on an especially low budget. Likewise, the budget for MGM's *Forbidden Planet* as compared to musicals like *Singin' in the Rain* (1952, budget: $2,540,800) and *It's Always Fair Weather* (1955, budget: $2,062,256) indicates that this science fiction film was given A-movie treatment.
3. *Invasion of the Body Snatchers* was made for approximately $417,000 – a comparatively low budget by mid-1950s standards.

4. Brosnan 1978, p. 118.
5. 'The Imagination of Disaster', in Sontag 1967, pp. 209–62.
6. See ch.3, 'Pods and Blobs', in Biskind 1983, pp. 102–59.
7. See 'Introduction to the First Edition', in Sobchack 1993, pp. 11–13. Here Sobchack justifies her emphasis on films from the 1950s onwards, stating that 'it was only after 1950 that SF film emerged as a critically recognised genre' (p. 12).
8. Henderson 1999, p. 1.
9. See Shapiro 2002.
10. Biskind 1983, p. 111.
11. Jancovich 1996, p. 17.
12. Ibid., p. 26.
13. Booker 2001, p. 4. It should be noted that Booker dates what he terms as 'the long 1950s' through to the early to mid-1960s, with the period coming to a close following the revolution in Cuba, the 1962 missile crisis, and topped off with the publication of Herbert Marcuse's *One-Dimensional Man* in 1964. Also, his dating through to the 1960s enables him to discuss Stanley Kubrick's cold-war satire, *Dr. Strangelove, or How I Learned to Stop Worrying and Love the Bomb* (1964). However, aside from the convenience of focusing upon the decade of the 1950s in terms of the reach of this book, I also take my lead from what was happening within the film industry as a whole and there is little doubt that production of American science fiction films fell off markedly at the turn of the decade and the film genre only really began recovering at the end of 1960s.
14. Booker's parentheses and italics; Booker 2001, p. 120.
15. See 'Transcript of Ed Murrow–Kenneth Arnold Telephone Conversation', *Project 1947*, http://www.project1947.com/fig/kamurrow.htm.
16. This demonstration is, of course, highly reminiscent of the call for brief periods of silence, stillness and reflection in remembrance of the dead in the postwar period.
17. Biskind 1983, p. 158.
18. Parallels between *Invaders* and the musical film *The Wizard of Oz* (1939) are unmistakable. For example, the winding pathway that leads to the field at the back of house is reminiscent of the 'yellow brick road'. However the nightmarish aspects of the boy's dream take precedence in *Invaders* in the creation of a far blacker fairy-tale scenario.
19. Gay 1995, p. 298.
20. Ibid., p. 299.
21. Ibid. 1995, p. 300.
22. Recent examples include 'Astounding She-Monsters: Femininity in Fifties Horror Films', in Hendershot 2001, pp. 117–27, in which she describes how a powerful and pervasive femininity was understood as 'progressively degenerating American men and society in general' (p. 118). Also Rachel Devlin's account of the growing attack upon the 'sanctity of the mother-child bond' in Devlin 2005a, p. 611.
23. LaValley 1989, p. 15.
24. At this point the saucer can be taken to represent an encroaching threat of feminisation. Indeed, the shape of the archetypal saucer is frequently juxtaposed with the masculine and phallic man-made rocket in these films.
25. Jancovich 1996, p. 28.
26. Of course, Jancovich's book takes issue with previous definitions of both science fiction and horror, preferring to see the 1950s invasion narratives as 'a distinctive transformation not only in the horror genre, but also in science fiction' (p. 13). Although he refers to many of the same films I have discussed, it is clear from the title of his book that he prefers an overall genre definition of horror. My point takes issue with his stance by reintroducing the way in which gender functions in these

narratives and the impact that this frequently has upon the visual presentation of the 'menace'.

27. 'Afterthoughts on "Visual Pleasure and Narrative Cinema" inspired by *Duel in the Sun*', in Mulvey 1989, p. 36.
28. Ibid., p. 36.
29. Devlin 2005b, p. 11.
30. Ibid., p. 10 (Devlin's emphasis).
31. Devlin 2005a, p. 610.
32. 'Kaiju' in its literal translation means strange or mysterious beast.
33. *British Cinema in the Fifties: Gender, Genre and the 'New Look'* (London/New York: Routledge, 2000), p. 156.
34. Geraghly 2000, p. 156.
35. Sue Harper, 'Hammer Films', in Harper and Porter 2003, p. 142.
36. Of course, the television series upon which this film was based was aired in 1955, so speaks to the awareness of growing unrest in the Middle East and an impending crisis.
37. *Father Knows Best* was a situation comedy based upon the trials and tribulations of the suburban, middle-class, Anderson family.
38. *Red Channels* (published in 1950) was a pamphlet listing the names of people in the entertainment industry who, it was claimed, had links with subversive organisations. Those mentioned had not previously been blacklisted and were subsequently called to a hearing of the House of Un-American Activities committee to state their case. The pamphlet was compiled by a former FBI agent, Theodore Kirkpatrick, and the right-wing television producer, Vincent Harnett.

3.   SPACED OUT: BETWEEN THE 'GOLDEN YEARS'

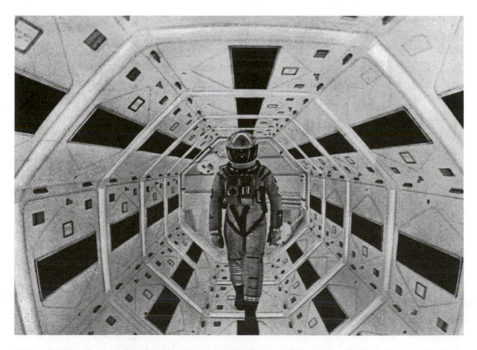

Figure 3.1   Transcendental tunnels in *2001: A Space Odyssey*. MGM / The Kobal Collection

After the B-movie boom of the 1950s, the production of science fiction films in America rapidly decreased during the early 1960s. Following the end of World War II, the paranoia associated with the earlier Cold War years began to give way to a sense of hot competition between the Russian and American super-powers in the 1960s. The so-called Space Race was central to this shift, becoming a major national and international preoccupation. This was the 'big science story' of the 1960s, right through to Neil Armstrong's first steps on the moon in 1969, and the NASA publicity/PR machine made sure that the public were supplied with a steady flow of visual images and media stories in the promotion of their work. For instance, the NASA Art Program began in 1962 and, in the years following, various artists were commissioned to create impressive images of rockets and colourful, epic representations of the planets, which were circulated in conjunction with media reports. Alongside this there were televised reports and official photographs of the missions undertaken. As early as 1962 close-up photographs of the moon were taken from Ranger 4 and in 1964 television pictures of Mars (recorded from Mariner 4) were available. The exploration of space was truly a spectacular media event.

Before the beginnings of the space programme, the utopian dream of scientific progress had been shattered by two world wars, culminating with the dropping of nuclear warheads at the end of World War II. But now media attention was focused upon developments in rocket science reputedly designed to enhance, rather than destroy, human life. In this sense, the 'story' of the Space Race helped reinvigorate the image and reputation of scientific and technological development in the popular imagination. Perhaps this further accounts for the decline of American science fiction films during the period: rather than passively 'watching the skies' (or the silver screen) in fear of alien invasion, the general populace was encouraged to engage with the real science story of the day in which the States was actively promising to conquer the skies. The competitive thrust of the Space Race therefore answered to the paranoia of the 1950s invasion films and promised to boost morale and reassert scientific superiority over the 'alien Other'.

In looking back at the science fiction films of the 1970s, Craig W. Anderson has commented that:

> The landings on the moon at the end of the 1960's and the early 1970's made the depiction of other worlds and the machinery required to get the characters (and the audience) to those worlds need to be at least as up-to-date as the technology seen weekly on television. People knew what computers looked like, how spaceships worked and something of the vast distances between planets.[1]

Unlike the fantastical space journeys to be found in the cinema serials of the 1930s, and unlike the sometimes laughable attempts at realism in the lower-budget 1950s films, the suggestion here is that the science fiction film now required more credible and convincing settings and effects for believable world-building. Anderson's notions are of course based upon the premise that the science fiction film necessarily falls under the rubric of Hollywood-style realism and, as such, must serve to encourage a suspension of disbelief in the building of a believable diegetic environment. Further, he also assumes a kind of 'hard science fiction' perspective, in which the fictional text rests upon believable extrapolations of actual scientific theory and technologies. So, according to Anderson, successful films of the genre needed to conform to some extent to the scientific images and information circulating at the time. If the science fiction film was somehow competing with reports of the Space Race in its attempts to attract an audience, then it would seem likely that budgetary constraints partly explain the genre's move away from depictions of space travel in the 1960s. Indeed, the relatively few science fiction films produced in America in the early 1960s were usually grounded in themes that explored worlds here on earth, such as the post-apocalyptic *The Time Machine* (dir. George Pal, 1960), *Panic in the Year Zero* (dir. Ray Milland, 1962) and *Fail Safe* (dir. Sidney Lumet, 1964). That is, until the virtuosity of Stanley Kubrick's high-budget *2001: A Space Odyssey* (1968) introduced images that both eclipsed and challenged the realness of those that NASA was providing in association with the space programme.

The noticeable reduction in the number of American science fiction films did not mean that the genre was disappearing from American screens in the early to mid-1960s; in a kind of return to its origins in the Saturday cinema serials, the genre found a more secure home on television with the airing of serials like *The Jetsons* (1962–8), *Lost in Space* (1965–8), *Star Trek* (1966–9) and *The Time Tunnel* (1966–7). Also, at the point where the American film industry largely abandoned science fiction, British and French films partially filled this generic gap. Offerings from Europe largely consisted of re-worked themes common to the American films of the 1950s. For example, 'alien invasion' was revived in low-budget British films like *Unearthly Stranger* (dir. John Crish, 1963), *The Night Caller* (dir. John Gilling, 1965), *Invasion* (dir. Alan Bridges, 1966) and the more prestigious *Quatermass and the Pit* (dir. Roy Ward Baker, 1967). The 1960s also saw a cycle of films adapted from the British novels and short stories of John Wyndham, beginning with the UK/US production of *Village of the Damned* (dir. Wolf Rilla, 1960) and closely followed by British productions of *Children of the Damned* (dir. Anton Leader, 1963), *The Day of the Triffids* (dir. Steve Sekely, 1963), and followed later by *Quest for Love* (dir. Ralph Thomas, 1971). While not rivalling earlier American invasion films in terms of spectacle and the scope of disaster visited upon the human populations, these films tended to suggest scale via the microcosmic situation. But, even though they were typically more understated in style, the British films of this period followed in the tradition set up by Hammer co-productions in the 1950s to the extent that they utilised plots that had become familiar to a public exposed to the American 'B-movies' in order to bring out particularly British concerns. For instance, just as the 'alien' children in *Village of the Damned* can be read as representing a burgeoning, post-World War II, 'generation gap' brought about by the baby boom of the late 1940s and 1950s, the film also harks back to the World War II era in the depiction of these Aryan interlopers as a kind of totalitarian, Hitler Youth. In addition, Britain produced two early 'spin-off' films based upon the science fiction television series, *Doctor Who* (1963–89, 2005–). In an attempt to cash in on the popularity of the series, both *Dr. Who and the Daleks* (dir. Gordon Flemyng, 1965) and *Daleks' Invasion Earth: 2150 A.D.* (dir. Gordon Flemyng, 1966) replaced William Hartnell as The Doctor and featured Peter Cushing in the title role, taking up the battle with alien invaders. Less austere and rather more light-hearted in style than both the *Doctor Who* series at this time and the more adult Wyndham films, these films largely failed to attract the kinds of audiences hoped for in the wake of the Dalek craze that had swept the country since their appearance in the series.

More formal re-workings of the genre came from French New Wave directors, with films like Jean-Luc Godard's *Alphaville* (1965) and Francois Truffaut's *Fahrenheit 451* (1967). In the spirit of the New Wave, the populist, 'low-art' productions of Hollywood were self-consciously appropriated, revisited and reworked. In part homage/part critique, Godard commented on both American film noir and science fiction by presenting an amalgam of the two genres and stripping them down to display underlying, essential characteristics. These films offered a simultaneously bleak and ironic replay of earlier science fictions by slowing down the pace of the action, taking emphasis away from exciting cinematic effects and action and foregrounding the alienating effects of life in a barren, totalitarian or authoritarian society. Like the American films of the 1950s, the genre continued to allow for a playing out of the underlying anxieties and concerns of the time, but unlike their more 'timid' American forerunners, in Europe it was ultimately co-opted as a vehicle to promote rather more unsettling perspectives.

It certainly seems plausible that the 1960s was a time when science fiction and science fact became remarkably intertwined, sometimes blurred, particularly within the context of an American national preoccupation with the story of the Space Race. This is attested to by the feverish debate and conspiracy theories that ensued concerning the believability of America's moon landing in 1969 and questions about the authenticity of photographic images of the event.[2] However, the growing demand for credible realism in American science fiction is thrown into relief in considering some of the highly playful, visually fantastic and eccentric films that emerged, largely from Europe and Britain, from about the mid-1960s through to the 1970s. The French-made, soft-core and stylishly kitsch *Barbarella* (dir. Roger Vadim, 1967) along with low-budget, sci-fi, sex farces like Britain's *The Love Pill* (dir. Kenneth Turner, 1971), played out the carefree, sexual mores of the 'free love' generation of the 1960s and the 'permissive society' of the 1970s. Here the genre offered a futuristic and playfully progressive framework within which to present the fashionable innovations of the day. As if in answer to the often pious science fiction films of 1950s/1960s America, *Barbarella*'s European impertinence was signalled from the outset by the cheeky exposure of America's then golden girl (Jane Fonda) performing a striptease behind the opening credits of the film. In minimal costumes designed by Jacques Fonteray, Fonda is irreverently paraded throughout the film in go-go boots, skin-tight cat-suits and skimpy leather, fur and PVC outfits, set against a busy backdrop of shag pile carpet, psychedelic light shows and an excessive array of designer paraphernalia of the period. Even though *Barbarella* was hardly the serious, laconic fare that non-European audiences had come to expect from the European 'art house' film, it certainly drew heavily upon contemporary artistic practices, particularly those associated with the counter-cultural youth movements of the day.

Of course, this was an era when America was bombarded with European, particularly British, culture, especially as produced by fresh young musicians, artists and writers who were, or became, associated with the hippy movement. The 1960s famously saw a 'British Invasion' of pop and rock music, epitomised by bands like The Beatles, The Who and Pink Floyd. As the decade wore on, the so-called 'progressive rock' of British bands like Procol Harum and the

Moody Blues also came to prominence and provided virtual anthems for the youth movements of the day. For instance, Procol Harum's 'Whiter Shade of Pale' and the Moody Blues' 'Nights in White Satin', along with the Beatles' release of the psychedelic album, *Sgt Pepper's Lonely Hearts Club Band*, provided the musical backdrop to the so-called 'Summer of Love' in 1967. Movements in modern art in America were also greatly influenced by European and British artists. The angst of American abstract expressionism (exemplified in the work of Jackson Pollock and the Dutch-born American Willem de Kooning) gave way to the sensorial, geometric abstraction, as witnessed in the work of Kenneth Noland, and the ocular illusions of the Op artists, such as the designs of British artist Bridget Riley. Op Art was seized upon my manufacturers of consumer goods and Riley's work in particular was reproduced and copied in designs for clothing fabrics, furniture textiles, wallpapers and so on. Op, or Op-inspired, design was extremely popular with the young and the trendy from 1965 onwards and it was certainly taken up by the counter-culture under the auspices of psychedelia, as can clearly be seen in the graphic art showcased on posters and LP covers of the time. The influence of the counter-cultural movements of the 1960s and its associated artistic practices also infiltrated science fiction writing. Moving away from the 'hard' science fiction line of 'classic' writers like Isaac Asimov, a 'new wave' of writing emerged in Britain under the leadership of Michael Moorcock, whose first book in the Jerry Cornelius series was later adapted into the British film *The Final Programme* (dir. Robert Fuest, 1974). Just as British and European artists and musicians had a noticeable impact upon the American cultural scene, the stylistic experimentation and thematic concerns of the 'new wave' science fiction writers were also strongly felt in American science fiction novels by the late 1960s (e.g. Harlan Ellison's writing is perhaps a prime example, whose 'new wave'-influenced, *A Boy and His Dog* [first published 1969] was later made into a film of the same name [dir. L. Q. Jones, 1975] in America). These science fiction writers turned their backs on the 'classic' themes of rocket science, intergalactic travel and the exploration of strange new planets; instead they were more concerned with exploring the 'inner space' of human subjectivity and perception. As outlined by Edward James, the 'manifesto' of the 'new wave' writers dictated that:

> Sf should not be an exploration of a hypothetical external reality, because objective reality is, in the post-Heisenberg world (and in the world of Timothy Leary and mind-altering drugs), a dubious concept . . . sf should be a means to explore our own subjective perceptions of the universe and our fellow human beings.[3]

This new generation of science fiction writers was clearly divorcing itself from what had gone before, especially the lowly forms of the genre, like the American pulps and comics, and was seeking to set itself up as a literary form that could be taken seriously. In this sense, the written genre was attempting to push itself into a literary mainstream. Likewise, the science fiction film was busy reinventing itself: both the speculative and fantastic components of the genre seemed to make it the ideal form with which to showcase the creative energies and sensibilities of the counter-culture, a point that was not entirely lost on a flagging American film industry busy looking for ways to revitalise its mainstream product and capture new audiences.

The late 1960s ushered in a big shake-up in the Hollywood film industry and the advent of what critics have come to call a New Hollywood. Alexander Horwath has characterised the years from 1967 to 1976 in Hollywood as a period of 'impure cinema', as a time of intense artistic experimentation and 'rejuvenation'.[4] Looking more broadly at changes within the Hollywood industry, Peter Kramer has pointed out that European films had 'an important influence on the 'new' Hollywood that was eventually going to emerge'.[5] Aside from the relatively large numbers of European film imports into America at this time, the interests of younger cinema audiences was being busily reflected in the American underground or independent art films of the 1960s (made by the likes of Kenneth Anger and John Cassavetes) or, at the other end of the scale, the low-budget, exploitation pictures that director/producer Roger Corman churned out during the 1960s (obvious examples being, the psychedelic extravaganzas, *The Wild Angels* [1966] and *The Trip* [1967]). Finally the Hollywood machine began to embrace the changes in film culture that were happening outside of the mainstream and started employing young filmmakers and directors whose vision was decidedly informed by the counter-cultural movements of the day. Films like the deliberately provocative *Bonnie and Clyde* (dir. Arthur Penn, 1967) and *The Graduate* (dir. Mike Nichols, 1967) successfully captured the interest of this rebellious young audience, but Hollywood's answer to the 'new wave' in science fiction, *Fantastic Voyage* (dir. Richard Fleischer, 1966), failed to appeal. In a rather literal translation of the 'new wave's' thematic concern with 'inner space', this film explored the inner workings of the human body as a miniaturised craft and crew are injected into the body of a dying man in an effort to clear a blood clot from his brain. In combination with this unusual plot, *Fantastic Voyage* featured aspects of popular modern art practices. For instance, the use of rotating and static coloured light (instead of traditional paint effects) in the creation of the organic setting reflected the 'hip' designs of contemporary abstract art and the interest in 'painting with light' in the work of the Lumia artists of the 1960s.[6] The light shows of Lumia artists, like London-based Mark Boyle and the USCO group who worked out of New York, were becoming increasingly popular among the young, as evidenced in the fact that both went on to design light shows for rock bands and, later, for discotheques.[7] However, although the look of *Fantastic Voyage* might have been designed to appeal to a younger audience, it is notable that the characters in the film were literally overwhelmed by these strange new surroundings (Donald Pleasence's character actually ends his days being consumed by a host of globular, white corpuscles); the psychedelic environment was therefore figured as threatening in terms of the film's narrative. Equally, even though the appearance of Raquel Welch in a skin-tight body suit indicated a loosening of the sexually conservative standards associated with American mainstream films, overall *Fantastic Voyage* did not compare well with the more alternative forms of cinema and entertainment that younger audiences were seeking. But this all changed with the release of *2001: A Space Odyssey* in April 1968.

In popular journalism, the first 'golden age' of the science fiction film is frequently placed in the 1950s, with a second 'golden age' typically dated from the late 1970s and early 1980s. Judgements as to what constitutes such an age are usually based on Hollywood's output and the sheer number of films produced, rather than on artistic merit or the influence exerted by particular films, small groups of films, or films from outside of the Hollywood nexus. Moreover, the large numbers of B-movies produced in America in the 1950s and the advent in the late 1970s/1980s of the science fiction blockbusters (discussion of which is to follow in the next chapter), has meant that these two periods have generally received more attention from film critics, historians and theorists. But one science fiction film provides a notable exception to this rule and has certainly attracted an unusual amount of critical attention: I am, of course, referring to the aforementioned *2001: A Space Odyssey*. Having outlined the cultural climate of the 1960s, this chapter therefore continues with a specific focus upon what I recognise as a cycle of films, partly inspired by the success of *2001*. I have come to call this cycle the 'new art' science fiction films, which are marked by the simultaneous display of the creative energies and sensibilities associated with the counter-cultural movements of 1960s/1970s and the industry's efforts to engage with a new and younger audience. Aside from *2001*, most of the films under discussion have been largely ignored by academics and they have certainly not been widely recognised as significant in the history of the science fiction film genre. However, these films are important in providing a fuller understanding of the development of the genre and, as I will show, are also important in a wider understanding of the cultural context of the 'impure' years of Hollywood production.

THE ODYSSEY BEGINS

The director of *2001*, Stanley Kubrick, had already made a name for himself in science fiction film with the British made satire, *Dr. Strangelove: or, How I Learned to Stop Worrying and Love the Bomb* (1964). Deciding that the time was ripe for a big-budget, high-concept, mainstream American film of the genre, MGM poured an unprecedented $6 million into the making of *2001* (the final budget came in at approximately $10–11 million). Its timely release in 1968, just prior to the Apollo moon landing in 1969, responded to the zeitgeist of the era and assured its eventual success at the box office, but critical opinion was markedly divided when it was first shown in America. For example, Renata Adler's largely scathing review in *The New York Times* described the film as 'the apotheosis of the fantasy of a precocious, early nineteen-fifties city boy', warning viewers that it was 'somewhere between hypnotic and immensely boring'.[8] In contrast, Richard L. Doe of the *Washington Post* took great pride in probing into what he saw as the deeply philosophical levels of the film and, in referring to Adler's review, stated that 'those who prefer to think of this as merely sci-fi must admit that it's marvelous sci-fi'.[9] Upon its initial release in April, audiences were reportedly confused by the intrinsic ambiguity of the film and reviewers were predicting that it was going to flop at the box office. But before long *2001* was adopted by the counter-cultural youth movements and gained a fervent following, prompting many critics to recant their harsh words.[10] In fact, in a later review of both *2001* and the musical stage show *Hair*, William Kloman lauded these two productions as examples of 'what might be called a sensory re-organisation among the younger generation'.[11] Although Kloman was not explicit in his review, the final section of the film was repeatedly read by critics and audience's alike as a direct reference to the kind of 'sensory re-organisation' brought about by the, so-called, 'mind expanding', psychedelic drugs that were fashionable at the time.[12] As John Brosnan testifies in his account of first seeing the film:

> I expected more story, a more event-packed movie. And I wasn't wild about the ending which I didn't really understand. I thought the light show went on far too long and I didn't even pick up on the fact that Bowman, the surviving astronaut, had gone through a 'star gate' and was hurtling through the universe at a terrific speed. I just thought he was having an alien-induced acid trip, as did many of the hippies who flocked to the movie and watched it under the influence of various substances.[13]

Marijuana use was relatively common among hippy communities of the time, but LSD (lysergic acid diethylamide) was the definitive psychedelic drug. With proponents like the writer and psychologist Timothy Leary, accounts of the reportedly positive properties of the drug abounded and descriptions of the colourful 'visions' and altered perceptions experienced during 'a trip' (a common expression at the time, used to describe the experience of taking LSD) became the subject of much discussion. An interest in what the parapsychologist, Charles T. Tart, called ASCs (altered states of consciousness) was central to the hippy movement and its serious attempts at imagining/creating a different or alternative world. For instance, Tart's edited collection, *Altered States of Consciousness*,[14] was presented as a scientific study of ASCs brought on by hypnosis, certain eastern forms of meditation and a variety of drugs, in which contributors gleefully explored, categorised and defined users' experiences. So, against the moral panic of an older generation, there was an overarching attempt to valorise these experiences (often in a comparison with religious or spiritual mysticism) and stress the positive effects of LSD use on intelligence, artistic creativity and attitude to life (usually involving a reported loss of ego boundaries and a sense of oneness with the world).

A variety of cultural artefacts became directly linked with the LSD experience and the apparently mystical states that it induced. Even though some artists denied ever having taken the drug, this did not prevent their work from being associated with its use and from being understood as a dramatisation of a drug-induced altered state, or even as work designed to induce an altered state of consciousness in the viewer/listener. Writing in 1968, Robert E. L. Masters and Jean Houston made chemical intoxication central to their very definition of psychedelic art, as: 'Works of art attempting in some sense to communicate psychedelic experience, or to induce psychedelic experience, or at least to alter consciousness so as to approximate aspects of the chemically induced state'.[15]

While inextricably linking LSD to the psychedelic art movement, the contributors to this book consistently stressed the need to guard against using this kind of art purely for, what they called, 'directionless escapism'. Even though they are less than clear as to the exact purpose in attempting to induce or communicate altered perception, it seems that they placed value on those artworks that promoted a kind of active engagement, rather than more passive pleasures. Indeed, Masters and Houston argued that 'an art movement that draws fundamental cohesiveness from an experience sometimes called escapist, addresses the world with an exuberance not suggestive of withdrawal'.[16] In furthering their claims, Masters and Houston drew a comparison with what could be seen as the movement's earlier forerunner: surrealism. Here they stated that where 'surrealism was exclusive; psychedelic art is inclusive'; that 'where surrealism is magical, psychedelic art would be scientific'; that where surrealism was concerned with madness and abandonment of reality, psychedelic art simply 'affirmed the value of inwardness as complementary awareness'.[17] So, it seems that the split between the active/passive use of the psychedelic experience is crucial to the consideration of the images I am going on to explore in this chapter. The low-art status of Hollywood films, in particular, has classically hinged on its ability to induce a dream-like state in the audience, and science fiction films have often been ridiculed as supremely escapist. Therefore, in choosing to focus this chapter upon the co-option of psychedelic imagery within the science fiction films of the late 1960s/1970s, you could say I am bringing to the fore one of the central issues in how the genre has been judged and assessed.

Of course, there is a long history of artistic works being associated with the taking of a variety of mind-altering substances or altered states of consciousness of one sort of another. Particularly prominent examples can be found in writing, especially writing related to fantasy or the fantasy genres.[18] In terms of science fiction, the novelist Aldous Huxley is famously linked with hallucinogenic or psychedelic drugs. Having written at length about his experiences with mescaline in *The Doors of Perception* (first published in Britain 1954), Huxley went on to experiment with LSD. The taking of drugs was a thematic concern in some of his science fiction novels and a change in attitude can be traced through this writing. For example, the use of 'soma' as an instrument of repression in the satirical utopia of *Brave New World* (first published 1932) revealed the contempt he had for drug use prior to his own experimentation with psychedelics. However, a shift in outlook can be located in his utopian commonwealth in *Island* (first published 1962); the mind lulling 'soma' is replaced with 'moksha', which is described in this later novel as the 'reality-revealer' or the 'truth-and-beauty pill'. Indeed, a plethora of science fiction novels appeared in the 1960s and 1970s that featured futuristic drugs as a central component in their narratives. These novels often revealed extreme attitudes on drug use, depending on whether the drugs in question were characterised as substances used to subdue and control human passion and/or intellect or to excite and stimulate the imagination. So, an interest in drugs and altered perception is certainly not new to science fiction, although it did became a more central and defining feature in written science fiction of the period. In addition, I would also contest that it became a defining feature of the 'new art' science fiction films; a feature that can be traced back to the so-called 'star gate' sequence in *2001*.

The Tunnels of Perception

Musically accompanied by György Ligeti's *Atmosphères,* the visual composition of the final section of *2001* (entitled 'Jupiter and beyond the infinite') begins with shots of the now famous black monolith floating tantalisingly across the screen before finally disappearing behind a symmetrical representation of Jupiter and its moons. This opening leads into the much celebrated 'slit scan' sequence, which is interrupted by occasional still, close-ups on the distorted face of the astronaut, Bowman, and several extreme close-ups of a single, blinking eye. The 'slit scan' effect was developed by a member of the special effects team working on the film, Douglas Trumbull, whose name later became synonymous with science fiction film throughout the 1970s. In simple terms, the 'slit scan' effect was produced by projecting bands of coloured light from a slide, through a thin slit, which were then recorded onto film. The camera was mounted on a track to allow for movement and the camera shutter left open to record, in continuous focus, the streaking of the coloured light across a single

Figure 3.2   Abstract imagery in the closing section of *2001: A Space Odyssey*.
MGM/The Kobal Collection.

frame. The recorded image gave the illusion of two planes of movement that
suggested Bowman was travelling through a deep and narrow corridor of
refracted, coloured light. In other words, in a construction that is highly reminiscent of the 3-D illusions of 1960s Op Art, the effect of a depth of field is
created by the way the streaks of colour appear to emanate from a centralised
origin within the frame, spreading outward in a linear formation, across the
two planes. At one point this corridor of light abruptly gives way to a more
fluid light sequence that resembles the kind of back or front projected light
shows that became common in the late 1960s and 1970s. Although many
artists were able to create these liquid effects using colour, light and oil, here
the images recorded the movement of chemical reactions mounted on glass
slides, with the aid of back lighting. So, the graphic depth and illusion of linear,
forward motion, set up by the 'slit scan' corridor, is juxtaposed with these
flatter, more painterly, organic images, which some have taken to represent
exploding stars and constellations. The corridor is also interrupted by a
sequence of travelling aerial shots of landscapes and bodies of water (introduced by the appearance of large, geometric diamond shapes), only the colouration of these shots is manipulated to make the terrain and water look
other-worldly. Bowman's literal trip through the corridor finishes with his
arrival in a starkly lit, Regency-styled, white room. Manipulation of time,
rather than space, colour and shape, becomes the focus of the final sequence,
as we see him observe himself at various stages of maturity, until treated to the
final shots of a rather decrepit Bowman, in his apparent death-bed, reaching
towards another giant monolith. The film then cuts to the image of a giant
embryo floating in space, whereupon the screen goes black as the final credits

play. This closing sequence raised the science fiction film in America to a 'new art' form in which special effects were art and art could be viewed as special effects.

Readings and interpretations of this sequence of the film abound and the sheer variety of explanations given for the ending speaks to the writerly nature of these closing moments. Certainly these images appear designed to raise profound questions about the nature of human existence as well as drawing upon the artistic innovations of the time. What I think is important to explore here is the way in which the final sequence serves to illustrate aspects of how the film, as a whole, has been constructed. By Hollywood standards at the time, *2001* was certainly seen as a radical intervention. The lack of a fully coherent narrative, the sparse dialogue, the shockingly elliptical editing, made it an unusual experience for audiences used to the codes and conventions of mainstream narrative Hollywood films. On the other hand, as presented to an audience in the late 1960s, the film's more accessible images of space travel may well have appeared supremely realistic, certainly in a comparison with visual material that NASA had pumped out over the years. In this respect it is notable that it was NASA artist Robert McCall's painting, *Orion Leaving Space Station* that was used for the advertising poster for the film. There are other aspects of the film that resolutely conform to the classical standards of Hollywood realism; most obviously the insistence on deep focus and centralisation in shot construction, which is emphasised by the consistent use of long shots, as well as spatial grids as a feature of the mise-en-scène. Indeed, this concentration on perspective and the exaggerated use of deep focus could well link the film to that other famous Hollywood masterwork, *Citizen Kane* (dir. Orson Welles, 1941). What seems clear is that *2001* was very self-consciously constructed, which is hard to ignore in thinking back through the film after viewing the assemblage of abstract images in the closing sequence. So, I am proposing that *2001,* paradoxically, sat comfortably between two camps: it was an art film that had many of the features of the European art-house film of the time in its style and attitude, but it was also a film that was self-consciously embedded within a Hollywood tradition. Although it is possible to read *2001* as deeply ironic, the irony was not of the kind seen in the earlier, blatantly satirical *Dr. Strangelove* and the sheer scale of the film can certainly be taken as a celebration, rather than critique, of both the genre and contemporary events. In addition, whether the film works to 'transport' the viewer/listener (in the escapist tradition), to encourage active/intellectual engagement, or to provide a purely sensory experience, is rather open to question and debate. However, my own view is that *2001* encouraged an active engagement on the part of the spectator, which is perhaps most clearly evidenced in the confoundingly abstract imagery in the long final sequence.

What is also clear about *2001* is that, for both academics and critics, it has served to mark a turning point in the science fiction film genre. For example, it provides a discernible division for J. P. Telotte in his brief history of the genre in America (he actually labels later films of the genre as 'post-*2001*' films),[19] and for Vivian Sobchack it was *2001* that proved that 'the film medium (could) accommodate 'adult' science fiction'.[20] What also appears undeniable is the way in which it influenced films that were to follow in the 1970s – many of which seemed to draw upon images and themes from *2001*. In fact, one of the most pervasive visual tropes in 1970s science fiction films was the tunnel or corridor; characters in these later films were frequently sucked into vortexes or seen journeying through fantastic corridors of light. Overall, after *2001,* the more decentralised and busy psychedelic aesthetic of earlier films (like the aforementioned *Barbarella* and even *Fantastic Voyage*) gave way to an aesthetic in which excessive depth and centripetal shot construction predominated. However, I would suggest that the vortex or tunnel effect in these later films continued to operate as a signifier of an altered state of consciousness, of the kind most commonly associated with the counter-cultural movements of the period.

Of course, this use of the vortex or tunnel image has its antecedents in literary fantasy; one of the most obvious example being the rabbit hole that Alice travels though in Lewis Carroll's (aka Reverend Charles Dodgson) *Alice's Adventures in Wonderland* (first published 1869). The vortex or tunnel has also been a common feature in the 'fantasy genres' of Hollywood: memorably illustrated in the swirling tornado that carries Dorothy to a magical fantasy land in the musical *The Wizard of Oz* (dir. Victor Fleming, 1939) and the repeated spiral motifs along with the famous 'zoom in, pull back' effect in Alfred Hitchcock's multi-layered fantasy thriller, *Vertigo* (1958). But, science fiction stands out in its use of the vortex or tunnel: concrete examples being the underground tunnels in *Metropolis* (dir. Fritz Lang, 1927), the alien tunnels in *Forbidden Planet* (dir. Fred M. Wilcox, 1956) that the crew travel along in order to reach the machine that maintains a fantasy life on Altair IV, or the whirlpool of sand that quickly sucks unsuspecting humans into an alien environment in *Invaders from Mars* (dir. William Cameron Menzies, 1953). Shifting closer to the time of *2001*'s release, the previously mentioned American television series, *The Time Tunnel* (1966–7), also featured a man-made vortex, which allowed travel to different time zones. The premise of the series was that two male scientists were trapped in the vortex and transported to different moments in history in each episode. Their counterparts in the present could only watch their adventures on a big screen and each time they tried to bring them back through the tunnel our two protagonists would be transported to another time. A further example can also be seen in the opening credit sequence of the aforementioned British television series, *Doctor Who*. When this long-running series began in 1963, what is known as a 'howlaround' effect was initially created by Bernard Lodge as an introduction to each episode. This involved the recording of images created by feeding the optical output of a video camera back on itself via its own monitor. The images created also resembled a kind of vortex or tunnel, designed to lead the viewer into the extraordinary worlds visited in each episode. In fact, the similarity between the 'star gate' sequence and the opening credits of this British series is evidenced by the replacement of the 'howlaround' effect in favour of 'slit scan' for series 11 in 1973. In looking at these earlier examples, it becomes clear that the vortex or tunnel trope has classically operated as a device that marks the crossing of boundaries between two worlds; the tunnel itself being a kind of liminal zone connecting the real with the fantastical. However, following *2001*, many of the 1970s films placed much more emphasis upon the journey through this liminal zone, sometimes to the point where it does not appear to lead to an alternative world or, for that matter, to anywhere at all.

Michel Chion states that '*2001* is, in spite of itself, an optimistic film'.[21] In large part, he sees this optimism encoded in the closing sequence of the film. Chion's reading relies heavily upon understanding the Star Child (the giant embryo in space) as signifying a new beginning: as though rising from the ashes of the more pessimistic world view to be found throughout the rest of the film, Chion asserts that the film is, in the end, life-affirming. My own assessment of *2001*'s overall 'message' is more ambivalent; taken on its own, the appearance of the Star Child may well signal a new beginning, but it could also be read as a symbol of recurrence, perhaps a recurrence of the same story. For me, optimism is not found simply in this image, but in the abstract nature of the 'slit scan' images in a comparison with the hyperbolic orderliness of much of the rest of the film. Rather ironically, there is a sense of stasis and confinement in this human odyssey; the characters appear fettered by a cold and preservational rationality that does not allow for change and meaningful movement. In contrast, the more abstract and colourful images of the final sequence work to excite and liberate the imagination, to suggest a kind of non-rational and transforming creativity.

In the context of the student uprisings at Columbia University (followed quickly by the riots in Paris in May of 1968 and accompanied that same year by various other student demonstrations in Mexico and across Europe), it is easy to see how the non-rational and creative force in the final sequence of *2001* spoke to a younger generation fighting for change and attempting to break away from the institutional authorities that had brought them the futile war in Vietnam. Following these uprisings, the revolutionary change that had been hoped for failed to materialise and there was a general sense of frustration among the young radicals, which was cemented in America when Richard Nixon took presidential office in 1969. In charting the movement from the late 1960s to the early 1970s, Bruce J. Schulman states that: 'Frustration and alienation pushed Americans toward the counter-culture, but also exerted a strong pull of its own: the conviction that it was possible to drop out of the polluted, corrupt mainstream and live according to one's values.'[22]

It is my contention that this 'dropping out' and reliance upon personalised and subjective viewpoints ('one's values') became emblematised by the trippy tunnels that were such a strong feature of 1970s science fiction films.

David Frum describes what he sees as a 'rebellion against rationality' in the 1970s,[23] but his line of enquiry quickly leads us to a picture of an age in which 'dropping out' meant selfish individualism. According to Frum, the hippies' search for alternative worlds and modes of being quickly turned into sensory decadence and the commercialisation of lifestyle choices. Schulman, on the other hand, repudiates what he sees as the conventional portrayal of the 1970s as the 'Me Decade'. Although he admits that 'the rebels would lose their lop-sided battle against a softened mass culture', he maintains that as the counter-culture expanded into the early 1970s, the 'utopian naiveté of the Sixties' gave way to an age of 'energy and experimentation', which reshaped the cultural landscape with a 'distinctively sceptical style'.[24] Indeed, a more sceptical perspective can definitely be located in the science fiction films that emerged in the early 1970s. An example of this can be found in *The Andromeda Strain* (dir. Robert Wise, 1971), in which a select band of scientists is brought together to find an antidote for an alien microbe that has wiped out all but two inhabitants of an isolated town in New Mexico. Employing the quasi-documentary style adopted in his earlier *The Day the Earth Stood Still* (dir. Robert Wise, 1951), Wise confines his scientists in this later film to an underground laboratory. The film's narrative then revolves around the scientists' quest for answers as to the nature of the alien microbe. A surprising proportion of *The Andromeda Strain* is taken up with the various scientists gazing anxiously at enlarged projections of the colourful crystalline patterns created by the growing microbe, while lengthy discussion takes place as to what these images actually mean. The colourful geometric projections in the film are juxtaposed with views of the bland or startlingly white tunnels and ducts in the lower levels of this underground laboratory. Depth and perspective are brought to the fore in many of these tunnel shots, in particular during a scene in which one scientist is forced into a deep, vertical duct in order to climb up to another level of the facility. Attacked by security lasers, the pain he experiences, along with the apparent vertigo caused by looking upward into the duct, toward the surface, warps and blurs his visual perspective (revealed to the viewer in a series of point of view shots). Indeed, the scientists' sense of perspective, reason and vision is consistently challenged in this film. Also, the logical and pedantic scientific testing of hypotheses seems to fail them, along with the high-tech equipment employed to help them in their search for the truth. This is made clear when the super-computer is unable to deal with all the data it is given in visualising and tracking the microbe's growth rate (as explained by the '601' read out registered on the projection screen when it breaks down, which also takes up the closing frame of the film). Although the narrative could be read as a veiled warning about the dangers associated with altered states of perception, it is the abstract images on the screen that act as the catalyst for communication and questioning throughout. Each of the central characters in this film appears to have a different viewpoint and perspective in regard to these images and what they might represent, confirmed by the inordinate amount of exposition in the film. It is almost as though *The Andromeda Strain* was in dialogue with the earlier *2001*; the discussions of the scientists illustrating the sorts of energetic debates that occurred between critics and audiences in their attempts to pin down the meanings surrounding the closing sequence of *2001*.

Later films reveal a shift to a more nihilistic view of altered states of being, although there remains an implicit challenging of the supposedly rational world in the way that they openly engage with the kinds of existential questions raised in earlier films. The low-budget parody *Dark Star* (dir. John Carpenter, 1974), ridicules the freedoms associated with the counter-cultural movements of the 1960s. This film presents us with a band of literally and figuratively 'spaced-out' hippies who have become isolated and irresponsible after such a long time in space and who can find nothing better to do than to roam the universe destroying supposedly unstable planets. A series of accidents and mistakes leads to a malfunction in the ship and a sentient nuclear bomb threatens to explode and kill them all. In an effort to persuade the bomb not to carry out this mission, one of the crew engages it in a philosophical discussion about the nature of existence and perceptions of reality. This tactic initially neutralises the bomb's desire to explode, but the introduction of this new logic simply culminates in the bomb forming a somewhat different perspective on its actions and exploding in a state of reverential fervour, convinced that this will bring about spiritual enlightenment. The two crew members who survive the blast end their days in a haze of apparent ecstasy; one taking his place among the colourful, glowing lights of the Phoenix asteroid cluster, and the other surfing joyfully to his death on a piece of debris from the exploded spacecraft.

The Terminal Man (dir. Michael Hodges, 1974) continues the theme of isolation in staging the demise of a lone scientist as he descends into a pleasure-induced, murderous psychosis. In an effort to control his brain seizures the man agrees to undergo a revolutionary new treatment that involves the placing of electrodes into his brain, designed to stimulate pleasurable feelings. The idea is that, upon the outbreak of a seizure, the electrodes will be jolted into action and will flood his system with tranquillising pleasure. However, things go badly wrong when his brain becomes quickly addicted to this artificial stimulation and a cycle of ever-increasing seizures, followed by stimulation, simply makes him violent and uncontrollable. Hovering in a nightmare state between consciousness and unconsciousness, he ends up shot to death by the law forces chasing him, having conveniently thrown himself into a freshly dug grave. There is an obvious reference here to drug-induced states even though the stimulation the scientist receives is, according to the narrative, brought about by the technological apparatus in his brain. The 'tunnels of perception' remain in my last example, but largely gone are the lingering, colourful, hallucinatory episodes; instead our protagonist seems trapped in a constant state of disbelief which leads nowhere.

Even if there was an attempt to present a united nation in the Space Race against Russia, with events like the rise of the Civil Rights movement, assassinations of major figureheads (John F. Kennedy, 1963; Malcolm X, 1965; Martin Luther King, 1968), previously mentioned student riots etc., America had already become a noticeably more factionalised nation in the 1960s. Traditional American values and confidence were definitely shaken to the core during the early 1970s: America's involvement in Vietnam did not end in any recognisable victory and, following the Watergate scandal, Nixon announced his resignation in 1974. It became harder to establish just who were 'us' and who were 'them', hard and fast dichotomies appeared to be breaking down in the 1970s, which is partly reflected in the bleaker and more ambivalent stance of these later films. Alongside this, following the drug-related deaths of several counter-cultural figureheads at the beginning of the decade (e.g. Janis Joplin, Jimi Hendrix, Jim Morrison) reports about the CIA's use of hallucinogenics in mind-control experiments and the use of LSD by soldiers in Vietnam were circulated widely in the media. So, it is possible to see these later films as engaging with viewpoints that stressed the more negative aspects of the psychedelic experience and the ways in which this was being co-opted as a coercive tool by various governing bodies. What had been a drug that was linked with creativity and enlightenment was now becoming indelibly associated with the very bodies that the counter-culture sought to distant itself from. But these are not complacent or conservative films; rather each forces a confrontation with traditional world views. There are no rescuing superheroes; there are no pat answers or masterly speeches from all-knowing scientists in these films. Instead, they pose complex questions and escapist retreat from a somewhat overwhelming, complex and unreliable reality is not an option. While it is possible to read these films as expressive of a kind of national trauma, brought on by the variety of destabilising events of the 1960s and early 1970s, there is evidence of a very conscious working-through of various social, political and cultural issues. Even though the worlds that are conjured up in these films are nowhere lands, there is a sense of process conveyed as the characters scramble about in their attempts to interact with what has become the disturbingly irrational nature of their surrounding environments. These films therefore express the frustrations felt by the youth movements of the time and they also actively explore the feelings of alienation that Schulman charts in his socio-political history of the 1970s. So, unlike the first 'golden age' films, many of the American science fiction films of the 1970s were unusually anti-establishment (of any kind) and offered up questioning critiques of contemporary life. It is also important not to forget that this was the period that saw the emergence of the individual director (rather than studio) being understood as the primary 'author' of a film. Borrowing from the French *Cahiers* critics, Andrew Sarris led the way in creating an 'auteur theory' applicable to popular American cinema.[25] In an attempt to valorise Hollywood films, Sarris focused upon the director as a critical criterion of value, largely ignoring the contributions of technicians, writers etc. Against this backdrop, the individualised experiences that the 1970s science fiction films explored could be linked to the vision of a single author. The 'tunnels of perception' could then operate as a kind of filmic code that indicated the perspective of the film's auteur, and the abstraction of images and highly stylised worlds created in the films could be connected to an artistic and personalised account of the world. However, the repeated use of this visual trope across a variety of films (not to mention the obvious importance of visual effects creators like Trumbull) is also suggestive of a more dispersed and inclusive artistic perspective in these films.

Vivian Sobchack's account of contemporary science fiction films stresses the arrival of a sense of depthlessness, which became inscribed within the genre after the 1950s. With reference to Fredric Jameson, Sobchack describes how the 'deep' and 'three-dimensional' spaces of 1950s science fiction films were replaced, in the late 1960s, by an aesthetic in which 'space (is) perceived and represented as superficial and shallow, as all surface'.[26] Having skipped over the films that appeared in the early to mid-1970s in this particular discussion, her descriptions of this new aesthetic are largely concentrated on the late 1970s blockbusters (like *Star Wars* [dir. George Lucas, 1977] and *Close Encounters of the Third Kind* [dir. Steven Spielberg, 1977]), before moving onto a more detailed account of the dystopian, cluttered and dispersed surfaces apparent in the mise-en-scène of *Blade Runner* (dir. Ridley Scott, 1982). I think her overall focus here leaves out an important phase in the development of science fiction films during this period. By inference, Sobchack explains away the effects of depth in many of the 1970s films by looking at films like *Tron* (dir. Steven Lisberger, 1982) and *The Last Starfighter* (dir. Nick Castle, 1984). In her analysis of these later films she describes a depth that is 'simulated' and 'electronically schematised rather than re-presented'.[27] While the excessive depth of field and Op Art effects apparent in the earlier science fiction films that I have discussed could be taken as forerunners to these later films, I would suggest that the 'tunnels of perception' did not operate in the same way as they did in later films. The 'new art' science fiction films of the late 1960s and 1970s were frequently discernable by their innovative use and manipulation of existing photographic and cinematic technologies to create psychedelic episodes and visions inspired by the counter-cultural artists of the period. These films were obviously produced prior to the kinds of computer technologies that became available to effects supervisors in the late 1970s and the 1980s (which will be discussed more fully in the final chapter). What is also apparent is that in later films the tunnel or vortex is commonly used in its classic function, as the road or portal between two different worlds, and far less emphasis is placed upon the journey than is placed upon the destination.[28] My point here is that rather than working to connote a kind of schematised inauthenticity, as was seen in Sobchack's later examples, the 'tunnels of perception' marked efforts to provide a strangely authentic account of human experience. In fact, I would argue that this kind of aesthetic construction became such a powerful and unruly signifier that it is not surprising that it was later co-opted and tamed upon entering the blockbuster era. It is therefore my contention that in the transition to the more conservative 1980s there was an attempt to restrain and stabilise the symbols and signifiers that had come to mark the 'impure' period in Hollywood cinema, to empty out the more radical meanings associated with the 'tunnels of perception' so that they could be controlled and sanitised for commercial use.

A film that illustrates my point is *Demon Seed* (dir. Donald Cammell, 1977). I will be coming back to this film in a later chapter in which I will offer a fuller account of the narrative, but there is a sequence here that is highly reminiscent of the closing moments of *2001*. The difference being that in *Demon Seed* it is made very clear in the narrative that these images are technologically produced and intended to seduce, pacify and placate the unwilling human victim in the film. While these images can certainly be seen as a celebration of psychedelia – after all they were created by the avant-garde film artist, Jordan Belson – according to the narrative, they were produced by an artificial intelligence and entrance into an altered state is brought about through interaction with computer technologies. The supposed freedoms associated with 'mind-expanding' drugs are reformulated and the 'tunnels of perception' are used to literally signify the rape of the female protagonist in this film. The freedoms from logic and the 'non-rational force' of these images are then translated into a literal and rationalised confinement. The 'life-affirming' qualities associated with psychedelic and abstract imagery becomes narratively reconfigured in this film as the 'star child' born out of this experience has a mind literally created and controlled by this aggressive and powerful technology. The tunnel effects created in the rape sequence are very obviously drawn upon to represent, if not the literal female sexual organs, then a feminised openness to the reception of the visions that accompany the rape. Both the character's mind and body are penetrated, made clear in the dialogue that leads up to this sequence and also in the literally graphic representation of the AI's drill-like appendage penetrating the tunnel.[29] So these images both draw the viewer in and aggressively thrust forward to meet them at the same time.

I would say that Cammell's film not only forecasts the arrival of computer generated graphics, but also indicates an impending re-masculinisation of the genre. By the time *Demon Seed* was released the feminist movement was in full swing and the film can be seen to engage with the reactionary responses that the movement endured. In fact, a very threatening femininity was clearly figured in later films like Disney's *The Black Hole* (dir. Gary Nelson, 1979) and the first 'Star Trek' film, *Star Trek – The Motion Picture* (dir. Robert Wise, 1979). I see these two films as prime examples of transitional films that, while drawing heavily upon the vortex imagery that had become such a central feature in the cycle of 'new art' science fiction films, seek to neutralise the radical psychedelic special effect. In *The Black Hole*, the evil scientist, Hans Reinhardt (Maximilian Schell), attempts to find immortality and the truth of all things by entering the largest black hole in space that has ever been found. His overwhelming desire and ambition to penetrate and conquer its mysteries is only matched by his aggressive designs on the female member of a visiting crew from another space ship, Dr. Kate McCrae (Yvette Mimieux). The hole in question thereby becomes heavily associated with this female character and it is marked as a dangerously alluring, all-engulfing, *feminine* force. The final section of the film is taken up with images of spaceships and crew members being sucked into this hole, culminating in their respective arrivals in an allegorical heaven or hell. Likewise, in the *Star Trek* film, the crew are faced with a 'phenomenon' that threatens to engulf and destroy all humanity. The majority of this film is taken up with highly colourful, psychedelic imagery (also created by the aforementioned Trumbull), as their spacecraft (the Enterprise) travels through the phenomenon's tunnels and chambers. Responding like a diegetic audience, the crew on the bridge of the ship stare in transfixed amazement at the screened images projected in front of them. In case we are in any doubt as to the gender assigned to the phenomenon, it later takes on the corporeal body of an alien, female member of the crew and announces her name as 'Vger'. During the course of the film the crew discover that Vger is in fact NASA's 'Voyager 6' space probe (presumably a futuristic version of Voyager 1 and 2, launched by NASA in 1977). The probe has accumulated so much data on its journey through space that it has developed into a sentient being. The crew come to characterise Vger as child-like, as possessing an insatiable curiosity and, crucially, as in need of fulfilment. The required 'fulfilment' is brought about once Vger is able to communicate with her creator and eternally bond with a lovestruck, young male captain from the crew of the Enterprise. Following in the style of the television series, Kirk constantly debates the nature of this alien force and acts as the interpreter of her/its actions. In his final round-up speech he masterfully deduces that in order to evolve Vger needed to acquire the 'human capacity to leap beyond logic', which, in this case, is firmly associated with the male character that she bonds with at the end of the film. So, while

The Black Hole simply figures an engulfing feminine threat in space, in the *Star Trek* film the crew of the Enterprise successfully re-territorialise or take back their space. At this point the blackness of space returns and the imagery created by the phenomenon disappears. The psychedelic imagery on offer is therefore strongly encoded as feminine and the narrative crises that these images are associated with seems to suggest that it was a feminine force that caused not only the aesthetic and narrative shifts within the genre itself but also the destabilising events of recent history.

My final example of the American 'new art' science fiction film, also looks back to the late 1960s early 1970s and provides a similarly negative take on the period. As the title aptly indicates, *Altered States* (dir. Ken Russell, 1980) clearly brings together the issues and areas that I have been focusing upon, offering a veritable treatise on the 1970s, not only in terms of the themes that the science fiction genre dealt with and how these intersected with the contemporary cultural and political context, but also in terms of the kind of visual impact of the films during this period. As the following interview testifies, the development of this film (based upon Paddy Chayefsky's novel of the same name, *Altered States* [1978]) underwent a number of problems and delays. After the director, Arthur Penn, pulled out of the project, Warner Bros brought in the British director, Ken Russell. With his reputation for visual excess and symbolic imagery, Russell brought an appropriate pedigree to a film that concentrated on the inner turmoil of its central character, Eddie (William Hurt), as played out in the numerous hallucination scenes throughout the film.

In *Altered States* we follow the 'progress' (or, more accurately, 'regress') of Eddie and his wife, Emily (Blair Brown). The beginning of the film is set in the late 1960s, when we are introduced to these two characters as fresh, young science graduates: we later see the couple marry, settle down and have children. Both Eddie and Emily start out as self-appointed 'whizz kids' and their common thirst for scientific knowledge along with an interest in philosophical issues initially makes them the ideal modern young couple. However, their research takes them in two distinct directions. While Emily's anthropological studies involve an affectionate fascination for apes and monkeys, Eddie's search for the ultimate truth leads him into experimenting with altered states of being. Although both characters display an interest in human evolution, Emily's studies keep her firmly attached to a material world of the present, whereas Eddie displays a desire to escape this reality and enter into a fantasy world of the past. At the beginning of the film Eddie pronounces that he sees life as a 'ridiculous ritual' and his burning ambition is to find what he calls the 'original self'. In a frantically excited speech he states:

> Everybody's looking for their true selves. We're all trying to fulfil ourselves, understand ourselves, get in touch with ourselves, face the reality

of ourselves, explore ourselves, explain ourselves. Ever since we dispensed with God, we've got nothing but ourselves to explain this meaningless horror of life.

He seems to be going through a kind of existential crisis and appears to be searching for truth in his life through some kind of scientific self-discovery. His later family life with Emily does not offer him the meaningful existence that he yearns for and he decides to divorce her, to devote his undivided attention to his para-scientific studies. Already alienated from his lived reality, his separation from the world is further indicated when he immerses himself in the various isolation tanks that feature in the film. Having chosen this path, he becomes frustrated when he continually experiences black-outs during immersion. He claims that, just prior to the black-outs he gets a 'feeling of acceleration', but 'no images' and says he wants to know what happens in the black-out states. The trouble really starts when he begins to experiment with an ancient Mexican drug that, having synthesised and strengthened, he takes during his periods of immersion.

The drugs that he takes, allow him not only to see beyond the black-outs and to remain fully conscious during this dream-like state, but to experience a more primitive existence. He begins to crave the simpler, more primitive world that the drugs and tanks allow him access to and the regression that he undergoes begins to impact upon his physical self in the contemporary world. After extended experience of this primal fantasy he finds it increasingly hard to return to the reality of his own world. For instance, during one sequence we see him literally metamorphose into a primitive 'proto-human' (resembling an ape or monkey), breaking out of the immersion tank and rampaging about the streets of the city in search of live prey. His search for a primitive and true mode of being leads him to a zoo and, still in his primate form, he quizzically surveys the range of animal toys and goods for sale in the attached tourist shop. Nature has been tamed and commodified and the primate Eddie takes his place among the caged animals on show in zoo. Reminiscent of Robert Louis Stevenson's *The Strange Case of Dr. Jekyll and Mr. Hyde* (1886), the bodily metamorphoses that Eddie undergoes become uncontrollable. His friends and colleagues, including his ex-wife, are very worried about his altered state of being and try to persuade him to stop the experiments. Against all advice, towards the end of the film we see him undertake yet another drug-induced immersion in his search for the beginning, the essence and meaning of life. The power unleashed by this final 'head trip' literally engulfs the entire laboratory and causes his fellow scientists to black out. Managing to stay conscious, it is Emily who finally saves him from himself by literally pulling him from the grip of the swirling vortex that threatens to reduce him to his micro-biological beginnings. Upon his return to present-day reality, he announces that 'the final truth of all things is that there

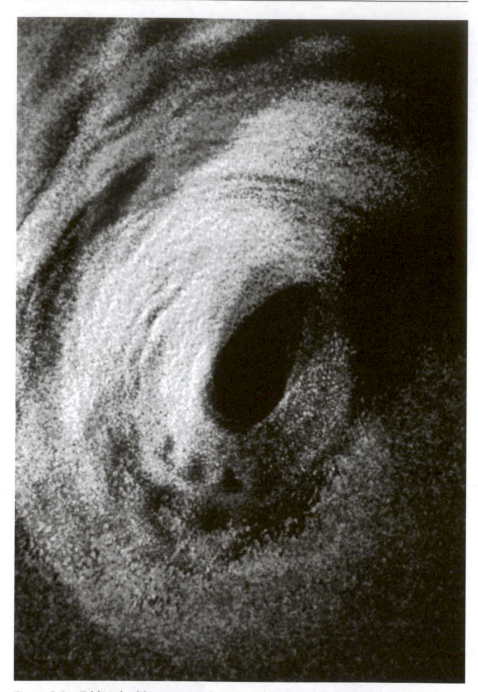

Figure 3.3   Eddie's bodily metamorphosis in *Altered States* (1980). The Kobal
Collection / Warner Bros.

is no final truth' and he describes the terror and horror that this regression has caused him to feel. But, the film does not stop here, and the sequence at the very end shows the couple both undergoing bodily transformation. This takes place in one of the many narrow corridors that are featured in the film. Having somehow infected Emily with the metamorphic effects he was experiencing, the scene features the couple struggling to retain their earthly bodies and return to normality.

Although this is very much an effects-driven film, it is also a film that is packed with heated dialogue about the nature of being human, as well as direct references to drug use and counter-cultural values. The main characters in this film are assigned long, quasi-philosophical speeches, which they often perform at breakneck speed. Even the purely visual, 'trippy' sequences are crammed with images that have been frenetically edited together. The sparse dialogue and languorous style that Kubrick instituted in *2001* are thoroughly vanquished and, by comparison, the protagonists seem to be in a constant state of hysteria. The hallucination sequences when Eddie first takes the drug outside of the immersion tank display the kind of surreal imagery with which Ken Russell has become associated. Here the 'lucid dream' is presented as a montage of apocalyptic and sexual symbols, which are clashed and melded together. These sequences are full of shocking, violent, sado-masochistic and religious imagery and are set up in comparison with later effects sequences, which ostensibly concentrate on the manifestations of Eddie's experiences upon his actual body. So the film's special effects ostensibly shift from a representation of Eddie's inner visions to providing visions of the traumatic affects that his experimentation is having upon his outer body. In other words, the perspective shifts from Eddie's point of view to looking at the spectacle of Eddie in his altered state of being. Having said this, the signature image of the film is a close-up on Eddie's metamorphosing and distorted face, with his mouth stretched wide in horror and agony (see Fig. 3.3). Although this can also be taken as a literal representation of his bodily metamorphosis, the first time we see this image it makes a very brief appearance during one of his inner dream sequences. Also, the likeness to Edvard Munch's famous painting, *The Scream* (1893), is unmistakable, which effectively alerts the knowing viewer to the way in which this screaming face is actually an artistic expression of Eddie's inner state of being. Although Russell denies consciously building in specific artistic allusions in *Altered States* (see interview on pp. 103–8), the film does display a dizzying array of references to a variety of artistic movements that have been associated with the genre since its inception. A colleague once suggested that Ken Russell seemed especially adept at bringing high-modernist art to the masses.[30] I think there is some truth in this statement, and perhaps Russell's work provides an especially clear example of the cultural shift from modernism to postmodernism in artistic practices. Indeed, the medley of images on offer in this film, as combined with

Eddie's experiences of what could be described as a postmodern-day sense of reality and the mix of British and American sensibilities that can be found in this film, presents a suitably climactic finale to the 'new art' cycle of American science fiction films.

NEW WORLDS AND OLD WORLDS

My primary focus so far in this chapter has been the development of the genre during, what I see as, a truly fascinating and influential period. I have, of course, been forced to set aside many films that I would deem as important and worthy of discussion, partly because I have chosen to concentrate the bulk of the chapter on those films produced by American companies (even if the personnel, directors etc. have not always been American), but also due to my focus upon the 'new art' cycle. For instance, two British films that immediately spring to mind are the long overlooked *The Final Programme* (dir. Robert Fuest, 1973) and more often discussed *The Man Who Fell to Earth* (dir. Nicholas Roeg, 1976), both of which were heavily influenced by the British 'new wave' in science fiction writing. These films are especially interesting in the way that they engage with features of late capitalist or postmodern society and an increasing commoditisation of counter-cultural mores and aesthetics. They are also important in terms of how they play out the sexual politics of the time, particularly in their figuration of androgyny and the performance of alternative sexualities as so much a part of European, popular youth culture of the time. This has not been the main focus of my attention in this chapter, but in moving into the 1980s and beyond, I will be looking at issues surrounding gender and identity in the next couple of chapters. Also left out are further examples of films that appear to answer to *2001* (the Russian-made *Solaris* [dir. Andrei Tarkovsky, 1972] being an obvious example), as well as the run of films that starred Charlton Heston (e.g. *Planet of the Apes* series [beginning in 1968], *Soylent Green* [dir. Richard Fleischer, 1973] etc.). In addition, I have not made mention of films like *Westworld* (dir. Michael Crichton, 1973) and *The Stepford Wives* (dir. Bryan Forbes, 1975). There are a variety of reasons for these exclusions; either because I have chosen to concentrate on American-made films, or because I do not see these films as especially linked to the 'new art' cycle. However, the racial issues raised in the 'Apes' series will be briefly covered in a later chapter, and mention will be made of both *Westworld* and *The Stepford Wives* in connection with gender issues in chapters to follow.

In concluding this chapter I have chosen to take a brief look at a couple of British films, *Zardoz* (dir. John Boorman, 1974) and *The Quatermass Conclusion* (which began life as a television series and was later edited for feature film release [dir. Piers Haggard, 1978]), in a brief comparative study with the American-produced films discussed above. These British films also represent the counter-culture as a feminine threat and can be read alongside films like *The Terminal Man* and *Altered States*. For instance, in *Zardoz* we find a literally feminised sphere of activity in the depiction of a society of immortal beings, called the Eternals. The Eternals live in a seemingly tranquil, pastoral commune, separated from the harsh reality of the outside world by an invisible and impenetrable dome called The Vortex.[31] Images of this feminine sphere are juxtaposed with the reality of the outside world, which is under male rule and populated by the Brutals. Control over the Brutals is exercised by bands of aggressive and murderous men called the Exterminators. One of the Exterminators, Zed (notably played by Sean Connery, of James Bond fame), penetrates The Vortex by crawling into the open mouth of the large stone head that conveys orders to the Brutals and transports offerings back to The Vortex. Upon discovering a Brutal in their midst, the Eternals variously attempt to tame him, educate him, have sex with him, and generally introduce him to their psychedelic and surreal world. The Vortex is matriarchal and the arrival of this supremely masculine and disruptive force provokes both fear and intrigue. A rather disgruntled male member of this society, Friend (played by John Alderton), is charged with controlling the Exterminator, although Zed's presence seems only to arouse his own disruptive masculinity. Even though the Eternals have created an idyllic 'pleasure dome' in the Vortex environment, Zed soon learns that there are members of this society who are not happy here; they feel that their lives have stagnated and many are so bored that they have descended into a psychologically remote and un-reacting state. A further complication arises as Zed forms an instant and obvious sexual attraction to one of the female leaders of the Eternals, Consuella (Charlotte Rampling), and thus a battle of the sexes ensues, during which they both vie for power and control. As the literal fabric of The Vortex begins to breaks down the brutal outside world rushes in and a band of Exterminators kill most of the Eternals. With her world collapsing around her, Consuella allies herself with Zed and, in a quick succession of shots, we see them have children, grow old and die together.

It is the male character in this film that is figured as a life-giving and creative, irrational force in this film; offset against a feminised, stagnant and dying world. However, the wonderfully surreal and psychedelic effects and imagery to be found in the world of The Vortex is truly captivating and provides the main focus of the film. Also Zed appears to learn much from his experiences of The Vortex. For instance, during one particular sequence he is forced to face himself, which is represented by his immersion into a kaleidoscopic world of mirrors. After this experience he appears to become more reflective and self-knowing. Life in The Vortex has civilised Zed in certain respects and the knowledge he has gained enables him to find his place in the real world. However, Zed's aggressive co-option of this knowledge and the experiences that this alternative world offers suggests the kind of re-territorialisation that was seen in the later American 'new art' films. In a similar fashion to *Altered States,* the mise-en-scène in The Vortex presents the viewer with a veritable bricolage of artistic imagery, in which old and new are placed together, side by side. For instance, Zed is led though several cluttered rooms containing ancient statues and paintings, and the images of reconstituting bodies floating in liquid space, behind glass walls, are reminiscent of epic religious frescoes (of the kind that Michelangelo undertook in the Sistine Chapel). In this respect, the film more obviously draws upon a history of European art and culture, and the presentation of some of these images also aligns itself with European surrealism. Indeed, the influence of surrealism is strongly indicated by the long opening shot (following the prologue) of the 'Zardoz head' floating in space, set against a panorama of sky. This image is repeated in the form of several framed pictures that Zed encounters upon entering The Vortex, at which point it is hard not to see a likeness to familiar and popular work by surrealist painters like René Magritte. Influenced by Sigmund Freud's theories, Surrealism aimed to break down the boundaries between conscious and unconscious states, between reality and fantasy, between the material outside world and an interior dream world, to bring the supposedly irrational and liberating force of unconscious desires into the artistic arena. However, although *Zardoz* is replete with surreal imagery, the boundary breakdowns that surrealism embraced are finally figured as dangerous and the dividing lines between worlds are kept in place throughout most of the film; the surreal imagery is created here to represent a literally separate world that is violently reawakened and finally destroyed upon the aggressive intrusions of a brutal reality. Although *Zardoz* luxuriates in a kind of postmodern mixing of artistic allusions, its attitude is not playful or celebratory. This film does not conjure up a 'new art' world of non-rational creativity, but an artistic world that is distinct in its cold and selfish rationalism.

The Quatermass Conclusion is not formally experimental, but it also offers a very negative, retrospective look at the counter-cultural movements of the 1960s and 1970s. Here we have a dystopian, near-future world in which society has largely broken down. The youth of the day are split between two diametrically opposed groups: the violent, marauding street gangs of the city and the catatonically pacifist cult called the Planet People (as unmistakable reference to the hippy movement of the 'flower power' years), who head out toward the countryside. So, the younger generation in this world are figured as either attacking the old world or opting out of the world completely. The Planet People are drawn to various ancient, stone circle sites around the country and they gather in their thousands to be 'taken up' by a burning white light that descends from the heavens. Our eponymous scientist, Quatermass, and a small cohort of followers, stand between the opposed irrational forces of the younger generation and attempt to return rationality and order to this disorderly world. Strangely, Quatermass is more anxious about the Planet People, whose motivations he proceeds to investigate, than the violent youth factions in the cities. Quatermass discovers that this cult believe that they are being transported to a new world when they are 'taken up'. However, he also discovers signals from space which correspond with the 'taking up' events that the young people are so eager to attend. Having disrupted this signal during one event, his findings reveal that rather than being a portal or tunnel to a new world, the planet people are being harvested, and the light rays that descend from the heavens before the mass disappearances actually bring about their deaths.[32] Needless to say, he saves the Planet People and, by inference, the Planet, this time by inserting an atomic warhead into the portal, thereby delivering a violent shock to the alien intruders. So, a younger generation obviously takes a hard bashing from both of these British films in what seems to be an aggressive backlash aimed at the counter-cultural movements that sprung up in 1960s and continued to exert their pull into the 1970s. 'Dropping out' in both of these British films, is not an option, but neither, it seems, is the existence of an alternative or 'complimentary awareness', as suggested by the psychedelic 'tunnels of perception' that were so pervasive in the 'new art' films: those who refuse to engage with the 'real world' are either killed off or violently brought back into the fold.

INTERVIEW: DIRECTOR KEN RUSSELL

C: Prior to *Altered States*, you weren't a director who was associated with the science fiction genre. Could you talk a little about how you came to direct *Altered States*? For instance, why, do you think, the producers felt that this project might interest you? What was it about the project that sparked your own interest?

R: I had made one science fiction film – well, a 'filmlet' – a fifteen-minute, short film, called *The Lonely Shore* (1964). I don't know who thought of the original story, but it was put up as an idea for *Monitor*.[33] The idea was that artefacts of the present day – we're talking about 1962–63–64 – might be puzzling to an alien intelligence, to aliens from outer space, who might come to the world years later. So the story was that a group of space travellers had collected together a kind of museum of artefacts that they found puzzling and that they were going to take back home. That was the preamble. The thing was that they didn't take them after all and left them all on a beach. So we covered a beach with a variety of things from furniture to fireplaces etc. that in the context of placing them in sand, just by the sea, made them look more surreal than they already were. For instance, we had one of those terrible 1930s fireplaces and on it we had tacky Alsatian dogs. So it looked like a shrine and the aliens were trying to work out what deity we were worshipping. We also had things like those red plastic tomato-sauce squeezers and manikins . . . and they were all in the sand that was blowing around them. In fact, the wind was blowing so hard we had to nail some of the objects into the sand, where it had turned into cement, or they'd bowl along. Anyway, I reckon you can call that science fiction.

Apart from that and aside from all the comics and so on, two of my favourite films were science fictions: *Metropolis* and *Things to Come*.

But I'll tell you why I was chosen for this film . . . I didn't know this at the time . . . I thought I was chosen for my artistry. There was a director called Arthur Penn, who had been involved in the project for a year. He was having problems with the producer and writer in realising the hallucinations. One of these was described as a black force travelling through black space at two miles an hour. Well, how do you show black on black? And also the fact that it was only travelling at two miles an hour puzzled Arthur Penn – it puzzled him for a year and he never came up with a solution. So, he resigned, or he was fired, according to what perspective you take. They needed another director. The writer, Paddy Chayefsky, had a reputation. He was an Oscar-winner; he had won an Oscar for the screenplay of *Marty* [dir.Delbert Mann,1955]. It became obvious to me later why he wasn't that easy to satisfy because he said to me one time . . . you don't do the usual shooting formula. You don't shoot wide shot, close-up, over-the-shoulder close-ups etc., which means that I can't cut the film when you've gone. He said: you often do scenes in one shot. Well, it turned out that other directors that they had approached had turned it down because they knew what I didn't know, which was his reputation for taking films away and chopping them up. Because he had written the story, he could never bear to let it go. I found out later that I was the twenty-seventh director they had approached . . . does that answer your question?

C: Released in 1980, *Altered States* provides a kind of journey back through the 1970s and late 1960s. What do you think it says about this period?

R: I haven't a clue . . . I am somewhat out of touch, deliberately out of touch with current affairs. I don't move with the times.

C: Is that an advantage sometimes?

R: I don't know, but I'm stuck with it. I mean I had to think up the hallucinations and since the writer said that the protagonist, Jessup, was a religious nut, and being a semi-religious nut myself I just looked in the Old Testament, where I found a lot of the imagery. The character, Jessup, didn't believe in the New Testament; that was too new for him. But all the old weird stuff he went along with . . . breaking the seventh seal and all that . . . So, for his state of mind, I used what I thought would be the correct imagery; imagery that he would be familiar with from the Old Testament; imagery that might have another meaning to it, that was symbolic of his problem or what he was searching for.

C: So, what about all the references to drugs?

R: Well, they were in the original novel from which Paddy wrote his screenplay. This was based very much on the Huxley book, *Doors of Perception*.

C: I've read in a *Cinefex* article that when you took over the project you decided that the existing sets looked too 'Space Odyssey-ish' . . .

R: Well, yes, they were glossy and they didn't bear any reference to reality. They looked like some of kind of sub-James Bond set or something and they weren't workman-like. They were left over from the previous director. Also, they didn't have the marvellous old copper tank that we used. I was very fortunate in having a very good production designer, who was also an artist. We got on very well and he said to me that they wanted me to use these sets. But then he said: well I think I can get around that. So, what he did was cut them to pieces and they were turned into the carpentry shop. Then we made the sets we wanted.

C: So, was there a sense in which you were deliberately moving away from the *2001* look?

R: Oh, yeah, I suppose, in a way, yeah. I suppose the original sets did look a bit like that, now I think. Our sets weren't like *2001*. We just had this old copper boiler that you might find in the basement of a hospital or university. Their sets were very spacious etc.

C: In your book on directing film, you talk about how important 'structure and development' is in filmmaking. For instance, you give the example of your film *Mahler* (1974) as structured like a rondo [a, b, a, c].[34] I wondered how you might describe the structure of *Altered States*?

R: Well, I just went along with it, chapter by chapter. The thing was that the script was the script and we weren't allowed to alter it. I nearly came to blows with Paddy Chayefsky when he started interfering with it during production and I said I couldn't work with him on the set. So, he went back to New York on the understanding that I would not change any dialogue, I would not change any scenes, and that he would see the rushes that were shipped to him. When we went to Mexico, I changed one line of dialogue. I think the line had something to do with the heat and the sweat that is meant to be pouring from one character's brow. It was raining at the time and I thought, well, that's ludicrous, so I changed it to something about getting out of the rain. Paddy said: well you've changed the dialogue, so let's go back and re-shoot. They had been bending over backwards to please him, but they weren't going to go back to do just that scene. As for the structure of it . . . I had no quarrel with that. It was a linear story. I thought it was well structured and the dialogue was very good. We did something with that . . . because the dialogue was so technical and had to be spoken with total credibility and expertise – and nobody knew what it meant anyway – we rehearsed for three weeks, just the dialogue, with everyone overlapping. Paddy was there for that. He had done stage plays and so on and he was very good at that. The thing was that apart from the hallucinations, the film was very chatty.

C: Yes, I was going to ask about the rapid pace and style . . .

R: Well, that was part of it. I mean, we rehearsed and rehearsed until it was no problem. It was incredible. They would cut into each other because they knew what the other guy was going to say, they were on the same wavelength. That worked very well and I think that made the whole thing quite credible.

C: It's interesting, because, again, it's quite different from what you might think of in terms of standard American science fiction. I mean, I think of the kind of stolid and slow speeches that you had in a lot of earlier, American science fiction films . . . and in *Altered States* there were long speeches, but they were . . .

R: Energetic . . .

C: What also fascinates me about the film is the use corridors and tunnels as a kind of recurring motif. Can you talk a bit about your thinking behind this?

R: Well, I think I've probably got things lurking in my mind that surface. For instance, I've been greatly influenced by *Metropolis,* which has lots of tunnels. I needed a sort of feeling of menace, of something lurking. This was the little ape. He was the presence of something . . .

C: Something primitive?

R: Yes, that's right. Similarly, when he has this adventure in the tank . . . we went to Oxford Scientific, who were into real scientific research, for images. We wanted to really go inside, in the veins almost, or the gut, going back to a primitive time.

C: But these images don't look horrific, they look sort of wondrous.

R: Yes, it was quite exotic.

C: Your earlier film, *Savage Messiah* (1972), was about Henri Gaudier-Brzeska – a sculptor associated with the Vorticist art movement. I was wondering whether your knowledge of this art movement had in any way influenced some of the imagery and design apparent in *Altered States*?

R: If it did it would have been subconscious. But, as I said, [Richard] McDonald was an artist who was familiar with that sort of art. In another film he did, *The*

Day of the Locust (1975),[35] he had Cubist people, groups of sort of Cubist, threatening people in that film. He draws upon his knowledge of modern art.

C: I know you've talked about this already, but I'd like to know more about the possible artistic influences behind some of the hallucination images. For instance, various critics have talked about how images in these scenes are reminiscent of Dali, Magritte, and, I can't help but think of Edvard Munch's *The Scream* in connection with the image that features Edward's distorted face and gaping mouth. Are these references or influences deliberately built into some of those images?

R: This question of influences comes up all the time. I absorb things. My first paying job was in an art gallery in Bond Street, as a salesman. I was very much into all that in my early twenties and I did a kind of crash course on the history of art, modern art in particular. So, I've always been a fan of modern art galleries. Whenever I'm in New York I always visit the Museum of Modern Art. You know, you just absorb these things and then they come out, consciously or not . . . I think it's mostly unconscious. I can't think of anything I've ever deliberately copied. That's not to say I haven't copied. It's true that I did consciously copy *Metropolis* in *The Devils* (1971), for the scene in the convent. Huxley was a great inspiration for that also, of course. He said the exorcism of Sister Jeanne was the equivalent of a rape in a public lavatory. I think that's such a blinding image of horror and that's just something else I've absorbed.

I've been a sort of visual freak all my life. I think it's significant that I realised cinema was cinema when I saw the early German expressionist films, which I showed in the war. So, there I was extolling German art, while our empire was reduced to ruins . . .

C: Bran Ferren's special visual effects are in evidence in the post-production work on the final two hallucination scenes – particularly the last one. What do you think he brought to the film? How did you find working on those two scenes?

R: Well, Ferren was an interesting guy, although he did mystify somewhat. He made this very expensive piece of equipment that looked really high-tech and that created a strange light. He was very secretive about it and it cost us a lot to use this amazing light. Then one day, someone dropped it. He wasn't there. One side of it dropped off and inside was just a piece of plywood with bits of broken mirror stuck on it. That was it. That cost about $250,000. There were really a whole group of people working on it. For instance, there was a man called [John] Dykstra, who is very famous. He worked on the *Star Wars* films and *Spider Man 2*. But they're all a bit hocus-pocus. Most of the Dykstra stuff was one liquid being pumped into another, which created weird clouds.

C: Oh, very 1970s.

R: Yes, but effects have got quite sophisticated now.

C: I have read that you like the work behind the image to be shown and that while the film's technicians were trying to cover everything up, to make it look it look slick and smooth, you liked it when it didn't look slick and smooth.

R: A lot of the effects were pretty straightforward actually. One of my favourite moments is the sequence when Jessup is in Mexico and he has that hallucination after having some of the local brew. This is the section when you see the atomic bomb, mushroom cloud, and there are references to magic mushrooms etc. The odd thing was that when we were in Mexico, at a location that was like a Mexican version of the Grand Canyon, the whole area was covered in great stone monoliths that were like mushrooms. I mean they were mushroom shaped. In fact, I began to wonder whether they were man-made. It seemed so extraordinary that they were brewing up all these magic mushrooms and there were these giant mushroom stones. It was a gift, I thought. The theme of this section was about creation and the Adam and Eve story – with the serpent and the umbrella . . . that was a mushroom too. Those images were very straightforward. Parts were just shot against a green screen background and then we just added images. That sort of thing was just very basic.

I remember I stayed behind for about six months, after the principle photography was finished, to oversee and make the special effects appropriate. It was in the days before CGI. I remember once that the same piece of film had to be differently treated with about twenty-seven runs through an optical machine. It could have got scratched and it often did on about the third runthrough, but you had to do the twenty-seven and then develop it to see whether it had worked. These days we have machines for that and we press buttons.

C: Again, I've also read that you apparently turned down the offer of making other science fiction films in America, after *Altered States* – why?

R: That was foolish. I didn't want to be pigeon-holed. I turned down certain science fiction films which went on to make a fortune. But that's life.

NOTES

1. Anderson 1985, p. 15.
2. For example, see Kaysing and Reid 1976. In addition, the film *Capricorn One* (dir. Peter Hyams, 1978) alludes to these conspiracy theories in a narrative about the staging of a mock Mars landing presented to an unsuspecting public as a real event.
3. James 1994, p. 170.
4. 'The Impure Cinema: New Hollywood 1967–1976', in Elsaesser *et al.* (eds) 2004, pp. 9–16.
5. 'Post-Classical Hollywood', in Hill and Gibson (eds) 1998, p. 295.

6. Osker Fischinger's Lumograph was featured as the 'love machine' in *The Time Travelers* (dir. Ib Melchior, 1964) and can therefore be seen a precursor to the innovative light effects in *Fantastic Voyage*. However, the light effects featured in *Fantastic Voyage* were on a far grander scale, as used in the creation of the setting/environment.

7. There was already a history in the Lumia arts of bringing music and light images together – some artists even described their work as 'visual music'.

8. '"2001" Is Up, Up and Away', *of New York Times*, 4 April 1968.

9. '"2001" Flings Man into Space', *of Washington Post*, 14 April 1968.

10. An example of this can be found in Gelmis 1968a and 1968b. In his first review he described the film as 'anti-dramatic', 'self-defeating' and 'patronizingly pedantic', a stance that he explains away in his second review as an inaccurate account of what he really felt, due to tight deadlines. He then goes on to applaud the film as 'a masterwork' that 'uncompromisingly demands acceptance in its own unique terms'.

11. '"2001" and "Hair" – Are they the Groove of the Future?', *New York Times*, 12 May 1968.

12. A neologism of the Greek words for 'mind' and 'manifest', a literal translation of the meaning of the term 'psychedelic' is taken to be 'mind-opening'.

13. Brosnan 1991, p. 144.

14. Tart (ed.) 1969.

15. Masters and Houston 1968, p. 18.

16. Ibid., p. 81.

17. Ibid., p. 97.

18. For instance, there is a direct link between Samuel Coleridge's fantastical poem, *Kubla Khan* (written 1797/98) and his addiction to opium. Coleridge claimed that the world of the poem presented itself to him in an opium-induced dream.

19. 'A Trajectory in the American Science Fiction Film', in Telotte 2001, p. 102.

20. 'The Limits of the Genre: Definitions and Themes', in Sobchback 1993, p. 26.

21. Chion 2001, p. 148.

22. Schulman 2001, p. 16.

23. 'Beyond Reason', in Frum 2000, p. 121.

24. Ibid., pp. 145, 146.

25. Reference can be made to Sarris 1968.

26. 'Postfuturism', in Sobchack 1993, p. 229.

27. Ibid., p. 231.

28. An obvious, more recent example would be the film *Stargate* (dir. Roland Emmerich, 1994) and the 'spin-off' television series, *Stargate SG-1* (1997 –). In the film the star gate is an ancient, circular device that allows for instant travel across the universe. There is far less focus on the journey through the tunnel – it is simply a convenient justification to place the protagonists within a strange and wondrous new world.

29. An understanding of the circle or tunnel as the symbol of feminine qualities was not lost on some of the abstract artists of the 1960s and 1970s. For example, the feminist artist Judy Chicago drew upon circular abstract forms in a celebration and expression of an essentialised femininity.

30. I am indebted to Justin Smith for this comment, which inspired me to consider Russell's films as 'transitional'.

31. References to *The Wizard of Oz* in science fiction had become ubiquitous by this point in the genre's history and the name 'Zardoz' is later revealed to be a neologism of the title this musical. If the Vortex then becomes an illusory, cinematic space of special effects and affects then, by extension, science fiction film is seen as feminised.

32. Given the rampant intertextuality inherent in the genre, it is not surprising that this section of the plot is highly reminiscent of the earlier *Logan's Run* (dir. Michael Anderson, 1976). Upon reaching the age of thirty, the subjects of the domed society in *Logan's Run* eagerly submit themselves to the 'carousel', which literally draws their bodies upward, into a vortex, for supposed reconstitution/rebirth, but actually simply kills them off. Although *Logan's Run* was produced by MGM, given that the two young protagonists were British actors (Michael York, Jenny Agutter), the casting suggests that a swipe is being taken at the British, as the feminised (counter-cultural) occupants of the dome.

33. *Monitor* was a television arts series produced by the BBC that began airing in 1958.

34. Russell 2001, p. 98.

35. Richard McDonald was credited as MacDonald in this film.

4. THE MASCULINE SUBJECT OF SCIENCE FICTION IN THE 1980s BLOCKBUSTER ERA

Figure 4.1   Masculinity in crisis in *Robocop* (1987). Orion / The Kobal Collection.

The Family Films

The late 1970s and early 1980s saw a popular rebirth in the science fiction film in America, leading to the genre's market dominance in the decades to follow. Following the experimental period of the late 1960s and 1970s, so-called New Hollywood entered its second phase of development, which was largely marked by the industry's embrace of the summer blockbuster in the 1980s. Thomas Schatz dates the arrival of the blockbuster with Steven Spielberg's *Jaws* (1975), closely followed by two major science fiction hits *Star Wars* (dir. George Lucas, 1977) and *Close Encounters of the Third Kind* (dir. Steven Spielberg, 1977).[1] In the wake of these films, Lucas and Spielberg went on to produce and direct a large number of science fiction films and were central figures in the re-creation of the film series. Witnessing their success, other producers and directors followed suit. For instance, the late 1970s also saw the beginning of the *Alien* series (1979, 1986, 1992, 1997), followed in the mid-1980s with *The Terminator* films (1984, 1991, 2003), the *Back to the Future* series (1985, 1989, 1990), as well as *Robocop* and its sequels (1987, 1990, 1993).

Lucas is, of course, famous for his ongoing *Star Wars* serial, currently numbering six films in all (1977, 1980, 1983, 1999, 2002, 2005), and after the success of the action/adventure, *Indiana Jones* series (1981, 1984, 1989), Spielberg's *Jurassic Park* films (1993, 1997, 2001, fourth film currently in production) continue to draw audiences and reap vast profits. There had always been an explicit tension between art and industry in Hollywood and, as previously stated in the Introduction, the marketability and repetitive nature of genre films can be viewed as emerging from an industry model in Hollywood that seeks to create a predictable and viable product and to maximise profit. However, in the 1980s many Hollywood mainstream films became decidedly commoditised, a tendency which was intensified by the blockbuster film series.

On one level, the blockbuster can be defined as a high-concept, big-budget film that reaches a mass audience and creates a very large profit return. But these elements alone do not necessarily differentiate it from certain earlier Hollywood films. More importantly, the emergence of the blockbuster represents a response that was very much bound up with political, economic and technological changes that began to occur during the late 1970s and early 1980s. For instance, economic growth in both Western Europe and some of the Pacific Rim countries, along with the development of cable television and the advent of home video, meant that not only were alternative markets opening up for films, but there was an increasing demand for 'product' to service these new outlets. So, Hollywood entered the beginnings of a period of globalisation, diversification across other media and widespread, ancillary merchandising. This all led to an exponential growth in profit returns surrounding certain films, increasingly coming from beyond the home market and beyond the revenues received purely from ticket sales. The major studios began running extensive pre-publicity programmes for their big features, both nationally and internationally. Along with saturation pre-booking and simultaneous release strategies, the aim was to create a level of media hype around an intended blockbuster so that the film's release could come to be regarded as a multimedia 'event'. The general return to markedly generic formats and other elements common to the blockbuster aesthetic can certainly be explained within this political and economic environment. As Schatz comments: 'From *The Godfather*, to *Jaws* to *Star Wars*, we see films that are increasingly plot-driven, increasingly visceral, kinetic, and fast-paced, increasingly reliant on special effects, increasingly "fantastic" '.[2]

These are considered the fundamental aesthetic elements of a blockbuster; a format that is intended to appeal to a diverse national and international market. The idea is that accessible and exciting visual spectacle can be more readily grasped than, perhaps, the complex unfolding of a dialogue heavy, character driven or psychological drama. Perhaps this partly explains why science fiction was so perfectly placed to become such a dominant and popularised genre, as its tradition of wondrous visual spectacle and effects, in many ways made it ideal for a global marketplace. In addition, science fiction's rather fluid and ambivalent boundaries as a film genre meant that it could more readily commandeer elements related to other genres; it could absorb elements from other genres in order to extend its reach and appeal. For example, this kind of borrowing is rampant in the *Star Wars* series, as the films frequently cut between 'dog-fight' scenes associated with war films, bar-room brawls reminiscent of a western, and acrobatic displays of martial arts related to popular forms that emanate from Chinese and Japanese cinema.[3]

The genre's more recent elevation in status in the late 1960s and early 1970s had, to some extent, already brought it into the mainstream and opened it up to new and wider audiences. However, while early blockbusters like *Star Wars* and *Close Encounters* retained aspects of science fictions from the immediately preceding, 'impure' period,[4] they were very different from their recent forerunners. *Star Wars* and *Close Encounters* were hardly the cerebral and thoughtfully ambiguous fare that had dominated the genre in the early part of the 1970s, instead these money-making machines presented audiences with straightforward, linear tales, calculated to capture a far broader audience than the films of the 1970s. Their simple but fast-paced plotting, along with the reversion to explicitly polarised, binary divisions (e.g. between good and evil, male and female etc.), may have seemed designed to serve a younger audience, but the myriad references to other films and other genres and their evident nostalgia for Saturday cinema serials, earlier television serials, as well as pulp and comic-book fictions, appeared calculated to please accompanying parents and older audience members as well. In comparison to the more radical films of the 1970s, the return to older traditions within the genre can certainly be understood as a rather retrograde step, which is confirmed upon close inspection of the films' narratives. Both of these films reveal a further level of reactionary nostalgia concerning traditional family structures and, in particular, the role of fatherhood.

Star Wars and *Close Encounters* present us with a picture of disintegrating family structures and absentee fathers, a feature that became common in science fiction films that followed in the early 1980s. As outlined in the previous chapter, the 1960s and 1970s brought with it not only an assault on established patriarchal power structures, but a related attack on traditional family values. Whereas family structures might have appeared relatively stable in the first half of the century, by the 1970s the breakdown of the family unit became a cause for concern: the divorce rate was on the rise, along with the number of single-parent families. Although the absent father figure in these films can simply be read as reflecting these social changes, in looking beyond the superficial logic of the films, it is clear that they signal the rise of a profoundly conservative era in American politics and a concomitant resurrection of some of the more traditional aspects associated with patriarchal power structures. For instance, Luke Skywalker's rite of passage into adult manhood basically involves him leaving the private/domestic matriarchal space of his youth to make his entrance into the public arena of aggressive, patriarchal, power politics. In order to take up his rightful place in the world he is presented with a choice between good and bad male role models, between the wise and spiritual mentor, Ben Obi-Wan Kenobi, and the evil overlord Darth Vader (revealed as his literal father in a later film). His passage into manhood is therefore predicated upon a choice as to how he uses his new-found patriarchal power, rather than offering any kind of challenge to the way in which this universe is organised. Luke's love object in the first *Star Wars* film, the feisty Princess Leia (revealed in a later film to be his sister), may pay some lip service to the changing role of women in the public sphere, but there is really no question as to who rules this empire and who has privileged access to the mystical 'force', as these powers are passed from father to son.

At first glance, Spielberg's more sentimental tale presents a picture of failed patriarchy in the portrayal of the literal father figure, Roy Neary, who renounces his responsibilities and leaves the family home. This is a figure who, like Eddie in *Altered States* (dir. Ken Russell, 1980), wishes to disengage himself from a domesticated reality in order to take up a mystical and fantastical quest. In this way, Roy can also be likened to Luke Skywalker as he relives his youth and rite of passage into manhood. In the process, Roy reinvents himself as the chosen human father figure within a wondrous universe populated by child-like aliens. As Vivian Sobchack succinctly describes the events of the final sequence of the film:

> Surrounded by the little and curious aliens, bathed in light, Roy Neary is a figure beatifically re-solved as powerful patriarch, loving father, and lovable child. He shines as he moves toward his imminent journey through the Star Gate, toward a culturally and politically 'positive' displacement, re-birth, and eventual return to earthly power.[5]

Sobchack makes direct reference here to the Star Gate sequence as the end of *2001* (dir. Stanley Kubrick, 1968), but it is my contention that even though *Close Encounters* manifestly borrows from late 1960s and early 1970s films of the genre, in Spielberg's film the aesthetic styles associated with the New Art science fiction films became assimilated into the undemanding blockbuster style and mode of address. Rather than engaging with serious and complex, contemporary 'adult' themes, as was witnessed under the influence of the 'new wave' in science fiction, these early blockbusters seemed to leap back in time (both generically and politically) in their return to highly fantastical tales that appeared far removed from reality. Unlike their immediate predecessors, these films became disengaged from critical confrontation with the real world into which they emerged.

For Robin Wood, the arrival of the Lucas and Spielberg blockbusters marked a definite reactionary swing for Hollywood, which he locates in a spectator – screen relationship that 'construct(s) the adult spectator as a child'.[6] According to Wood, the films' emphasis on spectacle and their simplistic narrative structures offer only regressive and passive pleasures. The regressive implications of removing oneself from a material/political reality certainly became a theme in the late 1960s and early 1970s science fiction films, however, in the shift toward a blockbuster aesthetic the more militant and 'irrational' aspects associated with the presentation of marvellous spectacle was reformulated. Extending Wood's hypothesis, it is possible to say that, far from the abstract and questioning spectacular visions offered in the New Art films, the early blockbusters utilised moments of spectacle in a way that invited the viewer to unquestioningly sublimate themselves to a patriarchal power within the narrative realm.

Robert Phillip Kolker's attack on Spielberg takes a similar approach when, in his critique of both *Close Encounters* and *E. T. the Extra-Terrestrial* (dir. Steven Spielberg, 1982), he argues that Spielberg 'disallows distance and objectivity'.[7] Kolker goes on to examine the ideological mechanisms through which the films achieve this aim. At the end of Jimmy Carter's presidency (1977–81), Kolker argues that the US was crying out for a period of increased security and certainty, which Carter was unable to provide or convey. This was instead delivered in the neo-conservative politics of Ronald Reagan's reign (1981–9). Reagan's project was, reportedly, to reduce reliance on government. It was ostensibly about decreasing governmental intervention, to allow for free market interaction and increased responsibility on the level of the individual. However, Kolker observes that during the Reagan administration:

> Patriarchy assume(d) a maternal position, of care rather than authority. In the process, an extraordinary event happens as the ideological material from the larger discourse of the government is given shape by its image-making arm, eighties film. Ronald Reagan (re)enters [*sic*] cinema as the guiding patriarch offering maternal care.[8]

So, in the light of Kolker's arguments here, the constant references to the domestic sphere and to the nature of fatherhood in many of these films can be linked to the political manoeuvrings of the period. Kolker obviously places great stress on the cultural and political power of cinema and assumes that, via the oedipal melodrama of the narratives, the viewer/subject is easily interpellated by the ideological underpinnings that he detects as particularly apparent in Spielberg's films. In looking more closely at the spectator – screen relationship encouraged by the films, he draws upon psychoanalytic film theory and appears to propose that the kind of security offered by the films is associated with a return to a pre-oedipal or imaginary phase. In brief, according to Freudian psychoanalysis the pre-oedipal phase is that which exists prior to the oedipal crisis and prior to the formation of the subject as a separate and gendered being. The pre-oedipal realm is traditionally understood as maternal, it is a realm in which the child is at one with the mother. The oedipal crisis then, at least for the male child, is based upon the recognition of difference and separateness from the mother and thereby involves a sense of loss and lack upon entering the oedipal realm of the father. It was this moment of loss and lack that Lacan concentrated upon in his reworking of Freud's theories. For Lacanian psychoanalysis, entry into the symbolic realm (roughly co-existent with Freud's Oedipal realm), into the social order, gives birth to the desiring subject, the subject who can never fill the void left by division from the mother. Desire then speaks to a kind of constant craving to return to the prior, imaginary realm; a craving that the differentiated subject is unable to satisfy. As applied to the spectator – screen relationship, one strand of psychoanalytic theory then proposes that the cinematic apparatus is designed to temporarily fill this void, to fulfil desire, to give the illusion of a return to the imaginary realm. Kolker's argument is therefore underpinned by the creation of this desiring subject and a cinema that taps into the gendered subject's desire for reunification. The crucial difference in Kolker's formulation is that, in terms of Spielberg's films (along with other films of the era) this reunification is with the lost father; the illusion of an imaginary realm that the films attempt to conjure is configured as patriarchal rather than matriarchal. The father figure here takes on the role traditionally played by the mother in psychoanalytic theory.

In as much as psychoanalysis can be understood as upholding a masculinist version of human psychology, I would suggest that what Kolker's reading of Spielberg's films actually achieves is laying bare the inconsistencies at the heart of Reagan's project. The gender confusion that he identifies points to the contradictions within a system of government that purports to allow for ever increasing individual autonomy, while simultaneously demanding levels of conformity and compliance. In order to maintain control, such a system really requires extended supervision, which Kolker believes was being attempted through a kind of psychologically underhand regulation of the film-going audiences' internal, fantasy worlds.

Kolker goes on to state that films like *E.T. the Extra-Terrestrial* (dir. Steven Spielberg, 1982) operate through the creation of a 'melodramatic oedipal machine, delivering protection, yet denying what it seems to offer, keeping the viewer attached to it all times, threatening/promising loss whenever the attachment is broken'.[9] This idea is highly reminiscent of Richard Dyer's arguments concerning the operations of popular, classical Hollywood cinema. Using the musical as a prime example, Dyer states that this sort of cinema works to resolve ideological contradictions related to inadequacies in society. Rather than offering up alternative worlds and alternative ideological constructions, the classical Hollywood musical achieves this by attempting to create a 'utopian sensibility'. In fact, on some levels, the classical musical has much in common with blockbuster science fiction. Although primarily aimed a female audience, lively and colourful spectacles were also central to the musical genre and it regularly featured a diegetic audience (a device I have already pointed to as common in science fiction), all of which worked toward offering a kind of escape or tonic that answered to the real-life situations of the audience. For Dyer, there is a kind of closed circuit of control in operation here, in which 'entertainment provides alternatives *to* capitalism which will be provided *by* capitalism'.[10] So, as a product of industrial capitalism, the Hollywood musical film is serving to sustain a system that promises to satisfy the needs created by this very system. In a similar way, Kolker proposes that Spielberg's films answer to various inadequacies in a neo-conservative and capitalist America, but he extends this notion by implying that the films themselves are offered as the solution, as the path to the fulfilment of those needs and desires created by this system of government. Dyer is careful to point out that the closed circuit he outlines in connection with the musical is not always successfully sealed. For instance, he says that drawing attention 'to the gap between what is and what could be, is, ideologically speaking, playing with fire'.[11] However, for Kolker, Spielberg's films appear inordinately successful in sustaining the myths of Reagan's conservative, capitalist project.

Kolker's argument is very persuasive, but I would say that he overestimates the possible effectiveness of the ideological coercion that he locates in the films of this period. Reception studies have surely taught us that the spectator – screen relationship is not a one-way path; readings of a film can differ depending on the specific subject position of individual viewers. In fact, his own reading implies that these films are capable of arousing very contrary effects to those he suggests. Indeed, Spielberg's films, along with many other blockbusters, all the way through to current releases, have regularly been derided as childish, patronising, as cynical and reactionary. Rather than representing an all-inclusive, magic formula for ideological coercion, opinion about many of these blockbuster films has been particularly intense and they have, on the contrary, provoked very active criticism. It also strikes me that certain criticisms could partially speak to the level of perceived threat that Spielberg's and Lucas's blockbuster films may actually represent to traditional masculine identity. After all, even though these films are very much *about* traditional masculinity, the kind of compliant consumption that they have come to represent, along with what is understood as the nature of their mode of address, challenges the very model of masculinity that the oedipal narratives espouse.

The *Back to the Future* series continues the themes of family and fatherhood, but, as if in answer to the criticisms levelled at earlier blockbusters, these films are laced with comic parody and self-conscious irony. Even though explicit mention is not made of their reliance upon the psychoanalytic model of the family romance (as in the case of *Forbidden Planet* [dir. Fred M. Wilcox, 1956]), the oedipal scenario that is central to the films' narrative trajectory is foregrounded to comic effect. The adolescent protagonist, Marty (Michael J. Fox), in *Back to the Future*, returns to the past and goes about trying to create an ideal father. Marty, is actually attempting to orchestrate his own rites of passage into the oedipal world of the father. If he sees his father as weak and unsuccessful, as less than ideal, at the opening of the film, then by the end of the film Marty has created a true patriarch: a man who is masterful and in control, a figurehead that he can respect. In such a way, he can complete his oedipal passage, turn his attention away from his mother to his new girlfriend, and re-establish patriarchal authority, an authority that he can therefore inherit.

The ideal father of Marty's dreams is one that is associated with an earlier period, namely the 1950s. Lynne Segal summarises the father of the 1950s as 'essential, but only, it seemed, for financial support, status and legitimacy: his wife and children relied upon him even when he totally ignored them'.[12] So, this was an emotionally absent father whose main role was as breadwinner/ provider for the family. However, by the close of the 1970s, partly in reaction to the 1950s father, the ideal of the 'nurturing father' was being widely pro- mulgated. Although this shift may have had its genesis in counter-cultural ideas concerning alternative modes of social life, this was the ideal that Reagan co- opted in attempting to redefine his political leadership into the caring and nur- turing, paternal leader of his subjects. But it seems to me that Marty's model father is closer to that of the 1950s ideal; after all, in the first film of the series, Marty seems rather more excited by the new car that he receives as reward for his efforts than he is in being reunited with his new family and his girlfriend. He is a yuppie in the making, who greedily accepts the prizes that this new- found father provides.[13] The shiny, new, 'nurturing' father here is really just a re-vamped version of the old-style, 1950s father.

Further films in the series continued with the themes and plot structure set up in the first film. So, Marty finds himself continually travelling back and forth in time in order to sustain his vision of the perfect family and the future of his patriarchal inheritance. Although the film's sequels can simply be read as cynical re-hashes of the first film, as commercial opportunism, the constant and repeated foregrounding of the oedipal moment suggests that Marty is less than successful in sustaining his fantasies, and less than successful in his entrance into adult masculinity via this oedipal route. Marty's passage into manhood is constantly deferred; he seems somewhat stuck in his own adolescence, which I would say adds to the comedic appeal of the sequels. On the one hand, Marty's struggles can be read as an endorsement of a Reaganite regime that delivers its glittering prizes to those who conform to its moral and social mores. But, on the other hand, Marty can be understood as an embodiment of the adult male interpreted as child-man, forever supervised and sublimated in a Reaganite world.

The 1980s Cyborg Film

What might be called the sentimental family films that I have discussed so far were not the only science fiction films during this period that displayed a particular concern with the masculine subject. In America, another, highly successful, cycle of blockbusters began during this period. I call this cycle the cyborg films and they really came to prominence with the relatively low-budget, 'sleeper hit', *The Terminator* (dir. James Cameron, 1984), which was later followed by *Robocop* (dir. Paul Verhoeven, 1987). In the interests of expediency, this chapter will primarily focus upon these two films, which are not only seminal examples of this sub-genre but also offer a convenient coupling for later discussion. Still, there were many other examples, as a procession of bigger-budget cyborg films followed *The Terminator*, including: two big-budget sequels, *Terminator 2: Judgment Day* (dir. James Cameron, 1991) and *Terminator 3: Rise of the Machines* (dir. Jonathan Mostow, 2003); the two sequels to *Robocop* and the later *Universal Soldier* (dir. Roland Emmerich, 1992) with its closely-packed run of three sequels that comprised two made-for-television films in 1998 and the big-screen follow-up in 1999. The comic book-references that were so much a part of the *Star Wars* series also found their way into the cyborg film. For example, the superhuman powers, 'special abilities' and hyper-muscular frame of American comic-book superheroes (e.g. Captain America, Superman etc.) were borrowed in the figuring of the lone and similarly taciturn cyborg warrior that emerged in the 1980s. However, unlike the family films, the cyborg blockbusters were largely marketed as science fiction/action films and were aimed at an adult audience (although the rating of later sequels frequently allowed for a juvenile audience).

Like many Hollywood genres, the action film has traditionally been built upon a structure of binary oppositions and definite distinctions. This structure has been especially noticeable in action films as it operates to provide the logic behind the genre's emphasis on displays of extreme combat between warring factions. Classically, the action genre presented visions of the male body engaged in direct and violent confrontation and the participation of female characters was usually kept to a minimum, even though they often functioned in the narrative to supply the motive or incentive for recurrent scenes of male aggression. This was the supreme masculine genre, in which the male hero/anti-hero of an action film became the embodied symbol of masculine endeavour. Drawing upon the conventions of the action genre, the cyborg films mentioned above presented the viewer with exaggerated visions of masculine subjectivity. The important difference was that in these science fiction/action films the action hero or anti-hero was replaced with the part human/part machine cyborg. Up to this point, Clint Eastwood's *Dirty Harry* films of the 1970s and 1980s, and Charles Bronson's vigilante in the *Death Wish* series (1974–94) had come to epitomise a cold and alienated masculinity, as indicated in their portrayals of emotionless, machine-like violence. So it is possible to say that elements that characterised the 'cool' masculinity of the 1970s action hero became literalised in the body of the cyborg. In addition, whereas female characters had been very much sidelined in traditional action films, in these cyborg films they were usually at the centre of the violence. In fact, the binary opposition of masculine/feminine was often foregrounded in the extreme masculine aggression visited upon the female in early renditions of the mainstream cyborg film. It is therefore easy to read these films as part of the hostile response to the rise of feminism in 1970s and the changing role of women in society. In a wider sense, they can also be seen as part of an aggressive conservative backlash against the now feminised counter-cultural movements and politics of the previous decades.

Susan Jeffords specifically relates the emergence of these figurations to the Reagan era and places the macho cyborg alongside other muscular heroes/anti-heroes that appeared in the 1980s (e.g. Rambo in *First Blood* [dir. Ted Kotcheff, 1982] and its sequels [1985, 1988], John McClane in the *Die Hard* series 1988–95 etc.). For Jeffords: 'The indefatigable, muscular, and invincible masculine body became the linchpin of the Reagan imaginary; this hardened male form became the emblem not only for the Reagan presidency but for its ideologies and economies as well.'[14]

So, as far as Jeffords is concerned, these cyborgs represented a dominant ideological formation and she traced their function to the political climate of the time. Taking *The Terminator* films as an example, she backed up her case by charting the modifications made between the first film and its sequel. She argued that, in the first film, the cyborg's 'hard body' stood for the aggressive militaristic and business strategies of the Reagan period, whereas, with the advent of the 'softer' Bush administration (1989–93), the terminating cyborg was refashioned into a powerful, protecting father figure. In this way, the film offered 'male viewers an alternative to the declining workplace and national structure as sources of masculine authority and power – the world of the family'.[15] What Jeffords appears to be articulating is how the narratives of the two films mediate in the ideological construction of the hard body on display. However, in concentrating so much on presumed intentionality or what she assumes as the preferred/dominant reading of these films, I think there is a tendency to imply an overly simplistic relationship between text and context in Jeffords' study. For example, the sight of the excessively muscle-bound, Terminator body may provide such a powerful visual metaphor of extreme masculinity that it exceeds the sort of narrative intent that Jeffords assumes. The visual excess associated with the hyper-masculine body of the Terminator can be easily understood as a highly defensive sign for a masculinity in crisis; a masculinity that is clinging to residual notions of gender. Furthermore, it is my contention that there are marked differences between the more 'impassioned' performances of 1980s muscular heroes/anti-heroes like Rambo (Sylvester Stallone) and McClane (Bruce Willis) and the 'colder' masculinities embodied in cyborg heroes/anti-heroes of this period. In important ways, these differences in performance actually mark the cyborg films apart from the action films that Jeffords discusses (I reserve further comment on these and other performance issues for a following chapter). So, the enormously threatening and coldly mechanical figure of the Terminator can be read as a critique of a then dominant, but warlike and dehumanised, masculinity. Moreover, the narrative consigning of these male characters to cyborg status not only serves to offer comment on the constituent features of past action heroes, but may even indicate a certain sexual/gender ambiguity at play in the 1980s action film. As Yvonne Tasker points out, the very fact that these spectacular male bodies are set up for visual scrutiny can be seen to problematise traditional gendered identity – particularly in terms of more conventional cinematic viewing constructions that position the female/feminine body as that which is to be openly gazed upon.[16] While there are certainly moments when the presentation of the passive male body may be offset by displays of extreme violence,[17] I would say that these cyborg films encourage a very consistent gazing upon the cyborg body in question. For instance, an invitation to gaze is hard to contest when, in both *The Terminator* and *Universal Solider,* the cyborg bodies in question are presented no less than naked to a viewer.

Using the body as a naturalising metaphor within a system of social organisation has a long history. In *The Body and Society,* Bryan S. Turner outlines a history of the human body as a central metaphor for social practices and, conversely (by drawing upon Michel Foucault's work), maps out the ways in which the body becomes disciplined through and by society.[18] Patriarchal society has been based upon hierarchical divisions and, what might be called patriarchal propaganda has certainly used the body in the way that Jeffords suggests – as a legitimating symbol. However, as Turner goes on to note, in contemporary, postmodern society the body has become more mobile and uncertain, less determined than Foucault's disciplined body might suggest. This complicates the idea that the body can be taken to provide, in any certain sense, a solid base upon which to support notions of an essential self. Even so, at the same time as ideas surrounding the 'natural' body are thrown into doubt, the material body also becomes a kind of signifier of contemporary selfhood, a site upon which individual identity can be located. For Chris Shilling this move towards the material body as the signifier of selfhood in contemporary society, is due to the uncertain nature of modern living: 'the body provides individuals with a "last retreat", an entity which *appears* [sic] to be a solid basis on which a reliable sense of self can be built'.[19] Nonetheless, I would maintain that even this supposed 'last retreat' becomes especially problematic in the figuring of the cyborg, as it presents a rather obvious challenge to the idea of the body as natural, as certain, and, even, as separate from other bodies. This challenge becomes clearer in looking back at the scientific and social theories and developments that support the appearance of the cyborg.

Manfred E. Clynes and Nathan S. Kline originally created the term 'cyborg', in 1960, by combining the words cybernetic and organism. In conjunction with NASA research concerning the literal alteration of human bodies to allow for survival in extra-terrestrial environments, Clynes and Kline were busy reconceiving the relationship between the human and the machine. Their use of the word cybernetics refers back to an earlier scientific discipline that was developed during World War II.[20] Replacing the linear, cause (leading to) effect model that underpinned a variety of scientific disciplines, cybernetics offered a model of causation that was based upon a circular exchange of information; an exchange whereby both fully automated systems, as well as systems that require the participation of a human being, could be conceptually enclosed within a given feedback loop.

Cybernetics can also be understood as part of a more general scientific and academic shift present in post-World War II theory, across a variety of disciplines. While the mathematician/philosopher, Norbert Wiener, is usually thought of as 'the father' of cybernetics, alongside its development something called Systems Science was also unfolding. Systems Theory was proposed in the 1940s by the biologist Ludwig von Bertalanffy who thought there was a need to think of real/material systems as open and in interaction with other systems or a given environment. Bertalanffy went on to introduce *GST* (General Systems Theory), which he proposed as a new meta-paradigm for use throughout the sciences.[21] But, in this postwar period, it was not only the sciences that saw the proliferation of notions surrounding the idea of feedback and open systems. For example, Stephen Pfohl points to some interesting parallels/similarities between Cybernetics/Systems Theory and existentialism. Pfohl also sets the general thrust of all these new theories in the light of a response to the war and what could be 'discerned as the deadly freeze-framings of fascism'.[22] According to Tiziana Terranova, Cybernetics (along with Systems Theory) presented a 'fundamental shift in the way the operation of power was viewed and organised'.[23] Perhaps, this was also part of a general shift in which new modellings/philosophies/theories provided a more fluid and reciprocal model of the world, whereby political and social control mechanisms could be understood as operating in a less deterministic, violent or repressive fashion.

Pre-World War II theories and practices of people management had been largely based on division of labour and hierarchical control (as exemplified in the factory model of organisation). This was underpinned by the biological image of the body as a collection of separate organs led, or managed, by the brain. However, the expansion of the cybernetic model, since the post World War II period, has affected the ways in which society is understood to operate.

Replacing a kind of hierarchical model of societal control, cybernetics has introduced a model that acknowledges reciprocity in the exchange of information and the operations of control. Alongside this, the scientific bodily models that have paralleled the growth of the cybernetic paradigm have altered. For example, the 'monarchy' of the brain (understood as the separate, organising/controlling force in charge of the rest of the body), has, to some degree, been replaced by the gene (now understood as the ultimate carrier of information), thereby offering the opportunity of a more decentralised notion of how the body functions. I would say that these relatively rapid shifts in how the body is understood to operate have made apparent not only the constructedness of what was previously seen as an 'essential body', but also the ideological imperatives behind the attempted use of the body as a 'naturalising metaphor'.

In the 1980s, the advent of the cybernetic society became particularly apparent, as the machines of a modern, industrial age were quickly being supplanted by the information technologies and biotechnologies of a postmodern age. This was a decade that saw a massive expansion in the home computer market and the further development of the internet (beyond its military beginnings) as the ideal tool for multi-national corporations and the furtherance of global capitalism. The cybernetic society now presents us with a body that is, both literally and metaphorically, de-natured. Not only have many of us become literal cyborgs (e.g. people with prosthetic limbs, electronic pace-makers, even people who have been immunised or receive hormone injections etc. can be said to fall into this new category), but we find ourselves involved in a cybernetic network of communication technologies. The cybernetic body is decentralised from within and from without; ideally, it is a body with fluid or permeable boundaries that allows for a constant exchange of information.

In coming back to the cyborg in science fiction films, rather than reading this body purely in alignment with the codes and conventions of the action genre, my point is that attention must surely be paid to the specifically science fictional aspects of the cyborg films in question. Therefore, in returning to look closely at the body politics on display in the figure of the cyborg Terminator, it is telling that he is most closely associated with industrial machinery, rather than technologies more readily allied with a post-industrial age. This is made clear in the first film of the series, in a dream sequence commencing after Kyle has fallen asleep while watching heavy digging, drilling and lifting machinery in a nearby yard. The sequence slips from the vision of the present to a vision of the future, in which similar machines, including Terminators, are tracking down and killing the human population. In addition, at the end of the first and second films, the Terminator is finally dispatched in a factory; once more aligning him with images of industrial age machinery. So, even though the Terminator is described as a cyborg in the film, my suggestion is that he is visually represented as a kind of 'old-style' aberration, an outmoded masculinity confronted by a cybernetic world that requires a rather more communicative and fluid subject: the very characteristics that he is forced to face in the literally fluid T1000 in *Terminator 2: Judgment Day* and the acrobatically agile female cyborg of the third film. And, it is not only the vision of an outmoded masculinity that is featured in the film. Sarah's 'old-style' femininity is signalled at the opening of the first film in her role as the servile waitress in the roadside family restaurant. What is interesting is that this begins to give way to a different kind of femininity, one that is associated with the 1960s; as signalled in the 1960s-style, tie-dye T-shirt that she dons just prior to the commencement of the chase. So, the showdown between the old and the new is played out both between and upon these two highly codified bodies.

Specific to classical science fiction are scientifically constructed, humanoid figures like the robot or the android. J. P. Telotte has proposed that it is possible to see these figures as human 'doubles', as a kind of self-projection or uncanny reflection of the self.[24] Telotte's understanding of the relationship apparent in the human/robot binary requires that these two images are understood as separate, even if he is indicating a kind psychical blurring of the divide between self, natural (human)/Other, constructed (robot). Clearly, the cyborg cannot operate in the quite same way. Here we have the literal melding of human self with mechanical Other – whatever characteristics were previously projected onto the image of the robot-Other are now figured as a part of the self. This poses a potentially more potent threat to the oppositions that underpin the psychoanalytic model of human subjectivity with which Telotte is working. Furthermore, if the central and founding opposition in psychoanalysis is one that is based upon the successful formation of gendered divides then the self/Other opposition that Telotte is referring to is also a gendered divide: self (masculine)/Other (feminine). It therefore does not take much of an imaginative leap to see how the erosion of boundaries that the cyborg represents comes to threaten further divisions, especially those between masculinity and femininity; a fundamental division upon which patriarchal power has been built. This may well be the reason why it seemed so necessary to re-establish, in such a prominent fashion, the traditional traits and confines associated with the most extreme, warlike and aggressive forms of male subjectivity in the 1980s cyborg films. In other words, because the cyborg is defined by a breakdown in the boundaries between self/Other, the hyper-masculinity on display becomes a hysterical attempt to recuperate the traditional distinctions that this figure threatens to erode. Seen this way, the fusion that the cyborg represents remains a powerful sign that problematises the very oppositions that the films so fervently attempt to uphold.

A comparison between the 1973 film *Westworld* (dir. Michael Crichton, 1973) and the later *Terminator* (1984) clarifies my argument. As a possible forerunner to these cyborg films, *Westworld* featured an android killing machine (played by Yul Brynner) who relentlessly stalked his human counterpart. The 'mild-mannered' Peter (Richard Benjamin) has been persuaded to holiday at a new kind of theme park in which it is possible for visitors to safely act out their fantasies. The park is populated by androids designed to enact the wishes of the human visitors: for the male visitors, the female androids are compliant sex objects and the male androids allow for the acting out of violent combat. The combat that takes place is between a male human and a male android and the androids are programmed to allow their human counterparts to emerge victorious. However, something goes wrong in this masculine paradise and the androids begin to act independently from their human programmers and dispatch all but one of the visitors to this glorified theme park. The latter part of the plot involves an extended chase scene in which Peter (as the only remaining human) is relentlessly pursued by the killer android. The android here is set up to be read as a kind of alter-ego figure for the human male. After all, according to the narrative, it is the servicing of innate masculine aggression that makes Westworld such a popular destination and Peter literally faces up to this aspect of his nature as embodied in the android gunman. But the narrative also makes clear that the reluctant Peter is forced to undergo a kind of rite of passage into 'proper masculinity' in order to survive the android's attacks: the film therefore foregrounds the creation of a masculinity that is suited to a fantasy world.

Although there are definite similarities between *Westworld* and *The Terminator*, the android and cyborg are not sutured into the same kind of human/machine binary. The most obvious difference being that, rather than pursuing a male counterpart, the Terminator is stalking a woman. It is Sarah who takes on the Peter role and it is Sarah who is forced to dispatch this macho killing machine at the end of *The Terminator,* thereby not only bringing to the surface the gender oppositions that remained latent in the earlier film but, at the same time, confusing these oppositions. Of course, until the end of the first film, Sarah is accompanied by the human male, Kyle (Michael Biehn), who has also travelled back from the future in an attempt to protect her. However, if the Terminator is meant to represent Kyle's fantasy double, then Kyle fails in attaining his proper masculine status (he is killed in his attempts) and is succeeded in his masculine role by Sarah (a scenario that is partially born out in the film's first sequel). This effectively means that both Sarah and the figure of the Terminator are seen to transgress traditional, gendered boundaries.

In the *Robocop* films, the association of the hyper-masculine cyborg with industrial-age machinery, of the kind witnessed in *The Terminator,* is unmistakable. Not only is the film set in Detroit (the home of Fordism), but the central hero has an obviously robotic appearance (what is left of his organic body is encased in metal armour). Like the Terminator, this mechanised masculinity is acted out in the delivery of his dialogue and the way he walks. For example, Robocop's speech and movements are predominantly separated, as he rarely moves and talks at the same time. Also, like the Terminator, Robocop's minimal dialogue is performed largely in monotone and he reveals a rather literal visualisation of a Cartesian-like head/body divide:[25] when he turns corners, his head or his body turn first, like an articulated truck. These movements are underlined by 'hydraulic' sound effects which further emphasise the character's alignment with construction and transport machinery, rather than the latest in communications technology. As Paul Verhoeven makes clear in the interview following this chapter, there was certainly a relationship between *The Terminator* and *Robocop* on a number of levels. In terms of the figuring of the central cyborg, it seems that outwardly at least, Robocop reveals the robotic side of his 'nature' for all to see. As compared to the Terminator, it is this outward display of armoured strength that is meant to make Robocop the reassuring representative and upholder of a masculine law. He is reassuring because he symbolises a certain masculine strength and masculine law, and also because, unlike the Terminator, in his outwardly robotic construction he can be seen as separate from the 'natural' masculine bodies that he represents. His presence is justified in the narrative because he ostensibly offers strong protection for the weak and innocent in the city's apparent battle with its criminal elements. However, it also becomes clear that Robocop is imperative as he disallows direct confrontation between the lawmakers and the citizens of Detroit.

The trouble begins when Robocop's 'inner humanity' begins to surface. This is initiated by the return of his human memories and dreams of the wife and child that he has left behind. His more human side is revealed in flashbacks of the 'soft' and caring emotions he once exhibited within this domestic environment; an environment that he has become disassociated from upon taking up his position as supercop. Unlike *The Terminator* the narrative therefore allows for comparison between the fully human Murphy and his metamorphosis into Robocop. Apart from the fact that the viewer is privy to the process undertaken in his transformation, direct links are made between these two seemingly separated characters. In particular, the repeated 'gun twirling' (gesturing back to the cowboy hero of the western film) is performed by Murphy both before and after he has been literally cyborgised. In terms of the plot, the 'gun twirling' performance outwardly indicates that the spirit of the human Murphy is still present under the armour plating. However, on another level, this device also indicates that Murphy's human masculinity was based upon a fantasy; a characterisation of a masculinity constructed according to the codes and conventions of the western film. This irony is underlined, of course, when the human Murphy is given the armoured body to back up his macho posturing, at which point his 'natural' humanity, along with his 'natural' masculine identity, are shown to be questionable. The battle between human and robot is therefore enacted within this single, cyborg body: a body that was socially constructed before it became literally constructed.

As human law officer, Murphy is but a cog in the wheel of the Detroit city law machine and the forceful masculinity that he embodies as Robocop does not afford him any more power to direct his own life; as Robocop he is even more controlled by the large conglomerate (OCP) that made him. It is evidently the search for a kind of self-directed control that fuels Murphy's masculine desires, and once he becomes Robocop this search takes on a renewed urgency. Interestingly, and ironically, it is when he learns to use the information technologies available to him that his battle for independence really begins to take a turn. The inference being that rather than the industrial technologies that provided him with his powerful armoured physique, it is engagement with these connective, cybernetic technologies that enable him to find himself. By the end of the film, having dispatched the villains of his peace, Robocop announces himself as Murphy: he has won back, if not his emotionalism, his identity. While it is possible to see this somewhat triumphant ending as an endorsement of the powerful masculinity that Robocop appears to represent, this is consistently undercut throughout the film: he has lost more than he has gained. Besides the links that are made between Murphy's masculinity and the constructed, fantasy images that he is subjected to in the OCP controlled Detroit, Verhoeven consistently calls attention to the pervasive television propaganda that is shown to be so much a part of the reality of life in this futuristic city. He achieves this in a 'direct address' device that has become a kind of directorial signature in his films (he later used this device in both *Total Recall* [1990] and *Starship Troopers* [1997]). At the opening of the film and interspersed throughout, there are moments when the narrative is interrupted by mock adverts and highly sensational news reports that are not only addressed to the inhabitants of the city, but also directly addressed to the viewer of the film. This device not only operates to shock the viewer into recognising the invasive and ideological aspects of screen culture in the diegetic world of the film, but also invites the audience to critically reflect on their own perception of reality and the screen culture of a present-day America. According to the narrative logic of the film, Murphy's desires are very much shaped by this screen culture and the world as created by OCP. So, there is a manifest invitation in this film to question not only the nature of Robocop/Murphy's victory over OCP, but the very nature of reality as a citizen of America in the 1980s.

In conclusion, I believe it is wrong to see either *The Terminator* or *Robocop* as unproblematically upholding the dominant ideology of the time. Having said that, it is notable that sequels to each of these films displayed certain recuperative strategies; in particular, their repeated attempts to re-establish binary oppositions in setting one *kind* of cyborg off against another. For example, in the succession of sequels that followed Verhoeven's *Robocop* the threat to the city does not come from the human criminal element but from other cyborgs.

Similarities can therefore be drawn between these films and *Terminator 2*, in that 'good' cyborg is pitched against 'bad' cyborg. In *Robocop 2* (dir. Irvin Kershner, 1990), Robocop is pitted against a cyborg that looks remarkably like the malfunctioning robot, Ed, of the first film. This cyborg's large and unwieldy, mechanical frame does not resemble a human body, but, unlike the fully mechanised Ed, is controlled by the implanted brain of a major criminal called Cain (Tom Noonan). The visual pairing implies that Robocop is not only more human but represents the lawful and acceptable form of a masculinity that is melded with machine. Evidently, the pairing also works to uphold some kind of dichotomy even if both sides are marked as fused beings. In fact, Cain is marked as the feminised opposite in this coupling because he has been created by a corrupt businesswoman.

By the time we reach *Robocop 3* (dir. Fred Dekker, 1993) the criminal force that opposes our hero comes from an oriental cyborg, figured as a ninja/samurai warrior. The warrior is almost impossible to eradicate: as one warrior is dispatched it is replaced by a cloned copy. So, the threat to law and order and to Robocop himself takes on an outwardly more human form here, but our American hero remains the same (even though Robert Burke replaced Peter Weller under the armour plating). Seen as a series, Murphy retains his outer body armour throughout and is repeatedly shown to lose and regain his human memories and his individual identity. Robocop remains constant while the world about him changes. Likewise, even though in *Terminator 2: Judgment Day*, there is a shift to a supposedly 'softer' characterisation, the body of the Terminator does not change and his function as super-violent, macho-machine remains. The consistency of these bodily figurations throughout the sequels suggests that this mechanical and hyper-masculine form is a requirement in these societies, as though the muscled cyborg warrior is somehow reassuring in a changing America. This is made quite clear when in *Robocop 2* a female scientist insists that Robocop be programmed in a more 'socially acceptable' way. He is then observed to be acting politely in his interactions with criminals and to avoid killing at all costs. Robocop's new-found sociability is played out to comedic effect and presented as being completely ineffectual in such a violent world.

Eventually, the iconographic terrain that marked the emergence of the mainstream cyborg of the 1980s shifted as the science fiction/action film gave way to what have been described as the 'cyber thrillers'.[26] The cyber-thrillers seemed less concerned with the body and more concerned with the psychical transformations of the human in their cyborgian interfacing with computer and virtual reality technologies. *The Lawnmower Man* (dir. Brett Leonard, 1992) can be taken as a relatively early example of this new breed of cyborg film, and in many ways it marks a kind of crossover to later cyber-thrillers. Having said that, although this film was concerned with computer enhancement of the mind the muscular male body was still very important in the figuring of the central character, Jobe (Jeff Fahey). With the aid of computer and virtual reality technologies, Jobe is shown to evolve into a threatening figure with dreams of godlike omnipotence. At the close of the film, he literally transfers himself into cyberspace. Although there is talk that he wishes to download his consciousness into the Net, this transference is actually shown to occur when his whole body is 'sucked up' into cyberspace – leaving his cyber-suit strung up, empty and flat on the gyroscopic apparatus he uses to simulate his bodies movements within the virtual reality environment. In the later cyber-thrillers, the shift away from the earlier visions of the hard-bodied, muscular cyborg was completed in the image of the slimmed-down, 'jacked-in', cyber-saviour, in films like *Johnny Mnemonic* (dir. Robert Longo, 1995) and *The Matrix* (dir. Larry and Andy Wachowski, 1999), both of which I will come to discuss in more detail in a later chapter.

SCIENCE FICTION AND THE GLOBAL FILM MARKET

In this chapter I have concentrated on images of masculinity in mainstream Hollywood films because these were so prevalent in science fiction cinema in the 1980s. Where examples of the science fiction genre could be found in European cinema in the 1960s and 1970s, this was largely not the case in the 1980s.[27] Certainly, the reach of the American blockbuster and the correspondingly high-budget aesthetic that became almost indelibly associated with science fiction cinema at this time might have made it difficult for less well-funded national cinemas to engage with the genre. For example, under the conservative Thatcherite government, British cinema suffered the loss of state subsidies and the industry went through a period of reformation. The removal of subsidies was partly offset with the involvement of Channel 4 television in filmmaking projects, leading to the production of many innovative films that engaged critically with social and cultural issues of the period (e.g. *My Beautiful Laundrette* [dir. Stephen Frears, 1985]). While the Channel 4 films reached an international audience (often via the art-house circuit), the production team of Merchant and Ivory were busy turning out a series of larger-budget, British 'heritage' and 'empire' films, specifically intended for an international audience. As John Hill notes, these films often had their first showing in the US and earned more abroad than at home. He goes on to suggest:

> Such films may be seen to be employing a familiar strategy available to national cinemas. Rather than attempting to compete with Hollywood directly by imitating its norms, this involves the adoption of aesthetic strategies and cultural referents which distinguish it from Hollywood and so foreground its 'national' credentials.[28]

So, if science fiction became associated with a particularly American sensibility at this time, then popular heritage and empire films projected a very different image of Britain in the historical images to be found in the likes of *A Room with a View* (dir. James Ivory, 1985) and *Heat and Dust* (dir. James Ivory, 1983). France, on the other hand, gave birth to a 'new new wave' in cinema in the 1980s, with films like *Diva* (dir. Jean-Jacques Beineix, 1980) and *Subway* (dir. Luc Besson, 1985); both of which came to be seen as epitomising a specifically postmodern aesthetic in film. Also known as the 'cinéma du look', this aesthetic was marked by its focus upon 'trendy' (or trend-setting) detail, lack of character development, pastiche of past cinematic stylisations and repeated use of quotation (in *Subway* there is a quotation from *Star Wars* when one character picks up a piece of fluorescent tube, which he wields like a light sabre). While it is possible to designate some of these films under a broad heading of fantasy and while they exhibited certain formal characteristics common to the American blockbusters, they were not recognisable as science fiction; their narratives were most often based upon the thriller genre and science fictional elements were kept to a minimum. It was not until the 1990s that France began to produce distinctly generic science fiction films that competed with the American product (e.g. *Delicatessen* [dir. Marc Caro and Jean-Pierre Jeunet, 1991], *The Fifth Element* [dir. Luc Besson, 1997]).

If European cinema had deserted the genre in the 1980s, the same could not be said of Australia or Japan. Taking Japanese cinema as my first example, by the 1980s, Japanese animation (commonly known as anime) was thriving in the home market, and science fiction became a dominant genre within this medium. In the mid-1980s Japanese anime returned in full force to the big screen (having been more prominent, since the 1960s, as a form embraced by television) with productions including the now famous cyberpunk thriller *Akira* (Katsuhiro Ôtomo, 1988) and the later adaptation of the manga (graphic novel), science fiction, *Ghost in the Shell* (dir. Mamoru Oshii, 1995). Also, in the mid-1980s, anime began to take advantage of the home video market and produced OAVs (Original Anime Videos) in large quantities. Once again, one of the most popular genres was science fiction, although the OAVs were known for their more 'adult' content (in terms of the violence and sexual activity depicted). So, science fiction was all the rage in Japan in the 1980s and many of the anime films revealed very similar concerns to the cyborg films. Indeed the flashback/flashforward dream sequence from *The Terminator* (discussed on p. 124) strongly resembles the futuristic and apocalyptic world of the cyberpunk, anime/manga hero. It was not only the backdrops that bore a resemblance to the cyborg films, the mecha sub-genre (so called because the narratives and visuals revolve around the featuring of humanoid robots or cyborgs) revealed an overwhelming concern with masculinity and the masculine body and regularly featured male cyborgs whose outer bodies were reinforced with armour plating. The battle of the sexes was another major theme in many adult mecha. Taking *Guyver: Out of Control* (dir. Hiroshi Watanabe, 1986) as a prime example, the central male character accidentally becomes engulfed in an armoured Guyver suit and is pursued by another cyborg-Guyver, the female head of security of the powerful Chronos corporation.

Japanese science fiction animations had been shown on American television, as part of children's programming, since the 1960s,[29] and the more adult amine had a following in other parts of Asia, America and Europe in the 1980s. However, its influence upon American science fiction was not generally acknowledged until the 1990s, when Japanese anime came to play a noticeably more global role in science fiction cinema. As Susan J. Napier describes it, Japanese anime has become 'a genuinely global phenomenon' and she goes on to state that it now 'stands out as a site of implicit cultural resistance' within a global marketplace often dominated by America.[30] Although Napier briefly acknowledges the flow of influences between Japanese and American animation and some similarities between science fiction anime and certain American films, in her estimation it is the 'otherness' of anime that has caused its more recent international appeal and success.

With the influx of the American film product onto the global marketplace in the 1980s, it seems that some national cinemas reacted by creating distinctly national films. However, this was not entirely the case with Australian cinema, which actively engaged, in one way or another, with the kinds of figurations emerging from American cinema. The Australian film industry had begun to thrive in the 1970s, after the setting up of the Australian Film Development Corporation (later to become the Australian Film Commission) and the introduction of government tax concessions in the early 1980s. But, by the mid-1980s the industry was in trouble and, for a variety of reasons, producers had to look to international distributors, who were not only able to guarantee large-scale distribution, but could pay up-front advances for a film. With an increasing dependence upon the international market, there was an inherent tension between objectives that began in the 1970s (to develop a specifically Australian national cinema) and the need to meet the demands of the distributors. In order to try to satisfy both of these demands, filmmakers started to explore a diversity of genres – borrowing from those already familiar Hollywood genres, but also altering these in order to preserve an Australian flavour. The low-budget *Mad Max* (dir. George Miller, 1979) had, in some ways, pre-empted the changes that came in the Australian industry in the 1980s. Here was a film that drew upon a variety of American genres: science fiction, action, the western, the 'road movie', and the American 'biker movie' (i.e. *The Wild One* [dir. László Benedek, 1953] and *Easy Rider* [dir. Dennis Hopper, 1969]). In this sense, it was perfectly placed to become a vehicle for a global market-place and the first film's international success was later followed by two higher-budget sequels, in 1981 and 1985.

Jonathan Rayner places *Mad Max* under the heading of 'Australian Gothic', which he describes as a 'mode' of filmmaking that has become common in Australia. According to Rayner, one of the features of the Australian gothic is the way in which it freely borrows from popular genres and then revises and parodies their conventions. Rayner goes on to look at the main 'thematic concerns' of the Australian Gothic and describes the way in which it questions established authority, social reality and is concerned with a search for identity. He says: 'These themes are interlinked, and reflect a doubt or dubiety in the assertions of national character and confidence in national institutions which characterised earlier examples of Australian films.'[31]

Mad Max engages with a specifically Australian masculinity in its references to earlier screen stereotypes (e.g. the young delinquents in the film can be traced back to the so-called, 'larrikin' figure of Australian literature and film). However, in his capacity as the 'lone avenger', Max also resembles the previously mentioned American hero/anti-hero figures of 1970s. Max's 'heroism' seems to be a point of debate in the first film, which is underlined by the repeated speeches that the police chief makes concerning the need for an Australian hero and Max's initial reluctance to take up this role. Also, whereas in classic American films a hero's actions have to be justified in some way, Max's actions as part of the policing force are undermined with each new car chase. While the police are still in operation, many of the cars and bike chases take place away from populated areas and even in those scenes when the public are threatened, their lethal pursuits only serve to cause more accidents involving law-abiding road users and pedestrians. These are personal feuds rather than heroic actions. Although Max's actions are justified as heroic or defending in the later sequels, the series continues to mark itself apart from American science fiction of the 1980s. For example, whereas the American cyborg films were largely set against an urban backdrop, the *Mad Max* films retain the 'apocalyptic' desert setting of the first film. This setting therefore doubles as a necessarily indistinct backdrop for home audiences, as well as feeding into a particular view of Australian life in the outback (an alien environment) for an international audience. Also, taking the trilogy as a whole, we see Max move from the loss of his family, to a nomad/settler conflict, to the beginnings of a new society based upon convict labour: the series is obviously looking to Australia's past history, as much as it is offering a kind of alternative form of science fiction hero.

In the 1980s there was much talk of a growing American cultural imperialism and the high-budget aesthetic of American blockbusters was often taken as a sort of nationalistic display of wealth and power. So, for some critics, the blockbusters came to signify a nationalistic attempt to dominate a growing cultural global marketplace. There were varied reactions to the shift toward global capitalism and the onset of cybernetic communication technologies that facilitated the growth of international corporations. Often, as a reaction to the increasing expansion of the global economy and the concomitant expansion of the mass cultural industries, what were understood as specifically national cultures took on a new importance in the 1980s. The science fiction genre allowed for the exhibition of the latest in technology and given that the diegetic technologies on display (as opposed to the cinematic, special effects technologies) in American science fiction blockbusters were often militaristic, it is, in some ways, easy to see how the science fiction/action films might have been understood as the cultural equivalent to an American invasion. However, as John Tomlinson points out: 'The problem with the cultural imperialism argument is that . . . it makes a leap of inference from the simple presence of cultural goods to the attribution of deeper cultural or ideological effects.'[32]

The cultural imperialism argument, as applied to films, therefore, does not account for the way in which cultural commodities are received and understood within different geographical and cultural settings. It assumes a passive audience that is somehow manipulated, once exposed to the alien ideologies of the film text. There are certainly pleasures to be gained from seeing a big-budget blockbuster, but their very commercial success does not necessarily mean an unproblematic transference of what are assumed to be their ideological messages. For example, I have already discussed why I believe figures like the Terminator and Robocop cannot be taken as some kind of direct expression of dominant American ideology, as the unproblematic embodiment of Reaganite power politics. In my view, the tensions and contradictions that are all too apparent in these cyborg bodies belies what some might take to be their inherent ideological message. Equally, although these science fictional figures may well have come to stand for American culture, then in their seemingly conflicted representation of masculine prowess it might be more accurate to put the overseas success of these films down to the fact that these figurations were actually playing out the contradictions and obscenities in American culture. In fact, the following interview with Paul Verhoeven makes clear the ways in which, as a European director, his own response to an alien, American culture came to be 'written' into the film.

INTERVIEW: DIRECTOR PAUL VERHOEVEN

C: Could you tell me about the distinctive style adopted in your science fiction films and the influences that you've drawn upon in films like *Total Recall* and *Robocop*. . .

V: Influences are certainly there. Although *Robocop* was written deliberately by the writer in a comic-book style – that was clear from the beginning. For *Robocop* I studied many comic books and also some English ones, like *Judge Dredd*. I think that for me it was kind of an easy way to do my first American movie. I knew enough about comic books from my youth and was highly influenced by comic books as a child – European comic books like *Tintin*. But I also read a lot of stuff like *Flash Gordon* and things like that, when I was eight, nine, ten, twelve years old, and other books that are only in Holland were very influential for me – comic books that were never published anywhere else in Europe – so they wouldn't mean much to you. When I was working in television, on a series called *Floris*, I did some, let's say . . . hyperbolic work, exaggerated work, which had a certain style. I'd describe it as grotesque or burlesque or whatever. I abandoned this style when I started doing my own movies – all the movies I did in Holland were pretty realistic. Although Americans and Europeans are supposed to be similar that certainly was not the case in my experience. So, when I came into this country and started to work here, I felt insecure about culture, language and many other things, and that's why, for some considerable time I would say, I felt much more secure when I could work in a genre that was not so realistic and was not so culturally defined. Where my lack of knowledge about cultural mores, and other things, would not be perceptible to an audience, because the style was anyhow 'futuristic', extremely 'over-the-top', 'stylised', which science fiction is of course to a large degree. I think the science fiction and the comic-book background rescued me from the chaotic world that I had entered – from an artistic point of view. So, it was a natural move for me to embark on science fiction, slash, comic-book adventures like *Robocop* and even *Total Recall*. Although *Total Recall* is based on a Philip K. Dick story, which is really not a comic book, we made it more comic-book than the original story. Mostly, we did this, of course, because of the presence of Arnold Schwarzenegger. I mean, if you see the difference between three films based upon Philip K. Dick's – if you look at *Minority Report, Blade Runner* or *Total Recall* – then you see *my* approach to Philip K. Dick . . . partly forced by having a superhero, bodybuilding-/-total film star in the movie, which led me to apply a more comic-book style to Dick than any body else.

C: I understand how science fiction might give you more leeway in a culture that you're unfamiliar with – that's interesting – but I wondered whether you could comment on the relationship that your science fiction films *might* have with reality – or maybe realism?

V: Initially, with *Robocop,* when I got the script, coming from a European background and from the kind of movies I had been making, I wanted to make the main character, called Murphy – played by Peter Weller – have an extra-marital affair with the Nancy Allen character. This was not in the script of course – the script was much more in comic-book style. The hero of the movie, following American puritan standards, would not have promiscuous relations with another woman while he was married. Because of the way I had been making my movies in Holland – most of them have promiscuous relationships and affairs, extra-marital stuff and whatever – I wanted these kinds of changes that I immediately proposed to the writers – I thought that this was more real to life. And it is of course, because everyone has extra-marital affairs, such as in the United States, on the highest levels, as we found out not so long ago. It took me time to realise that the comic-book style did not allow such digression, such an amoral attitude. So I backed off from that and then I re-read it and, probably in a moment of clarity, I realised that it was absolutely wrong and that I was mixing genres, and that basically I should stick to the puritan code that is mostly to be found in science fiction. For example, in general terms, when I was doing European movies, I made them realistic sometimes by necessity – we didn't have the money, especially in the case of *Robocop*, to create a new extravagant, futuristic world, like they did for example in *Minority Report*. I mean, any realism that is involved in *Robocop* was really, in the first instance, based on our budget – which is not a bad thing. So the budget allowed for money spent on the costume of Robocop and on Ed 209, but there was no money to do fancy buildings, or fancy production design a la *Blade Runner* or *Minority Report*. We were forced to shoot *Robocop* as if it was 'now'. Although the aspects of building a robot and building 'Ed 209' are clearly futuristic and were supposed to be . . . if you were going to be consistent, you would create a society, with buildings and all that stuff, more in keeping with the futuristic aspects of Robocop himself and with Ed 209. But we didn't have the money for that and, I think, ultimately, it turned out great to do it this way. I cannot imagine *Robocop*, in retrospect, done a different way. Like my producer told me, to do this we would have to create special effects – there were no digital effects at this time – matt paintings and all that stuff. He said, I can tell you this, you can have a good costume for Robocop or you can have futuristic buildings, but you cannot have them both. Even the cars that we wanted to make futuristic, when they were delivered to us, looked so stupid that I had to throw them away. Because the new Ford Torres had just come out, which looked a little bit futuristic, we decided to make a deal with Ford and to use normal cars. So, a lot of these artistic decisions were often based on lack of money. These constraints, ultimately, don't hurt. In this case, I would say, they were an asset. If you look at everything else, it's pretty much 1986 isn't it? I think it's as if there was a futuristic light thrown on the movie, but it only hit two places, you know (laughs). If you look, for example, at *Total Recall*, because there was more money, there was more of an attempt made to create a society – in buildings and other ways – that is where we tried more to extrapolate and to create an environment that was futuristic and that was, shall we say, not as predictable. All the little tricks and things . . . the walls that turn out to be screens, the finger nails that change colour etc. . . . they were all devices that were used, that were brought in, to make this idiotic proposal that you can buy a dream, seem possible. It's quite a strange proposal to an audience, isn't it, that you can buy a dream and have a holiday on Mars and then you think it's real, which was stressed I felt. We had to prepare the audience from the beginning so that they would accept that world and make a major leap of faith. So, what I did, when I was looking at the planet Mars, I went to NASA. I usually try to do these things as much as I can, but it depends how much money they give you. I asked the people at NASA, what exactly would be the kind of buildings that you would build on Mars. We got all the drawings from NASA and we applied that to the prediction side. Basically the vistas that you see, through the windows, these were based on designs that we got from NASA. But, of course, these designs were futuristic too – that's what NASA perhaps thought . . . we're still not there, we certainly haven't been building much there [*laughs*]. I think it's interesting to try to extrapolate, but in my opinion the human mind is too weak. Even with the help of computers, the possibilities to look into the future and to predict anything – apart from the war in Iraq – are extremely limited. I think it is hard to invent anything new – apart from what is nearly on the horizon. And to look beyond your horizon, I think, is often more of a retrograde movement – it's more to do with being influenced by something from the 1920s or the 1930s or the 1700s. Look at the light sabres in *Star Wars*, you know, they are completely stupid, but they work – it's a medieval sword, with a little light beam. You ask yourself why these people don't shoot each other – why they have all this complicated stuff with the light sabres. I mean, it's very difficult for the human mind . . . you can make small steps and a lot of scientists do of course . . . but for an artist to be really able to predict into the future, that's only given to a few – like Jules Verne, for example – who had pretty good intuition about the things that were already on the horizon – or Leonardo da Vinci. But these are people who have a knack for that in general. Every writer, producer, designer in Hollywood, would not be working on that level of genius. If you look at all the science fiction in Hollywood, I don't think you can see anything that's ground-breaking or that opens our eyes to something that we can't think of.

C: Given the differences that you've outlined between *Robocop* and *Total Recall,* how would you say the characters in each film fit into these worlds?

V: I would say that's already in the script. I had the feeling that in the script of *Robocop* there was a soul – whereas, in the script of *Total Recall,* there was a philosophy, but not too much a soul. I mean, the soul of Robocop is displayed in the movie at various moments. When he goes to his old house and when he takes his mask and his helmet off and he tries to remember his wife and they sit there together – the Nancy Allen character and him – there is a touching, emotional residue, there is something of a 'lost paradise' situation about the world that he had before – I mean his wife and his child and his house or what-ever – that is vaguely there, but it's not there any more. It's like everything about the past, isn't it. We look at the past and the past is there, it has a certain par-adise quality, but we can't reach it any more. And I think that 'lost paradise' was part of the attraction of the script. I think I chose or I dared to do the script because I understood the scene where Robocop comes to his house and redis-covers his old house and dwells in these empty spaces while memories of the past are suddenly jumping in. It's like the human mind – sometimes feeling that there have been other worlds. Some people would call this reincarnation, other people would say this or that, but sometimes you feel that there are other worlds inside you that you can't reach. I think that that kind of feeling is basi-cally a feeling of nostalgia, of loss, of the soul that is locked into a machine and tries desperately to come out. All these elements were inherent in the dramatic material of the movie. If you compare that to *Total Recall*, there was not so much a personal drama there – and anyway, bringing in an actor like Arnold, you would, let's say, go for a simplified version of human emotions – because that's the style, that is how he works as a superhero, isn't it? That's what his character is in *Terminator* and also in *Total Recall*, to a certain degree. But I think the essence of *Total Recall* was really a philosophy – the question of, what is the truth? Or, are there several realities that are parallel? It's really a philo-sophical movie – although done in an ironic and light style. I mean, it's not *The Matrix*, which takes things much more seriously and basically seems to refer to Hegel or Nietzsche. *Total Recall* is more to do with whether we are living in a dream. Is the dream life? Is my life real or is the dream real? I think the impor-tant thing with that movie, and what was challenging to me, is to have two par-allel tracks, in the movie, continuously available. So I think the power of the movie is not so much the personal emotion, but the confusion of the audience, not being able to separate, or to make a choice between two realities. So for me it was like, OK, this is, in retrospect, what I would call a postmodern film . . . you know what I mean? Because it states that we cannot know things or it states that nothing is absolutely true.

C: Do you think that your films are ambivalent?

V: I used a lot of ambivalence when I came to the United States. If you look at the European movies, the Dutch movies, that's never a theme. I think that the ambivalence that crept into my American movies and is even dominant in many of them – especially in *Total Recall* or even *Starship Troopers* – is about whether these people are idiots to do this, or whether are they heroes who will give their lives for the country? You have no idea because the elements of propaganda that are dispersed throughout the movie are so idiotic, or hyperbolic, I would say, that you must assume that these people are idiots, you know. But, the ambivalence there is about, let's say, what these people *think* that they're doing.

Johnny is resistant in *Starship Troopers* to joining the army, because he doesn't necessarily want to be a citizen, he's happy being a civilian. But, because all his friends go into the army to become first-class citizens – like we have examples of this now in the United States, and many other countries also – I think that Johnny ultimately gets convinced that this way of life is *the* way of life. Yet, at the same time, the way the surroundings are presented – I mean the media breaks – I'm pointing out that these people are victimised by propaganda. That kind of ambivalence is very strong in some of the movies, which might have to do with my ambivalence in being a person caught in between the United States and Europe.

C: As I'm sure you know, a lot has been said about the violence in your films and I wondered if you could expand a little on how you see violence operating or functioning in your films.

V: The violence is not very different from what you see on CNN. The world is filled with violence. The United States is politically promoting violence left, right and centre. After going for Iraq, we're now preparing for Iran, aren't we? I would say, what idiot doesn't want to use violence in his movies? That's the person that doesn't want to look around any more. That's the person that doesn't want to look at our world as it is. That's the person who is not looking at the violence that is visible in the universe.

C: So there is a relationship with reality, in a sense?

V: Well, yes. This universe is a very violent one, isn't it? It's not only life on earth, but life in all of the universe. To close your eyes to violence would be weird, in my opinion. That would be like looking continuously at your desk, where nothing happens, instead of looking over your desk and down on the street, where cars are crashing and people are dying all the time. So, I think it's a natural thing not only to be fascinated by violence – which I certainly wouldn't deny – but the fascination comes from my complete unwillingness to understand the necessity of a creation that is filled with violence. I think it's a protest, in general – the extreme measures that I take to portray violence in the most disgusting and horrifying way, which I normally do, is basically, an accusation, for me, against this universe.

C: Would you say that your science fiction films were in any way subversive?

V: I hope so – I certainly hope that *Starship Troopers* was subversive – it was certainly meant that way. In terms of *Robocop*, perhaps in a different way, because it was on an urban scale. That had more to do with the politics of the city – although there are lines of dialogue there. For instance, when, somewhere near the end of the movie, one character asks Jones if the corporation has access to the military – then Jones, the CO of the corporation, says that there's no fucking difference – the military and the corporation are the same. So, there are these kinds of statements in *Robocop* where, of course, the big corporation, which is the centre of the movie, is making deals with the other side to get things done. But really the most subversive film, for me, is *Starship Troopers* – especially because I used all sorts of Nazi imagery to express my conviction that the people who were basically our heroes were, at the same time, fascists. That was an ultimate accusation, I thought, towards a ripening fascism in the United States – which has been proven true hasn't it?

C: I know we've talked through this a bit, but you obviously set a lot of your science fiction films against a kind of televisual background culture, a propaganda culture, that's very pervasive and that creates quite a busy setting to the central dramas. I just wondered whether you could perhaps explain your reasoning a little bit more, specifically on the thinking behind this kind of mise-en-scène.

V: Well, this only happens in my American movies, not in the European ones. It was built into the script of *Robocop*, so I'm absolutely not the inventor of that, but I picked up on that and I emphasised it – having been confronted with American television, coming from a European background. When I came to the United States that year, the Challenger thing happened and I was so astonished about having reports of the most horrible things being interrupted by commercials and other things – with people laughing one minute and then, next thing, there were the anchor people saying 'Oh this is so horrible, it's a tragedy' and so on . . . you know. There was this open kind of atmosphere on television, where things are juxtaposed that have nothing to do with each other and convey completely different emotions and statements about life. I think I was totally amazed by that and that's why I started to use these commercials and these statements in the movie. When we did *Starship Troopers* it was more sophisticated because I then felt that I had seen so much of the way that the media and corporations are almost completely identical nowadays – I mean there's nearly no difference any more between the government point of view or the media point of view. Once in a while you hear a critical voice, but the rest of the time the media just tells you what the government wants them to tell you. So I think I started to feel that I had an insight, or I believed I had an insight, into the way the propaganda machine of the government was infiltrating our lives all the time – was continuously driving us to look at the world according to the prominent government point of view. So I think that was for me the reason to introduce, again, media breaks into *Starship Troopers*. It felt like the story really needed a commentary, another view that could not be expressed through the narrative, which had to be separated from the narrative, nearly counterpointing the narrative. This is so that you would not take the narrative, let's say, in the more old-fashioned way, as the story that we wanted to tell. In

Starship Troopers it's the story we want to tell, quote, unquote. And the quotes are visible through the interjections of the media breaks.

C: So would you say you were trying to 'wake up' your audience by doing that?

V: Sure, yeah, or seduce them to follow me and then hit them on the head – that was the essence – to follow me, to believe in these heroes and then to find out that, with them, you have been a fascist too.

C: So you put their position in question? So you make them self-aware?

V: Well I don't know if I succeeded – that's another question. I mean the commercial strength of the movie, unfortunately, was not similar to *Star Wars*, you know. It took a couple of years, even in Europe, for people to acknowledge this. For instance, when I came with *Starship Troopers* to Europe, to promote the movie, in general, in all the countries – with the exception of England, in fact – in all the European countries – especially the ones that had been fascist or Nazi, notably Germany, Italy and France – there was an enormous resistance and anger about this movie – they told me that I had made a fascist movie. I thought that I had made a movie about the United States, revealing fascist tendencies that were perceptible, in my opinion, in society – indeed, made clearer by this government of course.

C: You've talked a little bit about working with Arnold Schwarzenegger . . . but comparing *Robocop* to *The Terminator,* I wondered if Robocop's outer armouring was a kind of visual comment upon the muscled body of the Terminator?

V: That might be true, you know. I mean, that subject is not something I created because I got the script as it was, but I can tell you that I studied *The Terminator* many, many times before I shot *Robocop*. I was very much aware that *The Terminator* was a movie that had set a new standard and had created new openings into a certain way of thinking or of visualising and I felt that *Robocop* should, at least, be aware of that kind of way of thinking or of visualising. I think there are a lot of similarities between *Robocop* and *Terminator* – in fact, they were done by the same company, now bankrupt, that's Orion, and they were done in two consecutive years.

C: It's like there's a kind of dialogue going on in between these two films.

V: Well, I think there was. We, as the creators of *Robocop*, were very much aware of what James Cameron had done with *The Terminator*. In fact, at the very beginning, when we started the movie, there was a request from Orion that we might use Arnold Schwarzenegger as the hero. That was rejected for artistic reasons. We felt that Arnold was so big that this would be completely over the top, because the costume would have made him even bigger. We felt we needed a much more normal relationship between Robocop and the Nancy Allen character, or between him and anybody else, and we felt that if we took Arnold and built this costume over him that he would be completely giant, and that this would not function on the level of compassion or emotion that we felt should be in the movie. We decided that we needed a much more slender, slimmer person to do *Robocop*, so that with the costume around him he would not be too gigantic. So, the movies are different, but we were clearly influenced by *Terminator*.

C: How have you felt about the two sequels for *Robocop*?

V: I didn't like them as much as my own movie. In fact, I felt that they had not really perceived what we had done. I had the feeling that they had not really understood what exactly the premises were, the parameters within which we worked, and what our goals were, and why we did these media breaks. They seemed to be copied more for the reason that they had to be similar, without really knowing *why* they copied it. So I felt that they were just sequels, without adding anything and, in fact, what was there was lost – emotionally – I would say. The emotion was kind of gone and I think it's still possible to do a good sequel to *Robocop* but I don't think numbers two or three were. They milked it. This is what they call it here. It's a kind of depressing term used by lots of executives, who tell you, this scene is good, can you milk it a bit more? Make it longer or have the audience cry longer or whatever. They milk it like a cow . . . they pull these things . . . nipples . . . what do you call them . . . to get milk out?

C: The udders. They pull the emotional udders of the audience [*laughs*].

V: In general, all these sequels are that way – nearly all, with the exception perhaps of a couple of them. Prominently, of course, *Star Wars* – number two was certainly as interesting as number one. In general they always try to use the same copy twice – make it twice, or ten times, as long as the audience doesn't get disgusted – feed them, feed them with the same stuff.

C: It'll be interesting to see what happens with the new *Terminator* film.

V: I am very interested too, because it's a different director.

C: Yes, and apparently a female Terminator.

V: Yes, but that's a normal thing – I mean *Frankenstein* followed by *The Bride of Frankenstein* – that's kind of a pattern that has been used a lot in sequels.

Notes

1. Schatz 'The New Hollywood', in Collins *et al.* (eds) 1993, pp. 18–19.
2. Ibid., p. 23.
3. The sudden and elliptical editing style that is foregrounded in the *Star Wars* films can also be taken to be a reference to comic-book styles.

4. For example, the sheer epic scale found in *2001* is certainly present in *Star Wars* and the 'light shows' common to the genre in the 1960s and 1970s are to be seen in the closing scenes of *Close Encounters*. In fact, Doug Trumbull, who was so influential in special and visual effects during the 1960s and 1970s was also the visual effects supervisor for *Close Encounters*.
5. 'Child/Alien/Father: Patriarchal Crisis and Generic Exchange', in Penley *et al.* (eds) 1991, p. 17.
6. Wood 1986, p. 162.
7. 'Steven Spielberg and the Politics of Recuperation', in Kolker 1988, p. 238.
8. 'Steven Spielberg and the Politics of Recuperation', in Kolker 1988, p. 255.
9. Ibid., p. 294.
10. 'Entertainment and Utopia', in Nichols (ed.) 1985, p. 229.
11. Ibid., p. 229.
12. 'The Good Father: Reconstructing Fatherhood', in Segal 1990, p. 26.
13. The casting of Michael J. Fox in the Marty role supports my claim. Fox was known at this point for his role in the television sitcom, *Family Ties* (1982–89), in which he played the right-wing son of liberal, hippy parents.
14. Jeffords 1994, p. 25.
15. Ibid., p. 170.
16. For instance, reference can be made to Tasker's chapter 'Body in Crisis or Body Triumphant', in which she outlines the various approaches that have been taken in terms of the spectacle of the male body in association with 'gaze theory' in academic cinema studies. Tasker 1993, pp. 109–31.
17. Here I am drawing upon Neale 1983. In this article he suggests that displays of excessive violence in action films are designed to minimise the erotic connotations of the male body as object of the gaze and therefore as a feminised site of desire.
18. See 'Government of the Body', in Turner 1996, pp. 175–96.
19. Shilling 1993, p. 182.
20. See Wiener Clynes and Kline 1960, pp. 26–7, 74–5; 1948/1965.
21. For an easy-to-understand and accessible account of his work, see 'International Society for the Systems Sciences: Ludwig von Bertalanffy (1901–1972)', http://www.isss.org/lumLVB.htm (27th July 2000).
22. 'The Cybernetic Delirium of Norbert Wiener', in Kroker and Kroker (eds) 1997, p. 118.
23. Terranova, 1996, pp. 69–83, 77.
24. 'The Doubles of Fantasy and the Space of Desire', in Kuhn (ed.) 1990, pp. 152–9.
25. In some respects, this can be seen as a more exaggerated version of some of the Terminator's movements. For example, there are a number of moments when the Terminator simply stands, facing the scene in front of him, and turns his head from side to side to scan the area – as though his head were some kind of turning watch-tower, moving separately from the body beneath.
26. This is a term borrowed from Claudia Springer, 'Psycho-Cybernetics in Film of the 1990s', in Kuhn (ed.) 1999, pp. 203–18.
27. *Brazil* (dir. Terry Gilliam, 1985) being one notable exception – although this was a UK/US co-production.
28. Hill 1999, p. 79.
29. The 'mecha' anime series *Astro Boy* (Tetsuwan Atomu) is an early example, which began airing on American television in 1963.
30. Napier 2001, pp. 8–9.
31. Rayner 2000, p. 25.
32. Tomlinson 1999, pp. 83–4.

5.   GENDER BLENDING AND THE FEMININE SUBJECT IN SCIENCE FICTION FILM

Figure 5.1   Sarah in *Terminator 2: Judgment Day* (1991). Carolco/The Kobal Collection.

As the previous chapter indicates, the 1980s science fiction blockbuster exhibited an overwhelming concern with masculine identity and subjectivity. Both the 'family films' and the 'cyborg films' I have discussed seemed, in one way or another, to question, reinvent and/or preserve outmoded forms of masculine subjectivity in a world that was fast moving toward cybernetic connectivity and globalisation. At its most basic, the Freudian model of gender acquisition was based upon the bourgeois family and required the presence of both the father and mother in order for the boy-child to successfully complete his passage into manhood and take up his role within a wider, patriarchal society. As previously explored, notions of 'proper' family arrangements, and the demarcated roles that the father and mother traditionally played within this scenario, had been challenged by feminism and the counter-cultural movements of the 1960s and 1970s. However, in the late 1970s a 'politics of return'[1] emerged with the rising power exhibited by the New Right movement. Michael Ryan and Douglas Kellner describe the New Right as:

The combined call to return to pre-New Deal, pre-social welfare economics (with its faith in the free market), to the traditional, male-supremacist family (in which children were disciplined and women subservient to men), to fundamentalist religious values (especially as allied with the 'right to life' movement and with an eschatology that equated the Second Coming with the destruction of the Soviet antichrist).[2]

Ronald Reagan took up many of the movement's fundamental and reactionary ideals, and, as noted in the previous chapter, some critics saw his neo-conservative political agenda as unproblematically encoded in the films of the period.

Even though issues surrounding fatherhood and the masculine subject were central concerns in many 1980s blockbusters, anxieties surrounding mother-hood and the feminine subject can also be witnessed in the genre at this time. For example, the narrative of *The Terminator* (dir. James Cameron, 1984) revolved around Sarah's role as 'mother of the future' and, in *Back to the Future* (dir. Robert Zemeckis, 1985), although the figure of the mother is marginalised in the present-day life of Marty, she was definitely at the forefront of his mind once he returned to the past. But the films that stand out in their tackling of the 'mother problem' in science fiction came from the British director, Ridley Scott, with *Alien* (1979) and *Blade Runner* (1982). Mary Ann Doane sees both of these films as specifically dealing with 'the revolution in the development of technologies of reproduction (birth control, artificial insemination, *in vitro* fer-tilisation, surrogate mothering, etc.)' and she goes on to argue that it was the advent of these technologies that threatened 'to put into crisis the very possi-bility of the question of origins, the Oedipal dilemma and the relation between subjectivity and knowledge that it supports'.[3] These films were less about the forces of industrial or technological production than they were about the gen-erative capacities of reproduction. They were also less about the overt and aggressive display of traditional masculine prowess than they were about the role of the feminine in the creation of masculine subjectivity and identity.

In this chapter I will be following science fiction's treatment of the female through film examples that feature a central female character. To do this I will be returning to the late 1970s before moving on to discuss in some detail films made in the 1980s and then the 1990s. This chapter will therefore trace certain shifts in the representation of the female within the genre and will also unveil the recuperative strategies in play and attempts to contain the female protago-nist in science fiction through comparative analysis of certain films.

HORROR AND THE FEMALE SUBJECT OF SCIENCE FICTION AS 'COMPOSITE' BEING

Before moving on to discuss the *Alien* films, I am returning to Donald Cammell's *Demon Seed* (1977), previously mentioned in Chapter 3. In ways that will become clear, Cammell's 1970s film can be seen as formative for many later films that dealt with the female subject of the contemporary science fiction film. The narrative of *Demon Seed* revolved around Susan (Julie Christie), a psychologist, and her scientist husband, Alex (Fritz Weaver). Proteus 4 is an artificial intelligence created by Alex; a creation that exceeds the parameters of Alex's expectations and begins to act independently of his programming. Once it becomes evident that Proteus can no longer be controlled, it is decided to shut down the computer that runs this artificial intelligence, but this is not achieved before Proteus has managed to 'escape' via a forgotten terminal situated in the home of Alex and Susan. Proteus decides that in order to survive it must exist in human form and, to this end, proceeds to imprison and rape Susan.

Proteus is marked as a masculine intelligence, in the sense that the voice with which he speaks is performed by Robert Vaughn (although he is not given a credit in the film). The progeny that is produced from the 'union' of Proteus and Susan is a cyborg – machine intelligence melded with human body. Susan, having been impregnated by the computer, is only allowed to carry the child for a limited period; the later stages of the foetus's development and education are taken over by Proteus. The artificial womb that is created by Proteus to carry the child through to full term (which in this instance enables the production of a child at an age just prior to puberty) also acts as the vessel within which the computer can transfer his consciousness and knowledge into the child.

Earlier in the film the spectator sees Susan viewing some home-movie footage that shows a child playing. Susan is visibly upset by this and we later learn that her natural child died of leukaemia just after the home-movie was made. In order to coerce her into nurturing the progeny produced by the rape, Proteus reproduces a likeness of Susan's deceased daughter. In the closing moments of the film the cyborg child utters the words 'I'm alive', which is deeply ironic considering that this is precisely what she is not. In addition, even though the child outwardly resembles Susan's own dead daughter, when she speaks it is with the voice of the AI who spawned her. The female here becomes a mere vessel for the reproduction of a masculine consciousness: the computer representing mind while both Susan and the cloned copy of her deceased female child come to represent host bodies.

Alex is absent throughout most of the film, certainly from the point at which Proteus' consciousness enters into Susan's life, which suggests that this artificial intelligence is acting out his creator's desires. This becomes manifest when Alex returns to the house and hears of the existence of the child. As the couple enter the basement and see the artificial womb containing the child, Susan is suddenly struck with horror at the idea of its birth. As Susan's hysteria grows in intensity it is matched by Alex's enthusiasm and excitement over what has occurred. Susan tries to 'abort' the child by pulling out the cables and wires that feed the 'womb'. The room is then flooded with steam and fluids that gush from the disconnected tubes; visual clues that the film is drawing upon the codes and conventions of the horror film at this point. A metallic, plated body is ejected and Alex violently pushes Susan aside, proceeds to remove the plating and wipe away the gelatinous resin covering the fleshy surface of the child's skin. The final shots of the film reveal a hopelessly traumatised Susan who simply watches from a distance as Alex cradles *his* child.

At one level, the narrative action of *Demon Seed* can be read as an exposure of one of the commonest tropes in science fiction – the male/masculine endeavour to take over, or fully control, the procreative powers of the human female. After all, the suturing of production to reproduction is hardly new in science fiction; since Mary Shelley's *Frankenstein* (1818), connections between creation and procreation have been explored in the written genre. On another level, the birth of the cyborg in *Demon Seed* also serves to expose, or deconstruct, certain aspects of the cinematic apparatus itself. By this I mean that the evident split between body and voice, brought about when the cyborg child speaks the words 'I am alive', works to reveal the necessity of the voice/body, sound/vision synchronisation within cinematic 'realism'. Synchronisation of sound and vision usually functions as a naturalising device effacing the way in which cinematic technologies construct the aural as well as the visual. In *Demon Seed*, the sound and vision are synchronised to the extent that it is suggested that Vaughn's voice emanates from the female child's body, but here it operates as a denaturalising device, complicating traditional notions of a sex/gender unity. Further, a Cartesian mind/body duality is literally mapped onto a masculine (mind)/Feminine (body) divide in *Demon Seed*, which is foregrounded at the moment when the previously detached masculine intelligence of the AI takes up residence within the horrific materiality of the female body. Noel Carroll has noted that the horror genre is concerned with 'visceral revulsion', with impurity, with 'fusion'. Carroll goes on to state that 'horrific monsters involve the mixture of what is normally distinct',[4] which suggests that the cyborg can be understood as an appropriately horrific creation within the codes and conventions of the horror genre. But, what is significant is that, unlike the macho, male cyborg of the 1980s science fiction/action film, this outwardly female cyborg was born into a very different mise-en-scène; a visual terrain more readily associated with the science fiction/horror film than the science fiction/action film.

Although the character of Ripley in *Alien* is not figured as a literal cyborg (that is, until the fourth film in the series), I would contend that it is her presence that triggers the use of the horror codes in this film. Like the cyborg child in *Demon Seed*, Ripley is conceived in a horrific cyborgian environment, in which the melding of technology with the organic is made visually evident in H. R. Giger's design of the alien and the innards of the alien spacecraft that the hapless crew members investigate. While the interior of the Nostromo is initially presented with cleaner, harder surfaces than that of the alien vessel, the introduction of the alien aboard the crew's 'mother-ship' leads to a gradual organicisation in its appearance. The efficient calm of the futuristically equitable, de-gendered world of the Nostromo is invaded and this possible future is swiftly reconfigured as inhuman and horrific.

In an application of Julia Kristeva's ideas concerning the representation of the feminine as abject, Barbara Creed has explored the ways in which horror films propose a variety of forms of 'monstrous femininity', usually configured 'in relation to her mothering and reproductive functions'.[5] In *Alien*, Creed reads the presence of the parthenogenetic, archaic mother, and she goes on to say that this phantasmic figuration allows for 'a notion of the feminine which does not depend for its definition on a concept of the masculine'.[6] So, the archaic mother of *Alien* threatens to erase the gendered oppositions upon which 'proper' human identity has been predicated. Following on from Creed's comments, I would say that *Alien* articulates a masculine fear of gender dissolution, a dissolution that is initially presented under the guise of a progressive futurism and then quickly undercut with the introduction of the alien. In a comparison with the sight of the alien, Creed sees the character of Ripley as signifying the '" acceptable" form and shape of woman'.[7] However, I do not believe that Ripley is quite as 'acceptable' as Creed suggests. At the time of the film's release, the imposing figure of Ripley defied traditional gender roles and her very physical appearance suggested a disregard for the markers of sexual difference, as more normally encoded within mainstream cinema (she is 5′11″ tall and her body type could well be described as androgynous). Given the narrative trajectory of *Alien*, perhaps it is more accurate to read Ripley alongside Carol Clover's 'final girl': the girl left standing and the girl who single-handedly dispatches a pursuing, vicious killer at the end of a film. As Clover deftly illustrates, this was a characterisation that was common to the 'slasher' horror films that became so prevalent in the late 1970s and early 1980s (e.g. the *Halloween* series beginning in 1978 and the *Friday the 13th* series beginning in 1980). Clover discusses the inevitable gender complications that arise in the figuring of the triumphant female character in 'slasher' films and the way in which she was frequently presented as masculinised, as a 'tomboy'. However, for Clover, 'the discourse (of horror) is wholly masculine, and the female figures in it only insofar as they "read" some aspect of male experience'.[8] Clover therefore settles upon the idea that the 'final girl' be understood as 'a congenial double for the adolescent male' viewer.[9]

On the one hand then we have Creed's notion of Ripley as the reassuring face of womanhood and, on the other, Clover's idea that Ripley actually represents an adolescent male. Both of these readings are illuminating, but I do not accept either view as entirely accurate accounts of how Ripley functions, especially given the science fiction context of the film. For instance, in closing sequences of the film, Ripley's 'reassuringly' female form is exposed as she removes her clothes to don a spacesuit. Although she is voyeuristically presented in her near-naked state, this is immediately offset by the appearance of the alien and the violence of the actions that follow. The viewer is surely punished for the voyeuristic gaze here, in an operation that seems to deny Creed's assertion that Ripley is at all reassuring.[10] In addition, while I accept Clover's dynamic between male viewer and the 'final girl' of the 'slasher' film, I believe that Ripley functions in a different way, given the conventions of science fiction operating within *Alien*. The 'slasher' films' concern with sex (by this I mean the act of sexual intercourse or foreplay) is usually foregrounded, and it is the 'purity' of the final girl (her refusal to take part in sex acts) that marks her apart from the characters that fall victim to the monster. However, under the traditional codes of science fiction films, sex, in this sense, has been effectively denied. So the adoption of what could be taken as the 'final girl' to science fiction film makes Ripley a far more destabilising and threatening force within this context.[11]

As far as the aficionado and critic, John Brosnan, was concerned, the first *Alien* film was problematic as a science fiction. In an early appraisal he called it a 'botched job' and went on to state that 'as a science fiction film it's seriously flawed, but as a horror film it works perfectly'.[12] Brosnan therefore objects to what he sees as a generic boundary breaking, but I wonder if what he really objects to is the invasion of the feminine into the masculinist realms of the genre. Brosnan's position is strange, given that the figuring of frightening alien creatures has always been widespread within science fiction writing and film. In this respect, *Alien* most certainly takes its lead from the 1950s science fiction/monster movies (e.g. *The Thing* [dir. Howard Hawks, 1951], *Them!* [dir. Gordon Douglas, 1954] etc.), and, in terms of its narrative, is closely associated with *It! The Terror from Beyond Space* (dir. Edward L. Kahn, 1958). So why the refusal to accept *Alien* as a science fiction film? Brosnan goes on to justify his argument by stating that 'the main difference between *It!* and *Alien* is . . . at least ten million dollars',[13] and he expresses a concern that this later film 'create(s) the danger of the science fiction cinema going in the same direction it did in the 1950s when the genre was almost killed off by hordes of increasingly sleazy, cheap and shoddy monster movies',[14] But this ignores some crucial differences between the earlier *It! The Terror from Beyond Space* and *Alien*; differences that can be located in the representation of the human females as members of the space ship's crew. Apart from their very presence within the masculine environs of the spacecraft, the two female crew members in the 1950s version of this story are represented as in need of male/masculine protection and are largely servile to the men (they wait on table as the men eat and tend their wounds etc.). Ripley, on the other hand, appears to operate in a futuristically post-feminist environment, she is forthright and her nurturing instincts are focused upon the cat, Jonesy, rather than the male crew members. Therefore Brosnan's comments might be better understood as set against a time when not only had 1970s feminism challenged patriarchal structures, but feminist science fiction writing had dared to make inroads into the masculinist preserve of the written genre. The late 1970s had seen the advent of science fiction novels like Joanna Russ's *The Female Man* (1975) and Suzy McKee Charnas's *Motherlines* (1978); novels that ostentatiously undermined the idea of science fiction as a masculine realm and that extended the limits of the genre. Although it would be difficult to claim *Alien* as a feminist science fiction film, unlike its earlier pre-decessor (*It!*), this was a film in which the masculine fear of feminisation was made shockingly manifest in the notorious 'chest-ripping' scene where an alien is born out of the body of the male crew member Kane (played by John Hurt). Perhaps then Ripley's characterisation can be read alongside the written genre's 'invasion' by feminist writers and the film's appropriation of horror can be seen as an invasion of a 'feminine' force that threatened to 'soften' an otherwise 'hard' and masculine science fiction film genre.

Ripley has definitely reached iconic status in the history of the science fiction film genre, but that is not to say that she has remained unchanged in her various manifestations throughout the *Alien* series. Interestingly, the first sequel to Scott's original *Alien*, *Aliens* (dir. James Cameron, 1986), shifted from science fiction/horror mode toward science fiction/action film. Also, where *Alien* desta-bilised both sex and gender norms, *Aliens* reinstated differences based upon sex, even as the boundaries of traditional gendered roles were extended. For example, at the opening of the film a female foot soldier, Private Vasquez, pre-pares herself for combat under the watchful gaze of another male Private. The male Private asks: 'Hey, Vasquez, have you ever been mistaken for a man?' to which Vasquez replies: 'No . . . have you?' In other words, the sight of the female undertaking a role associated with the male becomes a source of humour and the comment works to assure the viewer that sexual difference still oper-ates in this world. Beyond this, whereas the mother figure was marked by her absence in *Alien,* she became rather more present in *Aliens:* not only does Ripley become substitute mother to a female child in *Aliens,* but sexed differ-ence among the aliens was introduced with the presentation of the egg-laying, alien queen surrounded by her drones. Sexual difference was also highlighted in the third science fiction/action film of the series, *Alien 3* (dir. David Fincher, 1992), in which Ripley finds herself the sole female among the all-male inmates of a penal colony. Facing threat from the rapists and murderers that populate the prison, Ripley takes tenuous control of the colony in their fight against the alien threat. What is most notable in this third film is Ripley's refusal of the literal mothering role in her final sacrifice at the moment she gives birth to an alien at the end of the film.

While there was a very clear relationship between Ripley and alien through-out the series, it was not until *Alien: Resurrection* (dir. Jean-Pierre Jeunet, 1997) that the character of Ripley became a literally 'fused' being; a synthesis of alien and human, technologically reproduced by the company scientists. The visual thematics of the first *Alien* (and, to some extent, the following two films) were extravagantly and very conspicuously explored in the fourth film. The themes of sexuality/birthing/abortion were brought together here in such a hyperbolic fashion that it could be seen as an almost parodic critique of the horror imagery in the previous films and the masculine fear of a feminine threat. For instance, an alliance of masculinity and technological power is underlined in this film in the shift from a 'mother' to a 'father' computer, which regulates the environment of the space station. This is a patriarchal environment in which great efforts are made to contain any threat associated with femininity. Further, it is ultimately revealed to be 'fusion' that threatens the scientists of *Alien: Resurrection,* as made evident in the scene where Ripley faces the pickled remains of failed attempts to clone her. The importance of this scene is signalled in the way that it brings the action to a tense standstill as the escaping group are halted in their tracks while Ripley investigates the laboratory containing the pickled 'specimens'. In looking at the progression from one specimen to the next it becomes obvious that the scientists were trying to clone her and the alien in a form that would allow for separation. The failed attempts at separation were marked in the way that the alien becomes visually integrated with Ripley (i.e. human body, alien head etc.). These clones could therefore be seen as an overt visual image of what the scientists understand as essential to Ripley; her monstrousness is written on the surface of these cloned bodies. So, what remained relatively covert in the preceding films was made ostentatiously overt here.

Following the series formula, Ripley again takes up a nurturing role, but this time her surrogate children represent the two sides of her 'nature': Call (a rebel android) and the human/alien offspring of the alien queen. In joining a band of renegade androids, Call has attempted to cut herself off from close communion with the masculine machines that constructed her. For instance, she sets herself apart from the ruling forces that created her by cutting the 'umbilical cord' that allowed her to 'jack into' cyberspace. However, her efforts to retain a distance from this world are reversed in the scene when she is asked to enter the space station's computer mainframe. She is very reluctant to do this as she says that this cyberspace is not 'real': within this masculine 'mind machine' she is faced with the fact that she is the literal product of a masculine imagination. Nevertheless, Ripley persuades her to go back in as this is the only way they can hope to return to their own spacecraft, The Betty, and escape the alien threat. So, a kind of necessary 'fusion' is apparently promoted here as a route to survival, Call's 'feminine' consciousness effecting a degree of control within a patriarchal cyberspace.

In opposition to Call is the monstrous figure of the alien/human offspring. Unlike Call, this 'progeny' is so demanding that it embarks upon a murder spree, effectively killing off rivals for Ripley's attention. Following a 'sibling spat', during which the monster attempts to destroy Call, Ripley is forced to abort the alien progeny from The Betty. Unlike the relatively clean dismissal of the alien from the escape pod in the first film of the series, this process is lengthy and messy. Via a small crack in a porthole, the alien progeny literally has the life sucked out of it, as its organic innards are drained out into the vacuum of space. Intercut with the repulsive sight of the alien innards dispersing into space, the viewer is shown Ripley's mixed response to her actions. There is melodrama in this moment, which plays out in gory and colourful detail the despair of the mature female, whose subjectivity rests upon her functioning role as patriarchal mother figure.

Having looked at the ways in which horror and the feminine have traditionally been brought together within the science fiction film, I believe that these images can be usefully compared to the films discussed in the previous chapter. For instance, the generic shifting from films featuring central male to those featuring female cyborgs indicates that issues surrounding gender were as fundamental within the genre as those raised by technological development. At the very least, a comparison based upon the use and adoption of generic codes suggests that powerful male protagonists in science fiction were often figured as *threatened* whereas the powerful female was frequently seen as *threatening*.

Replicating the Femme Fatale

Blade Runner is commonly cited as a seminal postmodern film, not only in terms of the cluttered and 'retrofitted' dystopian cityscape it offered the spectator, but also in the ways that it dealt with emerging questions of human subjectivity within a postmodern, post-industrial environment. The film sports a number of renegade, replicated bodies (replicants) designed to service their human counterparts. These are genetically engineered bodies; reproductions of human bodies that appear so real they throw into relief the supposed authenticity of being human. Although these replicants have been fashioned by a patriarchal mega-corporation, it is the figure of the absent mother that appears to be the key to their sense of selfhood. Even though the plot has them fervently seeking out the patriarchal figurehead (Tyrell) of the corporation that made them, the film also implies that what they are really seeking is the lost mother; a mother that will provide them with a secure historical lineage and a sense of subject-hood. So, unlike Creed's parthenogenetic mother in *Alien*, the absent mother of *Blade Runner* assures proper human identity. Rachel (Sean Young) is the only replicant who, initially at least, possesses a secure subjectivity; distinct from the renegade replicants, she has been implanted with the memories of Tyrell's niece and believes herself to be properly human. As the film progresses, Rachel learns that these memories are false and that she too is merely a replicated form of being; a condition that is extended to the Blade Runner, Deckard (Harrison Ford), in the director's cut of the film (1992). In this way, questions concerning the authenticity of human beingness and the socially constructed condition of human subjectivity are played out upon and around this female character.

Interestingly, Rachel's 'man-ufactured' identity is strongly signalled in an alignment with the 'femme fatale' of film noir. Like Robocop, Rachel's behaviour and her gendered identity are shown to be based upon a cultural fiction. Rachel is a fully encultured being, who, like the surrounding cityscape, has been retrofitted with an identity that harks back to film history. In drawing upon this genre, *Blade Runner* overlays the kind of doubleness that can be associated with the cyborg (in the human/machine confluence) with that of the dangerous and duplicitous femme fatale: Rachel is not what she appears to be. However, in contrast to the many, very active femme fatales of both the classical era and the later 'neo-noirs', it is notable that Sean Young's performance of the role seems particularly vacuous and passive. While this may well be justified by her replicant status in the narrative, her relative passivity also places greater emphasis upon her visual presence and foregrounds her function as fetishistic object. Upon learning of her replicated status, Rachel looks to Deckard for a sense of identity and acceptance – she is seen to acquiesce to Deckard's suggestions and appears eager to become what he wants her to be. Likewise, Deckard looks to Rachel in order to assert his own masculinity and to provide himself with a secure identity and future outside of his role as a killer. Judith Butler reminds us that 'the mark of gender appears to "qualify" bodies as human'.[15] So at a moment of crisis when both Rachel's and Deckard's identity is in question, they need one another. This is because they recognise that in order pass as human subjects they must act out what it means to be feminine or masculine.

There is a particularly interesting moment when Deckard and Rachel first kiss. Toward the end of the film, when they are alone in Deckard's apartment, he violently pushes Rachel against the wall. After this he tells her what to say to him:

Deckard: Say 'kiss me'
Rachel: Kiss me
Deckard: Say 'I want you'
Rachel: I want you

The aggression with which he approaches Rachel seems totally uncalled for and rather shocking in the context of their relationship up to this point. Kaja Silverman suggests that this moment obliges 'the viewer to confront the arbitrariness and the violence of what passes for "difference" within any culture'.[16] For Silverman, the scene's meaning hinges on what Rachel says immediately prior to the above exchange: 'I can't rely on . . .'. Although Rachel does not complete her statement, Silverman reads this as Rachel doubting her own feelings because the memories that provide her with an identity are not her own. Silverman goes on to suggest that Deckard is merely trying to prove to her that 'it is no less urgent or psychically real because it comes to her from the larger symbolic order'.[17] So, for Silverman, the film critiques the figuring of the female as a subject constituted by the law of the father. However, although *Blade Runner* certainly foregrounds the constructedness of gender it does, in part, neutralise any critique by allowing only the replicant who complies with this law to survive. In other words, Rachel survives because she acquiesces to her assigned role as feminine Other to Deckard's masculine subjectivity.

Later films also took up the figure of the femme fatale in their representation of powerful female characters in science fictional settings and the film *Eve of Destruction* (dir. Duncan Gibbins, 1991) is a particularly interesting example. The doubling associated with the femme fatale is literalised in this film when a female scientist (Renée Soutendijk) creates an android copy of herself called Eve 8. Eve 8 has been programmed with the memories of the human Eve and, on a test-run out in the real world, finds herself at the centre of male abuse. Eventually, goaded by the events she encounters, Eve 8's 'battlefield mode' is triggered and she actively defends herself. Having been let loose, Eve 8 begins a journey back through the human Eve's life in an apparent attempt to resolve those moments when the human Eve was forced to repress certain character traits. It seems that although the human Eve has attained a degree of professional prestige in her adult life, there are formative moments in her past which have stifled her character in the present. These moments are specifically connected to the way in which Eve has responded to various kinds of male abuse and, in some respects, continues to respond, as illustrated in her relationship with the military marksman sent to halt the runaway android. This marksman increasingly takes on the role of amateur psychologist as the film progresses and attempts, through a reading of Eve's innermost drives, to predict and control the actions of Eve 8.

There is, of course, a long history of female 'doubling' in connection with the femme fatale of film noir and much has been said about the way in which she is frequently juxtaposed or twinned with another female character, one who represents domesticity, safety, support to the hero.[18] Indeed, there are a number of examples in film noir in which this 'twinning' structure is made especially evident. *The Dark Mirror* (dir. Robert Siodmak, 1946) provides an impressive early example in which Olivia de Havilland plays identical twin sisters. In this film a psychiatrist is called in to decide which of the sisters has committed a murder and which is blameless in the affair. An interesting comparison with this earlier film noir can be seen in the later remake of *A Kiss Before Dying* (dir. James Dearden, 1991), which notably came out the same year as *Eve of Destruction*. Here, Sean Young (of *Blade Runner* fame) plays an identical twin who is obsessed with the death of her sister. In a reversal of noir conventions, she discovers that her sister's killer is none other than her own duplicitous husband.

Like *Blade Runner*, *Eve of Destruction* obviously draws upon film noir, but in the former film we are dealing with two identities, two distinct bodies

(Rachel and niece), sharing the same childhood memories, while in the latter both the physical and mental identities remain the same, although the actions undertaken by Eve and Eve 8 differ. Rachel's identity is assured through the replication of an assumed gender role, but I would say that Eve's identity becomes more fully authenticated through a process of replication, which allows her to perform outside of her assumed gender role. Where *Blade Runner* foregrounds the construction of Rachel as masculine fantasy, the way in which the narrative is set up in *Eve of Destruction* suggests that it is not simply designed as an exploration of the enigma of womanhood. In terms of the film's narrative, Eve 8 can be easily read as Eve's fantasy figure; an enabling figure through which she comes to terms with her own past and re-connects with dormant traits of her personality.

Claudia Springer states that the narrative of *Eve of Destruction* simply leads to a punishing of Eve 'for her sexuality and for engaging in technological rather than biological reproduction'.[19] For example, Springer implies that Eve 8 is the embodiment of a masculine fantasy, which is especially indicated in the placement of a nuclear warhead within the 'womb' of the android. Certainly, this suggests that she is meant as a representation of the 'phallic woman', but the plot also makes clear that this warhead has been insisted upon by the military men who funded Eve 8's development. In other words, their involvement in imposing a kind of phallic identity upon the android is made manifest. Springer states that at the end of the film the human Eve is forced to eliminate those threatening elements of her repressed being (in particular her repressed sexuality) in the destruction of her own creation, Eve 8. Eve is certainly forced into destroying Eve 8, but it is also clear that this is necessary in order to eliminate the threat of the nuclear warhead's imminent explosion; to eliminate that part of Eve 8 that has made her into an unwitting patriarchal weapon. What I am suggesting is that there is a separation between the Eve 8 as 'military weapon' and the Eve 8 as 'avenging female': these two perspectives are kept in play throughout the film. Therefore I believe that the ending of the film is far more ambivalent than Springer suggests. I do not see the human Eve's power or access to agency as conveniently quashed upon the destruction of Eve 8, but rather she takes control of the situation and does, in fact, take on behavioural aspects previously associated with Eve 8 at this point. In a comparison with a film like *The Stepford Wives* (dir. Bryan Forbes, 1975), which turned its rampaging feminists into compliant and servile robots, willing to undertake 'housewifely duties' for their husbands, *Eve of Destruction* reverses this logic by having its manufactured feminine object turn against its creators.

In *Star Trek: First Contact* (dir. Jonathan Frakes, 1997) we also find a notable example of a femme fatale in the representation of the Borg Queen (Alice Krige). Here the crew of the Enterprise comes face to face with the imminent threat of the Borg in their attempts to assimilate the human population of

Earth. In the television episodes when the Borg are fully introduced to the series (*The Best of Both Worlds: Parts 1 and 2* [dir. Cliff Bole, 1996]) they appear to be male and the voice that speaks for them is obviously masculine. When translated to the big screen, the Borg is led by a female cyborg who acts as the mind behind the more bodily actions of her male subjects. In fact, her representation as the 'brains' behind this collective 'brawn' is underlined when her separated head and spinal column are lowered into her female body. The figuring of the Borgian way of existence is an obvious reference to a kind of cybernetic 'hive world'. The way in which cybernetics, as a powerful paradigm as well as a working system, has been taken up varies according to context. However, as Kevin Kelly puts it, central to cybernetics is the idea 'that no one is in control, and yet an invisible hand governs, a hand that emerges from very dumb members'.[20] A cybernetic system can then be understood as operating itself; as responding on local levels to the needs of the whole without the necessity of centralised control or an overview on the part of individual members. Therefore the figuring of the Borg Queen not only seems to exceed the basic premise of the cybernetic model (by imposing a leader, a central brain), but also attempts to mark the Borg as feminised, as existing within a matriarchal environment.

Throughout the *Star Trek: New Generation* television series the android, Data, functions to illustrate a working-through of the tensions between the Enterprise crews' individual emotions/desires and a more mechanical obedience to the Federation. In the film *Star Trek: First Contact,* this is made all the more apparent, particularly in those scenes where Data is held hostage by the Borg and faces the Queen. Indeed, it these scenes which tellingly articulate the kind of danger she represents. The Borg Queen could be understood as Data's counterpart in the film and comes to embody those aspects that threaten to upset the order achieved by the Federation. Having previously stated that the Queen is meant to be the controlling *mind* behind her drones, it is interesting that her opposition to the Federation is largely illustrated in her physical aspects. When Data is taken onto the Borg ship it is not, primarily, the Queen's intellect which appears threatening, but rather her efforts to use her physicality in order to seduce and tempt him into 'assimilation' with the Borg. For instance, the very fact that she is literally lowered into her body when she comes to speak with the captive Data foregrounds the apparent need for a sexualised, female body to carry out her purpose.

In the earlier television episodes, the captain of the Enterprise, Picard (Patrick Stewart) also came into direct contact with the Borg and his 'assimilation' led to him becoming more mechanical and machine-like. In contrast, Data's 'assimilation' seems to involve the introduction of more human elements. The Borg Queen thus enables him to feel bodily sensation and in making him more human in this way she also makes him more vulnerable to attack: if the administering of pain does not work she tries to coax him by applying sensuous, bodily sensation or through the implied promise of sexual 'union'. At one point she even blows upon the new organic skin she has imposed upon him and after he responds with a kind of disturbed elation she says 'was that good for you?' In order to counter the 'assimilation' process it is up to Data (and, by implication, the rest of the Enterprise crew) to withstand these 'feminine' pains and pleasures. The Borg Queen is the duplicitous temptress, and if Data gives in to his newly acquired 'baser' desires, in an alliance with the 'feminine', he will suffer the consequences. If Data 'lets his guard down' he risks becoming one of her drones, losing not only his autonomy but his supposed individuality. Having said that, Picard states, later in the film, that the Queen is attempting to make Data more like her, in her quest for 'an equal'. Taking all of the above into consideration it seems that the cybernetic organism, in *First Contact*, the literal melding of human and machine, is affiliated with the feminine and the consequent blurring of boundaries can be read as a feminine threat to a masculinity that requires separation.

Unlike Sean Young's rather passive portrayal of the femme fatale, Alice Krige's performance of the Queen more closely resembles classic representations of this figure; she speaks using a low, soft, breathy tone designed to seduce her victim into compliance and a sense of security. Clearly, the low tones of the femme fatale voice represent a kind of aural fetishism – her voice becoming more 'masculine', allaying the anxieties associated with a powerful and insightful female, sexual being. The breathiness of her voice underlines her sexuality as this kind of tonal quality is highly suggestive of bodily involvement in the speaking process. The expiration of breath acts as a reminder of the breathing apparatus that lies below the neck/head, inside the body; breathiness, in this instance, becomes a kind of ghostly abject substance. Krige's delivery of the dialogue is also in marked contrast to Data's very measured and 'matter of fact' tone in that she makes use of a very languorous rhythm by placing more emphasis on a lengthening of vowels rather than clipped or plosive consonants. The elongation of the words she speaks, enhancing tonal quality, suggest that she is enjoying the very act of speech-making as opposed to merely imparting information. All of this has the effect of placing far more emphasis on actual sound quality (form), as opposed to word (content), as her voice envelops and absorb the listener. This delivery can therefore be understood in association with a long history of cinematic aurality connected to the fantasy of the maternal and all-engulfing voice. As Silverman points out, within cinematic practices the fantasy of the 'maternal voice' has been co-opted to connote both horror and ecstasy. In this instance it is drawn upon to connote horror, even though the promise of ecstasy is present. As horrifying, the 'maternal voice' comes to 'figure enclosure as entrapment and/or danger, and so represent[s] interiority as an undesirable condition . . . Trapped within the suffocating confinement of the mother's voice, the newborn child resembles a prisoner or prey'.[21] This works to emphasise the idea that union with the Borg will necessarily result in Data losing individual agency within this maternal realm. What the Borg Queen augers is the return to a pre-conscious, pre-oedipal state. Therefore, even though the technological worlds represented in *First Contact* are remarkably similar in some respects, the Borg realm is associated with a reactionary state of being, allowing the Federation's world, by contrast, to appear rather more progressive. In comparison to the 'mindless' obedience of the Borg 'drones', the crew of the Enterprise's obedience to their captain and the Federation appears as the outcome of free will and individual choice.

BEYOND THE FEMME FATALE

The 1990s saw the development of a different kind of female figure in science fiction cinema. Drawing upon a distinction that Yvonne Tasker makes between the 'active heroine' (of which a more recent version of the 'femme fatale' may be included) and the 'action heroine' (which I am choosing to call the 'female hero'),[22] I will be concentrating on female figures that emerged in science fiction/action films who appeared to take on a functioning role more normally assigned to the male hero. This new figuration was pre-figured in Ripley, but the female hero that emerged in the 1990s was more closely sutured to the codes and conventions of the modern action genre. Consequently, their heroic status was written upon their bodies, in terms of their pumped-up musculature and/or their physical fighting skills. The appearance of the female hero presented a striking break with the representation of women within the conventions of science fiction cinema. Powerful female figures were certainly to be found in the cinema 'serial queens' of the 1930s, but these tended to be depicted as evil and seductive and they were frequently pitted against a male adversary who eventually brought them under control. Of course, women were also represented in traditionally male roles in many of the films of the 1950s. However, as discussed in an earlier chapter, their potential centrality as scientists was usually undermined, either in their characterisation as love object or sidekick to a more commanding male hero or by the way their professional status was usually confined to those sciences that could more readily be associated with the 'feminine' (i.e. the medical or biological sciences).

More closely related to the female hero figures of the 1990s are the female superheroes (of which there were relatively few), like Wonder Woman, who first appeared in comic books in the early 1940s. Like the comic-book male superheroes, these characters were usually depicted as living out a split existence: they passed as 'normal' women in their everyday activities and, when needed, came out as superheroes to fight America's enemies (usually alongside or for government agencies or the military etc.). Their superhero identity remained a secret and with a swift change into body revealing costume they would unleash their powers. Like their male counterparts, their fighting abilities remained magical in some sense and, in terms of the narrative they were presented as 'exceptional' beings. However, unlike their male counterparts, their superhuman power was not marked by the kind of pumped-up musculature associated with masculine strength. In the exposing of the often exaggerated female form of the female superhero, they were codified as pleasingly sexual for the male viewer. In comparison, the authority of the female hero that emerged in science fiction films in the 1990s was, initially at least, marked upon her body in ways that have more traditionally been associated with masculine prowess; creating an arguably more ambivalent characterisation than her nonetheless dynamic predecessors.

In exploring the implications of this characterisation in science fiction cinema I will begin by carrying out comparative analyses of three films in which the female hero appears: the low-budget, British independent film *Hardware* (dir. Richard Stanley, 1990), the high budget sequel to *The Terminator, Terminator 2: Judgment Day* (dir. James Cameron, 1991), and a lesser known, direct to video film called *Nemesis 2: Nebula* (dir. Albert Pyun, 1995). As was the case in the last chapter with *The Terminator* and *Robocop,* these films make for convenient, comparative study, because there is a sense in which they can be seen as connected. The striking narrative similarities actually make the differences between these three films stand out; particularly in terms of how the female hero is visually presented and the specificities of her narrative function.

Beginning with *Hardware,* here we have a bleak futuristic vision of a dry and decaying world, in which humans struggle for survival amid the wreckage of a post-apocalyptic, industrial wasteland. At the outset, the audience is introduced to a standard (tall, dark and handsome) male hero called Mo (Dylan McDermott). It is Christmas and Mo buys the skeletal head of a junked robot in a scrap dealer as a present for his reclusive girlfriend, Jill (Stacey Travis). Refusing to subject herself to the harsh and poisonous outside world, Jill spends her time locked up in her heavily fortressed apartment, creating sculpture from the discarded metal debris of an industrialised past. Upon receiving her Christmas present, Jill spray-paints the head with the American flag and welds it into the centre of a large, recently constructed, sculpture. Complete with plastic baby dolls, melted and burnt by Jill's blow-torch, the sculpture not only expresses Jill's vision of the world outside but also marks her apart from the 'nice girl' image of Sarah as set up in the opening of *The Terminator.*

Mo and Jill definitely react differently to the wrecked world around them: Mo lives in a kind of fantasy world in which he sees himself as a soldier of fortune, while Jill seems to harbour no illusions about the harsh environment outside and is extremely sceptical about the politics behind up-beat television reports that she views through a haze of marijuana smoke and heavy metal music. Even though Mo and Jill are split along traditional lines in terms of the literal spheres they occupy (Mo = public sphere/labour/industry, Jill = private sphere/domesticity/art), gendered divides are also confused in the way in which these characters are represented. While Mo is somewhat passive, dreamy and idealistic, Jill is gritty, cynical and aggressive and adamantly rejects Mo's desires to start a family.

Jill is constantly under attack from the outside world, she checks everyone who enters the apartment for radiation levels and her privacy is invaded by a local peeping Tom who stalks her every move. Although Jill is adept at protecting herself and her environment, her hermetically sealed world is threatened when the junked robot head comes to life and rebuilds itself from the metal detritus that she uses for her artwork. The metal head is actually part of a military prototype designed to kill humans and having provided itself with a body it aggressively pursues Jill in a highly eroticised and bloody sequence of scenes. For instance, at one point the robot has Jill pinned to floor and we see it crawl up between her legs and attempt to impale her with a large drill head (shades of *Demon Seed* here). Eventually, Mo and a cohort of male followers break into Jill's apartment and Mo shoots at the robot until it crashes through her bedroom window. Believing he has destroyed the mechanical monster, Mo glories in his role as hero of the day. But, the robot returns, pulls Jill out through the window of her apartment, and kills Mo with a hypodermic injection that the audience has earlier learned induces death and euphoria. In an interview by Alan Jones for *Starburst,* Stanley stated that he wanted this film to be 'a psychedelic neo-fascist entertainment spiked for the Nineties'.[23] This description certainly seems fitting for the lengthy scene revealing Mo's death throes. Mo's euphoric demise is illustrated by a sequence of updated, paisley-style, psychedelic swirling tunnels (obviously based upon Mandelbrot's fractal geometric patterns) [24] and massively enlarged images of organic, cellular activity, intercut with distorted shots of the robot and the surrounding devastation. It is also during this sequence that the spectator is made aware of a kind of psychical link between the robot and Mo as the robot appears to record and repeat phrases that Mo has either uttered during the course of the film or appears to be thinking at that moment. The computerised brain of the robot is stealing Mo's identity at his point of death. The updated psychedelic imagery that accompany Mo's death very obviously refer back to the 'tunnels of perception' so prevalent in the 1960s and 1970s science fiction film, but within the context of the early 1990s these images also take on new significance as set against the growing number of reports of HIV and AIDS cases associated with intravenous drug use. Rather than heightened consciousness or mere regression, instant nirvana is, in this film, laced with the threat of disease and death.

It is upon Mo's demise that Jill assumes the full function of female hero in this film. Having momentarily escaped the robot's clutches she chooses to return to her apartment, ostensibly to rescue Mo. When she finds him dead she takes to the robot with a baseball bat and the fight between Jill and Robot continues. The Jill that emerges at this point is avenging and determined. During a lull in the battle, she uses her computer console to communicate with her adversary and hears Mo's recorded voice advising her of a defect in the robot's design. In a reversal of the famous 'shower scene' in *Psycho* (dir. Alfred Hitchcock, 1960), Jill finally wreaks her revenge by drenching the robot with water in the shower cubicle and short-circuiting his systems.

The influences and references to past science fiction films run riot in *Hardware*. Aside from the aforementioned reference to *Demon Seed*, the intrusion of the televisual images is highly reminiscent of Verhoeven's work, and the overall narrative is very similar to *The Terminator*. In fact, this film is like an excitedly uncensored version of its mainstream Hollywood counterparts and appears designed as an unashamedly shocking retort to macho science fictions of the 1980s.

In comparison to *Hardware*, the high-budget *Terminator 2: Judgment Day*, released the following year, looks rather polite, but it is nevertheless a central text in tracking the emergence of the female hero. This is largely due to the figuring of a new Sarah; a Sarah who has acquired aggressive 'masculine' traits and a pumped-up, muscular body to match. In the first film Sarah primarily functions as 'feminine' victim, whereas, in the second film she is visually transformed into a female hero. Also, whereas the first film saw Sarah as less than 'street wise' and largely unable to cope with the threatening world outside of her shared apartment, once set loose from the high security insane asylum where she begins the second film, this new Sarah has obviously become adept in occupying a public, 'masculine' sphere. She has acquired skills in the use of weaponry and views her body as a fighting machine. Sarah has certainly lost the victim-like qualities associated with her 'girly image' in the first film, but her more heroic characterisation in the second film is eroded in various ways as the narrative unfolds. For instance, her function as protector to her son is consistently undercut by the 'good' Terminator's superior tactical knowledge and even his superior parenting skills. In addition, it is also evident that her newly acquired physique is placed within a hierarchy of muscularity in which the Terminator's more bulky appearance signals his superior strength and importance. In other words, she is 'out-performed' by the Terminator throughout the film and instead of emerging victorious against him, the ending of the first film is rewritten as it becomes the Terminator's altruistic choice to sacrifice himself at the close of *Terminator 2*. Of course, according to the narrative of the first film, Sarah's main purpose was as the vessel for the birth of a future male saviour. Given the appearance of her son in the sequel, her warrior status is written into a narrative in which, like the comic-book female superheroes, she is predominantly characterised as fighting *for* patriarchy. In a comparison with Jill, who fights in defence of the space she has managed to carve out in an inhospitable world, Sarah is relocated to an outside world where she fights in defence of a patriarchal future. So, the threat that the female hero may offer to the stability of traditional gender hierarchies in *Terminator 2* is ensnared within a narrative that strongly upholds patriarchal values. At best, the attempts to recuperate and confine the image of the female hero in *Terminator 2* may signal her potential agency as a disruptive and threatening figure.

Arnold Schwarzenegger was obviously cast in the Terminator role for his physical prowess as a champion bodybuilder, well known as the several times winner of Mr Olympia and Mr Universe bodybuilding contests in the 1960s and 1970s. Verhoeven's characterisation of Schwarzenegger as a 'total film star'[25] therefore points to the degree that the Schwarzenegger star persona matches the characters he plays. There is a kind of hyper-realism apparent in Schwarzenegger's performances, due to the fact that the body and skills necessary to play the roles he has undertaken have been acquired outside of any dramatic training in acting, implying that he actually lived these roles prior to their re-enactment. Linda Hamilton (Sarah), on the other hand, was a known actor who had appeared in several relatively high profile film and television roles prior to undertaking the role of Sarah. Although much was made of the way that she trained and built up her body for the sequel, in comparison with the Schwarzenegger persona, the implication is that Hamilton's performance is less authentic, less real. This was not, however, the case with my third example, the female hero, Alex, who appeared in the final three films of the 'direct to video', *Nemesis* series. Alex is played by Sue Price, a professional bodybuilder who has competed in the Ms Olympia competition.

Within female bodybuilding there are basically three classes: Fitness, Figure and Physique. 'Fitness' concerns athletic body shape in conjunction with performance, 'Miss Figure' concerns a body trained to attain those physical characteristics closely associated with traditional ideals of feminine beauty (a variation on the old beauty contest), and 'Physique' is judged purely on particular muscle build and definition. Although 'Physique' is also split into lightweight, middleweight and heavyweight, it moves away from what are considered to be the realms of traditional feminine beauty. Even though male and female competitors are judged separately, the ideals within this category appear less gendered in that the female body shapes are sculpted through weight training and come much closer to the body shapes of male contestants. It could be said that these women were training to look more like men, but this ignores the irony that male bodybuilders actually acquire some of the traits associated with the feminine body (i.e. large 'breasts' and heavy thighs). Alternatively, I would suggest that the difference between female and male ideal body images within the Physique classes becomes far less marked.[26] In terms of female bodybuilding categories Sue Price comes under the category of heavyweight 'Physique'. She therefore presents an especially spectacular and excessive version of the built-up female body and is far more of a visual challenge to the macho posturings of the Terminator than Sarah's 'Fitness' body type. It seems that second *Terminator* film, placed Sarah's newly acquired physique within a hierarchy of muscularity in which the Terminator is figured as more powerful. We only need to imagine Sue Price in the Sarah role to reveal the recuperative tactics displayed in *Terminator 2*.

The narrative of *Nemesis 2: Nebula* is remarkably similar to *The Terminator* films, only in *Nemesis 2* it is Alex who is sent back through time, arriving in East Africa in the year 1980. We are told that Alex is a genetically altered female created to oppose the mechanical form of cyborg that has overrun an America of the future. Alex is taken in by a local African tribe and we see her adult life begin just as she is about to undertake a 'rite of passage' ritual in order to prove her warrior status. When initially introduced to Alex the viewer is shown a sequence of body and face shots, during which she describes her upcoming trial of strength and endurance to a female member of the tribe. None of these shots expose her as a female body and it may be quite a shock to the viewer when her sex is finally revealed. It is as though this sequence were intended to undermine the viewer's expectations not only in terms of what to expect of an action hero (that they be male), but what to expect from the muscularity achievable upon a female body.

In her article 'Traits of the Female Hero', Mary Ann Jezewski looks at the similarities and differences in the narrativisation of female heroes in Greek mythology as well as powerful women in history.[27] Jezewski looks at how the female heroes' legend revolves around the seemingly masculine deeds she accomplishes, but she also notes some significant differences in the structure of the stories accompanying these figures. One of these differences concerns the absence of the female hero's mother from many of these stories. She goes on to say that: 'The female hero most frequently received her power from her father or through her marriage and therefore it is her father and/or husband who becomes an important part of her legend'.[28]

Given Jezewski's insight, it becomes evident that Sarah has received her power from her lover, Reese, in the first *Terminator* film. For example, it is Reese who gives her a gun and who teaches her how to make incendiary devices. At one point Sarah does turn to her mother for help by calling her on the telephone, but the viewer learns that the Terminator has foreseen this action and killed her mother. Sarah is then tricked into giving out her location and her trust in her mother is shown to be misplaced in this situation. In the case of *Nemesis,* although the audience sees Alex's mother bring her back through time, she is also conveniently killed off at the beginning of the film. Along with this incident the introductory voice-over (performed by a male actor) announces that it is Alex's father (who is called Alex Rain in the first *Nemesis* film) who has performed the DNA alteration upon his child and even given her his name. This strongly indicates that the female Alex of the *Nemesis* series is primarily 'fathered' and has been given her father's powers. But even though the film presents this female hero as 'fathered', spectacle and narrative are also conspicuously set off against one another. The camera, seemingly without narrative explanation, constantly pans over Alex's/Price's body, inspecting the flex of individual muscles, and as Alex 2 meets each new character on her journey they almost invariably comment upon her muscularity. Alex is also seen changing her clothes on a number of occasions (most often into the clothes worn by a male adversary she has just dispatched), which provides the flimsiest of excuses for yet another look at aspects of her physique. This would seem to suggest that she is set up as an object for the male gaze. However, this is complicated when Alex rescues a character called Emily from a band of male rebels. Emily seems attracted by Alex's body and comments on how muscled she is. Thus follows the now familiar series of shots revealing various aspects of Alex's body seen from the point of view of Emily. This is a confusing moment due to the inherent ambiguities of applying a standard objectification scenario to a woman who looks like a man being looked at by another woman who looks decidedly androgynous.

So, both *Hardware* and *Nemesis 2* exploit the *Terminator* films, but each in its way also subverts the narrative trajectory of their blockbuster counterparts. What is notable about the lower-budget films is the way in which the active female wins out and is allowed to fully embody the function of the lone hero, a role normally assigned to a male performer.

Mind over Matter

The heavily muscled female hero has all but disappeared from science fiction films, which can partly be explained by the influence of cyberpunk novels and Japanese anime upon the genre. As stated in the previous chapter, the advent of the 'cyber-thrillers' ushered in a slimmed-down body and the focus of attention shifted to psychical transformation. Female heroes within this sub-genre might include Jane (Dina Meyer) in *Johnny Mnemonic* (dir. Robert Longo, 1995), and Trinity (Carrie-Anne Moss) in *The Matrix* series (dir. Larry and Andy Wachowski, 1999, 2002, 2003). Both of these characters are seen to be physically active and both appear to possess the bodily strength, skill and expertise that enable them to triumph in physical battles, often against male adversaries. Although the cyber-thrillers commonly sport an array of cyborgian characterisations, the heroic qualities of the male heroes become more closely associated with the mind, whereas the skills associated with our female heroes remain more firmly located in their bodies. For example, in *Johnny Mnemonic* our eponymous male hero (Keanu Reeves) has had a prosthesis implanted into his brain (enabling him to carry vast quantities of data) and he can also directly 'jack' into the Net. In contrast, his female partner and body guard, Jane, is cyborgised via technologies that enhance her bodily strength and skill. So a sex divide is underlined here in a way that is reminiscent of a traditional mind/body dichotomy: Johnny standing for 'mind' and Jane for 'body'. Even though Jane is a very active female hero in comparison with Johnny, she comes to represent the emotional, the bodily, the sexual and the material. This is in direct opposition to Johnny who is presented as logical and unemotional.

Like Jane, Trinity in *The Matrix* series is shown to be a particularly skilful opponent and she too becomes the partner and love interest to the male hero, Neo (Keanu Reeves). Toward the end of the first film she comes to believe, along with the rest of the rebel group with which she is associated, that Neo is the saviour they have been waiting for to lead them against the virtual 'agents' that defend the Matrix (the cybernetic system that creates the illusion of realty within the minds of its human inhabitants). Both Neo and Trinity are shown in physical battles against their adversaries but there are differences in the way in which their bodies are displayed. While both Trinity and Neo wear long black coats, during Trinity's fighting bouts the curves of her body are frequently displayed in a skin tight cat suit, whereas Neo's body largely remains cloaked. If we were in doubt as to the hierarchy of importance allotted to these characters then the final film of the series clarifies their ranking within the overall narrative. In *The Matrix Revolutions* much is made of Neo's demise as, accompanied by choral music, his outstretched body is rapturously carried away through a golden corridor by the machines. Trinity's death is downplayed in comparison; no heavenly choirs, no suggestion of transcendence, she simply dies because her body has been pierced by metal shards. So the mere borrowing, by a female character, of what have been previously understood as masculine traits does not necessarily lead to a representation of equality between the sexes; the lines of demarcation are simply redrawn.

FEMALE HERO MEETS FEMME FATALE

I have chosen for my final example a science fiction film which effectively co-opts both the female hero and the femme fatale. *Starship Troopers* (1997) has proved to be one of Paul Verhoeven's most controversial films. Based upon Robert Heinlein's 1959, gung-ho boy's novel, the narrative concerns the adventures of a group of young army recruits, fighting a war against the alien Bugs of another world. Heinlein's novel was originally intended for a juvenile market, but Verhoeven's film was given an 18 certificate in Britain and an R rating in America. If this film is read as a translation of the novel to screen then the visual rendering of the violence present in the novel, in itself, seems to uncover the naive attitudes to war and the horrors of the social Darwinism at the heart of the book. In this sense it is possible to say that the film presents a relatively accurate portrayal of the book, but when Heinlein's imagined universe is vividly literalised on screen in the 1990s it is judged as unpalatable viewing for younger audiences. In my view, Verhoeven's starkly comic-book approach renders this science fiction film as a kind perverse black comedy that comments upon Heinlein's known anti-communist and militaristic views as well as the contemporary state of affairs in America following the Gulf War. However, it seems that controversy ensued because the film was taken rather too literally by some critics as a straightforward call to arms against the alien Other (see interview, pp. 169–73).

The group of high-school leavers in the film buy into the militaristic ideology of the federalised world portrayed in *Starship Troopers*: signing up for service is sold to them as their route to full citizenship and adulthood, which motivates their actions in the film. The first half of the film is taken up with the recruits' training, which is depicted in true comic-book style and saturated with embarrassing, 'feel good' moments of social bonding that would not be out of place in a Hollywood 'teen movie'. On one level, the film adamantly addresses the spectator as a child, which makes the accidental and violent death of a recruit in training, along with the extreme punishments dished out by the officers, all the more shocking. If the sporadic displays of gory violence in the first half of the film fail to astonish then the ultra-violent battle scenes that take up most of the second half represent an almost unrelenting attack upon the audience. Having presented the viewer with a film that in look and style is not dissimilar to *Star Wars,* stripped of the celebratory ritual and complex narrative turns of the former film, *Starship Troopers* is presumably intended to provoke a less than reassuring and more distanced view of what is happening on screen.

Starship Troopers offers up two central female characters: Dizzy (Dina Meyer) and Carmen (Denise Richards). Both of these characters are attracted to the central male hero, Johnny Rico (Casper Van Dien). At the opening of the film it becomes apparent that Johnny's desire is focused upon Carmen and that Dizzy competes with her for his attentions. Carmen's seemingly selfish ambition is juxtaposed with Dizzy's unabashed loyalty and unswerving love for Johnny. As Verhoeven makes clear in the second part of his interview below, Dizzy's character has undergone a sex change between novel and film, which may partly explain her status as a female hero. Dizzy is shown to be athletic and, like Rico, she joins the macho infantry corps. Carmen, on the other hand, appears more 'feminine' in her approach to the world; she is not so physically active and thrives on the attentions of a variety of young men in life. These two female characters seem set up for comparison and it is therefore important that Dizzy does not survive to the end of the film, although she does succeed in her dubious ambition of forming a romantic alliance with Rico, but only after he has been dumped by Carmen.

According to Verhoeven, the response to the Carmen character by American audiences at the film's previews was very aggressive. It seems that these audiences saw her as a duplicitous figure, who does not respond in the expected way to the desires of the male hero. By the time Verhoeven's film came to the screen audiences had been treated to a number of well-known female hero characters and were more used to witnessing these active women on screen. In this sense, Carmen is somewhat out of place in this action film, whereas Dizzy's female action character can now be viewed as fitting company for the male hero. Seeing this film as embedded within generic conventions, it is possible to say that the figure of the female hero is played off against the femme fatale. The fact that it is Dizzy who dies for 'the cause' and Carmen who survives, although obviously disappointing to some audience members, provides a further shocking and irreverent twist in the narrative. The sight of the physically active and fearless Dizzy may well be taken as an enabling vision of a powerful female, but within the confines of this narrative she is also shown to be a tragic and misguided figure. Like the young male characters in the film, she uses her strength and power in the service of a patriarchal federal government and believes her desires will be met if she joins her love object on the battlefield. However, in Carmen we see a different kind of character; the femme fatale is revisited here as Johnny is lured into battle because of his sexual urges toward her. Unlike the faithful Dizzy, Carmen does not support our male hero, although she does function as a very willing representative for the patriarchal powers of the federal government. As is the case with so many of Verhoeven's Hollywood films, standard generic characterisations are co-opted, exaggerated and placed within an overtly patriarchal and aggressive setting, offering comment upon American ideology and the media machine that supports it, as well as on the values and ethics that familiar stereotypes have come to embody.

INTERVIEW: DIRECTOR PAUL VERHOEVEN (PART 2)

C: Recent years have seen a cycle of science fiction films featuring very active, what you might call, 'female heroes'. I wondered if you could talk about how you see the female characters that have appeared in your films.

V: In my movies I've had the pleasure of portraying women in a kind of strong way. I feel that this is more interesting for me than having women be victims or support systems for men. I mean there are so many movies where women are just added to a film so there is a sexual element. This was always boring for me. So, in my American work and in my Dutch work – in *Keetje Tippel* and *De Vierde Man* [The Fourth Man] and others – the women are generally portrayed making decisions and taking initiative and doing all the things that are normally given to men and acted by men. But that's my vision and my idea about women – that expresses what I feel about ideas supported by Judeo or Christian religion that the women are just basically support systems. I think that's completely false and should be destroyed as soon as possible.

C: I was thinking of Dina Meyer and her character in *Starship Troopers* – how did you approach directing her in that 'female hero' role?

V: Well you know that character in the novel was a male. I asked Neumeier [the screenplay writer] to change this, because I thought it would be more interesting to make the character a female. She was a bit of a rowdy kind of girl, a bit athletic . . . what do you call that – there is a term for that isn't there?

C: A bit of a tomboy?

V: Yes, she behaves a bit like a boy. Perhaps this is partly because of the way that the character started – as a male? So it's quite possible that some of the things she's doing or the way she's behaving might be influenced by the original thinking of Robert Heinlein, the writer of the book. She is, of course, for me, one of the most interesting characters of the movie, because she has a genuine touch, a genuine aspect to her, which in this case is projected onto Johnny Rico. He is rejecting her because of his presumed love for Carmen.

I based her on a girl from my high school – in fact, both of them, both Carmen and Dizzy – these were based on two girls that I knew at high school. One was the flavour of the school, the girl that was absolutely beautiful, intelligent and wonderful, the sweetheart, the love object of many, many young men. Like her, the Denise Richards character [Carmen] takes for granted that everybody loves her and every boy wants her. The other character was more into sports and a more attractive girl and both were in my class. The contest between them was always interesting to me and I think that's why they became that way in the movie. Dina's character is a person who seems to know what she wants. She accepts the burden of her convictions; she pursues what she wants, although not wanted by the male, in this case. She basically feels solace at the end because she ultimately fulfils her goal, even as she dies.

C: She's quite athletic isn't she?

V: Yes. When I did the tests, when I was auditioning, I did some of the football scenes – to see how they would react physically, you know – she's that kind of girl. The character of Carmen continuously goes from one guy to the other – first Johnny, then the other guy, the pilot – she takes what's available and she never seems to be able to make up her mind, because she feels that it is her right to have one or the other or whatever. It's interesting that when the movie was originally tested . . . when we first showed the movie there were still a couple of scenes there that were not in the final version, where she expresses even more this kind of promiscuity, feeling that she has a right to two men or ten men. That was expressed a bit stronger in the movie at that time. On the cards – the audience writes cards and give their opinion about the movie, that's how they do it here – and on many cards I read 'the wrong girl dies'. Others wrote 'kill the slut'. I would say in that version she was shown to be playing to the boys more – playing one against the other and whatever – and that ultimately didn't end up in the movie because the movie was too long or whatever. But it was also because the studio was frightened to death when they got these cards saying 'kill the slut'. Carmen was the survivor. And there was not just one card like that – there were many like that, you know, from the audience, feeling that Dizzy was the person who should have survived and the other girl should have been punished for her promiscuity or the fact that she had the audacity to abandon Johnny Rico.

C: The audience wanted her to be punished?

V: Well it's this puritan attitude in America, where the male should be free to do everything he wants and the females should not dare to do that. I mean, the fact is that Carmen behaves like a man – like so many men who go from one woman to the other and some of them at the same time. Carmen behaves that way. She takes one and then the other and she doesn't mind switching again. So, she behaves like a male – the way males are kind of seen – like Kennedy and his father, they fuck them then throw them away – that's the attitude isn't it?

C: So, taking those two characters together, she's acting, in some ways, in a more traditionally masculine way? And yet on the surface level, you'd look at the athleticism of the Dina Meyer character and say that she is the more masculine of the two?

V: True. That's strange, because Dina Meyer's character has a more conservative point of view – or romantic, if you want, or nineteenth-century – which is love for this one man that she will always love. Love for the man who she loves from the first moment in the class when we see them together. She is jealous of Carmen – that Johnny likes Carmen so much. She can't stand that. Dizzy is always with Rico, trying to follow him. She's like the conservative woman who follows the man of her dreams, until the very end even. So she behaves like people in the nineteenth century, or before that even, would have seen as the appropriate attitude of a woman. So it's interesting that Carmen – the woman who takes liberty and freedom and says, OK, it's my world and it's my rules, and I don't want to be courting your code of how a woman should behave – should be condemned by the audience for that. Especially, when she is, in fact, the more progressive person. She's the person that, in my opinion, is not caught up in the old-fashioned female paradigm.

C: I wondered whether there was a sense in which those two female characters play out different sides of the male hero of the film?

V: That's more for you to decide. I cannot decide about that myself. The two characters were based upon my own high-school situation and how far I use strong female characters to express parts of myself or to express a hate or love for women, that is more up to somebody on the outside to decide, because I cannot see that in myself, you know. I mean, for me, how I see things and how I feel about women and my perspective on women, and how far that is terrible, horrible or disgusting – that's up to you.

C: In terms of *Starship Troopers* then – how did you approach the performances there? You had these two very interesting, strong female characters and all the other characters and a lot of CGI going on – a lot of complex spectacle in the visuals – so how important were the performances?

V: They were important, but they were always worked within certain parameters . . . with the style of those movies where people were still victimised by the propaganda that was displayed by the global government. So they are always a little bit . . . you could call them all a little bit lobotomised, in a way. The characters were all part of the political perspective of the scriptwriter and me, about this world. If you look at the faces, you get the feel of those German movies of the 1930s, or Leni Riefenstahl's work in *Triumph of the Will* – where there was an attempt to streamline, basically, the male and the female – the male into these rock hard, edgy men with strong faces and the female into a certain kind of beauty which is so dominant in fascist thinking.

C: So there is a sense in which the characters are simple?

V: They are simple.

C: But political complexities are played out in the visual irony, the hyperbole and the violence?

V: But if you look at the characters in the Bible – all the characters have a hyperbolic quality. All the characters are close to life, but they are not life itself are they? They are written – they are not seen as real, full-fleshed, dimensional characters – they are really metaphorical characters. They are not three-dimensional characters like Shakespeare would write or something – or Dostoyevsky or whoever. They are streamlined in a certain way, I think, and you could also call it lobotomised. I think that's what we wanted to do. I don't know if that was a good idea, but that's what we had in mind – to portray these people as a little bit caught up in the parameters of their world. If you look at magazine covers – about 95 per cent are female – but they all look the same, don't they? They have all the same kind of beautiful breasts and lips. They are always a little bit naked, but not totally – so it's never shocking – but always promising a lot. And the males are all the same, although we always concentrate more on the women. So, basically, there's a prototype of looking fashionable or looking 'in'. That must have influence, because you are bombarded with these images. That makes everybody change their nose and chin here in some way.

C: Do you feel that you work differently with female as opposed to male actors at all? Are you aware of that?

V: Not really. Sometimes I like women or females more in general, you know. I am the kind of person who likes coffee with a woman, better than a beer with a man, you know. I'm sure there is a difference with the actors that I've liked better in my life. Especially in Holland, Rutger Hauer and even in America with Arnold [Schwarzenegger] and Michael Douglas – if you look at it on that level then perhaps there is not that much difference. I think I can project just as much warmth, and love perhaps, into my relationship with men as with women. Of course, with women actresses, there is an advantage – for me at least, there is always a sexual interest. I cannot take that away from myself – I am more a person who will stretch out his hand to a woman's shoulder than a man's shoulder. So I am sure I would approach women in a more direct, personal way, than I would a man. That's me. That's because I like women very much.

C: So there's always going to be that frisson?

V: Well I feel that I have a lot of freedom with women, more than with men, which might help a little bit. But on the other hand, I'm not Ingmar Bergman, who falls in love with all of his actresses and gets, really, the best performances out of them, you know. I mean, that has never been my style. I really have no idea if that expresses itself in the way they act or the way I direct them.

Notes

1. I have borrowed the phrase 'politics of return' from Ryan and Kellner 1988.
2. Ibid., p. 11.
3. 'Technophilia: Technology, Representation and the Feminine', in Jacobus *et al.* (eds) 1990, p. 169.
4. Carroll 1990, p. 33.
5. Creed 1993, p. 7.
6. Ibid., pp. 27–8.
7. Ibid., p. 23.
8. 'Her Body, Himself', in Clover 1992, p. 53.
9. Ibid., p. 51.
10. This is similar to Steve Neale's ideas concerning the offsetting of the erotic gaze upon the male body in action films by moments of extreme violence. See Neale 1983.
11. The narrative of *The Terminator* (dir. James Cameron, 1984) also resembles the 'slasher' films and it is possible to say that Sarah is a 'final girl'. However, Sarah is not presented in similarly problematic terms. She is continually represented as the

acceptable face of womanhood, particularly in her relationship with Kyle and in her state of pregnancy at the end of the film.

12. Brosnan 1979, p. 5.
13. Ibid., p. 6.
14. Ibid., p. 8.
15. Butler 1990, p. 111.
16. Silverman 1991, p. 113.
17. Ibid., p. 129.
18. Janey Place, 'Women in Film Noir', in Kaplan (ed.) 1980, p. 50.
19. Springer 1991, p. 320.
20. 'Hive Mind', in Kelly 1995, p. 16.
21. Silverman 1988, p. 75.
22. *Spectacular Bodies: Gender, Genre and the Action Cinema* (London/New York: Routledge, 1993), pp. 132–52.
23. Jones 1990, p. 30.
24. Benoit Mandelbrot was a mathematician who collaborated with IBM from the late 1950s onwards. He developed the famous 'Mandelbrot set' and also developed computer programs capable to displaying the fractal graphics created in the application of his geometric formula. These fractals became popularly familiar in the 1980s and 1990s, although they also resembled psychedelic art works of the 1960s and 1970s.
25. See interview on p. 135.
26. It is notable that moves have been made to remove the category of Physique from female bodybuilding competitions, in both Britain and America. In a brief interview with Alan Runacres (Director of Training with the Weightlifting and Bodybuilding Association [WABBA], 16th May 1999), he stated that this was because it encourages abuse of the body and a use of anabolic steroids. However, I note that the use of steroids is also rife among male contestants, which would seem to indicate that a double standard is in operation. At the time of writing this book, the female Physique category (in particular the heavyweight category) has not been removed from competitions, but has become far less popular with female contestants and is more frowned upon within bodybuilding circles.
27. In Jezewski 1984, pp. 55–73.
28. Ibid., p. 68.

6. ALIEN OTHERS: RACE AND THE SCIENCE FICTION FILM

Figure 6.1   Taking on the black mask in *Predator* (1987). 20th Century Fox / The Kobal Collection / Zade Rosenthal.

In science fiction ideas about human subjectivity and identity have traditionally been established in a comparison between self (human) and Other (non-human) characters. So, the alien, monster or robot of science fiction may provide an example of Otherness, against which a representation of 'proper' human subjectivity is established, interrogated and, on occasion, problematised. Images of Otherness in science fiction can be understood as a metaphor for forms of Otherness within society or between societies and in this way the genre can engage with the fears and anxiety surrounding a given society's Others. Preceding chapters have concentrated on the representation of gender and sexuality, but received notions of human subjectivity and identity are also bound up with issues surrounding race and ethnicity. Based upon classificatory models largely constructed in the nineteenth century, qualities and traits have often been assigned to particular races with the assumption that the race in question is homogenous and that individuals belonging to various racial groupings are the vessels of essential racial characteristics. So racial markers, as with the markers of sexuality, are frequently referred to as 'evidence' of an essentialised being that is separate and divided from other modes of being. However, divisions between self/Other have not always been based upon models of a clear cut opposition. For instance, as Robert J. C. Young points out:

> Racial difference in the nineteenth century was constructed not only according to a fundamental binary division between black and white but also through evolutionary social anthropology's historicised version

of the Chain of Being. Thus racialism operated both according to the same-Other model and through the 'computation of normalities' and 'degrees of deviance' from the white norm.[1]

Both of these classificatory models were imbued with value judgements which underpinned the attempt to naturalise various power structures: the dominance of one over another, even the right of one to define another. Since the rise of the civil rights movement and second-wave feminism in the 1960s, attempts have been made to challenge and disrupt the paradigms that have been used to support racial inequalities. The disruption has taken many forms but more recently the concept of hybridity has been used to draw attention to the falsity, both conceptually and literally, of traditional models involving precise division and essential difference.

One of the main academic areas to have explored and developed ideas surrounding hybridity is postcolonial theory. Like feminist theory, postcolonial studies has shifted from being dominated by a discourse of opposition to one that could be described in terms of negotiation; a kind of struggle from within as opposed to taking a stand from outside has emerged. In this sense the idea of the racial and cultural hybrid has been central to the growth of theories that aim to counteract concepts of purity and exclusivity as the necessary components in a claiming of selfhood.

Stuart Hall, in his article, 'New Ethnicities', succinctly outlines a change in the approach of political movements concerned with racial issues, from an earlier unifying stance to a greater acknowledgement of cultural differences among racial groupings. He states that:

> The term 'black' was coined as a way of referencing the common experience of racism and marginalisation in Britain and came to provide the organising category of a new politics of resistance, amongst groups and communities with, in fact, very different histories, traditions and ethnic identities.[2]

Hall goes on to note how various black activists, artists and cultural workers, in these early stages, fought against their marginalisation within society and also against the way in which they were represented/defined by a dominating white community. Activists therefore contested the 'stereotypical quality and the fetishised nature of images of blacks, by the counter-position of a "positive" black imagery'.[3] So, in these early days, the supposedly distinct opposition between white and black which had been used to underpin white supremacy, was co-opted and reversed.[4] Although Hall notes that this kind of strategy still exists, he describes a more recent move towards what he sees as 'a change from a struggle over the relations of representation to a politics of representation itself.'[5] He states that this shift has marked ' "the end of innocence", or the end of the innocent notion of the essential black subject'.[6]

This underlying transformation in approach has been influenced by post-structuralist theory and, in terms of postcolonial studies, the figure of the leading theorist, Homi K. Bhabha, stands at the centre of these debates. By drawing upon a mixture of Lacanian psychoanalysis and poststructuralist theory Bhabha expounds a model of hybridity as based upon 'a kind of "doubleness" in writing: a temporality or representation that moves *between* cultural and social processes' and calls this in-between interval, Third Space.[7] Bhabha goes on to say:

> It is significant that the productive capacities of this Third Space have a colonial or post-colonial provenance. For a willingness to descend into that alien territory – where I have led you – may reveal that the theoretical recognition of the split-space of enunciation may open the way to conceptualising an *inter*national culture, based not on the exoticism or multiculturalism of the diversity of cultures, but on the inscription and articulation of culture's *hybridity*. To that end we should remember that it is the 'inter' – the cutting edge of translation and negotiation, the *in-between*, the space of the *entre* that Derrida has opened up in writing itself – that carries the burden of meaning of culture . . . by exploring this hybridity, this 'Third Space', we may elude the politics of polarity and emerge as the others of our selves.[8]

So, in a practical sense, we can assume that Bhabha's notion of hybridity extends not only to the colonised, but also to the coloniser. For instance, if the racial Other is culturally hybrid, having taken on or negotiated with aspects of the coloniser's culture, then the traffic goes both ways – meaning that the coloniser, in a hegemonic appropriation of an-Other's culture, can also be understood as 'de-purified'.

Bearing in mind the body of work that I have referred to above and the enormous amount of academic focus upon the politics of representation, it is surprising that discussion of issues surrounding racial and cultural differences/resemblances in science fiction has remained marginal. While this is changing (recent studies have, for instance, paid some attention to the racial issues at the heart of the current crop of cyber-thrillers), the relative dearth of work in this area may simply reflect a lack of study, in terms of race, in connection with a whole range of science fiction images. Of course, this may be partly explained by the manifest concerns that science fiction films have exhibited. For instance, although some of the most iconic figures in the previously discussed, big-budget blockbuster films, were marked as foreign – usually in terms of extra-filmic associations via star persona (e.g. Schwarzenegger's

Austrian heritage, Van Damme's persona as the 'muscles from Brussels') – this has been conservatively drawn. As Richard Dyer points out, in his approach to the specificity of representations of racial and cultural 'whiteness':

> Attention is sometimes paid to 'white ethnicity' . . . but this always means an identity based on cultural origins such as British, Italian or Polish, or Catholic or Jewish, or Polish-American, Irish-American, Catholic-American and so on. These however are variations on white ethnicity . . . and the examination of them tends to lead away from a consideration of whiteness itself.[9]

So, for example, the hybrid/cyborg figures in films like *The Terminator* (dir. James Cameron, 1984) and *Universal Soldier* (dir. Roland Emmerich, 1992) are performed by white males and even though facets of their identity are 'uncertain', any exploration of racial aspects does not appear to move very far from a traditional concept of white, Western masculinity. Alternatively, racial issues have been frequently masked in science fiction. Where academics have tended to concentrate on the representation of characters and/or actors within the 'realist' genres, a classic convention within science fiction film involves a more or less covert coverage of racial and ethnic tensions. Therefore, in order to explore this somewhat overlooked area, the chapter will concentrate on how issues surrounding racial/ethnic identity and subjectivity are inscribed in science fiction films. In my view there is much that remains to be said about the genre's treatment of racial issues, but my forthcoming discussion and analysis will be largely confined to the representation of African-Americans or Afro-Caribbean-Americans and the figuration of the 'oriental' in science fiction films. In order to provide a cultural-historical backdrop to later discussions surrounding recent 'virtual reality' films, the following two sections will be split into sub-sections. The first begins by looking at the representation of black characters within the genre in American film and television of the 1960s and 1970s, pertinent film examples from the 1980s, before finally concentrating on films from the 1990s. The second is then similarly sub-divided, looking at the representation of the 'oriental' in American-produced films, leading to a discussion of the Orientalism apparent in recent 'virtual reality' films. The chapter then closes by taking a brief look at a recent cycle of European and/or American/European co-produced films, launched into a global market place in the 1990s.

REPRESENTATIONS OF 'BLACKNESS' IN SCIENCE FICTION OF THE 1960s AND 1970s

Since the early days of cinema, black characters (or 'blacked-up' characters) have been a regular feature in musicals and have also made a more limited appearance in horror films. Yet, even given the close relationship between these fantasy genres, science fiction has traditionally remained a remarkably white genre and it was rare to see a black character at all in films before the 1960s. However, marking a distinct shift from the usually all-white casts of 1950s science fiction films, the *Star Trek* television series (first aired on NBC in 1966) introduced audiences to the multi-racial crew on board a futuristic spaceship called the Enterprise, and an African-American woman (Nichelle Nichols) famously took up a central role as the communications officer, Lt Uhura. In parallel to the multi-racial, human crew of the Enterprise, *Star Trek* regularly featured encounters with alien beings from other worlds. Although many of the alien characters were initially played by white stuntmen/actors, as the series progressed racial and national lines were drawn in the casting of the aliens. Of course, it is too simplistic to assume that issues concerning race and ethnicity are necessarily more fully explored if central characters are replaced by actors of non-white descent, but this science fiction television series did provide employment opportunities for non-white actors on an unprecedented scale. Of course, the roles specifically offered to non-white performers usually required that they become all but unrecognisable behind heavy prosthetics and make-up or be represented as loyal supporters of the Federation. In other words, non-white performers were allowed human status within the narrative logic of the series if they were seen to conform to a dominant white ideology: they were allowed 'into the club' if they played by 'white rules'.

The *Star Trek* television series both engaged and disengaged with the burgeoning racial conflicts of 1960s America. Although the series acknowledged African-Americans in its casting, it also presented audiences with a kind of utopian future in which conflicts had been resolved and peaceful relations had been made possible under the 'melting-pot' governance of a liberal humanist government. On one level, the Enterprise's mission 'to explore strange new worlds; to seek out new life and new civilizations'[10] can certainly be read as an allegory enabling the series to engage with the international political manoeuvres of the period. On another level, engagement with internal racial conflicts was also neatly displaced onto conflicts between humans and alien beings from other worlds (read nations), in a kind of two-phase denial of contemporary America's domestic disputes.

Following the *Star Trek* television series and along with the emergence of the mainstream science fiction film in the late 1960s and early 1970s (as discussed in Chapters 3 and 4), the *Planet of the Apes* series of films (released in 1968, 1970, 1971, 1972, 1973)[11] also used allegory to explore racial conflict. However, in these films the location was Earth and oppositions and conflicts based upon race were not played out between terrestrial and extra-terrestrial beings, but via an inter-species war: apes (orang-utans/chimpanzees/gorillas) on one side and humans on the other. Even though the science fictional setting can be understood as another example of a safe space within which to investigate contemporary political and moral struggles, given the long history of racist discourse that likens the ape and monkey to peoples of African origin, it is hard to imagine that audiences at the time would really have missed the racial implications in these films.

Looking at the first film in the series, the narrative follows a group of human astronauts who are accidentally catapulted into a future world. *Planet of the Apes* (dir. Franklin J. Schaffner, 1968) initially sets up a binary opposition between ape and white human,[12] presenting the audience with a world in which orang-utans and chimpanzees rule over and enslave a more primitive human population. Simian superiority and dominance is marked in their power of speech, as offset against the mute human population of this future world. This binary balance is disrupted upon the arrival of the speaking astronauts and, in a racial reversal of the civil rights struggles of the period, the surviving white astronaut, Taylor (Charlton Heston), is forced to fight for freedom and recognition as an intelligent, thinking being. Significantly, it is a couple of chimpanzee characters (Cornelius and Zira) who befriend Taylor and who enable him to escape the wrath of the orang-utan leader Dr Zaius. In his detailed account of the series, Eric Greene reads these chimpanzees as the 'jewish apes' in this film[13] and I would suggest that they were therefore located in a kind of 'Chain of Being' in between black ape and white human. Cornelius and Zira are marked apart from the chimpanzee guards who also feature in the film. Much darker in complexion, it is the guards who blithely mete out punishment and who act as the enforcers of orang-utan law. In contrast, the orang-utans have blond hair, are paler in complexion than the chimpanzees, and dictate the law of the land. Complexion therefore dictates certain behavioural characteristics: the dark chimpanzees represent an extreme unthinking, animalistic violence and the pale orang-utans represent a cold and controlling rationality. The positioning of the 'jewish apes' sandwiches them in between these two extremes, between orang-utan and dark chimpanzees and also between ape and man. The paler chimpanzees' understanding, empathy and less violent approach to inter-species tension indicates that they are civilised and perhaps closer to a human ideal. However, in associating the 'properly human' subject with whiteness, white rule and white subjectivity is also critiqued in the film in the aligning of the white man with the ruthless and domineering orang-utans.

On the one hand, the species war that ensues in the film obviously draws upon racist myths and can be read as playing out the fears of white Americans concerning the civil rights movement and the violent, racial confrontations of the period. On the other hand, the films can be understood as working to expose the essentialist myths at the core of interracial antagonism and inequality. Unlike patently liberal films of the time that also approached race relations, like *Guess Who's Coming to Dinner* (dir. Stanley Kramer, 1967), the *Planet of the Apes* series does not present audiences with ready-made solutions to racial conflict. For example, by the end of the first film inter-species conflict is not resolved through peaceful understanding and a conclusion is only brought about upon the geographical separation of ape and man. Distinct from the *Star Trek* series of this period, the *Apes* series of films did not present audiences with a futuristic vision of a peaceful society in which harmony is restored or difference subsumed by an all-encompassing Federation. Instead, they presented audiences with a future/present world in which racial difference equalled inequality, violent discord, division and conflict.

THE AFRICAN AMERICAN ALIEN IN 1980S SCIENCE FICTION FILM

What I would call the 'conspicuous allegory' witnessed in the late 1960s and early 1970s *Apes* films was also adopted in a later cycle of films released in the mid to late 1980s. Mainstream films like *Enemy Mine* (dir. Wolfgang Peterson, 1985), *Predator* (dir. John McTiernan, 1987) and *Alien Nation* (dir. Graham Blaker, 1988) all presented thinly disguised explorations of race relations through the device of white human male coupled with alien. In both *Enemy Mine* and *Predator,* a heavily suited and facially disguised black male actor is coupled with a white male actor. In *Enemy Mine* the human male (played by Dennis Quaid) plays opposite a lizard-like alien (played by Louis Gossett Junior) and in *Predator* our white action hero (played by Arnold Schwarzenegger) is set off against the dreadlocked, eponymous alien (played by Kevin Peter Hall) featured in the film. Racialised oppositions were obviously indicated in the costuming and casting in these films. It is also interesting that the degree of threat posed by the black-alien figures is signalled in the respective height of the actors chosen to play these roles (Louis Gossett Junior is 6′ 4″ and Kevin Peter Hall is 7′ 2½″), making the white human male appear vulnerable by comparison.

Enemy Mine opens with human and alien in violent conflict, but then proceeds to focus upon a growing understanding and mutual affection between the human, Davidge, and alien 'drac'. Separated from their compatriots, the two are forced to form an uneasy alliance in order to survive the harsh environment of a distant planet on which they have crash landed. Violent tension between the couple is eased through interpersonal contact and education in each other's culture and beliefs. The narrative then takes a turn when the alien reveals that s/he is pregnant, at which point they take up their respective roles of contented mother-to-be and nervous, expectant father. Although this is played partly for humour, their differences become manifestly re-inscribed in sexual/gender terms, resulting in the feminisation of the alien. As Frantz Fanon's early work teaches us, the colonised subject has often been situated within sexualised discourses in which the Other is frequently feminised.[14] It would therefore be easy to see the feminisation of the alien at this point as reiterating, along sexualised lines, the power relations of a colonial discourse. However, the harmony reached in this gender re-balance is short-lived when the birth of the baby drac (called Zammis) brings about the death of the adult alien. Davidge, as sole parent of the alien off-spring, feeds and cares for the baby and effectively becomes both father and mother to the drac. This ambiguous gender role appears to parallel the uncertain sexual identity previously assigned to the adult drac. Once the infant drac reaches puberty,[15] further humans and dracs return to the planet to set up a mining colony. At this point, the dracs have become enslaved and ruled over by the humans, who force them into hard labour. Davidge realises that the mining colony presents a danger to both him and the drac and attempts to stay hidden, but Zammis yields to curiosity and travels to the mine. There Zammis witnesses the savage treatment that his fellow dracs are forced to undergo at the hands of the human slave masters and he is also captured and forced into slavery. The violent rift between human and alien is repaired when Davidge turns against his fellow human beings to rescue the child, eventually returning Zammis to the drac home planet and overseeing the drac's rites of passage into adult society.

This film is obviously calling for racial harmony and understanding, but the way in which it draws upon the sort of sexualised discourse, recognised by Fanon, in its dramatisation of race relations is especially interesting. It seems that in order to overcome the oppositional conflicts brought about by racial difference, the film requires that both human and drac take up an ambivalent role in terms of their gendered identities. So, tolerance and understanding becomes a feminine trait that each has to acquire. Having said this, it is notable that the adult drac's feminisation is essentialised, while the human's is articulated simply in terms of the role he undertakes as father/mother to the drac. Even though erosion of difference is offered up as a possible solution to racial conflict, the film therefore remains predicated upon an essential self/Other divide.

While *Predator* is structurally similar to *Enemy Mine*, it certainly does not present audiences with the same kind of liberal humanist message. Given *Predator*'s obvious references to the Vietnam film (i.e. many of the scenes appear to reference films like *Apocalypse Now* [dir. Francis Ford Coppola, 1979]), it is interesting that the alien is not marked as 'oriental' but as Afro-American/Black. The black character here is figured as the polar opposite to the white human, allowing for a direct and simplified mode of adversarial combat as the fight for supremacy begins. This is set up clearly at the beginning of the film when Dutch meets with his former friend, Dillon (Carl Weathers), and they greet each other with a ritualistic arm wrestle. Needless to say, the white hero, Dutch, emerges as victor over the black man, Dillon, who concedes defeat.

In *Predator*, apart from a female hostage and Dutch, the special forces team sent into the jungle to investigate strange disappearances are all killed off by an alien hunter. In order to survive, Dutch is therefore forced to learn about this enemy. However, unlike *Enemy Mine*, this process is not undertaken in order to reach peaceful settlement, but in order to gain strategic advantage. The alien initially has a strong tactical advantage because he wears a highly technological camouflage suit that makes him all but invisible. But, in the closing stages of their battle, Dutch realises that covering himself in black mud means that this also makes him invisible to his adversary. This is justified within the narrative as producing a cooling effect that does not allow for the alien's 'heat seekers' to detect Dutch, but, visually, it makes Dutch look black; thereby aligning him with this adversary. While the alien is obviously technologically superior the implication is that he is essentially more primitive as Dutch eventually proves his 'natural' superiority in defeating this predator.

I am not suggesting that this is the first time that this kind of conjunction has cropped up in film. Indeed, this is all highly reminiscent of the closing scenes in *Apocalypse Now* when the American captain (played by Martin Sheen) 'goes native' just prior to dispatching the renegade colonel (played by Marlon Brando). Of course, *Apocalypse Now,* in turn, pays homage to Joseph Conrad's novel, *Heart of Darkness* (first published 1902), in which the jungle native comes to stand for the 'primitive' side of white masculinity. However, in *Predator,* Dutch's return to this primitive state suggests that he becomes more fully and authentically human; his 'natural' strength and fighting prowess is thereby pitted against the 'unnatural', technologically enhanced skills, of his alien adversary. Dutch becomes a kind of 'noble savage', a figure that can be traced back to Jean-Jacques Rousseau's philosophical writings of the eighteenth century. Very briefly, even though Rousseau upheld that civilisation was necessary in providing a system of law that was moral and just to govern social existence, he also contended that man is essentially an uncivilised 'noble savage' when surrounded by a natural environment and living according to the rules of nature. The 'noble savage' was seized upon in later novels and stories and developed into a European myth. Colonised natives could then be understood as primitive but pure, as a more authentic version of humanity in a comparison with the civilised Westerner. The 'noble savage' is therefore simply a projection of a white fantasy written onto the body of a colonised people and the black man's 'primitive authenticity' is realised only as represented by the white man or seen through the white man's eyes. In classifying people according to the colour of their skin, there is also a sense in which the subject is reduced to a 'body'. As Victor Burgin has commented, ' "people of colour" are embodied people. To have no colour is to have no body'.[16] In other words, to be white suggests a disembodied positioning, which can be placed in opposition to the body of the native. Therefore, the black body can stand in for the displaced body of the white man. In *Predator* it seems that Dutch's 'return to the body', his return to a primitive and more authentically 'human' state upon his entrance into the jungle and upon his fight for survival against the alien, is marked by taking on the 'black mask' of the 'noble savage'.

As discussed in Chapter 4, blockbuster science fiction films of the 1980s were inclined towards setting up simplistic binary oppositions. In comparison, the relatively small numbers of American independent science fiction films made in the 1980s tended to articulate a more complex account of the social worlds they presented. For example, inhabiting that shady world of art house/cult/low-budget/auteur filmmaking, films like *The Brother from Another Planet* (director/writer/editor: John Sayles, 1984) and *Repo Man* (director/screenplay Alex Cox, 1984) can be more readily allied with films released in the early to mid-1970s in their representation and concern with the experience of alienation and estrangement in a decaying, urban environment. But, given the focus of this chapter, *The Brother from Another Planet* is of particular interest in its overt and ironic examination of racial difference. Here an extraterrestrial alien (played by Joe Morton) escapes from slavery and crash lands on Ellis Island (the official gateway for immigrants arriving in New York Harbour between 1892 and 1954). Although the film is loosely held together by a narrative involving the alien's escape from two white slave masters (played by John Sayles and David Strathairn), it is largely an assemblage of episodic encounters in which the alien's identity is continuously constructed, deconstructed and reconstructed.

After making his way over to New York City, our illegal alien wanders the streets of Harlem and is finally befriended by the African-American regulars in a local bar. At first they find his behaviour odd, but quickly embrace him as a brother (a fellow African-American): his three-toed difference from them remains hidden inside his shoes and his inability or unwillingness to speak allows these Harlem residents to self-project and welcome him into the fold. Eventually put to work fixing pinball machines, his fellow worker, a Puerto Rican called Hector (Jaime Tirelli), attempts to ascertain where the alien is from. Speaking to him in Spanish (notably subtitles are not provided), Hector asks him if he is from Puerto Rico and eventually assumes he comes from his own home town. So, Hector also projects his own racial/geographical origins onto the alien. 'Black', as a resistant and oppositional 'organising category' is ironically revisited and acted out in these two scenes, simultaneously highlighting and compounding resemblance and difference. However, the alien's muteness does not always result in unquestioned acceptance. For instance, it was earlier read as 'guilt' by a Korean shopkeeper, when the alien could not explain himself, and is understood as 'ignorance' by his white employer (played by Michael Mantell), whose own brand of glib essentialism allows him to stress an assumed superiority and difference from his employees. For these characters the alien is not accepted as a 'brother' and judgements about his character are made purely based upon skin colour.

A crucial moment occurs later in the film, as the alien travels back to his new-found home on the New York subway. As passengers get off at one particular stop, it is pointed out to him that only black people are left on the train, travelling to uptown New York, towards the Harlem ghetto. Given Morton's performance, this appears to be a bemusing but revelatory moment for the alien, as he is made aware of both the literal and metaphorical space he inhabits and the boundaries that dictate his existence. The scene in the train is quickly followed with the introduction of two white men who have accidentally wandered into Harlem. The men deduce that this is where they are because of the number of black people they see in the vicinity. Lost and uneasy, they end up in the same local bar that the alien first entered and now frequents. They try to strike up a conversation with him and appear to read his lack of speech as evidence of his contempt and their own outsider status in this environment. In contrast to the pinball shop owner, the men attempt to 'communicate with the alien' by stressing their supposed lack of racial prejudice and peaceful intent. One of them talks at length about his youthful adoration of a black baseball player, called Ernie Banks (who came to fame in the late 1950s and early 1960s). The man repeatedly states that when he was seven years old he wanted 'to be Ernie Banks' and then goes on to say that, at this time, he did not realise that Banks was black. So, as he later understands it, the inhibiting factor in his youthful dream of transcendence was not the impossibility of literally becoming or taking the place of another person, but the impossibility of a white man becoming a black man. Representing the white, liberal elite, their clumsy attempt to find some common ground with the alien actually results in further underlining how they have come to define themselves as essentially different in opposition to the men that inhabit this Harlem bar.

At the end of the film, 'brother' appears to make contact with other alien escapees and, in the closing moments, when he faces recapture by the slave masters, he is joined by a group of what could be taken to be African-Americans from the surrounding neighbourhood or fellow aliens or both. Faced with overwhelming odds, the slave masters give up the chase and simply vanish. On one level, as was seen in both *Enemy Mine* and *Predator,* a separation based upon racial difference is re-established at the end of this film. However, given the film's oscillation between science fiction fantasy and documentary style account of life in Harlem, this ending takes on an obviously ironic aspect. Fact and fantasy become both clearly separated and irrevocably intertwined here, and, overall, the film establishes the arbitrariness of what comes to stand for difference and the confusions that arise when difference is misunderstood as essential and secure.

It is interesting to compare the role of the alien 'brother' with a later role that Joe Morton undertook in *Terminator 2: Judgment Day* (dir. James Cameron, 1991): Dr Miles Dyson. Although Morton denies that there was any connection between the two films (see interview on pp. 208–12), aficionados of the genre are likely to be aware of his previous performance in *Brother* and may well read the Dyson role against his role in the earlier film. In some respects, his appearance in *Terminator 2* pays homage to *The Brother from Another Planet* and might even be seen as an attempt to indicate that Hollywood is now offering African-American actors roles outside of the confines of the traditional stereotypes associated with black characters; the kind of stereotypes that Morton states he has avidly avoided in his career as an actor. Certainly, it was unusual at this time to see a black character presented as a powerful and respected scientist. However, while I agree with Morton when he says that Dyson was 'central to the plot' in this film, I believe that the character also functions as a scapegoat. Morton's comments regarding Richard Pryor's joke about black characters in science fiction films (see interview on p. 210), are quite telling, since Dyson is indeed 'killed off' in *Terminator 2*. Also, according to the 'time-loop' narrative logic, the Terminator becomes Dyson's creation in this second film and the threat that cybernetic technologies raise is therefore placed at Dyson's feet. At the same time as Dyson's middle-class lifestyle and professional standing could be taken to indicate that race is no longer an issue in this society, Dyson is forced to sacrifice himself to save this society; in effect, he must 'bow out' in order to maintain a status quo.

Issues of Authenticity in the 1990s Virtual Reality Film

The home computer market expanded rapidly in the 1980s and the 1990s witnessed the further development and global proliferation of the internet. The novels of a science fiction sub-genre, collectively called cyberpunk, anticipated the reach of the internet and the kinds of virtual worlds, identities and communities that might arise as a result. Cyberpunk provided a populist language with which to articulate and conceive of the imaginary spaces created by computer and related technologies. In fact, many of the terms coined within this sub-genre were taken up by the cultures and discourses surrounding computer and internet technologies that came to prominence in the 1990s. For example, the word 'cyberspace', coined by the writer William Gibson in his novel *Neuromancer* (first published 1984), became the common term used to describe the virtual spaces of interaction between the individual and the computer, or groups of interconnected people communicating via the internet.

Exploring the complexities and shifts that a cyberspatialised world might bring, it was not only cyberpunk that acknowledged the impact that these imaginary, interactive spaces might have upon received notions of human subjectivity and identity. For example, Fredric Jameson famously outlined a newly formed sense of self within a postmodern culture that arises under the conditions of 'late capitalism'. For Jameson, computer and internet technologies are utterly sutured to an age of American militarism and economic domination and have come to represent the 'whole new decentred global network of the third stage of capital itself'.[17] So his description of the 'decentred' self that arises from the experience of postmodern living can be taken as critical of the technological shifts and changes of recent years.[18] However, Sherry Turkle points out that 'the internet has become a potent symbol and organisational tool for current grass-roots movements – of both left and right'[19] and she goes on to emphasise the transformative and therapeutic effects of life in cyberspace. For Turkle: 'Internet experiences help us to develop models of psychological well-being that are in a meaningful sense postmodern. They admit multiplicity and flexibility. They acknowledge the constructed nature of reality, self, and other.'[20]

Placing computer and internet technologies at the heart of her inquiries into a new sense of fragmented but extended postmodern self, Turkle stresses a kind of emancipation from confining, essentialist principles. Indeed, perhaps the global proliferation of computer and internet technologies makes more readily available a kind of literal version of that interruptive 'Third Space' that Bhabha proposes we should explore.

Certainly, the explosion in the domestic use of the internet in the 1990s meant that increasing numbers of people were in instant and regular contact with others: geographic borders were not an obstacle to communication and exchange of information. Along with this, further development in satellite and cable technologies offered delivery platforms for entertainment products across national and international borders. While the possibilities of diminishing state power and political instability had been a major issue with the arrival of global corporatisation in the 1980s, I would suggest that in the 1990s concerns revolved around increasing levels of cultural exchange and the fragmentation of traditional forms of subjectivity on a more interpersonal level. Although these technologies supported a specifically American global expansionism it became harder to 'police' and control flows of information. National borders appeared to be blurring and a sense of selfhood and identity once sutured to the nation was therefore understood as threatened. Under these conditions it became harder to formulate clear-cut divisions between self and Other. In other words, globalisation and the kinds of fragmentation that both Jameson and Turkle propose could be understood as destabilising to ideas of identity built upon essentialist notions of race and ethnic allegiances. However, the perceived weakening in the power of the nation-state as a unifying category also led to a renewed sense of importance for ethnic identity, resulting in what Jonathan Friedman identifies as 'a shift from assimilationism to multiculturalism'.[21] For example, these technologies supported the formation or re-formation of de-territorialised identities, whether these are identities based upon pre-existing diasporic communities or the emergence of new affiliations and cultural identities dislocated from geographical location. It is no surprise then that by the mid-1990s there was a flurry of American science fiction films concerned with the social implications of virtual reality/internet technologies. On one level these films engaged with technologies that had now become a familiar part of professional as well as domestic life across the world and, on another level, the depiction of a futuristic form of virtual reality provided the perfect plot device with which to explore issues surrounding identity and postmodern culture. The following section will look at how two films, released in the same year, *Virtuosity* (dir. Brett Leonard, 1995) and *Strange Days* (dir. Kathryn Bigelow, 1995), dealt with race/ethnicity and identity alongside the figuring of virtual fantasy worlds within the 'real' world of the film. Although both of these films feature virtual spaces into which characters immerse themselves, the narrative makes clear that these are localised spaces and that entrance into them is highly controlled. So, these two films are not ostensibly concerned with the kind of virtual spaces created by dispersed communications networks, but rather they concentrate on the individual's psychical interaction with a boundaried, alternative environment, even as those boundaries are crossed and interaction with a virtual world comes to have wider consequences.

In dealing firstly with *Virtuosity,* this film tells the tale of an ex-cop, Parker-Barnes (Denzel Washington) who has been convicted of murder and sentenced to a long and harrowing imprisonment. During the course of his custodial sentence, he is used by government authorities as a guinea pig in experiments with virtual reality, police training programmes. This involves his immersion into a virtual city environment predominantly populated by white-suited businessmen. Within this environment Parker becomes the adversary of a white male, serial killer called Sid 6.7 (Russell Crowe). Sid is a virtual character who has been programmed with the memories and traits of a number of real murderers in order to prove a most demanding and complex adversary. Like *The Brother from Another Planet* the film makes heavy references to the history of black slavery and the colonisation of America. Images of the slave trade are evoked as Parker is shackled, chained and paraded through the prison. The figuring of the serial killer (statistically 'serial killing' is a crime committed predominantly by white males), can be understood as a reference to the violence of the white male coloniser and slave trader. So, there is a sense in which Parker and Sid play out both past and present battles between black and white races within the game. The trouble really starts when Sid becomes fully embodied and escapes the confines of his virtual world. Parker is then offered a pardon if he takes up his law enforcement role once again and agrees to track down and curtail the killing spree that Sid has embarked upon in the real world. Underlining the fact that Parker is once more operating on the right/white side of the law, he becomes romantically associated with a white female, criminal psychologist (played by Kelly Lynch) who accompanies him on his quest. Sid kidnaps the psychologist's daughter and a replay of the abduction and murder of Parker's own wife and child gives Parker an additional and more personal reason for his pursuit. Eventually, Parker saves the day by returning Sid to his virtual world and rescuing the psychologist's daughter.

Throughout the film there are images which place Parker on one side of a literal divide while his adversaries take up their position on the other side. This is set up in the opening sequence, which the viewer later learns has taken place in the virtual world of the program. Towards the end of this sequence, Parker is seen pursuing Sid through an oriental-style restaurant sectioned off by thin paper walls (I will return to the relevance of the 'oriental' space in the following section). The walls allow for shadows to be seen, but they also obscure and confuse the identity of the people on either side. These flimsy divides are later broken down by flying bodies and gunshots until Parker faces Sid in the closing showdown in the game. Apart from being a portent of the violent collapse between fantasy and real worlds that occurs later in the film, these images serve to accentuate the impression of Parker as positioned on one side of a flimsy divide based upon race and legal standing. The false start in the film operates to thwart the expectations of the viewer. Having witnessed Parker in the hero role within the game, the audience then learns that he has been classified a criminal by the authorities. This abrupt disclosure, when the virtual reality world is shut down and Parker's consciousness returns to the diegetically real world, is notably echoed in his appearance. Within the virtual world he is seen wearing a policeman's uniform and has short hair, in marked contrast to his dreadlocks and unkempt appearance as the criminal guinea pig. Here, it becomes obvious that his criminalisation is associated with his ethnicity and racial origins: his dreadlocked appearance allies him with the Rastafarianism of Jamaicans and the references to slavery provide a historical backdrop to his own personal traumas at the hands of the white authorities.

A later scene within the 'real' world echoes the opening game sequence as Parker attempts to gain entrance to a television studio in which Sid has taken hostages. Although Parker is now working for the law enforcement agencies, the security guards assume he is a criminal and proceed to shoot at him along a corridor sectioned off by large portions of plate glass. Parker runs from the shots down one side of the glass partitioning while the guards shoot at him from the other. The glass is shattered but Parker manages to elude the bullets being fired at him. Again, he is shown to be on the wrong side of a divide, but the walls between him and his adversaries do not offer protection, they simply mark him apart. The implication being that the breaking down of various divides (most essentially those between black and white) is dangerous. Along with this, both the opening and closing sequences (those that take place within the virtual world) make it difficult to judge the content of the rest of the film by the codes normally associated with 'realism'. To a certain extent meaning is made ambiguous as fantasy and reality fold in on one another, but this is offset by the re-establishing of a clear opposition between Parker and Sid. Evidently, in conjunction with Sid's construction from a multitude of personalities, Parker is portrayed as more 'authentic' than his white adversary. If identity is fragmented and multiple in postmodern society then Sid is the simulated result of a post-modern cultural and political logic. In contrast, although Parker has a prosthetic arm, the relative simplicity of his split embodiment/identity can be read off against Sid's totally simulated and fragmented embodiment/identity (Sid is constructed from a mass of microscopic robots called 'nano-bots'). Sid therefore comes to represent the falsity and corruption of the dominant and pervasive white culture that surrounds Parker, while Parker comes to stand for a kind of human truth and authenticity.

The authentic/inauthentic opposition which is evident in *Virtuosity* is also noticeable in *Strange Days* (1995), only here our 'authentic' black character, Mace (Angela Bassett), is female. *Strange Days* presents us with a futuristic underworld dealing in the buying and selling of human experience. The experiences are both captured and replayed using 'Squid' technology, which consists of a headpiece (commonly hidden under a wig) that records the 'real-life' experiences of the wearer. The resulting footage is not only viewed as though through the eyes of the wearer, but the recipient is also treated to the feelings and emotions that the original wearer experiences. Most of the characters in the film are shown to use this technology, but Mace consistently refuses to engage with it (until this becomes absolutely necessary at the end of the film). In what appears to be an updated reworking of the seminal *Peeping Tom* (dir. Michael Powell, 1960),[22] Bigelow attempts an exhaustive critique of voyeuristic, cinematic practice while also suggesting that the development of more immersive technologies (e.g. virtual reality, interactive computer games etc.) may result in an excessive extension of these practices. Carol Clover, in her study of the modern horror genre, has referred to *Peeping Tom* as a horror 'metafilm' that 'has as its task to expose the psychodynamics of specularity and fear'.[23] Like *Peeping Tom*, Bigelow presents the audience with a very extreme version of diegetic voyeurism in which the act of voyeuristic viewing is linked with literal violence.

Although gender issues are obviously foregrounded in this film, the way in which these intersect with race is particularly interesting. Mace is intimately associated with the white male protagonist Lenny (Ralph Fiennes), who is an ex-cop and peddler/maker of recorded experiences (known as 'clips') using the Squid technology. He is a 'wheeler-dealer' who will lie, cheat and manipulate in his attempts to sell his wares. He has a particular patter and mode of self-presentation which he is seen to utilise in order to con his customers and extract favours from his friends. He is therefore marked as fraudulent and dissembling in his interaction with others, but this is also extended to the way in which he fools himself; particularly in his constant reliving of a past romance with the character of Faith (Juliette Lewis). He has self-recorded highlights from his past relationship with Faith and repeatedly plays back these scenes, effectively blocking his chances of 'moving on'. He is living in a perpetual present fed by his own recent past, which, in turn, becomes his present and conceivably his future; past, present and future conflating when he sees/feels the tapes. Like Fredric Jameson's schizophrenic, postmodern subject he is 'unable to focus on [his own] present, as though [he had] become . . . incapable of dealing with time and history'.[24] Although Faith has long since left him he has set her up as an idealised figure, frozen in time, who has become the site of his own transcendence.

In direct contrast to Lenny, Mace is presented as candid and earnest. She possesses a personal and political consciousness and is shown to have a serious interest in the well-being of others. Mace's sense of empathy can then be compared to the literal empathy experienced vicariously through the 'clips'. Indeed, Mace consistently espouses the harmful effects of indulging in Squid. For example, toward the end of the film, just after she has stumbled upon Lenny's recordings of Faith, she angrily tells him:

> This is your life – right here, right now. It's real time, time to get real – not playback – you understand me. She doesn't love you. Maybe she did once, I don't know, but she doesn't now. These are used emotions – it's time to trade them in. Memories were meant to fade Lenny – they're designed that way for a reason.

In trying to persuade him to face certain realities Mace is attempting to bring him out of his fantasy world to enable him to properly engage with his material existence. Lenny's use of the Squid technology allows him to escape his lived reality, he is resistant to the transformative potential of virtual reality; that is, until he becomes inadvertently involved in a cover up concerning the murder of Jeriko One (a 'black power'-rap artist and community spokesperson). The appropriately named Iris (Brigitte Bako) passes a 'clip' of Jeriko's murder by two white LAPD officers to Lenny. Iris, in turn, is murdered and a 'clip' of her death is also passed to Lenny. Lenny's 'transformation' appears to begin on viewing the 'Iris clip' and along with Mace's comments at this point he recognises how he has become complicit in a system of extreme exploitation. His reaction to the viewing of the 'Iris Clip' indicates his transformation: whereas, at the opening of the film, upon the viewing of a snuff clip, his response appeared minimal, here he reaches a state of panic and rushes to the scene of the murder in order to avert it. Forgetting that this event is in the past, by the time he arrives he sees her body being wheeled out by medics, which forces him into the present in the most dramatic of ways.

After Lenny has seen the 'Jeriko clip' he insists that Mace also see it. Having adamantly refused to use the Squid apparatus she asks him to tell her what is on the tape, to which he replies: 'I can't tell you – you gotta see it – it's that important'. It is as though he does not believe he has the right to tell this story (to mediate) and that she will not understand its impact unless she sees/feels it for herself. Lenny places the 'Squid-set' on her head and it is her viewing that is shown in the film. Unlike most of the previous Squid segments this is shown without intercut shots of the wearer's reactions and at the end of the clip it is Mace's response that takes precedence. So, Mace takes centre stage here and from this point on there is an overall shift of perspective within the film itself: Mace becomes a more centralised character along with becoming more proactive – the film follows her story. After the viewing she states that the clip 'is a lightning bolt from God'. Mace sees the tape as indisputable evidence of a racially motivated attack by the LAPD. Given the obvious reference to the 'Rodney King' video recording,[25] the irony is that her confidence in the justice system at this point may be viewed as hopelessly optimistic. Of course, Jeriko's killing in the film also recalls the killing of black leaders Martin Luther King and Malcolm X in the 1960s and, in a kind of replay of all these past events, the couple eventually place the clip in the hands of a trustworthy police official, and a kind of justice is enacted at the close of the film.

The setting up a diegetic distinction between virtual and real space opens up a potential for playing one off against the other in a variety of ways: foregrounding the interplay between fantasy and reality, blurring or reconfiguring the relationship between fantasy and reality and so on. However, while *Brother from Another Planet* made use of the codes and conventions of science fiction to complicate received notions of essential difference and racial divides, both *Strange Days* and *Virtuosity* simply map racial divides onto the divide between the virtual and the real. It would be easy to read the 'genuine' qualities that both Mace and Parker come to signify as examples of a positive representation of the African-American subject. Alternatively, these characters can be read as playing out a resistant political stance, opposed to the hegemonic incorporation of their being into the whitewash of the virtual worlds on offer. On a more cynical note I would say that in the context of these science fiction films their characterisations can be related to earlier representations in which the black body was utilised to connote the animalistic or the primitive. In this sense, they become updated versions of the 'noble savage' within these highly technologised societies. The black protagonists in these two films then act as a kind of reminder of what the white community appears to have lost or, perhaps, never had.

THE ASIAN AMERICAN AND THE 'ORIENTAL'

Visions of the 'oriental' in science fiction film can be traced back to the canonical works of George Méliès. Settings in Méliès' films are repeatedly constructed from an assortment of exotic images that evoke Middle and Far Eastern culture. In 'trick films' like *Illusions Funambulesques* (aka *Extraordinary Illusions*, 1903) and *Le Thaumaturge Chinois* (aka *Tchin-Chao: The Chinese Conjurer*, 1904) Méliès even casts himself as the inscrutable 'oriental' magician who conjures up and presents the illusions made possible by the wonders of cinematic technology. Of course, Méliès' association of the fantastical and magical with an exotic East can be seen as part of a long-standing Orientalist tradition. In his ground-breaking book, *Orientalism*, Edward W. Said identified the ways in which the Orient became both a European and American invention, represented in academic and literary fiction as 'a place of romance, exotic beings, haunting memories and landscapes, remarkable experiences'.[26] For Said, Orientalist discourse offered a way for Europe to come to terms with its 'cultural contestant(s)', and operated 'to define Europe (or the West) as its contrasting image, idea, personality, experience'.[27]

Méliès' inscrutable magician seemed to live on in later American science fiction cinema, reborn as 'Ming the Merciless' (played by white actor, Charles Middleton) in the *Flash Gordon* cinema serials (released from 1936 to 1940). Here our orientalised adversary exercised his superior technological wizardry in his battle with the Earth. Although Flash (Buster Crabbe), our athletic, all-American hero, always succeeded in his struggles, unlike the kind of 'noble savage' associated with the black characters, Ming was presented as a formidable and advanced, alien opponent. In the 1960s and 1970s the 'oriental' was again present in science fiction cinema, in the aesthetics and philosophies of the counter-culture, expressed either in terms of psychedelic imagery (discussed in Chapter 3) or in the thinly veiled references to East Asian culture (e.g. *Star Wars*' references to the mystical Chinese, Ch'i [Chinese]/Ki [Japanese], life force and the alien 'samurai master', Yoda). A more recent example can be found in *Blade Runner* (dir. Ridley Scott, 1982). Here marginalised 'oriental' characters are consistently seen to be the makers/producers of technologies surrounding the manufacture of the Replicants, even though it is a Western male who plays the part of the 'overlord/creator' in charge of the whole operation. Whereas Ming was clearly set up as an alien Other (e.g. he was evil and inhabited a separate geographical domain – the planet Mongo), in *Blade Runner* the 'oriental' Others, although ghettoised, occupy a proximate space and are relied upon by the white elite for their skills and intelligence. The 'oriental' therefore forms the underbelly of a commercial and technological culture in this futuristic city, which suggests that the threat to human authenticity that the Replicants represent is associated with an underlying Eastern menace. At the time of *Blade Runner*'s release certain Eastern economies were growing fast and countries like Japan and Korea were becoming known for their manufacture of computer components and other cutting-edge technologies. Over the course of the 1980s it became apparent that the so-called 'Tiger Economies' were outstripping Western economies, in terms of growth, and that they were fast moving from being the copiers/providers of Western led technology to becoming inventors/initiators of new technologies. Alongside this, Eastern financial intervention in American corporations was on the increase and particularly pertinent in terms of the film industry was Sony's later takeover of both Columbia Pictures in 1989 and, more recently, MGM in 2005. But this view does not, of course, account for traffic in the opposite direction, an example being the exploitation of various Asian markets for the American film product (Japan being one of the most lucrative expansions for American film producers at this time). Either way, *Blade Runner* engaged with an increasing American fear of orientalisation; a fear that American dominance was being undermined by a growing Asian economy and that American culture was being diluted or de-purified through increasing interaction and involvement with East Asian companies and markets.

Drawing upon Said's work, David Morley and Kevin Robins argue that the association of postmodern technologies with 'oriental' imagery can be understood as a continuation of an Orientalist practice in the West and they coin the useful term 'Techno-Orientalism' to describe this phenomenon. For Morley and Robins, this latest form of Orientalism serves as a disavowal mechanism that 'defers . . . the encounter with Western self-identity and self-interest'.[28] It is this kind of disavowal and deferral that *Blade Runner* appears to exhibit and that became acutely prominent in science fiction from the early to mid-1990s onwards. For example, even though the race relations explored in *Strange Days* and *Virtuosity* are ostensibly those between white and African/Afro-Caribbean Americans there are moments in both films when interactive technologies featured in the films are associated with the 'oriental'. As previously mentioned, in *Virtuosity* it is an orientalised space that Parker finds himself within in his opening, virtual battle with Sid. Also, in *Strange Days*, there is a sequence of scenes in which Lenny attempts to sell Clips to a visiting businessman, Mr Fumitsu (Jim Ishida). However, it is revealed that the businessman already possesses the latest model of 'player', putting him at the cutting edge of this technology. The two Japanese corporations Nintendo and Sega had dominated the video/computer game market since the 1980s, but the mid-1990s saw the beginnings of a much publicised 'console war', when Sony entered the market with the PlayStation in 1994. Although the virtual play spaces created by video/computer games are but one form of cyberspatial interaction, the games themselves have presented the strongest challenge to the dominance of feature films as the most privileged form of commercial entertainment. Commercial links between games and films have increased substantially and video/computer game versions of films now frequently outrank the films in terms of returnable profits. So, the names Sony, Nintendo and Sega have become indelibly associated with the virtual spaces created by the games. Obvious allusions to existing games apparatus can therefore be taken as a reference to these Japanese corporations, in what would appear to be an ongoing disavowal in which the decentring of a formerly centred subject is blamed upon the intrusion of oriental technologies in these films.

As if to confirm increasing links between games and film industry, film versions of existing computer games were released in the mid-1990s. *Mortal Kombat* (dir. Paul Anderson, 1995) and *Streetfighter* (dir. Steven E. de Souza, 1994) presented the audience with markedly exotic spaces; spaces that could be read as corresponding to the magical worlds of cyberspace in which the games are played. In a manoeuvre that can be traced back to Méliès, the wonders and excesses made possible by new technologies are associated with the 'oriental' and cyberspace becomes an exotic state where the 'tourist' can be freed from Western rationalism and taste the 'mystical essence' of the East. Taking *Mortal Kombat* as a prime example, although the film is based upon the popular computer game, it also heavily references *Enter the Dragon* (dir. Robert Clouse, 1973) and, indeed, features an Asian-American hero who is pitted against an evil oriental overlord. Cyberspace is then likened to the mystical island in *Enter the Dragon* that operated as a meeting place and place of combat for various national emissaries. The central characters in *Mortal Kombat* have all been lifted from the 'Mortal Kombat' game and each clearly represents a racial stereotype. According to the logic of the game, any one of these stereotypical characters could end up facing the evil overlord Shang Tsung (played by the Japanese American, Cary-Hiroyuki Tagawa) in the final 'showdown', making it especially relevant that Liu Kang (played by the Chinese American, Robin Shou) is chosen for this dubious honour in the film. While the casting might suggest a happy acknowledgement of the debt owed to East Asian culture by this film (more specifically, Hong Kong action films and Japanese martial arts video/computer games) and may also work to signal the film's transnational status, it is well to pay attention to the way in which Liu Kang is represented. For example, there is a notable split set up between good (Chinese) and bad (Japanese) Asian characters in this film, which is then conflated by the suggestion that Tsung actually represents an aspect of Kang's character: Kang is specifically told that he has to face three challenges in fighting Tsung: he has to face his enemy, face himself and face his worst fear. Also, during their final fight scene, Tsung even becomes Kang's murdered brother and Kang is only able to set the spirit of his brother free once he has dispatched Tsung. Of course, the battle between Tsung and Kang avoids the depiction of direct confrontation between the all-American Johnny Cage (Linden Ashby), and the Japanese representative, Tsung, in the film. Instead, the fight becomes a kind of sado-masochistic ritual in which our Asian American hero is forced to dismiss a part of himself in order to uphold American justice and dispatch an oriental threat.

It is revealing to compare the final 'showdown' in *Mortal Kombat* with a similar 'showdown' in the low-budget, 'direct to video', science fiction film released the following year. Called *Virtual Combat* in the US and *Grid Runners* in Britain (dir. Andrew Stevens, 1996), the titles obviously allude to the earlier *Blade Runner* and *Mortal Kombat*. However, unlike these mainstream forerunners, *Virtual Combat* initially separates futuristic, immersive game space from diegetically real world. Like *Virtuosity, Virtual Combat* then becomes a film *about* game play and *about* the racial identities caught up in the interplay between these two worlds.

Virtual Combat is set in a near-future America in which various cities and states are sectioned into geographically policed areas called Grids. Surveillance and control is centrally guided from a computerised policing station and the boundaries between each urban Grid and between the real and virtual world are patrolled by the Runners. These Runners are like border guards and it is their job to make sure that no one crosses between urban grids without permission or between the virtual and real world without payment. The narrative is set in motion by the illegal crossing of these boundaries and follows the exploits of the Runner, David Quarry (played by the ex-world champion Kick Boxer, Don 'The Dragon' Wilson). In exploiting elements associated with the earlier *Blade Runner, Virtual Combat* effectively refocalises the former film and offers us an Asian-American perspective. Our hero's ordeals begin when, in a similar way to *Virtuosity*, scientists develop a process called 'cyberplasm', which allows for the replication and material embodiment of virtual characters. A powerful white businessman (played by Ron Barker) plans to use the cyberplasm technology in order to enslave the female replicants of a 'cybersex' program and to sell their bodies for sexual services. He is thwarted when a dangerous martial arts game character, Dante (played by the Canadian martial artist Michael Bernardo), also escapes into the real world. Initially Quarry takes his orders directly from the policing force that employs him, but the murder of his white partner (played by Ken McLeod) by Dante, justifies Quarry's divorcement from the police authorities as he takes up the quest to avenge this killing.

The film opens with martial arts fighting scenes in which Quarry faces a number of opponents. In a now familiar device, it is not until Quarry requests a move to another 'level' that the viewer is alerted to the fact that this is a virtual game environment (indicated by the instant change of scenic backdrop). Having successfully fought off several opponents, Quarry faces Dante in the final level of the game. Distinct from previous opponents, Dante is able to predict Quarry's fighting tactics and communicates telepathically with Quarry throughout their battle (indicated by voice-over while the camera fixes on Dante's unmoving mouth). The use of voice-over here could certainly imply that Dante is a manifestation of Quarry's imagination and it becomes apparent that there is an intimate connection between these two characters. At one point Dante communicates: 'You can't kill me, it would be like killing a part of yourself', further indicating that he represents an aspect of Quarry's own character. If Dante represents a connection to Quarry's East Asian heritage (a connection that may have become repressed due to his involvement with a dominant white American culture and underlined by his positioning as an agent of the American law machine) then it is interesting that this is embodied by a character of more Western appearance. If Quarry is meant to represent a fully 'consenting' American, it is also telling that this manifestation of his own, personal Other be projected upon one of Western appearance. Alternatively, Dante might be taken to signify an American-made stereotype; a projection of how Quarry understands he is seen within this American world; an image that Quarry has perhaps internalised and is forced to face. Needless to say, there are several possible readings available, but these moments serve to draw attention to Quarry's hybrid characterisation.

The final 'showdown' between Dante and Quarry takes place in the diegetically real world of the film, although divides between real and virtual worlds begin to blur prior to their battle. The blurring is signalled by the introduction of a postcard picture of the 'Japan Town' Grid, which is telepathically transmitted to Dante by way of an invitation to combat, suggesting that Japan Town is less a real place than an imaginary construction. Quarry finally dispatches Dante at the headquarters of the American owned Burtech Industries that created the cyberplasm process. However, it remains unclear as to exactly how we should understand this finale. Perhaps the casting indicates that Quarry exercised his claim as an authentic Asian martial artist set up in opposition to an inauthentic copy? Alternatively, as an Asian American, has he exorcised the fantasy image of the 'oriental' that American culture has forced upon him? At the very least, I would say that *Virtual Combat* uncovers some of the complexities that *Mortal Kombat* attempts to gloss over.

Since the mid-1990s the more decentralised image of the fighting body that the martial artist provides has been avidly taken up to connote a flexible mode of being in an age of information technologies. In fact, the use of martial arts in science fiction films has become a persistent signifier of the interaction between human and computer technologies. The increased inclusion and centrality given to Asian Americans and, on occasion, guest stars borrowed from Hong Kong action cinema, in the casting of science fiction films, can be taken as a way of addressing overseas Asian markets as well as Asian American and fan markets within the USA. In addition, an increasingly globalised marketplace for commercial films and related products has certainly encouraged the use of the martial artist as an expedient and familiar national stereotype associated particularly with a Japanese entertainment product.[29] However, the consistency of the coupling of the 'oriental' with cyberspace still indicates a degree of disavowal and anxiety, which is repeatedly played out in terms of the position assigned the Asian American in many American science fiction films. What is noticeable in a further comparison between *Virtuosity* and *Virtual Combat* is that the simplistic black/white – real/virtual divide that is dominant in the former film becomes far less certain upon the introduction of the central Asian American character in the latter film.

In looking back at how 'oriental' characters have been depicted in Hollywood films, it is possible to trace conflicting and paradoxical characterisations; the two most prevalent stereotypes being the oriental as ruthless, fighting machine and the oriental as wise and spiritual. In recent years, especially in terms of the science fiction film genre, I would suggest that the 'oriental' has been figured as inherently dualistic; a conflation that serves to displace the kind of hybrid consciousness that may arise in the formation of a global aesthetic in science fiction onto an 'innately' paradoxical Orient/oriental. This is currently played out in two different ways. For instance, in *The One* (dir. James Wong, 2001) the Asian-American protagonist, Gabe Law (Jet Lee), literally faces himself when an alternative Gabe Lawless (also played by Jet Lee), from a parallel world, pursues and attempts to dispatch our hero. Thus follows a series of spectacular martial arts scenes in which Gabe is literally seen to fight himself. Certainly there is a playful conceit present here in the suggestion that Lee is so proficient in the martial arts that no one else could hope to match his skill: he is 'the one' of the title. However, once again, the 'good Gabe' is discernable in his role as an American security officer. In what has become an almost hysterical and therefore unconvincing trope, the 'good oriental' is seen to use his 'special powers' in the service of an American law machine. However, the threat that the 'oriental' represents is palpable and a perceived duality remains in the persona of Lee as both 'bad' and 'good' oriental.

A racially particularised duality can also found in the figuring of Neo in *The Matrix* series of films (dir. Larry and Andy Wachowski, 1999, 2003). Drawing heavily upon cyberpunk,[30] these films appear more concerned with internet communications and the mediated interactions between a variety of individuals (as opposed to the more localised gaming scenarios discussed above), which is echoed in the sheer number of central protagonists and the multi-racial casting. In these films the protagonists are all represented as adept martial artists, but it is Neo (Keanu Reeves) who is figured as the ideal mediator between the diegetically real and virtual worlds of the film and between the human and machine. Once more, a real/virtual opposition is mapped onto a black/white racial divide. The real world is largely marked out as an African or Afro-Caribbean American space, while the unreal world is governed by a band of 'special agents' who take on white male personas.[31] It is Neo who stands as the sole saviour in between these two states of being. Much has been made of the fact that Reeves was born of a British mother and Chinese-Hawaiian father in media reporting, which is undoubtedly drawn upon to underpin this characterisation. *The Matrix* films therefore deploy the Reeves persona to suggest a literal and essentialised embodiment of an 'in between' mode of being. On one level, Reeves' mixed heritage appears to literally place him in a 'chain of being' between black and white poles and on another level his interaction with technology, his cyborgian hybridity, is sutured to his known racial hybridity. As neither clearly oriental or occidental (or as *both* oriental and occidental) his uncertain 'in between' status allows him unusual access to both the real and virtual worlds at the same time as it threatens the binary balance that separates these worlds.[32]

In the final film of the series, there is an interesting scene in which Neo has to undergo a kind of rite of passage in order to access information and advice in dealing with his predicament. This involves an extended martial arts fight sequence with Seraph (Collin Chou),[33] in which Neo/Reeves' suitability and martial arts skills are tested prior to his audience with the Oracle (Mary Alice). This sequence functions to emphasise Neo/Reeves' 'oriental side'; not only does it echo the many scenes I have discussed above, but it also signals his acceptance by a character who clearly represents an idealised image of the 'oriental' martial artist. What I find interesting and rather telling are the later sequences in this final film, in which both Seraph and Neo separately face the agents. Seraph attempts to escape from the agents in an effort to protect an Indian child, called Sati (played by Tanveer K. Atwal). The child is known to be the artificial offspring of two AIs (Artificial Intelligences) in the film, and has emigrated from the world of the machines to the world created by the Matrix. What is significant is that while Seraph's encounter ends rather abruptly (he is not seen to deploy his martial arts skills), Neo's later fight with the multiple Agent Smiths is fought through to the bitter end. Neo takes up the battle where Seraph left off and the audience is treated to a long and spectacular fighting sequence in which Neo emerges victorious. Here the hybrid character of Neo/Reeves becomes a necessary and superior element in retaining the balance of power between these two worlds. Having said that, even though *The Matrix* films borrow heavily from cyberpunk, the written genre's embrace of human/machine interaction is ultimately disqualified in the film: in order for the human race to survive, Neo is required to sacrifice himself and the human/machine divide is once more set in place. Therefore, even as Neo's cyborgian and racialised hybridity qualifies him as the perfect ambassador, he is finally forced to relinquish his in-between status. Hybridity is finally denied as a viable position in this film, as survival requires separation and sacrifice. So, at least in terms of the film's narrative, rather than presenting us with a new world order which recognises and celebrates an ongoing hybridity on all sorts of levels, the 'blurrings' of the postcolonial, postmodern world are presented as a glitch in the program which needs to be overcome in order to return to a period of stability and parallel co-existence. Although the ending of the first film of the series suggested that Neo continued to exist in that interzone between two worlds, the challenge that the Reeves persona might offer to an ideal of what constitutes American subjectivity is recouped in his final sacrifice.

The 'Oriental' in the Euro-American Science Fiction Film

Relatively large, multi-racial, central casts became a feature of American-made virtual reality films from about the mid-1990s onwards. These films were obviously intended for a global marketplace, which their casting affirmed. Recalling the multi-racial cast of the *Star Trek* television series and films, whether this recent shift indicates that a variety of viewpoints are on offer in these films, or whether it simply indicates the assimilation of the Other by a liberal, democratising (Western) power depends largely on the way in which the narrative orders these characterisations. For instance, in the *Star Trek* films there is a chain of command that informs the functioning of the characters on board the Enterprise, as well as within the narrative. The multi-racial cast is therefore captained by our all-American, white hero, James T. Kirk (William Shatner), later replaced Jean-Luc Picard (played by the British actor, Patrick Stewart), and the inference is that it is a masculinist Western ideology that oversees and guides this futuristic world order. Conversely, power, in terms of leadership, becomes more dispersed in *The Matrix* films. In some respects the first film of the series is closer to the *Star Trek* model, albeit in inverted form, in that the African-American Morpheus is the leader of the rebels on board their craft, the Nebuchadnezzar, even though he places his faith for the future in Neo. But, as the series progresses, the audience is presented with a multitude of leaders, each arguing their position and viewpoint in their fight for survival against the agents. No one seems to have a complete picture of events, including Neo, who, until the very end, does not fully understand his role as their sole saviour. This kind of dispersal of power can be accounted for in terms of the excessive spin-off marketing associated with the two sequels: the inclusion of separate, 'teaser' storylines and featuring of parallel battle scenarios under different leaderships works to introduce the various games and spin-off storylines that were marketed heavily alongside the films. But, whatever the underlying economics behind the narrative structuring, the two sequels are closer in form to the kind of dispersal of agency and power evidenced in many cyberpunk novels. In Gibson's *Neuromancer,* for instance, the 'console cowboy', Case, consistently struggles to gain an overview of the situation he finds himself within and is guided by a profusion of seemingly unrelated characters (both human and artificial). In Pat Cadigan's cyberpunk novel, *Synners* (1991), we get an even clearer example, with a large ensemble cast of characters, operating from various locations, chiefly linked via their involvement with futuristic internet communication.

Even as there may be frequent efforts to contain the plurality of viewpoints that an ensemble cast might offer, this format nevertheless provides a perfect vehicle for transnational production and marketing. I am not suggesting that transnational production practices are new to cinema. As Andrew Higson points out:

> The film business has long operated on a regional, national and trans-national basis. . . . Since at least the 1920s, films have been made as co-productions, bringing together resources and experience from different nation-states. For even longer, film-makers have been itinerant, moving from one production base to another.[34]

What I am instead suggesting is that co-productions, multi-national casting and, in particular, narratives that allow for a relatively large central cast became exceptionally prevalent in the 1990s science fiction blockbuster. One only needs to take a brief look at the listings available on the popular website of IMDb (Internet Movie Database) to view the array of science fiction, blockbuster co-productions that were made from the early 1990s through to the present day. Although this database locates country of origin based upon the national affilia-tion of a particular production company (it follows the money rather than the artistic talent and even the primary shooting location), the rise in the number of science fiction co-productions during this period suggests that companies from outside of Hollywood were prepared to sink their money into the genre. Examples include: *Terminator 2: Judgment Day* (dir. James Cameron, 1991, France/USA), *Until the End of the World* (dir. Wim Wenders, 1991, Germany/France/Australia), *The Lawnmower Man* (dir. Brett Leonard, 1992, UK/USA/Japan), *Stargate* (dir. Roland Emmerich, 1994, France/USA), *Event Horizon* (dir. Paul W. S. Anderson, 1997, UK/USA), *Lost in Space* (dir. Stephen Hopkins, 1998, USA/UK) and so on. In addition, the late 1990s and early 2000s have also seen the proliferation of a number of multi-national, science fiction film co-productions: *Virus* (dir. John Bruno, 1999, France/UK/Germany/USA/Japan), *Alien Vs Predator* (dir. Paul W. S. Anderson, 2004, USA/Canada/Germany/Czech Republic/UK), and so on. The intended global appeal of many of the blockbuster films listed above is signalled in the casting: many of these films featured an ensemble cast of performers who hailed from a variety of nations and were well known on a local, national and, sometimes, international level.

As outlined in Chapter 4, the 1980s had seen science fiction lead the way as Hollywood's number one global film genre, set against the 'heritage films' of Britain or the French thrillers of the period. This shifted in the 1990s, as other national cinemas, particularly in Europe, began to re-engage with the genre. The co-production route offered one way in which national cinemas, outside of America, could enter the science fiction film arena and, as evidenced in the list above, this was certainly a route repeatedly taken up by French, British and German production companies. Although it would be hard to detect a specifically French influence in a film like *Terminator 2*, there were co-productions that could be argued as manifesting a European influence. *Stargate* provides an interesting example. As a French/USA, English-language, co-production, this film sports a multi-national cast: surrounding the two American stars, Kurt Russell and James Spader, are a central cast including the Swedish-born Viveca Lindfors, the Israeli actor Mili Avital and, fresh from the British film *The Crying Game* (dir. Neil Jordan, 1992), Jaye Davidson (born in California and relocated to Britain at two years old). The Orientalism, which was so much a feature of American 'virtual reality' films of the period, was also very much present in *Stargate*. But, whereas the American science fiction films more usually exhibited a vague and stereotypical notion of Japanese or Chinese culture, the Orientalism in *Stargate* is unmistakably associated with Middle Eastern culture. The film opens with an archaeological dig in Egypt, in 1928, where an ancient artefact (the 'stargate') is unearthed, before shifting location to a secret military installation in present day Colorado. Scientists deduce that the 'stargate' is a highly advanced alien device and a small division from the American Air Force, accompanied by one intrepid American Egyptologist, soon find they have been transported across the universe to a desert planet, peopled by direct descendants of ancient Egyptians. This division is led by Colonel Jack O'Neil (Kurt Russell), whose young son has recently died in a shooting accident. Blaming himself, the Colonel has sunk into a deep depression and, having become alienated from the world, is about to commit suicide before being called up for duty once again. Interestingly, the American Egyptologist, Daniel Jackson (James Spader), has also reached a low point in his life; discredited by the academic world, he is broke and alone before being coerced into taking part in the mission. Also, like so many of the 1990s films, *Stargate* features an 'in between' character, an alien who has taken on the body of an Egyptian boy and who the primitive locals fearfully worship as the sun-god Ra. This character is played by Davidson and, drawing upon his famous performance as the transvestite in *The Crying Game* as well as his known racial heritage (Davidson's father was Ghanaian and his mother was English), Ra's inherent duality is echoed in his sexually ambivalent appearance and behaviour. Recalling the Lucas/Spielberg action-adventure *Indiana Jones* series (1981, 1984, 1989), Emmerich makes use of Spielbergian establishing subtitles and editing style at the opening of the film. So, *Stargate* is formally designed to evoke a well-known American formula. In addition, America's eventual liberation of these Egyptian descendants from the alien/Ra can definitely be read in the light of the 1991 'Desert Storm' battles and the Gulf War. However, as set against contemporary, 'virtual reality' films of the 1990s, the substitution of the Far East for the Middle East in the location of the mystical oriental may also be taken to relate to a specifically European Orientalist tradition.[35]

Until the End of the World provides a rather different example from *Stargate*. This film was produced without the involvement of an American production company and draws upon the traditions of European art-house cinema. Although the film can certainly be viewed as an example of 'second cinema', as an alternative to the Hollywood mainstream, the casting of the American actor, William Hurt, in one of the central roles also indicates a desire to reach a wide audience. Along with Hurt, the cast includes a number of internationally known French and German actors, as well as less well-known Australian actors. Situating the film within director, Wim Wenders' oeuvre, and putting to one side Australian involvement, Dimitris Eleftheriotis reads *Until the End of World* as attempting to provide a particularly European perspective in film: 'a balanced combination between anxious European soul-searching and a reaffirming demonstration of global sensitivity'.[36] Certainly, I would agree that the film does seek to present an alternative perspective from the discernible American/Americanised viewpoint in science fiction. Indeed, viewpoint is of uppermost concern in this film as the narrative centres around the Hurt character (Sam Farber, alias Trevor McPhee) and his efforts to collect a visual family record with a device designed to allow his blind mother to see through his eyes. The device that he uses resembles the Squid technology in the later *Strange Days,* recording the reactions of the wearer (as one character describes it: 'the experience of seeing') as well as the visual images he sees. The information is then translated by a computer and directly imputed into the receiver's brain and projected onto the visual cortex. Sam's family is dispersed around the world, which provides the justification for a quest that takes him across several continents in pursuit of these personalised recordings, before returning to his parents who have settled in the rocky, desert terrain of the Australian outback. At the same time, Sam is also relentlessly trailed by a multi-national cast of characters, including a bounty hunter (played by Ernie Dingo), a young female drifter called Claire (played by Solveig Dommartin), Claire's ex-lover, Eugene (played by Sam Neill), and a private detective (played by Rüdiger Vogler). Sam continually deceives his pursuers in an attempt to escape their grasp and continue on his journey. Each of his pursuers has a different viewpoint on Sam's true identity and during the first half of the film it is Sam/Hurt who becomes the enigma that fascinates and frustrates those who try to track him down. Even as Sam's true identity emerges, he remains elusive. For example, if the point of view shot is taken as an indicator of subjective perspective then it is notable that Sam's point of view shots are usually distorted and mediated by the recording technology he uses, and that he proves deficient in his ability to re-envision the subjective data that he has so avidly collected. The inference here is that Sam is incapable of a clear subjective perspective because his subject-hood has become fragmented and uncertain. Underpinned by the oedipal scenario played out in Sam's devotion to his mother and the difficult relationship with his father, he could well be taken as the embodiment of an immature American addiction to the image and image technologies. This addiction is then passed on to Claire, as, upon the death of Sam's mother, the couple sink into a narcissistic and alienated state, feeding upon recorded images of their own dreams.

In its travels across Russia, Siberia, China, Japan, America and various parts of Europe, the film avoids the representation of Arab nations: the Aboriginal desert therefore takes the place of an Arabian desert as an image that evokes both an apocalyptic erasure of Western rationalism and control and a hope for new beginnings. Indeed, once the characters have reached the desert, the long-awaited apocalypse results in the elimination of the global network of computer-generated, image technologies. The orientalised desert then becomes a place of healing and renewal for these Western travellers.

My final example is not a co-production, but the French-produced, English-language film, *The Fifth Element* (dir. Luc Besson, 1997). French cinema has a long history of 'dialogue' with its American competitor, popular Hollywood cinema; a dialogue that became especially noticeable with the conscious reworkings of American themes in the French New Wave of late 1950s and early 1960s and the coming of the New New Wave, as exemplified in the so-called 'cinéma du look' in the 1980s. Distinct from other European cinemas, where national film industries have remained relatively small, or have become very much eroded in the face of Hollywood competition, French cinema has managed to retain a respectable portion of the home market. Partly due to quota systems, government subsidies and staunch protectionist policies, the French cinema industry continues to thrive and is also in the position of being able to support occasional blockbuster productions that have entered into the global arena. While the early 1990s saw the French-produced, science fiction fantasies, *Delicatessen* (dir. Jean-Pierre Jeunet, 1991) and *Les Visiteurs* (dir. Jean-Marie Poiré, 1993) achieve notoriety on a global scale, in turning to the use of the English language and in the casting of the American star Bruce Willis, *Fifth Element* was obviously intended as a French produced rival to the Hollywood science fiction blockbuster.

Like *Stargate*, *The Fifth Element* reproduces a familiar Hollywood format and offers a blockbuster display of spectacular special effects and fast moving, action-adventure. Also, following in *Stargate*'s footsteps, the film establishes a literally alien and mystical Middle East in its opening scenes. After a brief shot of a spacecraft entering the frame, the film cuts to the opening scene set in Egypt in 1914, in which an archaeologist is endeavouring to unlock the secrets of an ancient pyramid. An Egyptian priest becomes nervous as the archaeologist successfully translates the hieroglyphs on its walls. At this point, our friendly aliens revisit the pyramid, which turns out to be their hiding-place for a weapon designed to combat evil alien forces. The weapon is powered by four stones, representing the elements of earth, fire, air and water, and a fifth element is contained within a sarcophagus (later revealed to be a humanoid female called Leeloo). The Egyptian priest is in league with the aliens and is charged with passing the secret knowledge about the weapon and Earth's impending invasion to the next generation within this religious order.

Following this opening scene the film cuts to a futuristic New York in the year 2214. The narrative then revolves around the appearance of the prophesied evil force and follows the escapades of our rugged American hero, Korben Dallas (Willis) in his attempts to save the world. In addition, the design of the vertigo-inducing, multi-layered cityscape makes specific reference to the urban science fiction films that dominated the Hollywood genre in the 1980s and 1990s. However, in contrast to the dark and dystopic urban settings of films like *Blade Runner* (dir. Ridley Scott, 1982) and *The Terminator* (dir. James Cameron, 1984), the city in *Fifth Element* provides a stimulating, bright, colourful and multi-cultural environment against which the action unfolds. Influenced by French comic books (bande dessinée) and the adult science fiction comics created by the French artist, Jean Giraud (under the alias Moebius), *Fifth Element* recalls the Franco-Italian production, *Barbarella* (dir. Roger Vadim, 1967) and reclaims the comic-book style so heavily associated with Hollywood science fiction since the late 1970s and early 1980s.[37] The eclectic excess of *Fifth Element's* colourful design is also intrinsic in Jean-Paul Gaultier's immoderate costumes for the film and is mirrored in the overtly theatrical and highly mannered performances given by the cast of characters that surround Dallas. Richard F. Kuisel suggests that 'the evolution of the French cinema has been toward a kind of hybridisation that blurs, without entirely obliterating, a "national" style'.[38] *Fifth Element* therefore confronts Hollywood on its own turf, but also marks itself apart from the American blockbuster. Moreover, in overlaying its references to American science fiction with the exotic and comic campness evidenced in the film, I would suggest that *Fifth Element* successfully 'queers' its Hollywood forerunners. In an analysis of the dance styles employed by the choreographer, Jack Cole, in a variety of Hollywood musicals, Adrienne L. McLean suggests that 'Orientalism was part of an often transformative and empowering Camp discourse'.[39] In this way, the 'oriental' provides a playfully irrational space in which alternative modes of expression and behaviour can be articulated. So, what I am proposing is that *Fifth Element* conjures up this brand of 'transformative Orientalism' as an appropriate vehicle to advance an alternative Euro-French perspective within the science fiction genre. Although the narrative revolves around Dallas and even though he provides the audience with a central point of identification, his reactions to those around him are crucial to an understanding of the perspectives at play in the film. For example, Willis' performance relies heavily on a kind of ironic incredulity in reaction to the exploits of his fellow city-dwellers.

Figure 6.2   Korben Dallas (Bruce Willis) out of his depth in the exotic surroundings
of *Fifth Element* (1997). Columbia Tri-Star / The Kobal Collection.

In many respects he is the true alien in this environment and much of the
humour is created in the film in watching Dallas apply an absurdly gung-ho
and macho approach to the situations he encounters. It is as though Willis's
'John McClaine' character from the *Die Hard* films (1998, 1990, 1995) had
been inappropriately dropped into the completely alien environment of this
French film, an environment that he is none too successful in dealing with until
the appearance of a female in apparent distress provides suitable motivation
for his actions. Dallas's actions and lack of appropriate etiquette are also paralleled in the response of the American-style military to the alien threat that
approaches the Earth. Without proper consultation, the military bombard the
approaching threat with the largest nuclear missiles they can muster, but this
only succeeds in making the threat more palpable.

The Middle Eastern theme introduced at the beginning of the film is carried
through in the musical sound track. Upon Dallas's first meeting with Leeloo, his
allegiance with this mysterious female is sealed when he refuses to hand her over
to the police who are trying to take her into custody and, instead, takes off at
speed in his flying taxi-cab. The high-speed chase that ensues is accompanied by
the Algerian-born musician Cheb Khaled's 'Alech Taadi'. As compared to the
preceding scoring by Eric Serra, the distinctly Arabic tones of Khaled's music
operates in the film to signify not only Dallas's seemingly irrational attempt to

break away from the forces of law and order in this city, but also his roman-
tic/sexual attraction for this exotic/erotic female. These 'oriental' undertones are
then taken up in Eric Serra's song, 'A Little Light of Love', at the close of the
film, which accompanies the consummation of Korben and Leeloo's relationship. While it was fairly standard practice in classical film noir to evoke the 'oriental', this usually signalled the arrival of a dangerous eroticism, but here the
'oriental' becomes a protecting and healing power. The mystical powers of an
ancient Middle East are therefore pitted against the corruption and inhumanity
of American-style capitalism (represented in the character of Zorg as the greedy
and unfeeling capitalist) and the mindless violence of a militaristic government.

Although the examples above represent a variety of responses by a European
film industry to Hollywood science fiction there are also clear similarities
between these otherwise diverse films. The most obvious similarity occurs in
the frequency of the desert motif across these films and direct/indirect reference to an ancient Middle Eastern civilisation. Also, each film presents us with
the markedly estranged central male hero who seems out of place in the world
in which they find themselves. In all three films this character is an American
who, initially detached and distanced in some way from his surroundings,
finally embraces an exotic new world. In the context of an increasingly global
film industry, the bizarre mix of 'oriental' images serves a doubled purpose in
the Euro-American science fiction film, simultaneously signalling the films'
uncertain national status as well as working to reinstate division and dissimi-
larity.

Interview: Actor Joe Morton

C: How would you describe your working relationship with the director of *The
Brother from Another Planet*, John Sayles?

M: John and I have done three films together and each was a joy and a real collaboration between actor and director. I look forward to the next venture whenever that might happen. John is greatly responsible for putting my career on the
map.

C: John Sayles is often reported as adopting an 'ensemble' style in his working
methods. How would you describe the methods of working on his films, particularly in *The Brother from Another Planet*?

M: John definitely works on an ensemble basis. Most of us came from a theatrical background, including John. This makes for an ability to communicate
easily and efficiently. John has grown as a director. When we did *The Brother
from Another Planet* John wanted actors who could take care of their own emotional life within the film. He wasn't interested in background stories or how

the actor got from A to B. He no longer holds that opinion. He goes as far as providing background for you. I think partly we've all gotten to know each other better. The more you work with someone the better you know them – witness Scorsese and De Niro for example.

C: In what ways, perhaps, has your experience of working on a film like *Brother* differed from, say, the more mainstream film productions you have been involved with?

M: With John, the script you are given at the beginning of principal photography is the same as the script you finish with. Most mainstream film suffers rewrites throughout the entire course of shooting. Mainstream films are shot by committee, for the most part. John's films are John's films.

C: Reviews of your work in *Brother* have likened your performance to stars of the silent era, Chaplin and Keaton . . .

M: I think because the character does not speak and I was given the opportunity to use my face and body in similar ways as Chaplin and Keaton, the tendency was to make the comparison. The most difficult part in doing the role, however, was not its silence but the fact that I could not recognise a world that I, the actor, knew well. Also, doing theatre in general was helpful in all kinds of ways. For instance, there is a scene when John, as the bounty hunter, 'reels' me in as I try to escape. I used a mime technique to perform that moment as opposed to allowing John to use a 'special effect' vis-à-vis the camera.

C: I'd like to know more about how you prepared for this role and more about your thinking behind this characterisation.

M: 'The Brother' was a man who had to learn a great deal in a short amount of time while surrounded by a world with which he was unfamiliar. I studied babies, puppies and anything or anyone who had to learn the way that he did.

He starts off as a character that is more reactive than showing initiative. He begins to study earthlings more intensely once he discovers the kid who overdoses. He wants to know why someone would purposely take something that ends their life. The result is he follows the drugs to the dealer and takes things in hand and kills the dealer. He enters the world in an extremely active way.

John is a social commentarian. The film takes us into a world most white people would not normally enter. We see this world through the eyes of someone who is at once accepted into this world and is a stranger at the same time. It talks about people who have talents and no outlets for those talents due to oppression and racial prejudice. Because he can not speak, people tell him secrets. We hear things we might not normally hear, for instance, the conversations in the bar.

C: Who do you think the film was 'talking to'? Do you regard it as having been an effective film?

M: John's audience is made up of people on the political left, intellectuals and artists. I don't know that any film has any real cultural effect. In most cases you are speaking to the already converted no matter where you, as the filmmaker, might be coming from. You are appealing to people of like minds, in most cases.

C: Do you think your role in *Brother* has affected the kinds of roles you have been offered since?

M: After the movie opened I got lots of auditions, but people didn't know me or what I sounded like – some even thought I was a mute. I have no regional accent. I am an army brat I travelled around the world as a kid. So when I came in not sounding 'black', directors would always say, 'Loved you in that *Brother*'. That meant I was not going to get whatever it was I was auditioning for.

C: Do you think there is any kind of connection in your playing of Dyson in *Terminator 2* to your previous role in *Brother*?

M: There was no connection between the two films other than they were both sci-fi. I told James Cameron I wanted to play Miles Dyson because of a joke Richard Pryor told. Richard said that obviously Hollywood didn't think black people were going to be around in the future because we were never in futuristic movies or we were the first to be killed. Miles Dyson was central to the plot and the most human character in the movie.

C: It seems that *Brother* primarily uses the science fiction genre to make a broader social comment, but I wondered how you might feel about other science fiction films.

M: Science fiction is definitely a way to talk about the human condition. All you need do is look at everything from *The Time Machine* to *2001* to *Star Wars*. Each, in its own way, tries to talk about humankind's needs, habits, psychologies and drives . . . spiritual or otherwise.

C: Even though mainstream science fiction films are often regarded as spectacular, mindless fun, they often (either implicitly or more explicitly) deal with issues surrounding race, in one way or another. I wondered what your views were on the way particular films of the genre have dealt with racial issues.

M: Personally I never feel they deal with it a way that is satisfying. I always feel as if, because race is such a sensitive issue in this country, most sci-fi skirts around it or treats it predictably. *Brother* is one of the few that deals with it head on.

C: Bob Westal, in reviewing your work, praises your performance in *Brother* and says that this should have propelled you into becoming a major film star.

He goes onto say: 'In a colour-blind, less looks-obsessed world, this would have been a star-making performance for Joe Morton'.[40] He says that although you remain an 'outstanding, character actor' you were never really given the chance to become a major star, which he is suggesting was due to the fact that you are an African American.

M: American film has a tradition. Sidney Poitier has been substituted by Denzel. There can only ever be one of us in a dramatic category. Will Smith has proven to be an interesting actor but again most of his credits are action/adventure films like Wesley Snipes. I have done well to play as many different kinds of black people as I have. That will be my 'claim to fame'. Film is based on images. Most images in America are produced by white males. Consequently most opportunities are given to males who fulfil that profile.

C: Some of the roles you have undertaken suggest a particularly attuned aware-ness of issues surrounding race and ethnicity and a political consciousness – to what extent would you say you brought a political consciousness to your work?

M: Pretty much every role I have taken or sought was based on the idea that I wished to present a wide range of African Americans who have some stake in the emotional thread of the story being told. I have not played many villains, despite the fact that they are usually the most interesting. But, in the case of black villains, they are more often than not clichés.

C: To what extent would you say that your profession as an actor has allowed you to express a political consciousness?

M: Certainly, the parts I have done for John are obviously political. Most every-thing else has been political either in the fact that they were not necessarily written for a black person to do or due to the nature of the circumstances speak-ing to something controversial, for instance, Miss Evers' Boys (dir. Joseph Sargent, 1997). Sometimes I took a role because it was fun and good money.

When I first started working professionally I decided I would not play certain kinds of roles (the drug dealers, the pimps, the 'boogey-men'), unless they were unique and interesting. I figured someone would take those roles, it just would-n't be me. I have spent my whole career pursuing roles and in many cases getting roles not written for black people, both on stage and in film. I was involved in a published debate with John Simon after Mr Simon's review of me playing Lysander in A Midsummer Night's Dream commented that a conspicuously white role should not be played by a conspicuously black actor. I basically said that Shakespeare was about metaphor, not literal translation, and if he were correct then there should be no women on the stage either. The public got involved and wrote in their opinions as well. Most were on my side. He never gave me a bad review after that. I think he respected my intelligence.

C: So an awareness of issues surrounding race has affected your decisions over whether or not to take a role?

M: Of course. It's a shame I would ever have to think about it, but sometimes you do.

NOTES

1. Young 1995, p. 180.
2. Ashcroft *et al.* (eds) 1999, p. 223. Although Hall is mostly referring to Britain here his analysis also holds true within an America context.
3. Ibid. 1999, p. 224.
4. For example, the slogan 'black is beautiful', which emerged in the 1960s and early 1970s was designed to encourage a renewed sense of pride in Americans of African origin.
5. See Ashcroft *et al.* (eds) 1999, p. 224.
6. Ibid., pp. 224–5.
7. 'DissemiNation: Time, Narrative, and the Margins of the Modern Nation', in Bhabha 1990, p. 293 (my emphasis).
8. Bhabha 1988, pp. 5–23 (p. 22 Bhabha's emphases).
9. Dyer 1997, p. 4.
10. This is part of the voice-over 'manifesto' spoken by the captain of the Enterprise and repeated at the beginning of each episode of the original series.
11. I am obviously not including Tim Burton's recent re-make, released in 2001.
12. As if to underline a self (white)/Other (black) dichotomy, the only astronaut to be played by an African-American (Jeff Burton) is killed off near the beginning of the film and the rest of the narrative focuses upon the white astronaut, Taylor (Charlton Heston) and his struggles.
13. Greene (ed.) 1998, p. 150.
14. See Fanan 1970, pp. 78–82.
15. 'Bumper' Robinson, who played the drac infant, Zammis, was 10–11 years old when he appeared in this role.
16. Burgin 1990, pp. 62–73 (p. 68).
17. Janeson 1991, pp. 37–8.
18. Ibid., p. 15.
19. Turkle 1997, p. 243.
20. Ibid., p. 263.
21. 'Global Crisis, the Struggle for Cultural Identity and Intellectual Porkbarrelling: Cosmopolitans Versus Locals, Ethnics and Nationals in an Era of De-hegemonisation', in Werbner and Modood (eds) 1997, p. 84.
22. Although this technology is also reminiscent of the 'feelies' in Aldous Huxley's novel, *Brave New World,* and the 'stimmies' which feature in Marge Piercy's *Body of Glass.*
23. 'The Eye of Horror', in Clover 1992, p. 169 (Clover's emphasis).
24. 'Postmodernism and Consumer Society', in Foster (ed.) 1983, p. 117.
25. The recording of Rodney King being beaten by police was televised in 1991 and the later acquittal of the officers involved, in 1992, set off a series of riots in Los Angeles.
26. Said, *Orientalism* 2003, p. 1.
27. Ibid. 2003, p. 1–2.
28. 'Techno-Orientalism: Japan Panic', in Morley and Robins 1995, p. 167.

29. For example, Darrell William Davis has explored a kind of 'auto-orientalism' in the Japanese film, *Hana-Bi* (dir. Kitano Takeshi, 1997), as a marketing ploy, in order to sell this film to an international market. See Davis 2001, pp. 55–80.
30. Many critics have read the films as a successful 'translation' of Gibson's *Neuromancer* to the screen. See Barnett 2000, pp. 359–74.
31. It is certainly possible to read this the other way around, as an ironic inversion of real and fantastical. However, a distinct racialised divide remains and even given the ambiguity of which world should be considered 'real' (especially in the first film of the series), the fact remains that the black characters function to bring Neo back to a sense of his own humanity.
32. This 'in-between' status was, of course, also assigned to the 'Jewish apes' in *Planet of the Apes*, who could equally be seen as orientalised.
33. Collin Chou is also known as Sing Ngai. He was born in Taiwan and began his film career in Hong Kong, where he is a well known actor/martial artist. He moved to the US in 1999.
34. 'The Limiting Imagination of National Cinema', in Hjort and Mackenzie (eds) 2000, pp. 67–8.
35. Said argues that European Orientalism largely revolves around Middle Eastern culture, whereas American-style Orientalism more frequently concerns Far Eastern culture. See 'Introduction', in said 2003, pp. 1–28.
36. 'Global Visions and European Perspectives', in Sardar and Cubitt (eds) 2002, p. 177.
37. The Moebius cityscape featured in the influential, adult French comic 'Métal Hurlant', heavily influenced Syd Mead's urban design of *Blade Runner*. Also, Jean Giraud worked on American science fiction films from the late 1970s throughout the 1980s (e.g. *Alien, Tron, The Abyss* etc.).
38. 'The French Cinema and Hollywood: A Case Study of Americanization', in Fehrenback and Poiger (eds) 2000, p. 217.
39. 'The Thousand Ways There Are to Move: Camp and Oriental Dance in the Hollywood Musicals of Jack Cole', in Bernstein and Studlar (eds) 1997, p. 149.
40. Bob Westal, 'The Brother from Another Planet' (review), *Film Threat*: http://filmthreat.com/index.php?section=reviews&Id=2796.

7.   GENERIC PERFORMANCE AND SCIENCE FICTION CINEMA

Figure 7.1   Sensual surfaces in Cronenberg's *Crash* (1996). Columbia Tri-Star / The Kobal Collection / Jonathan Wenk.

Science fiction writing has traditionally dealt with ideas; often subordinating characterisation (or creating what are commonly called 'flat' characterisations) to a more overarching premise. As Alexandra Aldridge puts it: 'Whilst individual experience in a fragment of historically familiar world constitutes the principle subject matter of the traditional novel, in SF individual experience recedes into the background.'[1]

Similarly, the kind of characterisation found in film genres more readily associated with cinematic realism (as adopted and adapted from the novel) is not the central concern of the science fiction film genre. Although a film narrative might revolve around a relatively small number of central protagonists, they are often understood as generic archetypes or one-dimensional characters representing particular views, beliefs or principles. Consequently, performances given by actors working within the genre are not taken seriously and receive little critical attention. Indeed, it is generally assumed that the genre does not require what is considered to be 'proper' acting and performances are commonly denigrated or completely disregarded.

Richard de Cordova, in an article addressing the lack of performance analysis in Film Studies as a whole, states that: 'The examination of the ways that different genres circumscribe the form and position of performance in film is an important and underdeveloped area of genre studies.'[2] He goes on to argue that a variety of genres actually foreground performance and that these, in particular, cry out for a level of reading and analysis that takes performance strategies into consideration. Although de Cordova points to examples such as film noir and melodrama, which often require the flamboyant playing out of unre-strained or overstated human emotion, I would suggest that performance is equally as important to the science fiction film genre. For instance, what amounts to the highly stylised acting repeatedly witnessed in science fiction fre-quently operates to defamiliarise aspects of supposedly 'naturalistic' acting, thereby making questions of human performance or the performance of being human integral to the genre. This is perhaps most clearly affirmed in the way that the film genre has consistently questioned what stands for 'proper' human behaviour within a given technological environment, often established in a comparison between seemingly human and non-human behaviour or through the general adoption of what I would call a vacuous or blank style of acting. For instance, *Metropolis* (dir. Fritz Lang, 1927) is clearly critical of encroach-ing industrialisation in its depiction of a dehumanised and robotic underclass who serve as cogs in the machine of a futuristic state. In direct contrast, the sci-entific romanticism exhibited in the later *Things to Come* (dir. William Cameron Menzies, 1936) is also played out in similarly regulated perfor-mances, as witnessed in the inhabitants of a vast underground city. But here the behaviour of the city's occupants denotes a relatively stable and peaceful utopian world of scientific rationalism, rather than a vision of metropolitan misery and despair. In both of these films, recognisable human passion might not be detailed through performance, but is reassuringly represented by the blossoming of romance between a young heterosexual couple: humanity is thus restored through the love between Maria and Freder in *Metropolis,* and the hope for the future is represented by our pioneering young couple, Maurice and Catherine who take off into space at the end of *Things to Come.*

Many of the American films of the 1950s also relied upon romantic encounter as a device to explore human behaviour within an increasingly conformist and controlled environment. In these films the successful romantic union usually sig-nalled the reintroduction of a traditional human order into an alien scientific environment (e.g. *The War of the Worlds* [dir. Byron Haskin, 1953], *This Island Earth* [dir. Joseph M. Newman, 1955], etc.) or, alternatively, the failure of the heterosexual union marked the founding of a new order of systematic restraint and collaboration (e.g. *The Day the Earth Stood Still* [dir. Robert Wise, 1951], *It Came from Beneath the Sea* [dir. Robert Gordon, 1955], *Invasion of the Body Snatchers* [dir. Don Siegel, 1956],). As if to suggest that scientific rationalism had won the day, the calmly coordinated and passionless behaviour exhibited by the inhabitants of Santa Mira in *Invasion of the Body Snatchers* reappears in Stanley Kubrick's *2001: A Space Odyssey* [1968]. Here the contently serviced and amenable subjects of a highly technologised environment are represented through an equally 'blank' or underplayed performance style. My point is that there is a clear history of this performance style which, repeatedly utilised, has contributed to and served the film genre in a number of different ways.

More recently, these blank characterisations have re-emerged with the introduction of the cyborg to blockbuster films like *The Terminator* series, *Universal Soldier, Johnny Mnemonic* (dir. Robert Longo, 1995) and *The Matrix* series (dir. Larry and Andy Wachowski, 1999–2003). Star performers like Arnold Schwarzenegger, Jean-Claude Van Damme and Keanu Reeves are hardly applauded for their acting skills in these films and, as detailed in previous chapters, are more usually judged in terms of how they look and the body politics that each displays. Certainly these blockbuster science fiction/action and science fiction/thrillers concentrated on bringing thrilling spectacle to the screen through their use of cutting-edge special effects along with the fast-moving physicality of fight and flight sequences. Consequently, studies of the cyborg in cinema have concentrated on the spectacular technological aspects surrounding the actor's performance rather than on the acting style employed in conjunction with these technologies. However, in the light of the history of generic performance I have outlined above, I would say that this 'blank' style takes on new meaning when associated with the cyborg. Importantly, the cyborg in film can be seen to operate as a foregrounding device, indicating how an actor's cinematic portrayal is always already cyborgian. The actors involved in depicting a given cyborg can be understood literally as cyborg actors; their performance being so obviously enmeshed with the technological apparatus of the cinematic machine. It follows then that the performing cyborg brings into contention what has traditionally stood for human authenticity in both the *real* and *reel* world.

Scott Bukatman boldly states, that 'it is the purpose of much recent science fiction to construct a new subject-position to interface with the global realms of data circulation' and he famously calls this new subject-position 'terminal identity'.[3] In addition to this, he argues that 'cinematic style becomes a part of social and gestural rhetoric, an integral part of the presentation of self in the era of terminal identity'.[4] He is therefore suggesting that the various behaviours and etiquettes acquired by subjects of a postmodern technological society are highly influenced by cinematic portrayals. It seems that, in this panoptic era, our self-presentations are not only becoming increasingly mediated by and through visualisation technologies, but postmodern identities may also be, somewhat literally, bound up with various performed images – especially those presented by cinema. So surely a figuration that can be seen as enacting emerging forms of subjectivity could be usefully analysed through the filter of performance theory? And in order to prove this point I will be offering an examination of David Cronenberg's *Crash* (1996), followed by his later film *eXistenZ* (1999). These films are instructive examples because they foreground performance and because they can be instructively read in conjunction with more familiar, mainstream films; especially the blockbuster science fictions featuring central cyborg characters, some of which I have discussed in previous chapters.

Based upon J. G. Ballard's novel, *Crash* (first published in 1973), Cronenberg's film is episodic in construction, dealing with the sexual exploration of a band of people brought together by their shared experiences as the victims of car accidents. Vaughan (Elias Koteas), the leader of this cult-like group, is driven by a desire to replay the car crashes of various famous film stars. Having introduced James and Catherine Ballard to the possible pleasures gained from a literal collision with technology, the proceeding scenes concentrate on the way in which the characters' sexuality is played out in a melding of flesh and metal. *eXistenZ*, like *Crash*, is also concerned with the human/ machine interface, but here the technology in question is a futuristic version of the so-called virtual reality computer game. At the beginning of *eXistenZ*, Allegra Geller (Jennifer Jason Leigh) introduces an assembled audience to the 'eXistenZ' game world that she has apparently created. The assembly are eager to try out this new product, but just as volunteers are about to enter her world there is an attempt on Geller's life. Thus ensues a tangled narrative in which Geller, accompanied by a young and seemingly inexperienced security guard, Ted Pikul (Jude Law), attempts to avoid assassination and recoup the game software trapped in her injured pod/computer. Toward the end of the film, it becomes apparent that during the opening scenes the players were already in a game world called 'transCendenZ' and that both Geller and Pikul were simply members of the audience at the premier tryout of this game. However, following this revelation and echoing the opening of the film, Geller and Pikul are then exposed as assassins on a mission to kill the creator of 'transCendenZ'. They apparently succeed in this mission, but not before it has become questionable as to what is, after all, diegetically real and what is a constructed game scenario.

eXistenZ sits securely within the science fiction genre and provides an alternative vision to the kind of cyborg presented to us in films like *Johnny Mnemonic* (dir. Robert Longo, 1995), *The Net* (dir. Irwin Winkler, 1995), or *Virtuosity* (dir. Brett Leonard, 1995). *Crash*, on the other hand, may seem more difficult to define under the heading of science fiction, but can be read alongside earlier depictions of mainstream cyborgs, which concentrated on technology's impact in more bodily terms (i.e. through technological prosthetics, the development of the artificial body etc.). In this sense, my choice is justified by the way in which the characters in *Crash* depict a kind of 'low-tech'[5] precursor to cyborgs found in films like *The Terminator* (dir. James Cameron, 1984) and *Robocop* (dir. Paul Verhoeven, 1987).

Both *Crash* and *eXistenZ* cry out for analysis at the level of performance. Both films place questions of performance at the heart of their projects, which is made abundantly clear in the reference to past film performances. For instance, this occurs in *Crash* with the scene in which Vaughan 'replays' the death of James Dean and in *eXistenZ* when the 'characters' critique their own contributions within the virtual game. I will come to discuss both of these scenes in more detail, but my point is that if there remained any doubt about the centrality of performance in the two films, these moments definitely serve to concentrate attention on this area. In addition, these two films make for an interesting comparative coupling, given the markedly different performance styles adopted by the actors: the diverse and blatantly 'flat' theatrical style adopted in *eXistenZ* is diametrically opposed with the previously discussed blank or vacuous style that dominates the performances in *Crash*. Given the moral outcry that *Crash* engendered, I am left with the impression that Cronenberg may well have penned the later *eXistenZ* in answer to the almost hysterical critical response that *Crash* received, especially in the UK.[6] For instance, the device of the virtual reality game in *eXistenZ* along with the constant reminder that the characters are acting out their roles within it, makes it easier to understand as a fantasy piece. But a relationship between the two films is also indicated in the obvious references to *Crash* in *eXistenZ* (e.g. when a character is seen to purchase a virtual reality game called 'Hit by a Car'), ironically demonstrating that the earlier film was taken rather too literally. So, although I would argue that both films comment upon the ways in which technology impacts upon social interaction and human psychology, the teasingly playful *eXistenZ* appears far less shocking than the bleaker and more direct approach taken in *Crash*. However, both of these films present the audience with a world in which self-reflexive performance has become central to the way in which the characters respond as cyborgised subjects in a technologically mediated environment.

Paul Patton has suggested that urban living has increasingly led to a kind of individual role-playing among city dwellers and has argued that to facilitate a life spent in such close quarters with so many strangers, people are increasingly encouraged to indicate their 'role' within society. He goes on to state that:

> In cities, people identify other people on the basis of their appearance, their social role or other singular characteristics. In turn, this mode of relating to others reacts back upon their sense of self and they experience themselves as actors.[7]

In other words, the degree of self-reflection exhibited by the actants in both *Crash* and *eXistenZ* can be understood as an illustration of the extent to which performance is fast becoming a recognised constituent of postmodern subjectivity. Indeed, in an interview about *Crash*, Cronenberg has been quoted as saying:

> The conceit that underlies some of what is maybe difficult or baffling about *Crash*, the sci-fi-ness, comes from Ballard anticipating a future pathological psychology. It's developing now, but he anticipates it being

even more developed in the future. He then brings it back to the past – now – and applies it as though it exists completely formed. So I have these characters who are exhibiting a psychology of the future.[8]

Similarly, a 'psychology of the future' is also explored in *eXistenZ* as all of the 'characters' appear to internalise aspects of their roles within the game, which, melded with their existing psychological make-up, compels them to literally act out their roles. Any idea of a fundamental human nature thus becomes complicated as characters in both films are both excited and traumatised in a collision with technology.

Externalising Performance

During the opening shots of Cronenberg's *Crash*, the camera slowly pans across an airport hangar, surveying the smooth metallic surfaces of the planes before finally focusing upon a man and woman having sex. Catherine is shown caressing the metal surface of a light aircraft; in fact, her attention seems more fixed on these caresses than the man who stands behind her. Throughout this scene her expression remains distant, as though she was somewhat removed from the situation or, at least, remained relatively unaffected by the man's attentions; she does not display the more usual signs of arousal that a filmgoing audience may have come to expect. There is very little sense of emotional connection here and the way in which the scene is set up encourages a viewing of the surfaces of their bodies and clothing as though these people were simply an extension of the surrounding mise-en-scène. Even Howard Shore's accompanying musical score forestalls any depth of inquiry: it is minimal, repetitive and does not have a dominant melody line. In this sense, the score does not offer the more familiar kind of musical hierarchy (with the melody lines supported or underpinned by other lines) and does not operate to connote emotional subtext or any kind of hidden undercurrent; it simply echoes the somewhat detached view from the camera.

This opening scenario sets the tone of the piece and as the film progresses it becomes apparent that there is a similar sense of surface, of superficiality, of lack of depth, inherent in the performance styles of the featured actors. There is little indication of emotional or psychical depth being played out and the performers/characters seem most concerned with their own externality as well the external natures of what surrounds them. Also, any sense of characters' personal history is not so much marked in terms of nuances of performance as by the outward scars, tattoos and injuries they sport. For instance, following their head-on collision and just prior to their first session of sexual intercourse, the character of Ballard (James Spader) has a brief conversation with Dr Helen Remington (Holly Hunter). While Ballard drives Remington to work the ensuing conversation consists primarily of exchanges of information, notably about their professions or comments on their surroundings, as opposed to how they feel. In many films this kind of dialogue would have been played for what lay 'under' it, giving the characters a deeper level of emotional connection. Indeed, it is a common acting exercise to play different underlying emotions/motivations, behind a few lines of mundane dialogue, but here the delivery is direct, without any indication of particular tensions or censored thought. There are also moments when an unusual camera angle is adopted in short cutaways, detailing certain movements, but even these do not seem to signal subtext and, at most, simply reaffirm the way in which these two people are coolly sizing one another up. The nearest instant to a demonstration of underlying motivation in the performances is at the point when Remington very deliberately starts to smoke. This is followed by a close-up on her cigarette. The smoking woman (in particular the femme fatale of film noir) is a classic indication of a kind of phallic or repressed sexual undercurrent, but here it operates to highlight a cinematic coding, with the inference that Remington is using her knowledge of this code in order to quickly and efficiently communicate her desire for sex with Ballard.[9]

In terms of the way in which these particular performances were elicited it is interesting to note that Cronenberg replayed the rushes and had the best colour monitors installed for the cast to refer to during rehearsal and recording.[10] Although it is not that unusual for actors to view the rushes for a day's filming, or to have access to the monitors, it is unusual for these things to be set in place so specifically as an aid to the process of performing. Even though this further suggests the importance that Cronenberg placed upon performance in this particular film, it also implies that the actors were encouraged to focus their attention on outward appearances, as though they were being asked to see themselves as objects or bodies in conjunction with the other objects and technological bodies of the surrounding mise-en-scène. While this production technique may well have been used to encourage a particular style of performance (almost as though it were reproducing, or emphasising, a pervasive panopticism within postmodern society), the resulting vacuous quality could also be seen as allowing the director more freedom to impose meaning. However, the camera work and muted colouration (among other things) in *Crash* simultaneously signal a very detached point of view. Then perhaps these performances are designed to promote a more thoughtful and critical engagement on the part of the viewer? Does the vacuous quality provide a more writerly performance for the audience? On the contrary, I would argue that the audience is discouraged from reading underlying symbolism or metaphorical meaning: the metaphors have been literalised and are simply there to see.[11]

In the final chapter of *Screening Space,* Vivian Sobchack talks of a shift in the aesthetics of contemporary science fiction film. Drawing upon Jameson,

Sobchack describes the way in which a depth model has been replaced by a surface model in science fiction. She looks at how 1950s science fiction films inscribed space as 'deep' which, she argues, is now replaced by an exploration of space as shallow, all surface, displaying rather than concealing, and she goes on to detail the ways in which this surface aesthetic manifests itself.[12] What is missing from her description is any detailed discussion at the level of performance. Jameson basically states that this shift from depth to surface is expressive of postmodern subjectivity and has resulted in the repudiation of four crucial and fundamental depth models in contemporary theory. He names these areas as 'the dialectical one of essence and appearance . . . the Freudian model of latent and manifest, or of repression . . . the existential model of authenticity and inauthenticity . . . and, most recently, the great semiotic opposition between signifier and signified'.[13] He continues to explore models of postmodern subjectivity and comments that:

> As for expression and feelings or emotions, the liberation, in contemporary society, from older *anomie* of the centered subject may also mean not merely a liberation from anxiety but a liberation from every other kind of feeling as well, since there is no longer a self present to do the feeling.[14]

By drawing upon Jean-François Lyotard, he goes on to say that 'feelings' seem to have been replaced by 'intensities', which are 'free-floating' and 'impersonal', but what is of particular interest is the way in which he illustrates his discussion with reference to film and film performance. Although his illustration is fairly short and relatively cursory, he at least acknowledges the usefulness of a focus upon acting styles. I would contend that closer analysis of performance styles, particularly as present in recent science fiction film, reveals how performance styles engage with these postmodern shifts, which Cronenberg emphasises with reference to one of the leading Method actors of the 1950s.[15]

As previously mentioned, there is a scene in *Crash* during which Vaughan replays the death of James Dean. Vaughan's introduction to this enactment involves a retelling of the events that led up to the Dean crash and various details of the road accident itself. While narrating these events, Vaughan's body moves around the 'stand-in' Porsche Spyder (the model of car that Dean was in at the time of his death) as he caresses various areas of its bodywork. His rather languorous body movements are reminiscent of the way in which Dean uses his body as a performer. For instance, in *Rebel without a Cause* (dir. Nicholas Ray, 1955), during one particular scene when the Dean character is talking with Judy (Natalie Wood), he uses unusual body movements that signal what he feels (which is not really present in the dialogue) and that also suggest that his whole body is being affected by his surfacing desires toward Judy. In some ways, this is an example of the classic Method style, particularly of the 1950s era, in which the body language of the actor was often juxtaposed with the spoken dialogue. The classic Method style that emerged during this period focused on the psychological apparatus of the individual actor and the motivation that lay 'behind' a character's action. Based upon an interpretation of the first of Stanislavski's three books on acting (*An Actor Prepares* – first translated and published in America in 1936), the Method took some of its central tenets and placed a great deal of importance on preparation work, in isolation from the script, rather than the rest of the mechanics of performance. So, during this period, one of the main features in the development of this style was its emphasis on the physical/emotional body of the performer as opposed to the spoken dialogue. This marked a move away from intellect, as denoted by clear vocal utterance of dialogue, to a kind of inarticulate, bodily responding as a supposedly more authentic approach to acting. In terms of the preparation techniques the style advocated, the Method drew heavily upon a popularised form of Freudian psychoanalysis and included exercises that aimed to help the actor recall past emotional events in order to use these in performance. So, the Method was based upon a depth modelling of being human and Dean's performance in *Rebel* was intended (or can be read) as denoting a characterisation of psychological depth.

At first glance, although there seem to be similarities between Dean's and Koteas's performances here I would argue that they are vastly different, largely due to the overall contexts in which they appear. During the replay scene Koteas's performance can well be read as a kind of pastiche of the Method style, which, bearing in mind the circumstances of this re-enactment, can further be seen as an extreme extrapolation of some of the tendencies presented by this style. Vaughan tells the assembled audience that he is aiming for as much 'authenticity' as possible in his replay. Indeed, the search for an authenticity of feeling seems to have led Vaughan to literally 'live his role'. Having said that, Vaughan later undercuts the authenticity of his performance when he asks: 'was I glib . . . "James Dean died of a broken neck and became immortal"?' In fact, throughout the film he consistently undercuts the 'truth' of earlier statements. Vaughan's enigmatic insincerity is further underlined by Remington's comments immediately following the replay: when Ballard asks if the participants in the re-enactment are really hurt, she replies: 'I don't know. You can never be sure with Vaughan. This is his show'.[16] So, although the Method is evoked here, its associations with inner 'truth' and 'authenticity' are simultaneously undermined throughout. Ultimately, Vaughan's taking up of the Method style is not intended to denote a depth of character, but rather to indicate a lack of character. Seemingly, the Freudian assumption of interior impulses (most notably the sex drive and the death drive) articulated by the Method's bodily performance have been thoroughly externalised in the characters in *Crash*, reducing the characterisation of the human subject to a surface rendition of what was previously assumed to be basic underlying drives.

The Method has, of course, moved on since its heyday, when stars like Marlon Brando and James Dean were at the height of their 'anti-hero' fame. As Virginia Wright Wexman has stated:

> In place of the anxiety-fraught romantic relationships suggested by the neurotic male Method stars of the fifties, newer Method stars like Robert De Niro, Dustin Hoffman, and Al Pacino typically project a cold narcissism that suggests they are beyond romance.[17]

Bearing this in mind, perhaps the performances in *Crash* can be read as a further development in the Method stylisation? For instance, in a discussion of *A Streetcar Named Desire* (dir. Elia Kazan, 1951) as a seminal film in which the style fully emerged, Marianne Conroy talks of the way the Method 'foregrounded how social and cultural categories are acted out'.[18] In her closing statement she notes how: 'The significance of Method acting for our time lies in the way its middlebrow mix of heterogeneous cultural styles prefigures a differentiated and perhaps distinctively postmodern perspective on national identity and culture.'[19]

Along with these comments, the emphasis apparently placed on the body, as opposed to the spoken word, in Method, could allow the style to be read as a precursor to later performance practices. Further evidence of a link between later styles and Method acting can be found in its apparent association with Existentialism. It was not uncommon for the anti-hero in films of this era to be understood as enacting a kind of existential version of subjectivity. The acting out of this kind of subjectivity was previously more readily associated with avant-garde practices. For example, in his comments about the emergence of alternative forms of performance from the 1950s onwards and these forms close associations with Existential philosophy, Peter Gorsen (writing in the late 1970s) states:

> There is something striking about the unsymbolic reflection on one's own corporeality and its nonverbal language, on the aesthetics of an unseemingly unconditional 'naked existence' (Sartre), which shows similarities with the modern '*I am in my body*' tautology, and, in connection with, the determined stand against declarations that crop up to assert the claims of the scientific approach, of finality, and of exclusiveness.[20]

The kind of alternative forms that Gorsen outlines in his article certainly influenced the Method style at this time, but I do not believe that developments in the Method style fully account for the performances evidenced in *Crash*. Although the behaviour exhibited by the characters in *Crash* may operate to comment upon past and current styles, within the context of this film a different approach sheds more light on the performances adopted here and, by extension, the characterisations under discussion.

Karl Toepfer, in an article entitled 'Nudity and Textuality in Postmodern Performance', has stated that the sight of a nude body in performance produces a tendency for the spectator 'to collapse distinctions between the "real" body of the performer and the "imaginary" body of the "character" textualised out of a theatrical code'.[21] Toepfer goes on to call this effect 'an extreme form of realism which seeks to dissolve difference between reality and representation'.[22] Although he is largely talking about live stage performance (nudity in films might operate somewhat differently), it is interesting to consider his comments in association with the bodies on display in *Crash*. Perhaps then the nude bodies paraded in *Crash* could be taken to indicate that the presentation of the material body is the only element left in an account of what can be seen as authentically human. Having said that these authentic human bodies do not remain intact for long, due to the way in which the characters seek to collude/collide with mechanical technologies. On the contrary, I would say that the nudity in *Crash* allows the bodies in question to be re-inscribed, particularly in conjunction with the vehicular technologies also on display. For instance, there is a fascinating moment when Remington's outstretched muscled arms are heavily associated with the bumpers on the front of the car in which she is having sex. So it seems that although the nude body may be understood as 'un-inscribed' there is a re-inscription here which potently foregrounds the conceptual amalgamation of human body/technological car. If read as a fetishistic metaphor then there is also a confusion as to its primary or originary source: the kind of feedback loop between car–body/body–car explored in the film makes it difficult to detect which each acts as a signifier for the other. A further example can be found in the way that, following his first crash, Ballard replaces his damaged vehicle with the same model and colour of car that he had driven previously. Although this certainly indicates that Ballard has a compulsion to repeat the trauma of the first crash this also implies that he now sees this type of car as somehow an extension of his body (if not his actual body). Likewise, Vaughan's identity is consistently associated with the 'beat-up' Lincoln, to the point where the body of the car and Vaughan's body become literally interconnected: just as his car becomes covered in his own and others' bodily fluids and segments of his fleshy epidermis, his organic body is also covered with a tattoo of a steering wheel and marked by the scars of previous crashes. Given this kind of rampant literalisation in *Crash*, I am reminded more of recent developments in the area of performance art. To look to these developments also seems appropriate due to Cronenberg's own comments about the characterisations in the film. In an interview with the director, Gavin Smith asked if the characters in *Crash* are the first (compared to characterisations in his earlier films) to consciously and

actively attempt to shape their realities. Cronenberg agreed that this was probably the case and commented:

> Their project is a creative one, but it's less formally an artistic process, it's
> almost performance art . . . to use one's art to explore the purpose of one's
> existence, while at the same time giving one a purpose. Suddenly seeing
> your life as an artistic process automatically invests it with some shape.[23]

The characters in *Crash* actively insert their bodies into this hyper-technologised
environment and, in turn, express/perform their experience of this world in a
similar fashion to the way in which a performance artist can be understood as
working. Certain mechanisms inherent in performance art are echoed in the
actors' performances in *Crash* and perhaps in the way in which the performances were elicited in the first place.

Richard Schechner, in his book *The End of Humanism: Writings on
Performance* describes a kind of linear development in performance techniques
from 'naturalism to alienation-effect to autoperformance'.[24] Autoperformance
was basically a term coined to describe the rise in solo theatrical work in the
late 1970s and 'the more radical sense of using the one person who is performing as the source of the material being performed'.[25] The term also carries
with it connotations that the performance is narcissistic in nature; not only is
the performer using their self as source material, but is also acting as their own
director and even audience in the production of an externalisation of their inner
being. I would suggest that a similar approach has been taken in *Crash*, as evidenced in the excessive self-reflection instituted by the constant self-viewing
through monitors and tapes and the presentation of an ironically literal form
of autoperformance. Although it is amusing to consider the pun involved in the
use of this term in connection with this particular film, the car also has clear
associations with ideas surrounding individualism. As a technology the car
allows for individual control, it also creates a hermetically sealed world around
the driver, thus separating the individual from direct contact with the outside.
So, the driver of a car, looking out at the world from a privileged position,
enacts some of the extremes of a humanist trajectory. According to Schechner,
the two-sided nature of humanism means that, on the one hand, it seeks to preserve the rights and freedoms of human individuals and, on the other hand, it
is 'as an ideology . . . connected to the sense that human being, male human
beings especially . . . are the lords and masters of the world'.[26] Therefore, the
humanist project is based upon the assumption that the self-contained and
boundaried human being (in particular the male/masculine subject) is at the
centre of their world. The irony, as it is revealed in the characters in *Crash*, is
that the very technology that allows for an enacting of separation, of human
individuality, of mastery, also becomes the vehicle of human dissolution.

Philip Auslander, in his book *From Acting to Performance*, charts a similarly linear, historical shift from a transcendent, logocentric ideal in Western philosophy toward a more decentred, deconstructed view (as proposed by postmodern and poststructuralist theories) and he goes on to discuss how this has affected notions of the self. Auslander basically attempts to account for the way in which shifts in philosophical perspective, along with social and cultural changes, have altered how being human is understood and have impacted upon approaches to performance theory and practice. He notes that:

> Whereas modernist and avant-gardist theatres of the late nineteenth through the mid-twentieth centuries conceived of their work in terms of innovations in acting, subsequent postmodernist innovations have resulted from a reconsideration of the very nature of the activity that takes place on the stage, and the development of performance art.[27]

Auslander also looks at how acting is commonly understood as an expression of the actor's/character's true, inner self and he refers to 1950s Method acting as an example of a style that was judged in these terms. For Auslander, the Method is logocentric and he moves on to compare this approach to seemingly more radical, oppositional styles, which often purport to explore the more material nature of human being. But, as he later states:

> If, as Michel Foucault and others have argued, a part of the manageable, modern performance theory as a social discourse is to discipline the body, to make it manageable, modern performance theory as a social discourse has managed the body by robbing it of its materiality, subjecting it to the discipline of text, whether the dramatic text or the text of archetypal psychic impulse. Although avant-gardist performance theory frequently claims to liberate the body and thus to challenge the social or political hegemony, it fails adequately to conceptualise this liberation by failing to see the body as ideologically produced.[28]

Auslander goes on to argue for resistant forms of performance that retain a degree of reflexivity, remain at the level of the superficial, the surface, while somehow avoiding a reification of the very surfaces they present.[29] Taking his stance into consideration, the performances in *Crash* could well be seen as resistant, in that the definite emphasis upon the body and upon surfaces does not deny the very literal impact of social conditioning. However, given that these performances are filmed (which suggests some form of reification is likely to be taking place) it is probably more accurate to say that the characters in *Crash* are, paradoxically, attempting a resistive practice through a transgressively literal embrace of the cyborgisation process.

Rebecca Schneider, in her book *The Explicit Body in Performance*, talks of the way in which a number of recent performance artists appear to 'render the symbolic literal'.[30] Schneider contends that this effectively 'confuses the space between the symbolic and literal reading, and in so doing it both plays with and questions dominant habits of comprehension'.[31] Throughout her book Schneider looks at examples of contemporary performance artists who, rather than widening the gap between signifier and signified have a tendency of 'making "the gap" . . . apparent by provoking its implosion across the visceral space of their own bodies'.[32] She suggests that this use of literality:

> Disrupt[s] and make[s] apparent the fetishistic prerogatives of the symbolic by which a thing, such as a body or a word, stands by convention for something else. To render literal is to collapse symbolic space . . . it is to pose . . . a 'direct threat' to the naturalised social drama of 'comprehensibility'. To render literal is also to interrogate the notion that relations between sign and signified are fundamentally arbitrary. Denying the arbitrary, a notion at the very base of modernist and capitalist sensibilities of abstraction and meaning, invites a kind of hysteria, or psychosis of the overly real.[33]

If my understanding of Schneider's analysis is correct then, unlike a Brechtian approach, (which widens the space/gap between player/performance) and unlike certain forms of 'naturalistic' acting in which deeper levels of meaning are played out within the performance, these artists, if I may borrow a phrase from Schneider, make the latent blatant. Schneider also goes to some lengths to stress that the bodies of the performers in question should not be considered as in any way essentialised, but remain immersed and entangled within systems of representation. This 'making literal' does not, therefore, divorce them from discursive systems of representation, but draws attention to the reality effects of the symbolic. I believe that Schneider's analysis of a literalisation tactic among certain performance artists is very useful in considering exactly what is happening in *Crash*. For instance, although the play with surfaces in this film might ridicule certain metaphors and analogies, it does not deny their power as conveyers of meaning. Indeed, *Crash* distils ideas that remain more latent in other cyborg films and makes palpably literal the effect of these ideas across the bodies of the performers involved. Indeed, the representation of the cyborgisation process in *Crash*, as compared to films like *The Terminator*, *Robocop*, *Universal Soldier* is far 'messier' than the relatively 'clean' images presented in the three former examples. Also, the mainstream examples portray the process of unification with the machine through the fully formed and boundaried body of the cyborg. In other words, these images present the viewer with a kind of reunification whereas the characters in *Crash* are bound up in a constant process of change and alteration in which their bodies are seen to be more vulnerable and more fragmented. If a comparison were made between the now famous shot of Arnold Schwarzenegger's muscled body framed against a Los Angeles skyline (in the opening sequences of *The Terminator*) and the scene in which Ballard's newly disabled body can be seen, on his balcony, looking out across the motorways of the city, then it becomes evident that the bodies at the centre of these two shots are very different. Ballard's cyborgisation does not make of him a macho, armoured, hyper-masculine figure; instead his newly disabled body is revealed as vulnerable and only enabled through the medical and mechanical technologies, which, at this point, maintain its tenuous coherence while simultaneously signalling its fragmentation.

In reading the obsessively 'driven' characterisations and the vacuous quality of the performances in *Crash* alongside the depiction of cyborgs in my mainstream examples, the context of these performances becomes a crucial determinant in how each is understood. In *Crash* the audience is given little opportunity for comparison with alternative characterisations or performance stylisations. The viewer is immersed in a world in which, with the possible exception of the Car Salesman (who features in only one scene and whose authenticity is questionable due to his sales role), all participants are working toward a sexualised synthesis with the machine. However, in films like *The Terminator*, *Robocop* and *Universal Soldier*, the vacuous and mechanical performance of a lone cyborg is set up in comparison with the 'fussier' and more recognisably 'naturalistic' performances witnessed in the 'fully human' characters that populate the film world. Here, the vacuous style is simply employed to separate the human from non-human or superhuman, therefore limiting its possible challenge to traditional conceptions of being human. Equally, in the figuring of the members of the Borg Collective in *Star Trek: First Contact* (dir. Jonathan Frakes, 1996), the extreme regulation of their actions and general lack of individualised response is ostensibly opposed to the human subjectivity of the crew of the Enterprise. The members of the Borg Collective have been 'assimilated' against their will; a process that removes their individuality and allows for swift, telepathic communication and extreme efficiency in carrying out their colonising expansion into the universe. As previously discussed in Chapter 5, the Borg become femininised in the transition from small to big screen and, apart from the Borg Queen, individual Borg are visually indistinguishable. In contrast, distinction between members of the Enterprise crew is visually accentuated through costuming and make-up. However, what is interesting in the case of this film is that the cosmetic individualism exhibited by the Enterprise is rarely echoed in the performance of these characters. It is not unusual for key crew members to be shown collectively working through a crisis situation, to the point where each performs a line of dialogue in a long sentence. Even when lapses occur in the normal presentation of this 'regulated' self these are quickly recuperated or used to display how each crew member freely returns to being an instrument of the Federation, once more aligned with the collective 'mindfulness' of the 'modulated' self. So, the Borg's extreme vacuity actually mirrors the subjugated self required by the Federation, while simultaneously making the mode of being presented in the crew of the Enterprise appear more desirable. In *Crash,* however, the disorderly conduct of the main characters marks them out as highly active participants in the cyborgisation process. These are not the slave subjects of a highly mechanised world, like the Borg in *Star Trek: First Contact* or the underclass in *Metropolis.* Nor are they the compliant subjects of *Star Trek*'s Federation or Kubrick's contentedly serviced 'space cadets' in *2001: A Space Odyssey.* Instead, the protocyborgs in *Crash* use their new-found status as performers to actively reinsert themselves into a world which, prior to their crashes, constructed them as passively alienated.

INTERNALISING PERFORMANCE

The existential questions set up in *Crash* are also approached in the appropriately titled *eXistenZ*. Jean-Paul Sartre, the recognised 'father' of Existentialism, stated that '[m]an is nothing else but that which he makes of himself'[34] and the philosophy is generally understood as placing emphasis upon 'individuality' and 'agency'. Before his conversion to Marxism (which seemed to come with his writing of *Critique of Dialectical Reason* in the early 1960s), Sartre's philosophy emphasised 'subjective' experience as the locus from which arises our understanding of the world and, through self-reflection, an understanding of ourselves. He saw 'man' as the centre of his own universe believing that '*existence* comes before *essence* – or, if you will, that we must begin from the subjective'.[35] He, therefore, rallied against certain of Freud's notions; in particular the idea that individuals are led by unconscious drives and desires that are ultimately pre-given and beyond their control. Indeed, he believed that Freud's formulation of the unconscious was entirely false and that explaining human actions in terms of underlying drives was simply an act of 'bad faith', a lie that enables man to escape from the responsibility of freedom.[36] Sartre stated that 'the existentialist does not believe in the power of passion . . . He thinks that man is responsible for his passion',[37] and in formulating an alternative to Freudian psychoanalysis, he rejected 'the hypothesis of the unconscious . . . mak[ing] the psychic act coextensive with consciousness'.[38] So, for Sartre, the reasons for a particular behaviour, or choice, could be ascertained consciously by the individual and he went on to state: 'We are not dealing with an unsolved riddle as the Freudians believe; all is there, luminous; reflection is in full possession of it, apprehends all'.[39] In some respects, you could say that Sartre levelled out Freud's depth modelling of subjectivity. By discounting deep-seated, deterministic structures he believed that human beings are left with a freedom to choose; to make conscious decisions, for which they are responsible.

Sartre also renounced the notion of an all-powerful and overseeing God. However, he did not discount the notion of a certain form of transcendence, but suggested that this was 'not in the sense that God is transcendent', rather, as linked to a kind of striving in which man projects himself into the future; in which 'man is thus self-surpassing . . . he is himself the heart and centre of his transcendence'.[40] He went on to say:

> This is humanism, because we remind man that there is no legislator but himself; that he himself, thus abandoned, must decide for himself; also because we show that it is not by turning back upon himself, but always by seeking, beyond himself, an aim which is one of liberation or of some particular realisation, that man can realise himself as truly human.[41]

Of course, this liberation assumes a unified and self-sustaining identity and does not account for any limiting factor in the making of individual choice; a weakness that, as David A. Joplin points out, he addressed in his later work when he considered how these freedoms might operate within the bounds of certain essential human limits. As Joplin puts it: 'this means that we are free to choose who [but not what] we are'.[42] Then again, events in recent years seem to have overturned this equation; choosing 'who we are' is not the only freedom open to us any more, as technology increasingly promises us choice in terms of 'what we are'. Where Sartre acknowledged that a self-conscious capacity to formulate our own, individual psychic identities was bounded by human materiality, the existential questions raised in *Crash* see our performance artists attempt to dis-integrate these bodily boundaries in their collusion/collision with surrounding technological apparatus. But, where *Crash*'s exploration of postmodern fragmentation is externalised in the bodily imagery on display, the ostensible focus in *eXistenZ* is upon the psychological dissolution of human identity. Certainly, the kind of technology referred to in *eXistenZ* (both as it exists now and how it is imagined to exist in the future), has been discussed by various theorists in ways that suggest it allows for a greater degree of individual agency for the user (see Chapter 6). In fact, virtuality is often sold as offering an extended form of freedom to the subject that ignores, or transcends the limits of human biology and the constraints of normal social subjectivity. At the same time, if the predominance of violent and sexual imagery in the games is anything to go by, virtual reality is also sold as playing to basic Freudian drives – namely sexual libido and the death drive. Unlike the audience of a feature film, the player of a virtual reality game is able to interact with the fantasy world on offer. But, as will become evident, this association with a 'free-willed' and unconstrained form of individuality is complicated, in *eXistenZ,* through the various moments when the players' true identities are brought into question. Instead, the film deals with the way in which new cyborgian technologies make a lie of both deterministic and transcendent models of humanity, both Freudian and Existentialist versions of being human.

In the opening sequence of the film, Allegra Geller announces that 'eXistenZ is not just game'; after which several volunteers are chosen to 'product test' the alternative reality on offer. Each player is plugged into a gaming 'pod' (a fleshy computer built from organic material) via an 'umbycord', which is 'jacked' into the players' 'bioports' (a surgically created, 'anus-like' hole) that allows for connection directly into the human nervous system. Just as the game is apparently about to start a protester makes an attempt on Geller's life and, in the process, injures her 'pod', which contains the only master copy of the game. Geller then goes on the run with the young and inexperienced security guard, Ted Pikul. Having discovered the injury to the pod she decides that the damage can only be assessed by playing the game and persuades Pikul to enter this virtual world with her. Pikul is an apparent novice who has never undergone a 'bioport' operation, but he agrees to undertake the procedure in order to comply with Geller's wishes. As the game proceeds, it becomes increasingly difficult to detect what is meant to be understood as 'real' and what is actually taking place in the gaming world. Also, the behaviour of the central characters' is brought into question when each professes to be overtaken by the actions necessary to the role they play within the game. The 'pod' can access memories and hidden desires within each player, which are then melded with the standard roles and characterisations set up within the game's various scenarios. For example, at several points Pikul claims to be shocked by his own words and actions; whereupon, Geller informs him that they are due to his 'character set-up' and explains that certain dramatic turns are required of him to 'advance the plot'. So the game players seem to function as characters within a classic realist film (particularly of the Hollywood variety) with the assumption that 'action will spring primarily from *individual characters as causal agents*'.[43] Later Pikul exclaims: 'Free will is obviously not a big factor in this little world of ours'. Geller responds: 'It's like real life – there's just enough to make it interesting'. The confusion that all this sets up for player and audience alike spirals until, at the end of the film, a member of the diegetic audience, when facing his apparent death, asks if they are still in the game. Psychical immersion into the game is shown to directly impact upon the player's ability to distinguish between reality and fantasy.

In his book *Cyberia: Life in the Trenches of Hyperspace*, Douglas Rushkoff describes his meeting with a number of young 'gamers' (reportedly in their twenties) in New Jersey, commenting that these players 'live the way they play, and play as a way of life'. Rushkoff goes on to describe the type of 'fantasy role-playing game' (known as FRPs) in which they are involved, as a forerunner to the type of virtual games now played on the internet or via game consoles. In order to play this game, Rushkoff states that players must behave according to their 'character profile'. The game has no set rules but merely acts as an 'interpretative grid' within which the players improvise (in a similar way to an acting exercise). The object of the game is not only 'to keep their characters alive' but also to create entertainment largely by 'getting into trouble and then trying to get out again'.[44] The players are, therefore, encouraged to create a number of dramatic (often adversarial) situations in which they can work through their character. However, according to Rushkoff, these players appear to have extended their experiences of the gaming world to encompass their actual lives, in the creation of what he describes as 'designer reality'. For Rushkoff, the players have therefore 'adopted the cyberian literary paradigm into real life'.[45] The literary paradigm he is referring to was primarily that set up in the cyberpunk novels of the 1980s and Rushkoff goes on to state that 'fantasy role-playing served as a bridge between the stories of cyberpunk and the reality of lives in Cyberia'.[46] So, Rushkoff's account argues that these fictional worlds and the performed behaviour that ensues from the playing of these games can actually become the reality that the player lives by. The players appear to 'internalise' their performances to such an extent that they become their game characters. On the other hand, of course, it could also be said that the game simply acts as a mechanism through which the players can disavow their own 'urges', desires and even actions.

Likewise, Howard Rheingold discusses the idea that players within a virtual reality environment are prone to 'internalise' various traits of the characters they take on within a given virtual world. Rheingold, like Rushkoff, is focusing on a similar type of fantasy game scenario, only these are played on the Internet and are known as MUDs. He goes on to describe them as:

> Multi-User Dungeons – imaginary worlds in computer databases where people use words and programming languages to improvise melodramas, build worlds and all the objects in them, solve puzzles, invent amusements and tools, compete for prestige and power, gain wisdom, seek revenge, indulge greed and lust and violent impulses . . . kill – or die.[47]

Rheingold also says that users 'testify passionately that the feelings they have about their characters and worlds are real to them and often quite intense'.[48] By drawing upon a number of critics and theorists, he speculates that the media saturated environment of modern living has brought about what he terms a 'social saturation', which has led to an internalising of a vast number of characteristics and roles. This process of internalisation is self-consciously sought out and made readily available to the players in *eXistenZ*. In fact, the players in *eXistenZ* are not only aware of the process taking place, but seem to embrace the actions/emotions that their 'character profile' excites. This is most clearly displayed after the participants have exited the virtual world of 'transCendenZ'. At this point the game's designer, Yevgeny Nourish (Don McKellar), and his female assistant chair a discussion session in which the players comment on their experience of the game and their own performances. All the players sit on a platform in a semi-circle and rather awkwardly go through a process of self-criticism. The player who undertook the role of Gas (Willem Dafoe) within the game comments: 'I was really bummed out at first – I got knocked out of the game so soon'. But this is soon followed by another player's commendation of his performance and there is a round of tentative applause, which appears to both embarrass and appease him. Another player then states: 'I sucked, but you guys (referring to Geller and Pikul) were great. You were like game divas. Personally I think you both deserve to win'. This young player seems to elide the quality of their performances with their ability to compete within the gaming scenario. Speaking to Nourish, Geller then admits: 'the game picked up on my ambition to be like you'. Nourish replies: 'you were so good in that role that I suspect it won't be long before Pilgrimage (the game manufacturer) is after you to sign a design contract'. His comments suggest that her very performance of the role indicates that she has the skills to take on this position in reality. Following this session, Geller and Pikul turn on Nourish and reveal themselves as the assassins sent to kill the creator of 'transCendenZ'. This echoes the actions set up at the opening of the film/game and is partially explained by the game within a game scenario. Nourish had previously confided to his assistant that he was troubled by the degree of 'anti-game' sentiment evident during the test run. Worried that the hidden desires of the players have been brought to the surface by the game, he also shows some concern about his own safety. Certainly his worries seem well-founded when Geller and Pikul turn on him, but, in keeping with the rest of the film, this narrative turn is ambiguous, as an alternative reading might suggest that our two protagonists were so affected by the game that they now see themselves as the undercover agents of its destruction. In other words, while the game allows for the 'playing out' of a Freudian model of subjectivity, this comes to be bound up with narrative and character construction rather than being understood as essential or authentic.

Claudia Springer has pointed out that in a number of Hollywood films featuring virtual reality 'cyberspace is constructed as an instigator of wild instability, and simultaneously as a therapeutic device to restore conventional order'.[49] If cyberspace is understood as threatening to conventional notions of a fixed and unified identity then, in the mainstream films that Springer cites, this threat is contained through 'asserting the primacy of "the real", of restoring or attaining an identity that exists "outside" of the electronic arena'.[50] Of particular interest is Springer's reading of *Johnny Mnemonic* (dir. Robert Longo, 1995) as a film that 'takes Johnny from fragmentation to unification, and defines the process only in conventional terms of a resolution of the oedipal crisis and attainment of heterosexual romance'.[51] Picking up on Springer's point here, I would suggest that a traditional, depth modelling of the psychoanalytic self therefore triumphs against the threat of the post-humanist, postmodern subjectivity that is played out, and contained, within the cyber-technologies featured in these mainstream films. In looking at *Johnny Mnemonic,* it is notable that the performance given by Keanu Reeves in this film is highly reminiscent of those seen in *Crash*: a literally 'vacuous' characterisation is indicated in the absence of subtextual enactings. Of course, this is explained in *Johnny Mnemonic* as due to Johnny's 'dumping' of long-term memory in order to make room for his implants. The inference here is that Johnny is cut off from his own inner drives (those associated with the psychoanalytic model) and is left totally reliant on a technological environment to guide his actions. The suggestion being that it is only when he regains his psychoanalytic self that he regains his essential humanity. So in *Johnny Mnemonic* the psychoanalytic assumption of what is really human remains largely unquestioned. In comparison, it would seem that the virtual reality technology in *eXistenZ* operates rather differently, to the point where a depth modelling as an essential part of human nature becomes questionable.

An earlier film, not mentioned in the Springer article, is also worth a comparative mention at this point. The narrative trajectory of *eXistenZ* bears some resemblance to *Total Recall* (dir. Paul Verhoeven, 1990), in that by the end of the film the Schwarzenegger character is so affected by his memory implants that he chooses to retain his implanted identity as an underground agent. However, in *Total Recall* our hero replaces one fixed identity with another. The various roles that he plays out in the film are kept separate and, although he is eventually made aware of their existence, there is little indication that this impacts upon his final sense of a unified self. That is not to say that this unified self is in any sense 'deep'. What Paul Verhoeven called 'a simplified version of human emotions' (see p. 138) as played out in Schwarzenegger's performance, can be aligned with the 'flat' characterisation common to science fiction. For Verhoeven, *Total Recall* was 'really a philosophical movie – although done in an ironic and light style', and he also commented that 'the power of the movie is not so much the personal emotion, but the confusion of the audience in not being able to separate or to make a choice between two realities'. So the flat performances here work to place emphasis upon the ideas proposed by *Total Recall* and upon the spectacle of the fantastic environments created in the film. Dean Norris's comments (see pp. 238–44) also testify as to how these performances were elicited and to the 'inauthenticity' that Verhoeven sought to bring to this film. Unlike those films that create a distinct separation between diegetically real and fantasy worlds, often signalled through performance, *Total Recall* refuses to clearly signal which of these worlds is intended as real and which as fantasy. Confusion is encouraged in following the attempts of the hero, Douglas Quaid/Hauser (Arnold Schwarzenegger), to disentangle fact from fantasy in his own mind. Further, even though the narrative resolves this issue at the end of the film, it is significant that the hero chooses to adopt what finally turns out to be a fictional persona, leaving both Quaid (and viewer?) immersed in the fantasy world that Hauser created, internalised, and now lives. While the 'therapeutic' power of the cyber-technologies in *Total Recall* might have turned a money-grabbing capitalist (Hauser) into a people's saviour (Quaid), this film also fails to uphold 'the primacy of "the real" '.[52]

In a similar manner to Quaid's 'virtual holiday' in *Total Recall*, the progression of the game in *eXistenZ* is associated with standard, generic film plots and the character profiles are likened to familiar stereotypes in various film genres (especially the action and thriller genres). For instance, Geller's search for an illegal bioport implant for Pikul takes them to an isolated gas station, where the resident mechanic, the aforementioned Gas, is willing to undertake this operation. After fitting the import, Gas produces a gun and turns on Geller, claiming that her dead body is worth millions to an underground movement. Geller attempts to talk him out of killing her by saying: 'Do you really expect them to hand over five mil. cash . . . don't you ever go to the fucking movies?' To which Gas replies: 'I like your script – I want to be in it'. It is as though Geller attempts to take back control of the narrative by indicating what the outcome of his actions are likely to be – as though the game plan were analogous to a standard movie plot. This strategy fails because the character playing Gas reverses her logic by indicating his willingness to be a part of this plot; to fulfil his character's function. Had he succeeded in killing her, it might be assumed that he would have earned a more central role in the unfolding story. But, as it is, he fails and is left behind as the narrative continues to follow Geller and Pikul. The players/characters are, in fact, vying for control of the narrative in competing within the game. In this respect, I find Norris's repeated use of the game metaphor fascinating, as he explains his experiences of acting in films like *Total Recall* and *The Lawnmower Man* (dir. Brett Leonard, 1992). As Norris puts it:

> It's more of a power study. What power do I have versus what power do other characters have and how can I use it to my advantage to get what I want – as opposed to trying to find out the Stanislavski kind of emotional thing, which is great for other things, but not for science fiction.

The kind of game play that Norris suggests is a central feature of the contemporary science fiction film genre is not dissimilar to the kind of game play that both Rheingold and Rushkoff discuss in the FRPs and MUDs. Rushkoff implies that the organiser of the FRP group he interviews is, in fact, in control of the game's trajectory when he comments that he is 'unable, it seems, to accept a role in life other than "Gamemaster" '.[53] And, in looking at the MUDs, Rheingold notes how '[g]aining the power to modify the environment in which the game takes place is a primary goal for newcomers' in these virtual worlds.[54] It is as though the players of MUDs and FRPs wanted more than simply to function as characters within these worlds; their goal appears to be the attaining of a kind of omniscience analogous, perhaps, to the director of a film. If *eXistenZ* is foregrounding this element of the role-play game then it seems that authorship is the real goal of the players. But, authorship is shown to be an illusive prize in the film because the degree of interaction allowed by the game means that control over the virtual world and the narrative's progression within the game is constantly shifting.

Throughout my analysis of both *Crash* and *eXistenZ* what has become apparent is a certain play with an established 'depth' formula of being human and visions of a constantly emerging techno-human. While many of the mainstream cyborg movies present the viewer with a fully re-embodied and unified version of future subjectivity, Cronenberg's two films leave open any sense of a final outcome or finalised state of being. To a large extent, the films' self-conscious focus upon performance not only speaks to previous representations of the techno-human, but seems to allow for more contingency in the evolution of the techno-human being. In these two films, the performative aspects of performance are emphasised not in the sense that a 'deeper' subjectivity is reintroduced into the realm of the technologically constructed world, but in the sense that uncertainty and possibility is kept in play.

INTERVIEW: ACTOR DEAN NORRIS

C: According to my research, you trained as an actor at the Royal Academy of Dramatic Arts in London.

N: Indeed, yes, I spent some time over there in England. I was actually on a three-year programme, but about a year and half into it I got a job offer with an American Repertory Theatre – so that's why I opted out of the last year and a half and went back and started working.

C: To what degree do you think this training prepared you for the film roles you later undertook, specifically within the science fiction genre?

N: I think it did a lot. While you're there and you're young and rebellious, you think that you really don't need any training. Then, as the time goes on, the kind of discipline that you have learned – with the voice and just the really kind of basic things like relaxation techniques – really come out later on. Film is really interesting versus the stage, but it's no less pressured in its own way.

People are often say 'oh it must be really easy to do that' – and it is true that if you mess it up then you get to do it again, but it's also true that there's a huge pressure pouring down upon you because of the time and money that goes into film. You don't have unlimited time, so you do have to be able to perform under pressure.

C: Do you think it was advantageous to train in England, given that you work mostly in America?

N: It was for me, because I kind of got plenty of training, in my teens and stuff, in the ways of American acting and I was really glad to have gotten accepted – and I made a particular point to apply there as I wanted to get a different type of training.

C: How do you approach a film role? Is there a common process that you undertake each time?

N: I guess the common denominator is obviously to try to find out what the role is about, what the character is about, and what the character's position is within the film. That's kind of the back research. It's important to me, particularly, to find out what the character's role is, not only what he is, what his history is and all that stuff, but what his role is in the movie.

C: In terms of, maybe, the way he functions within the whole story?

N: Yes, that's right. It's important to talk to the director to reach an understanding, to find out the director's view of how the movie looks or what it is about. It's not your job to go and say, 'hey this is my interpretation and this is the way it goes' – it's your job to understand your function in the film. I think you have more of an opportunity to explore those things in a film than perhaps in television, TV comes so quickly – directors are hired at the last moment – it's less of a director's medium.

C: So would you say that there was a degree of 'self-directing' in television, more so than in film?

N: Absolutely.

C: What kind of guidance do you generally receive in preparing for a film role? Does this vary a lot? I mean you've kind of covered that, but I'm thinking of the brief character synopsis you might get with a script, or on set rehearsal, if any, and even the audition process, if you undertake that. What kind of other guidance would you get from others working around you or would this only come from the director?

N: It's usually only from the director unless there is a senior actor who's there and who is willing to open up to you. You know I've had some great advice from guys like Donald Sutherland and Anthony Hopkins. One would be a fool not to take advice from them. But other than that, it is essentially from the director and the director will say how he sees your role and how he sees that character and how it fits into the movie and what the scene means to the movie and what we need to get out of it in order for that to work . . . and things like that.

It's important not to set things in stone in your mind – while you're working on it in the bathroom, you know.

C: So you have to remain malleable in a sense?

N: And I think that's an important trait and something that I try to work on. I mean you might try to work on a part one way and then you get onto the set and it's very loud and everything else and the way you wanted to do it completely wouldn't work. I hate to use these sports analogies, but they always seem to work so well . . . it's best if you train yourself really well and then you kind of relax into the game and what the game gives you. If the game give you that then you react that way and if the game gives you this then you react differently, whatever the exact moment is at that point. Amazingly some of the best things come out when you just relax into the situation. You can tell if an actor is not relaxed in the situation if he doesn't react to whatever input comes along – either from another actor or from something happening on the set and you realise that the goal is to be as relaxed as possible while maintaining your character. Then anything that happens you hope to react to it as truthfully as possible.

In film you generally don't have two cameras going. So, one person is filmed and then they turn the camera around and film the other one. So you need to try to find, in the early part of the day how you're both going to do it – so I'm reacting to the same scene that he is. Even though the person will be there, he may filmed in three different kinds of ways – little tweaks – four or five different shadings of that scene – and then they turn around and film me. Neither one of us know which of those will be edited together. My performance might be edited with a performance that he did in the different way. That gives the process over to the editing person as well, which is the nature of film.

C: So you're very much at the mercy of the editor in that sense.

N: That's right – and a lot of other people as well. For instance, when the music track is added it can change the tone of the scene completely from what you thought you were playing. Music has a very powerful impact on the mood of the scene and you have no idea what that music will be. Sometimes you wish you did, but then again it's the director's job and whoever else's, to put it all together.

C: Although some directors use music on set I've heard?

N: Yes they do, but I haven't had that experience – and I think that's great because music affects me a lot and I would love to know what the music is going to be on a particular scene.

C: That's interesting, especially in looking at blockbuster science fiction films, which often use a lot of music. You have worked very extensively in science fiction films as well as science fiction on television. I wondered whether there was a sense in which you had actively sought out science fiction as a genre?

N: I'm not sure whether I've actually sought out science fiction, as much as I think that because of my 'look' I've been seen as a kind of archetype. I'm able to represent a certain kind of authority. Archetypal is the only word I can think of, as opposed to really naturalistic.

C: Yes, I was going to say that you've played a lot establishment figures, government figures, authoritative types, and you think that there is a physical stereotyping here?

N: The physical is part of it. For whatever reason, you know, the bald pate and, I don't know, the set of the jaw or something. I think establishment figures like that exist, by virtue of force, power, ultimately, and I think that that kind of look projects that kind of thing. So they get an easy buy, if you understand – let this guy project that. Particularly in science fiction where the establishment, the government, is often portrayed as a sinister force.

C: So it wouldn't necessarily be simply due to physical appearance? Are there a particular set of demands in terms of the science fiction genre? For instance, a particular vocal delivery that you might often be required to perform in playing those kinds of authority figures in that setting.

N: Yes, other than the physical, they all demand a vocal part to be precise, and they want it to be articulated, almost over-articulated, to the point where it seems a little unreal. It's not naturalistic . . . it's all about precision.

C: More mechanical?

N: More mechanical – right.

C: More theatrical maybe?

N: Maybe theatrical. Again coming back to the archetypical sort of acting, it's almost that I portray a lot of those things – a closeness to the machine. For instance, in *The Lawnmower Man*, the humanity is what Pierce Brosnan represents, with his scruffy hair and scruffy beard. And he's dealing with feelings and everything else, whereas my character is really the opposite of that whole thing. In that role, my voice appears to be an unreal, or fake, with an affected accent to the point where it's kind of jarring.

C: Playing 'the director' in *The Lawnmower Man,* you use a lot of almost quirky pauses as part of the effect and a very mellifluous, it seems to me, monotone – which suggests a kind of un-humanity and a sort of lack of authenticity. It's obviously very deliberate and I wondered what your thinking was with that performance?

N: Again, I think I wanted to produce a contrast with the fear expressed by the other characters. I mean there was also a great deal of fear surrounding virtual reality – particularly back then – and the internet wasn't even a viable public thing at that point. The film kind of played on all those fears. Fears in science fiction seem to revolve around the unfeeling machine and the fact that computers reduce everything to zeroes and ones. All of that informed that character. We wanted him to be creepily mellifluous – you know what I'm saying? It allowed him to seem completely at ease and to be completely unruffled, which again is unreal and unfeeling. I think if a person is so unfeeling then those sort of odd pauses come out. It's almost like a psychopathic person – they have to try to imitate feeling as opposed to actually feeling it . . . if they're trying to hide the fact that they're psychopathic. That's how people look when they're trying to be sympathetic and the fact that this guy maybe tries too hard means that it doesn't quite come out right.

C: As though he's constructing it as he's going along?

N: Yeah, right.

C: I see similarities here with later performances by other actors. I'm thinking in particular of Hugo Weaving as Agent Smith in *The Matrix*. He uses exactly the same kind of pausing technique.

N: He was great in that. I loved that film.

C: I'd like to know a little about the differences or, indeed, similarities in working within the science fiction genre as opposed to other genres. Do you think there are differences in approach in working within one genre as opposed to another genre, which perhaps produce a certain sort of stylistic in the performance?

N: Well, working in science fiction is almost more like working within experimental theatre, as opposed to other film and TV genres where you really are trying to be naturalistic, charmingly personable, a real person. This is particularly true of TV – American TV, I should say. One is rewarded for being particularly charming and personable in American TV. You have to bring more of a personality to it, a true personality if you can, in regards to whatever character you're playing. In terms of other movies I've done, mostly action films, the goal or the idea is to be more of a real guy – if you will. I have not got the sense in any of the science fictions that I've done that I need to know the history of the character – in terms of whether his father beat him as a child and things like that. With other genres, whether you're married or your wife is bothering you etc. . . . that can inform your character. But the only history, in terms of the science fiction characters, that seems necessary is the position of that character within the government and his reasons for manipulation and things like that.

C: So it's much more a present moment that you're dealing with? You're not thinking back and constructing a life for this character – you're dealing with a present moment and broad set of circumstances within that present moment?

N: Yes, I think so – it's more of about manipulation. Generally those characters want something. I guess that's true of any role or any character, but in particular they're intense in their needing to have or change or manipulate something. It's more of a power study. What power do I have versus what power do other characters have and how can I use it to my advantage to get what I want – as opposed to trying to find out the Stanislavski kind of emotional thing, which is great for other things, but not for science fiction. I mean, Paul Verhoeven, who did *Total Recall*, that's exactly his approach. He says, I need you to look this way – it's not the old 'well what's my motivation for this or that' – it's just 'look this way' or 'I need you to take a pause here'. I'm not opposed to that because I like him, I think he's great. I like the artificiality that he brings to his films. That's his vision. That's the way he wants to do it and he's certainly done some of the great ones – I mean *Robocop* and *Total Recall* – not to mention his earlier work in Europe. You know, you say 'hey great, let's play his game'. And his game is such to say 'what I need from you here is a big presence this way or a big presence that way'.

C: Of course, in *Total Recall* you were dealing with some very heavy, facial construction make-up. How did you find that?

N: Yeah, it was clearly a challenge, but it was fun as well. To try to make those little pieces come alive. I guess that was the challenge of that role.

C: Did you find yourself concentrating on other areas of your body in order to perform? A bit like mask work?

N: Exactly, and also once I'd got the make-up on I'd take it in front of the mirror and see what I could do. Because what you think in your mind, might not be reflected outwardly. You might have to exaggerate a certain something in order to make the mask work correctly. I mean we have to work with mirrors anyway a lot, but you want to know what your face can do. How far you need to go, how much less you need to do. But with a mask on like that it was important to really take some time and see how your face looked when you thought something. You might have to exaggerate the expression a bit because you have this big hunk of plastic on your face.

C: What about other special effects, like CGI that is used these days. I mean do you ever find yourself acting with, or against, nothing at all? Special effects are so integral to science fiction, I wondered if that created any particular demands?

N: Yes, it does. It continues to do so to this day. Even with *Total Recall*, the backgrounds were blue screen (or green screen now). So you really don't know what's going on. You depend on the director to feed you right . . . they essentially talk you through it. They turn the sound off and say, OK, 'this is happening and now it's happening more – so it's really coming at you this time', or something like that. Again that goes back to coming into the role with some flexibility, so you are prepared to deal with whatever comes at you. However the ball is thrown at you, to try to catch it or to take a swing at it the right way.

I actually did a little piece in this movie called *The One* in which nobody (dir. James Wong, 2001) was there, ever. They literally had these balls hanging down from the ceiling and those were the points you were meant to look at, or fire at, or take a swing at etc. Then magically they were turned into characters in post-production.

C: And what have you thought when you've seen the final product?

N: I've always been amazed at the fact that it works out so well.

Notes

1. 'Science Fiction and Emerging Values', in Myers (ed.) 1983, p. 16.
2. 'Genre and Performance: An Overview', in Butler (ed.) 1991, p. 117.
3. Bukatman 1993, p. 8.
4. Ibid., p. 43.
5. This is a term borrowed from William Gibson's cyberpunk novels and is used to define groups of people who use older technologies, either through lack of access or through choice (low-techs).
6. Following Walker's review of *Crash* in 1996, the *Daily Mail* began to lobby for a ban on the film. For a detailed account of the initial reception of *Crash* see Barker *et al.* 2001.
7. 'Imaginary Cities: Images of Postmodernity', in Watson and Gibson (eds) 1994, p. 117.
8. Rodley 1996, p. 8.
9. This is also a fascinating moment because of the way in which recent mainstream films have attempted to re-code the act of smoking as 'evil', as 'un-sexy'. Aside from the way in which this can be read as Cronenberg playing with the censorship mechanisms of mainstream film and societal taboos, this moment may also indicate how this code has been emptied of its subtextual meaning.
10. Rodley 1996, p. 7.
11. Of course, given that audiences have become so accustomed to the enacting of underlying motivation and emotion in film acting, this does not discount that many may still project underlying meaning of one sort or another onto these performances.
12. 'Postfuturism', in Sobchack 1993, pp. 223–305.
13. Jameson 1991 p. 12.
14. Ibid., p. 15 (Jameson's emphasis).

15. It is notable that Cronenberg replaced the figure of Elizabeth Taylor in Ballard's book with that of James Dean.
16. It is interesting to compare this dialogue with comments made by the character, Plato, in *Rebel without a Cause*. When asked about the Dean character Plato says of him: 'He doesn't say much but when he does you know he means it . . . he's sincere'. Of course, within the context of this film, sincerity was being highlighted by these comments as a kind of extra-filmic selling point of the Method style.
17. Wexman 1993, p. 179.
18. Conrey 1993, p. 256.
19. Ibid., 1993, p. 258.
20. 'The Return of Existentialism in Performance Art', in Battcock (ed.) 1984, pp. 136–7.
21. Toepfer for 1996, p. 77.
22. Ibid., p. 77.
23. Smith 1997, p. 17.
24. Schechner 1982, p. 44.
25. Ibid., p. 45.
26. Ibid., p. 9.
27. Austander 1997, p. 1.
28. Ibid., p. 91.
29. Ibid., p. 85.
30. Schneidor 1997, p. 2.
31. Ibid., p. 2.
32. Ibid., p. 23.
33. Ibid., p. 6.
34. Sartre 1974, p. 28.
35. Ibid., p. 26 (Sartre's emphasis).
36. Reference can be made to Chapter 2, 'Bad Faith', in Sartre 2000, pp. 47–70.
37. Sartre 1974, p. 34.
38. Sartre 2000, p. 570.
39. Ibid., p. 571.
40. Sartre 1974, p. 55.
41. Ibid., pp. 55–6.
42. 'Sartre's Moral Psychology', in Howells (ed.) 1992, p. 105.
43. Bordwell and Thompson 1993, p. 82 (Bordwell and Thompson's emphases).
44. Rushkoff, 1995, pp. 243–4.
45. Ibid., p. 251.
46. Ibid., p. 252.
47. Rheingold 1994, p. 145.
48. Ibid., 1994, pp. 155–6.
49. 'Psycho-Cybernetics in Films of the 1990s', in Kuhn (ed.) 1999, p. 206.
50. Ibid., pp. 214–15.
51. Ibid., p. 213.
52. This is certainly ironic given Schwarzenegger's promotion of capitalist ideals and his known affiliations with the Republican party.
53. Rushkoff 1995, p. 253.
54. Rheingold 1994, p. 149.

8. CONCLUSION: THE TECHNOLOGY OF SCIENCE FICTION CINEMA

Figure 8.1 Old-style effects meet computer graphics in *Independence Day*. 20th Century Fox / The Kobal Collection.

Since the inception of the science fiction film, the genre has been built upon a thematic interest in the social and philosophical delights and dangers associated with industrial, communications and biological technologies. This is a characteristic that it shares with the written genre and, to an extent, with the science fiction comic book, graphic novel and television series. However, science fiction films are also known for their devotion to technological display and for the presentation of phenomenal spectacle. These are characteristics of the film genre that can be traced back to the beginnings of cinema. As outlined in the introduction, early forerunners of the science fiction film genre often featured the new technologies of the industrial age at the same time as they showcased the illusions made possible by the advent of the cinematic apparatus. Although George Méliès' *La Voyage dans la Lune* (1902) is probably the most famous proto-science fiction film, on a structural level many 'trick films' displayed a two-fold convention of presenting new and fantastic technologies within a formal composition that foregrounded cinematic intervention and invention. While audience members in 1895 may well have run away from the screen in fear and panic upon viewing Auguste and Louis Lumière's short 'actualité' of a train approaching the camera in *L'Arrivée d'un train à la Ciotat*, viewers quickly learned to distinguish the experience of seeing a film from the reality of modern life. The reported effect of the Lumière's film was even parodied in Robert W. Paul's *The Countryman and the Cinematograph* (aka *The Countryman's First Sight of the Animated Pictures*, 1901). This film within a film showed a shot of a stage, a proscenium, and framed screen upon which is playing a film of a dancing girl.[1] An over-excited country yokel takes to the stage and is seen reacting to the girl in the film. This is then replaced by a film within the film showing a train rushing toward the screen as the yokel runs to the wings in fear. The yokel has not learned to distinguish the special effect that is film from concrete reality and is ridiculed for his improper behaviour and stupidity. The final insult comes as the film he views changes for the last time and the yokel sees his own likeness clumsily seducing a milkmaid. In a comic rendition of audience responses to the very first films, *The Countryman and the Cinematograph* is addressed to a more sophisticated viewer and calls attention to film itself as a technology of the new industrial age.

By the time Paul produced *The '?' Motorist* (dir. Walter R. Booth, 1906), many filmmakers were making extravagant use of effects like reverse motion, multiple exposure, extreme close-ups, stop-motion and so on. In this later film stop-motion camera techniques and special effects using miniature models are combined with the featuring of a motor car. This is but one example of an early film that shattered the laws of space and time in its use of cinematic effects alongside a playful extrapolation of the extended speed and scope of travel made possible by industrial-age vehicles. The narrative follows the passengers of a car as they exceed the speed limit and run down a policeman who tries to stop the reckless driver from proceeding further. Due to the wonders of cinema, the policeman survives this ordeal, but eventually gives up the chase as the car is seen driving vertically up the side of a building and launching into space. In an obvious reference to Méliès' *La Voyage dans la lune*, the rest of the film follows the car's journey around the solar system. After circling the moon and racing round the rings of Mars, the car eventually runs out of petrol and crash lands in the middle of a court house. Once again, the comic disposition of this film indicates that it is addressed to a knowing audience and the fantastical nature of the plot accentuates the technological wizardry of cinema at work for their pleasure and amusement.

Of course, many of the practices instituted by these early film pioneers were later appropriated as part of an almost imperceptible film language in the construction of narrative realism, but the overt display of cinematic effects continued as a crucial element of the fantasy genres that emerged when the film industry began to establish itself as a major form of popular entertainment. While musical, horror and science fiction films all made spectacular use of technically clever cinematic effects, the science fiction genre was usually distinguished by its frequent creation and display of fantastical new technologies as a central component and driving force within the narrative world of the film. In an essay entitled, 'The Cinema of Attractions: Early film, Its Spectator and the Avant-Garde',[2] Tom Gunning re-evaluated the form and function of early film. Up until this point academics had tended to think of early films as primitive precursors to a later, 'fully mature', classical narrative cinema. Gunning contested this view, arguing that early cinema aimed to exhibit the novelty of film as an attraction. Initially films excited audiences purely in the presentation of a moving and active photographic image of the world. However, this simple thrill soon wore thin and early cinema had to renew its novelty value by offering more unusual sights and spectacular displays in order to draw an audience. For Gunning the main attraction attributable to early 'trick films' was of a specifically cinematic nature and he goes to state that 'to approach even the plotted trick films, such as *La Voyage dans la lune* (1902), simply as precursors of later narrative structures is to miss the point. The story simply provides a frame upon which to string a demonstration of the magical possibilities of the cinema'.[3] Even as both *La Voyage dans la lune* and *The '?' Motorist* tell a story, these unfold in an episodic fashion and it is the featured special effects, rather than the characters, that appear to motivate the action in each of these films. As Gunning puts it: 'The cinema of attractions expends little energy creating characters with psychological motivations or individual personality . . . its energy moves outward towards an acknowledged spectator rather than inwards towards the character-based situations essential to classical narrative'.[4]

Given the centrality of the science fiction film in the birth of the so-called New Hollywood and given the genre's special connection with early film, it is hardly surprising that academics turned to Gunning's article in their efforts to explore the aesthetic shifts and modes of address that emerged with post-classical cinema. This is a cinema that frequently places emphasis upon the thrills and spills that film can evoke and upon the big-screen spectacle that effects can create, so it seemed to many critics that the form and style of Gunning's 'cinema of attractions' had re-emerged to dominate popular cinema in the post-classical era. As discussed in Chapter 3, although the peculiar artistry of special effects in many science fiction films of the 1960s and 1970s was certainly held up for inspection by the viewer, the mode of address adopted by the 'new art films' is not suggestive of the 'outwardly' moving energy that Gunning details in his article. Rather the viewer was invited to look inward, to meditate upon the meanings evoked by the on-screen image. A more obvious example of the kind of energy that Gunning refers to was reinstated with the coming of the later blockbuster films. For many, George Lucas's *Star Wars* films (1977–2005) and Robert Zemeckis's *Back to the Future* series (1985–90), among others, re-created the 'cinema of attractions' in their vigorous action and delivery of exhilarating special effects. It was the science fiction blockbusters that emerged in the late 1970s and early 1980s that more readily reaffirmed cinema's 'roots in stimulus and carnival rides'.[5]

COMPUTER GRAPHICS IMAGERY AND CONTEMPORARY SCIENCE FICTION

While special effects have always been a foregrounded attraction of the science fiction film, it is no accidence that the arrival of computer graphics in film was an important component in the apparent reappearance of the 'cinema of attractions' as a dominant form. Computers had been used in the creation of effects and unusual images since the 1970s. For instance, animators Gary Demos and John Whitney Jr, from the computer technology company called Triple I, created 2-D digital images for *Westworld* (dir. Michael Crichton, 1973), which represented the view of the robot gunslinger (played by Yul Brynner) as he tracked his human prey. 3-D computer graphics imagery was later featured in *Star Wars* (dir. George Lucas, 1977), during a 'briefing scene' when the Starfighters are shown a large computer screen containing a mock-up of their forthcoming attack upon the Death Star. The later *Alien* (dir. Ridley Scott, 1979) also used computer animated graphics, which were inserted into the ready-made frame of the Nostromo's navigational computer as their spaceship comes into land near the wreckage of an alien craft. So, these films presented this new technology in cinema on both a formal and narrative level: the earlier film revealed its 2-D imagery as the literal point of view from the computerised systems of the robot and the latter films demonstrated the 3-D imagery by showing a diegetic audience concentrating on the framed off effects emanating from computer screens. The two-fold convention of presenting new and fantastic technologies within a formal structure that foregrounds cinematic intervention and invention returned with renewed impetus in the science fiction films that followed.

Following the success of *Star Wars*, George Lucas set up a special-effects company called Industrial Light and Magic, which continued to develop CG imagery for this series of films as well as producing effects for other films. For instance, the all-digital 'genesis' effect in *Star Trek: The Wrath of Khan* (dir. Nicholas Meyer, 1982) was of epic proportions, representing the devastation wreaked by a futuristic doomsday, terraforming device as it sweeps across an entire planet. However, in the same year, the Disney Studios made a much more ambitious attempt to introduce audiences to the wonders of computer graphics in cinema. Disney's *Tron* (dir. Steven Lisberger, 1982) follows the exploits of a scientist (played by Jeff Bridges) who has been transported inside a video game. Here he repeatedly fights for his life against characters created by the game and battles to return to reality. The majority of the film's action is set within the virtual world of the video game, but even though the film did make relatively extensive use of CG images, much of the computer-generated look of this world was created using backlighting and the introduction of colour. For instance, a lot of the live action footage was shot is black and white and later overlaid using a traditional colourising technique. Against the starkly linear setting of the computer world, the actors' action is both simplified and accentuated by their strangely luminous attire, which echoes the neon-like light streaks that mark out the game's pathways. The film was launched onto the market on the strength of its cutting-edge computer effects, but it was not a success with audiences. It seems that while CG effects could provide a gratifying supplementary element within a film, audiences would not accept the complete immersion into the world of computer imagery proposed by *Tron*.

After the box office failure of *Tron*, mainstream science fiction films of the early 1980s remained relatively cautious in its use of this new technology. But convinced that CG had a place in live-action cinema, Gary Demos and John Whitney Jr separated from Triple I to form the effects company Digital Productions. Moving away from the aesthetic path laid out in *Tron*, Digital Productions produced photorealistic CG effects for *The Last Starfighter* (dir. Nick Castle, 1984). Substituting CG objects for what might have previously been achieved using models, the metallic spacecraft that swept our boy-hero off on the rollercoaster adventure of a lifetime looked solid enough, as did the rest of the computer generated, technological hardware that was inserted into the frame at various points in the film. These effects were visually integrated with other elements within the frame of the film. In other words, rather than seeing the human element ostensibly submerged within a computer world, *Starfighter*'s CG effects were subsumed within the otherwise naturalistic setting of the film.

Starfighter performed well at the box office, but further developments in CG came from the animation sector of the industry. Companies such as Pixar went on to design new rendering and animations software and produced a number of feature-length animations from the mid-to late 1980s (e.g. *Luxo Jr.* [1986], *Red's Dream* [1987] and the Oscar-winning *Tin Toy* [1988], all dir. John Lasseter). In live-action cinema, ILM's developments continued to be showcased in the *Star Wars* and *Star Trek* films, but their most notable addition to the field came with the introduction of the digital morph for the fantasy film *Willow* (dir. Ron Howard, 1988). Departing from the scientific pretext for CG effects displays in earlier films, the narrative incentive for showcasing the morphing technique in *Willow* is magic. In his efforts to save a human child from evil forces, the would-be wizard, Willow (Warwick Davis), ineptly wields a magic wand that changes a sorceress into a series of animals. Similar kinds of metamorphoses had been previously achieved using cross-fades (e.g. a number of early 'Jekyll and Hyde' films used cross-fades to show character transformation), but morphing presented the viewer with a slower, more seamless change between characters. Like *Tron*, *Willow* did not match up to expectations at the box office, but the morphing effect took on a life of its own in later science fiction films. Building upon Pixar's developments in the 'RenderMan' software, ILM went on to create both the watery pseudopod alien for the film *The Abyss* (dir. James Cameron, 1989) and the T1000 metamorphosis effects in *Terminator 2: Judgment Day* (dir. James Cameron, 1991). Unlike the simple wireframe images seen in the first *Star Wars* and *Alien*,[6] and unlike the tangible and rigid CG objects that populated *The Last Starfighter*, the rendering of these two characters not only allowed the obviously impossible to appear visually believable, but also to perform organically within the frame of the film. Paradoxically, both of these generated characters took on a reassuringly human face at the same time as they were unable to settle upon a meaningful identity; their slippery status echoed in the appearance of their liquid surfaces and fluid dimensions. While the alien pseudopod momentarily mimics the features of human faces, it remains translucent and quickly returns to its watery state. The T1000 is more dissembling as it transmutes into a variety of human characters. Nevertheless, the viewer is alerted to its true nature when the creature is seen in its literally liquid form between transformations. So, the morphing in these two films does not simply involve the visual change from one recognisable character into another, as was the case in *Willow*; instead the effect lingers on the intermediary stage between one concrete form and another. Rather than the magical process associated with the fantasy film, the morph in *The Abyss* and *Terminator 2* effectively concentrates the viewer's attention on the space in between familiar images, giving fluid form to the technological process at work and suspending belief (as opposed to disbelief) in the reality of the image.

On one level, these mutable images suitably represented a technology that was caught up in constant state of becoming. The manifestations of digital morphing in *The Abyss* and *Terminator 2* signalled that although CGI was adapting to the narrative world of cinema, it also remained at odds with the diegetic 'reality' of film image. Inhabiting the space between the familiar and the unfamiliar, the pseudopod and T1000 caught the public imagination and the computer-generated morphing effect turned into an endemic emblem of the transformative potential of CGI. Indeed, morphing was not confined to science fiction cinema and became a prominent element in other areas of popular culture. For instance, the same year that *Terminator 2* was released, the morphing effect appeared in Michael Jackson's pop-music video, *Black or White* (featuring a multi-racial group of people seamlessly changing into one another), and was also used in the Exxon advertisement in the US in which a car slowly warps and changes into a tiger. I believe that the fascination with constant conversion and elastic boundaries, as exhibited by the morphing effect, resonated with wider cultural concerns in the late 1980s and early 1990s. Taking the T1000 as an example, the visual plasticity offered in the image of the T1000 as it morphs into characters and objects in order to carry out its purpose, spoke to a new style of living in a highly interconnected, computerised and cyberspatialised world. On a number of levels, the morphing metal man could be seen as an anxious sign of the subjective flexibility demanded by a corporate postmodernity of the 1990s.

Throughout the 1990s the continued use and development of CG effects and computer technologies in mainstream science fiction film followed two parallel routes: the figuring of human characters interacting with computer-generated or computer-controlled objects/characters in a 'real world' environment or the human/post-human character immersed within a computer generated environment. Of course, these are false distinctions in many respects, but I am referring to the way in which characters, objects and environments appeared and functioned within the narrative of individual films. Steven Spielberg's blockbuster hit, *Jurassic Park* (1993), for example, placed its human protagonists within the, albeit fantastic, material world of a futuristic theme park. The park is populated by dinosaurs, which, we are informed, have been re-created using cutting edge, genetic technology. Several scientists, a lawyer, and the grandchildren of the park's creator, are treated to a preview of the wonders produced by this new technology, in the hope that they will approve the park for public access. Before entering the dinosaur enclosures they are taken on an instructive ride that explains how the creatures were created. Following a short film, the moving platform upon which they are seated gives them a momentary glimpse into one of the working laboratories set up behind the scenes. In a reversal of *The Countryman and the Cinematograph,* the lawyer mistakes the human workers for animatronic models, but is sharply informed: 'we have no animatronics here'. Immediately following this scene, the group are led into a laboratory where they witness the birth of a velociraptor. Since they are able to hold and stroke the baby dinosaur, it is obvious that this is an animated model of some kind. Even as this witty self-reflexivity places emphasis upon the model

Figure 8.2   Stan Winston's T-Rex looks down upon the human victims trapped in the car below, from *Jurassic Park*. Amblin / Universal / The Kobal Collection.

work, it also alerts the audience to the imminent arrival of the computer-generated dinosaurs that the group encounter once they have entered the park.

The dinosaurs were brought to the screen through the amalgamation of CGI and the latest in model work, puppetry, robotics and animatronics. The Stan Winston Studio was responsible for building and operating the 'live action' dinosaurs, while ILM provided the CGI. As Winston points out in the following interview (pp. 267–75), the building of moving models allows the actor to interact with a literally fabricated character. So, rather than being isolated against a blue or green screen,[7] the actor is given the opportunity to react to the model character that is fully present within the scene. Winston upholds that his main interest is in the creation of characters rather than effects and he sees his mechanical models as fantastical creatures that function within the narrative in much the same way as the human actor. Together with Winston's mechanical models, ILM was credited with the design of the 'full-motion dinosaurs', which were predominantly featured in those scenes where the creatures are viewed in long shot, chasing, flocking, and generally moving freely around the terrain. Stop-motion, model animation, of the kind that Ray Harryhausen made famous in his science fiction and fantasy films of the 1950s and 1960s (e.g. he created the six-legged octopus mentioned in Chapter 2, in *It Came from beneath the Sea* [dir. Robert Gordon, 1955]), was therefore replaced by both the mechanical model and CGI in *Jurassic Park*. In a move toward greater realism, where stop-motion created a kind of staccato rhythm in the apparent movement of models, the animated models from Winston's studios reproduced a more even flow of creature movement and the 'motion blur' that CGI software was able to simulate gave the impression of smoother, 'naturalistic' movement in the 3-D dinosaur images.[8]

Aside from the CG creature/object inserted into a 'real world' mise-en-scène, science fiction films of the 1990s also began to re-imagine the immersive computer world introduced by *Tron*. Fuelled by the growing appeal and consumption of computer and video games in the late 1980s and 1990s, as well as the increasing domestic access to the internet in the 1990s, the genre attempted to visualise the interaction between the human or post-human subject absorbed into the virtual space of a fully computerised environment. The UK/USA/Japanese co-production of *The Lawnmower Man* (dir. Brett Leonard, 1992) is most often credited with igniting audience interest. Recognising the topicality of its subject matter, this relatively low-budget film was treated to a hyped-up advertising campaign, implying that the experience of viewing the film would be far removed from anything audiences had previously encountered in cinema.[9] The narrative follows a simpleton called Jobe (Jeff Fahey), who mows lawns for a living, and a scientist called Dr Angelo (Pierce Brosnan), whose work is funded by a clandestine government agency. Dr Angelo persuades Jobe to undergo a treatment of 'mind-expanding' drugs along with extended sessions in his virtual reality machine. As previously outlined in Chapter 4, Jobe is eventually transformed into a megalomaniac and finally downloads himself into the virtual realm of cyberspace. In contrast to *Tron,* this later film alternates between a 'real world' setting and cyberspace sequences. Initially introduced to virtual reality via a computer game, Jobe's education continues as he is seen 'downloading' vast quantities of information from a futuristic version of the internet. Learning and apparently evolving through these experiences, he graduates to a more immersive VR environment when he is hooked up to a bodysuit and suspended in a gyroscopic contraption. Earlier VR sequences in the film strongly resembled an increasingly familiar video/computer game setting in both the use of simple shapes and colour as well as the chase and competition scenarios. However, the later sequences are different and owe more to effects created in the 'new art' films of the 1970s. During these sequences the viewer is shown a world of whirling patterns and complex geometric designs. However, while the viewer may be given the opportunity to retain a kind of distance from these abstract images, the 'personalised viewpoints' that might be offered by this 'new art' are arguably channelled through a tight identification with Jobe. Also, rather than 'dropping out', the narrative makes clear that Jobe's mind and body has become completely immersed within the pre-programmed world of the computer.

The Lawnmower Man performed extraordinarily well at the box office, grossing $7,751,971 in domestic revenue in its opening weekend and going on to gross approximately $150 million worldwide.[10] Nonetheless, reviews for the film were very mixed. Richard Harrington of the *Washington Post* derided the film as 'short on plot and long on derivation', although he grudgingly admitted that it boasted 'some dazzling computer animation sequences'.[11] Alternatively, Gary Arnold from *The Washington Times* could not see any redeeming features in the film; describing it as 'more of a tribute to drug abuse than computer animation', Arnold claimed that he watched 'the movie fizzle while trying to pump up a computerized monster'.[12] And as far as Richard Scheib was concerned, the film amounted to nothing more than 'eye-candy'.[13] Although there was certainly an audience for VR films in the 1990s, the episodic construction of *The Lawnmower Man* might partly account for its mixed critical reception. If this construction was unfamiliar to the critics, what *The Lawnmower Man* augured was a tendency towards 'video game logic'.[14] This tendency became prevalent in the science fiction films of the 1990s as the industry attempted to negotiate with the new entertainment medium. Using *The Fifth Element* (dir. Luc Besson, 1997) as an example, Thomas Elsaesser and Warren Buckland have looked at how both its visual and narrative construction exhibits the rules associated with the video game. For Elsaesser and Buckland the 'serialized repetition, disguises, the attempt to move to the next level, feedback loop (in which unsuccessful characters are immediately eliminated and successful ones rewarded), and a space warp'[15] are characteristics of video-game logic, which they read as present in *The Fifth Element*. Arguing that the film is 'a hybrid between the classical (psychologically motivated cause–effect) narrative logic and digital (video game) logic',[16] they detail moments of correspondence between film and game logic. Of course, this correspondence is particularly evident in films in which the narrative openly engages with VR in one form or another. For instance, the previously discussed *eXistenZ* (dir. David Cronenberg, 1999) takes the clash between 'digital logic' and classical film conventions (e.g. realism, narrative motivation, linear construction etc.) as its main focus. So, on a simple level, you could say that this is a film *about* 'video game logic' and the ways in which it comes to bear upon filmic realism and character construction. Returning to *The Lawnmower Man*, here we have a film *about* VR, in which the kind of game logic detailed by Elsaesser and Buckland is also very much in evidence. Although the narrative line of *The Lawnmower Man* is held together in following the 'evolution' of Jobe, it is also broken up into sections, which could be said to mirror the levels of a video-game world. Viewed as a game, the film seems to make more sense: Jobe's advance to each level of difficulty is achieved as he learns the rules of both virtual reality and the real world and his reward comes with the increasing exhilaration experienced as the adventure intensifies. Interruptions in the narrative come with the repeated and abrupt shifts from the real world setting to the world of computer. In contrast to a film like *The Last Starfighter*, the computer animation featured in these sequences does not attempt to look real or naturalistic, which makes the shift between worlds all the more disruptive. For example, the real-world sex scenes with Jobe and his love object, Marnie (Jenny Wright), are strikingly juxtaposed with their final sexual adventure in cyberspace. Here the couple's mutual caresses are visualised as they morph and meld into each other, finally fusing to become a single insect-like creature with wings. The temperament of the sequence changes when Jobe becomes sadistic toward Marnie; ignoring her pleas, the visuals strongly suggest that Jobe rapes Marnie. Thus follows a swift and rude awakening which underlines the disturbance caused by these images; after the rape we are returned to the real-world setting where it becomes apparent that the whole experience has been so traumatic for Marnie that she has lost her mind. Also, towards the end of the film the computer graphics begin to invade the real-world setting, but even here there is no attempt at invisible integration. For example, the computer-generated swarm of bees that attacks the armed guards at the secret facility where Angelo works might look impressive and certainly have the desired effect upon the guards, but they do not look real. Likewise, when Jobe turns his atomising (or perhaps digitising) gaze upon a number of special operatives from the government, a striking effect is created as their bodies slowly disintegrate into globular particles. Again this effect does not look real; instead it is very obviously a computer-generated manipulation of a photographic image. So, in contrast to the relatively seamless insertion of CG objects, this film offers up a disrupting CG aesthetic that is closer to comic books or anime in its look. In terms of the film's narrative, the realism of film as compared to the very graphic computer-generated effects in *The Lawnmower Man* implies that this new technology is dangerous, particularly as associated with viewer perception and the threat of over-stimulation. But, on a more basic level, although many of these images are incredibly violent and alarming, the use of computer graphics during these passages allowed the film a greater leverage in the display of violence, while retaining a reasonably wide potential market. After all, *The Lawnmower Man* was only given an R certificate in the United States and received a 15 certificate in the UK. In comparison it is interesting to note that even though *Jurassic Park* was awarded a PG or 12 certificate in most countries, it was criticised for the violence shown in the computer graphics and was forced to curb this aspect in order to retain its certification in later films of the series. At this time, a naturalistic aesthetic in CGI ironically limited what could and could not be shown.

In her book on special effects, Michele Pierson maps out the ways in which CGI was 'bracketed off' in films of the early to mid-1990s.[17] While I would uphold that the 'bracketing' of CGI can be witnessed in films as far back as 1973, this tactic did become especially apparent in the 1990s. As CGI increasingly became a practical alternative to more traditional methods of creating both naturalistic and non-naturalistic effects, its use was not only a distinguished element within the narrative world of the film, but was proudly announced in pre-publicity, 'the making of . . .' documentaries and later 'special features' additions to the DVD releases of effects-driven films. *The Lawnmower Man* and *Jurassic Park* are clear examples of the two main aesthetic strands followed in CGI in films of the period: the first being the obviously graphic and designed and the second marking an urge towards photorealism. While a kind of 'bracketing' was an almost automatic result of graphic effects as juxtaposed with the photoreal, photorealist CGI was also presented as a special effect in science fiction films of the period. It is perhaps not surprising that, as the decade wore on, the photorealistic CGI aesthetic began to dominate the screens, in what could be taken as a move toward the total subjugation of this new technology to an already familiar aesthetic of filmic realism. However, immersion into a kind of computer game world also became all the more pervasive and although the diegetic worlds in many films increasingly looked real, the 'truth' of the image was continuously challenged. For example, immersion into a computer-generated world was a predetermined aspect of those films based upon pre-existing video and computer games. I mentioned both *Street Fighter* (dir. Steven E. de Souza, 1994) and *Mortal Kombat* (dir. Paul Anderson, 1995) in Chapter 6, but more recent examples include *Lara Croft: Tomb Raider* (dir. Simon West, 2001), *Resident Evil* (dir: Paul Anderson, 2002) and *Doom* (dir. Andrzej Bartkowiak, 2005). The genealogy of these films is frequently exhibited in the breaking or extension of the natural laws of time and space. For example, the frames of the shots tend to be far more mobile and the standard horizontal 'eye line' is often extended to include points of view from and across several planes of action. The 'virtual cameras' of computer-generated effects, as sutured to a character's point of view, allow these shots to appear realistic if not naturalistic. Indeed, the multi-planed movement within a computer world is often highlighted as the film's protagonists traverse an otherwise familiar, often urban, terrain in an eccentric fashion. In his study of the American comic-book superhero, Scott Bukatman sees the city and the superhero as intimately connected; they both embody the utopian aspirations of modernity. The rationality imposed by the grids and borders of a city like New York is both transcended and policed by the superhero: 'Superheroes preserve the order of the city but need not submit to it'.[18] What becomes apparent in his brief account of this relationship is that the fantastic freedoms awarded the superhero are supported by the concrete reality of the modern metropolis: superman can only defy the laws of physics if these laws are first set in place and obvious to the viewer. So, the zero-gravity worlds of the 'game films' award their protagonists the freedoms and powers that were previously associated with comic-book super-heroes. The frequent featuring of highly defined spaces is therefore no accident as the sharply horizontal and vertical design of these concrete worlds serves to accentuate the exceptional movement that the viewer witnesses in these films.

Aside from the 'game films',[19] other recent science fiction films have tended to indicate immersion into a computer generated space in a rather different manner. In these films the direct dynamic between concrete surroundings and superheroic action is irrevocably altered. For instance, films like *Dark City* (dir. Alex Proyas, 1998), *The Matrix* (dir. Larry and Andy Wachowski, 1999), *Artificial Intelligence: AI* (dir. Steven Spielberg, 2001) and *Minority Report* (dir. Steven Spielberg, 2002) often signal immersion rather than transcendence, through the warping and bending of the concrete lines of a familiar cityscape. A clear example can be found in *The Matrix* when Neo is alerted to the imma-terial nature of his surroundings by Morpheus. During a training programme, Neo is taught to regard his erstwhile reality as mutable: when he tries to leap from one concrete skyscraper to another he lands heavily on the highway below, which easily yields under his weight. This is a rubber reality, one that Neo must learn to control and bend to his will. While the famous 'flo-mo' or 'bullet time' effect in this film allows for the kind of mobile viewpoint featured in many of the 'game films', the use of this technique basically means that the movement of elements within a scene can be separately controlled. The distinct mobility awarded to the likes of Superman is undercut by the mobility extended to other objects and characters in the shot. In fact, the apparently dynamic camera that circles Neo and captures his movement in slow motion as he dodges bullets and leaps into the air, works less as a demonstration of Neo's transcendence than as a device to fix him in the moment.

The concrete materiality of the city is also resolutely disputed in the Australian/USA co-production, *Dark City*. Here we have a world that appears real, if only in its hyper-cinematic presentation. The viewer could be forgiven for thinking that they were watching a standard film noir, but it later becomes apparent that this environment is literally a living reconstruction of a classic film noir setting. In fact, *Dark City* makes very sparing use of computer graphics and much of the urban backdrop was constructed using miniatures. But the most telling and effective moment comes after our central protagonist, John Murdoch (Rufus Sewell), wakes up to the fact that his surroundings are not all that they appear to be. The human subjects who exist here have been abducted by aliens and are actually living on the surface of an alien craft, floating in space. Murdoch's world and even his memories have been fashioned by voyeuristic aliens, who are busy studying human behaviour. In their search for 'human essence' the aliens regularly modify the city through a combined act of willpower, which they call 'tuning', and alter the roles allotted to test subjects by injecting them with false memories. These changes are imperceptible to most of the captive humans as the aliens induce a deep sleep during their 'tuning' sessions. Murdoch manages to stay awake and not only witnesses the city grind to a halt as everyone falls asleep, but sees the spectacular transformation that it undergoes during the 'tuning' process. The main 'tuning' sequence begins as the aliens gather in their underground laboratory. Their combined will is concentrated upon a large metallic head, which groans into action and spirals upwards toward the city surface. During this sequence buildings literally shrink and grow; twisting upwards and outwards, shifting sideways and back, vast skyscrapers lurch towards the heavens like strange mechanical plants seeking sunlight. The dimensions of the city are mutable and the reliable realism of cinematic space is severely undermined by this demonstration of digital delirium. The aliens are seen to float above and between buildings as they seek out possible subjects for experimentation and, following their point of view, the spectator is given multiple perspectives of the scene. The whole procedure is wildly fantastic, but the effects are also designed to look solid and believable. To accentuate this visually realistic and yet unbelievable effect, the buildings' movement is accompanied by cranking, metallic sound effects and at one point we see steam spew forth as the vast underground machine is set in motion. This spectacular sequence does not so much dramatise a clashing as a marriage of past and present/future technologies; a combining of industrial images and sound effects with the computer-generated morphing effect. The transcendence made available to the old-style superhero depended upon the rigid materiality of the city, but this discrete luxury is no longer available in such an uncertain environment. Rather than transcendence our new-style superhero is overcome by a city that refutes his very existence.

Along with Murdoch, the viewers' sense of space and time are irrevocably altered upon witnessing this transformation. The rigid permanence of the city, demonstrated in its towering apartment blocks and skyscrapers, is challenged by this alien technology; a technology that undermines the very foundations of perceived reality. In spite of this, after a mighty battle of wits with the aliens, Murdoch learns to harness the 'tuning' power exhibited by the aliens. Emerging victorious against the aliens, he eventually asserts his superhuman authority and brings happiness and light to the city. Murdoch's literal intervention in the narrative design of the city and the control he is able to exert over his somewhat limited surroundings might emulate the experience of an interactive computer game, or life within a yielding cyberspace. However, it is also important to note that he restores a sense of familiar permanence to this cinematic world, even if it is shown to exist within a protected bubble in the nothingness of space.

A kind of bending and mobility is also witnessed in Steven Spielberg's recent contributions to the genre: *Artificial Intelligence: AI* and *Minority Report*. In the creation of the CGI for these two films ILM made conspicuous use of the kind of fluid effects that they introduced with *The Abyss* and *Terminator 2*. The Manhattan cityscape is literally engulfed in water in *AI* and the fluidity of this environment is emphasised when, towards the end of the film, our central characters (the 'mecha' boy David [Haley Joel Osment] and Teddy) are submerged in water. This gives birth to the imaginary world of David's dreams and the translucent CG creatures that supersede both the mechanical constructions and cartoony animations in the film (e.g. Dr Know and the Blue Fairy) are especially liquid and graceful in appearance and movement. Equally our central hero, John Anderton (Tom Cruise), in *Minority Report*, is led into the watery world of the Precog characters. Floating in a tank and suspended in a kind of lucid dream state, the Precogs can supposedly predict violent crime. As the chief of police, it is Anderton's job to interpret the images they transmit and stop these crimes from actually occurring. Like *Blade Runner* (dir. Ridley Scott, 1982), *Minority Report* was also based upon a Philip K. Dick story, and like its predecessor the truth of the photographic image is also placed in question in this later film. But here our detective is dealing with the moving images created by the Precogs, rather than the still frame photographs of the replicants. These images are transmitted onto a flat transparent screen and Anderton is seen to carry out a kind editing process in order to highlight relevant information. The imprecision of these moving images is signalled using a 'squishy lens' device, which frames and disturbs the Precog's fragmented visions. The 'squishy lens' consists of a soft plate containing fluid, through which the camera records images onto film. The flexibility of the lens allows for the peculiar distortion of filmed images, which in the case of *Minority Report* blurs and fans the outer edges of a central image or creates ripples of movement across the frame. This look is therefore primarily created at the point of filming rather than through post-production CGI and these sequences are interestingly offset against the CG environments of the futuristic city (in particular those scenes in which the backgrounds are almost exclusively created using CGI – the multi-levelled environment of the prison that houses the criminals and scenes featuring the twisting multi-planed motorways). So, the supposedly real world that Anderton inhabits is actually juxtaposed with the literally flat and fluctuating photographic images that he handles throughout the course of the film. In an interesting reversal of the framing devices used to introduce CG effects in films like *Star Wars, Alien* and so on, it is the photographic which is 'bracketed off' in *Minority Report*. Also, in both *AI* and *Minority Report* CGI is shown to supplant the photographic in the provision of a 'real world' environment.

Rather than the 'bracketed off' CG imagery associated with earlier films, it is as though the human characters in these films are 'bracketed within' a synthesised world of their own making. In fact, I would contend that the use of CGI in the creation of environments in many recent science fiction films has the effect of throwing into relief effects based upon more traditional methods. This is evident in a film like *Independence Day* (dir. Roland Emmerich, 1996), where old-style models and camera techniques are mixed and matched with CGI. Pierson sees this film as marking a turning point in the genre's use of CGI and she goes on to argue that 'none of the special effects images in *Independence Day* are treated to the presentationist style of exhibition that was so much a part of the art-and-effects direction just a few years earlier'.[20] While I agree that the film contains an excessive array of types of effects, I do not think that the presentationist style has disappeared in this film. What I see happening here is that the focus of attention is at times directed toward the more traditional effects. The most obvious examples are found in the film's use of large-scale models in the scenes of destruction. For instance, in the sequence showing the alien's first attack, skyscrapers in Los Angeles fall, followed by the Empire State building in New York, and finally the destruction of the White House. The blowing up of the White House is given a privileged position, as the scenes of destruction build to this point: the rhythmic visual rhetoric of the sequence culminates in the destruction of the White House. The viewer was not only alerted to this scene in the trailer to the film, but the accompanying documentary to the DVD focuses upon the large and expensive model that the crew lovingly built and then rudely destroyed to create this effect. Of course it is the CG alien craft that apparently triggers the destruction, but the importance of the model effect is made plain and the real risks involved in using explosives and the filming of the event are also made known. As opposed to the relative ease with which CG effects can be altered, re-run, reconfigured, the pressure was on to get this particular effect right first time around. So the audience is primed to recognise the special thrill associated with this scene as set against the relatively safe CGI in the film.

To summarise, the protagonists in all of these films find themselves immersed in a kind of computer-game world. Having discovered the true nature of their surroundings, like the players in *eXistenZ*, Neo, Murdoch, David, Anderton and the motley crew in *Indpendence Day* all struggle to gain control of their environments. These films announce a post-celluloid era in which the characters' dreams and nightmares are played out against changing and mutable cityscapes. With the exception of *Minority Report*, all of these examples also envision the destruction and decay of the high-rise city as representative of a postmodern and post-celluloid world superseded by the malleable constructions of a wondrous but overwhelming digital environment. The inevitable insecurity that this promotes in our protagonists is evidenced in their struggles to retain a firm foundation upon which to build a sense of self.

As Susan Sontag has taught us (see p. 32), 'the imagination of disaster' has been a common feature of the genre since the 1950s;[21] a feature that took on renewed importance following the attack on the World Trade Center in Manhattan and the Pentagon in Washington DC on 11 September 2001. It is hardly surprising that *ID4*'s (*Independence Day's*) palpable pyrotechnics were reportedly recalled when television viewers across the world bore witness to the demise of the Twin Towers of the Trade Center. The quasi-prophetic quality of science fiction was endowed with renewed significance in the light of these events. Of course, as Steven Keane has stated in connection with his study of the rise and fall of disaster films, repeated scenes of destruction in film 'are born out of times of impending crisis'.[22] So, on one level, the rising tensions between East and West in the lead-up to al-Qaeda's attack were partly expressed in the scenes of disaster included in many science fiction films that preceded the event. But beyond this, immediately following 9/11, the 'what if' of science fiction was retrospectively transmuted into a 'what next'; a shift that was partly confirmed by the much publicised meetings between Hollywood executives and representatives of the Republican government in the weeks that followed 9/11. A form of self-censorship was also quickly set place in Hollywood. Films featuring the New York skyline were held back while post-production alterations were made to exclude the Twin Towers.[23] Likewise, a number of projects were cancelled due to what was now seen as the sensitive nature of their subject matter.[24] As Emmerich made clear in the interview below, (pp. 275–9) following 9/11 it was not possible to include the kinds of explosive effects in films that had been a feature in *ID4*. The reality of the albeit edited images of destruction that appeared on television during and following 9/11 seemed to both replicate and supersede the scenes of destruction in fiction film. Emmerich's later 'ice age' film, *The Day after Tomorrow* (2004), can be read as a response to the events of 9/11. Rather than blowing up buildings, this film literally covers landmark American buildings in a blanket of computer-generated snow and ice. Ostensibly, the 'big freeze' in the film feeds into a growing concern with global warming and the systematic destruction of our natural environment. But equally it can be read as a allegory expressing the trauma felt in America after

9/11 and as a comment on the arrogant and aggressive policies of the Bush administration.

As outlined in the Introduction, science fiction film exhibits a very particular and somewhat troubled relationship with reality, a relationship that is often articulated in the genre's simultaneous rebuke and commemoration of realism as a filmic style. Although the irreverent blowing up of buildings in a film like *ID4* paid a sort of homage to realism, the scale of destruction represented a fantasised and libidinal response to life under the Clinton administration: as Emmerich noted in his interview, 'people were very frustrated with Washington and we expressed that'. The destruction of the skyscrapers and the White House was obviously not real as these recognisable buildings still existed. Rather it was what these buildings symbolised that was being attacked within this fantasy setting. While the film is based upon a representation of reality, illusion is foregrounded in the continued existence of the referent in an extra-filmic concrete reality. This, in part, explains how science fiction can work to reassure audiences at the same time as the viewer is bombarded with images that herald change and sometimes devastation. So, simply put, what happened with the events of 9/11 was that the delicate balance between fantasy and reality was upset: fantasy appeared to become reality in the most traumatic of ways and the potentially reassuring function of a film like *ID4* was undercut by the reality of what television viewers were now witnessing.

For Slavoj Žižek the televised images of the events of 9/11 should be seen as part of an already constructed and imagined reality. Drawing upon Lacanian psychoanalysis Žižek understands 'the Real' as unknowable; what we call reality is the constructed and symbolic world, which is increasingly known through the images we encounter on television screens, film screens and so on. So, as Žižek characterises it:

> We should therefore invert the standard reading according to which the WTC explosions were the intrusion of the Real which shattered our illusory Sphere: quite the reverse – it was before the WTC collapse that we lived in our reality . . . and what happened on September 11 was that this fantasmatic screen apparition entered our reality. It is not that reality entered our image: the image entered and shattered our reality (i.e. the symbolic coordinates which determine what we experience as reality).[25]

In other words, our sense of reality, as partly constructed and informed by media, was shaken after the events of 9/11. I was not in New York when the Twin Towers collapsed and like Žižek I experienced the event through images presented on a television screen. Tuning in to watch an afternoon film, I momentarily assumed that the advertised feature had been replaced by a disaster or science fiction film. Quickly realising that this was not the case, I was forced to accept these images as part of a new reality. At one remove from the live event, I could not say that these broadcast images, in any direct sense, impinged upon my immediate sense of a material reality; I was after all sitting safely in Southampton in the comfort of my living room. However, they did inform my wider sense of reality, as I was forced to seriously consider the death and destruction that was being wreaked as well as the wider implications of what I was seeing. E. Ann Kaplan, on the other hand, was living in close proximity to the World Trade Center at the time and experienced these events in a more direct way. Kaplan's reading of these events is therefore unashamedly personal in working through the meanings and implications of 9/11 for herself and for a traumatised world. In studying what she calls 'cultural trauma', Kaplan briefly refers to early cinema's intimate relationship with the 'shock' of modernity, before moving on to discuss the peculiarly visual nature of trauma symptoms (hallucinations, dreams and so on).[26] Although Kaplan does not detail specific films, it should be apparent from my discussion above that early cinema was bound up with the presentation and representation of the new technologies of the industrial age. The reportedly hysterical reactions to some of the very first films therefore speak to the violent disruptions caused by the introduction of a newly manufactured sense of reality. On one level, as audiences learned to accept the moving images placed in front of them they were also rehearsing reactions to the machines of the modern age as well as forming collective fantasies for the future. Making a distinction between direct and secondary trauma, Kaplan's study looks at how the media and wider culture deals with reality changing events and how 'the reader or viewer of stories or films about traumatic situations may be constituted through vicarious or secondary trauma'.[27] So, as much as cinema has a long tradition in working to both register and relieve our fears, trauma can return as a response to visual images that disrupt our sense of lived reality.

Immediately following 9/11, although the news media repeatedly replayed the falling of the Twin Towers, in an act of conscious forgetting, fiction film stayed well away from any image that might be directly linked with 9/11. As opposed to the futuristic visions of destruction in science fiction cinema, Hollywood saw the comeback of the war film (e.g. *Black Hawk Down* [dir. Ridley Scott, 2001], *Hart's War* [dir. Gregory Hablit, 2002], *We Were Soldiers* [dir. Randall Wallace, 2002]) and the historical and biblical epic (e.g. *The Passion of the Christ* [dir. Mel Gibson, 2004], *Alexander* [dir. Oliver Stone, 2004], *Kingdom of Heaven* [dir. Ridley Scott, 2005]). Destruction and conflict on a large scale was still featured in Hollywood, but removed to a past setting, This sense of re-visiting the past could also be extended to those science fiction films that did feature scenes of mass destruction: unlike the irreverent irony of a film like *ID4*, the pious remakes of *The Time Machine* (dir. Simon Wells, 2002) and *War of the Worlds* (dir. Steven Spielberg, 2005) also returned us to a cinematic past even as they featured futuristic events. In an act of remembrance, Hollywood cinema appeared to be returning to the past both stylistically and politically. Perhaps all of these films were intended to heal the rift in reality caused by the traumatic events of 9/11 by reminding viewers of the response to past traumas, at least as represented in cinematic memory. Furthermore, as Wheeler Winston Dixon has pointed out, these films seemed designed to 'create a sense of unity out of deeply disparate factions'.[28] Cinema was therefore a central component in an organised cultural response that sought to remember a unified and coherent American society fighting against a clearly opposed Other.

These political aspirations were also played out in the numerous war games released after 9/11. With titles like *Call of Duty, Command and Conquer, Medal of Honor* and *Rise of Nations* these video games were marketed toward a young male audience and generally took place within a quasi-World War II setting. But, aside from the historical war games and films, 9/11 seemed to clear a path for what might be called pure fantasy films. Indeed, the various elves, wizards, pirate monsters, and other fantastical underworld creatures in the blockbuster hit series' that followed 9/11 clearly came from the generic realm known as fantasy. Awarded PG or 12 certificates (or equivalent), films like the New Zealand/USA co-production, *Lord of the Rings* series (dir. Peter Jackson, 2001–3), the UK/USA *Harry Potter* series (variously directed by Chris Columbus [2001, 2002], Alfonso Cuaron [2004] and Mike Newell [2005]), and the USA-produced, *Pirates of the Caribbean* series (dir. Gore Verbinski, 2003, 2006) noticeably relied upon CGI to create both characters and settings. Here the technology was not so much used in the service of a recognisable realism, but in the creation of complex visual designs that recall the so-called fantasy fine art (of the kind produced by Terese Nielson and R. K. Post), frequently used to illustrate fantasy books. This represented a distinct shift away from the photorealist aesthetic of previous science fiction films. Also, Pixar (in combination with Disney) produced a number of highly successful children's animations. Following in the tradition of American cartoon animation, the CGI in *Monsters Inc.* (dir. Pete Docter, 2001), *The Incredibles* (dir. Brad Bird, 2004) and *Cars* (dir. John Lasseter, 2006) was economical in style. As Kristin Thompson has pointed out, fantasy films provide the perfect vehicle for tie-ins and foster fan cultures that seek out further products and information associated with the films.[29] However, these fantasy film franchises also took over in many ways from the science fiction blockbusters that had previously dominated the market, which seems to indicate something more than purely economic factors was at work. The most obvious explanation is that Hollywood was offering a complete and distinct escape from the confusing and changed reality that followed 9/11; these alternative digital worlds were at a far remove from the televised images that accompanied 9/11 or from the simulated scenes of destruction in science fiction. CGI was now developing a number of alternative aesthetic strategies that marked it apart from the photorealism of film.

After a five-year 'grace period', Hollywood has finally returned to mark the events of 9/11. At the time of writing, the films *The World Trade Center* (dir. Oliver Stone, 2006) and the French/UK/US co-production, *United 93* (dir. Paul Greengrass, 2006), have yet to be released in the UK but the advent of these films does suggest that the industry is more directly, albeit cautiously, re-engaging with our new reality. Quite what all this means for science fiction as a dominant film genre is hard to say as yet, given that the mainstream industry has become so polarised over the last few years. With pure fantasy on the one hand and a kind of neo-realism on the other hand, a genre that has happily inhabited the space in between fantasy and reality might currently be viewed as outmoded. Alternatively, perhaps the science fiction film genre has become a victim of its own success. For instance, if one of its functions over the last couple of decades was to introduce and acclimatise a viewing public to a newly digitalised world, then having achieved this it now finds itself redundant. I am not suggesting that science fiction has disappeared as a film genre, in many ways it has managed to hold onto a large share of the market because of its close association with video games. The genre is also thriving in recent television series like *Eureka* (2006–), *Invasion* (2005–), *The 4400* (2004–), the remake of *Battlestar Galactica* (2004–) and so on. Nevertheless the pre-eminence of this film genre is currently disputed by the phenomenal success of the fantasy film in recent years. It seems ironic to suggest that a film genre that has challenged and pushed at the limits of both filmic realism and the medium of celluloid for so long might now become obsolete, just as we enter a post-celluloid age. But, I would tentatively suggest that we may be witnessing the beginning of the end of the second 'golden age' for the science fiction film, an age that began with the late 1970s and early 1980s science fiction blockbusters. That said, even if popular cinema as we know it is coming to an end I strongly suspect that science fiction will continue to visit our screens in one form of another.

INTERVIEW: SPECIAL EFFECTS TECHNICIAN STAN WINSTON

C: You are, of course, very famous for your creature designs, in films like *Aliens* [1986], and the *Predator* [1987, 1990] and *Terminator* [1984, 1991, 2001]. You have often been quoted as saying that the challenge is in giving the audience something they haven't seen before.

W: Yes, this is crucial and you have to create that opportunity. If you wait for someone to hand you the opportunity to do something special, you will never do it. It's a requirement of every job that comes to me to find a way to do either something that hasn't been done before or to do something that has been done before, but in way that we haven't seen it. To create a character that is new and fresh. If we are doing what we did yesterday it would be boring for you and for me. The brilliant creative minds that have been working with me – many of them for over twenty years – wouldn't be in this business creating fanciful and wonderful characters if I was a boring person or wanted to do things that weren't exciting and special. So part of that is doing something that is challenging to yourself. If you're not challenging yourself, you're not doing the best you can. Therefore, every job is a challenge – must be a challenge – to create a creature or a character in some kind of artistic and dramatically new way.

I don't consider myself a special-effects man. I know many people do, I don't. It's not what my mind is about. I am actually techno-ignorant, although I own and operate one of the most advanced companies, as far as creating character and creature effects, in the world – be it anywhere from make-up effects, to animatronic effects, to robotic effects, to puppet effects, to CG effects. I use all of the technology at hand, but it's not for the purposes of special effects, it's for the purpose of creating characters. I came out here as an actor, which has influenced my entire career. I have also been a fan of science fiction, fantasy movies my entire life – from *King Kong* [1933] to *The Wizard of Oz* [1939]. Anything that had a fanciful or fantastic or wonderfully dramatic character in it, I was drawn to – all the original horror movies from Universal, like Boris Karloff in *Frankenstein* [1931], to Spencer Tracy in *Dr. Jekyll and Mr Hyde [1941]*, to Charles Laughton in *The Hunchback of Notre Dame* [1939]. Every time there's been a fantastic character that has either been created by an actor in make-up, or an effect, like King Kong, it's always been about that character – it's never been about the technology. I get the same excitement from a character like King Kong as I get from Charles Laughton as the Hunchback of Notre Dame. They're just fantastic characters.

I came out to create characters as an actor and I failed dramatically, but at the same time I was a fine arts major in college, a drama minor and I was a painter and sculptor. I was always interested in fantastic make-up. So, I decided that instead of parking cars or waiting on tables, I would try and work within the industry – so I could work with actors, so I could work with the people that I wanted to eventually be and help create characters. I decided to take up an apprenticeship as a make-up artist, which would allow me to work with actors, to help them create characters that I wanted to do and also use my artistic skills as a painter and a sculptor and a sketch artist. It just snowballed – I became very successful at what was originally my sideline. I'm still doing my sideline, still waiting to be an actor, but, in fact, I have done everything I always wanted to do. What I thought I was going to do as an actor I did behind the scenes.

I've always wanted to create fantastic characters that tell fantastic stories and the methods that I use to do that can be as simple as a prosthetic make-up on an actor to as extensive as the 12½ ton robot Dinosaur that is in *Jurassic Park* [1993]. That Dinosaur, for me, is not an effect; it's an actor, a character. The Terminator was an actor – it's about what he looks like, how he performs. The technology behind it is, for me, the job of how I bring it to life.

C: And what you have available is what you use to create a character?

W: Also, to create what I don't have available. In my studio we've broken ground through the years, as far as technological advances, and so what we have done, in the world of quote/unquote 'Special Effects' is ground-breaking. But it's all been about creating characters for film, not about Special Effects. The art must lead the technology. If you are going to be a part of the filmmaking business, you must understand the priorities of what makes a good movie. There are three of these that run parallel to each other. Firstly, there is nothing more important than the script and the story. If you are not telling an interesting story, I don't care how good anything else is, it's going to be forgettable movie, because it's a forgettable story. So the script is the most important thing. The characters, the actors that are telling that story parallel that importance. Stories are about characters. Characters tell the story. The better the performance of the actor and the more wonderful the character is that is telling that story, the more involved the audience is when they are watching it. So, a wonderful story told by dramatic and wonderful characters, directed by a creative and cohesive director who understands how it all has to come together. The director is the master of the ship – without the director everything is chaos. So, script, actors, director – nothing else is important.

C: So you are working with the director's vision even though you see your role as being extremely creative.

W: Yes, of course. If you are going to work in this position you must serve the director. Film is a director's medium, so you must serve the director. There are many different ways of serving the director, but you must serve the director. The fact of the matter is that movies are not about effects. The point is that films are about stories, characters and direction. Now, effects are tools that are used to tell that story. I use those effects to help create characters that help tell the story.

C: How do you feel then about films where effects, whatever their nature, are foregrounded?

W: If they don't exist, then it's irrelevant. If they do exist, then wonderful effects are fantastic if they help tell a wonderful story. *The Lord of the Rings* [J. R. R. Tolkien, 1954–5] is probably the most well-read book and one of the most universal stories since the writing of the Bible. So, it's obviously a classic, memorable story. The performances in *Lord of the Rings* were wonderful and the direction by Peter Jackson was brilliant. Now, in order to tell that story, they needed to create a world we've never seen, to create creatures we've never seen. There was an absolute need for special effects, but it wasn't *about* special effects. Those same special effects, given a weak story with poor performances by actors and poor direction, are meaningless. I embrace special effects. I embrace what I do. I embrace all of it. I embrace CG. I embrace animatronics. I embrace puppets. I embrace make-up effects and prosthetics. I embrace creative set design. I use all of that, but you must understand ultimately what you are serving. You are not serving the effects; the effects are serving the film. For instance, I'll be brutal, I thought the first *Matrix* [1999] was an extremely interesting story and used effects in ways that we had never seen before to tell an extremely interesting story. I think *The Matrix Reloaded* [2003] is just a lot of effects.

Effects being in the forefront is fine with me. For example, you can't imagine telling the story of *Jurassic Park*, which is a movie about dinosaurs coming back to life, and not having the effects be important. It was a dinosaur movie; it wasn't *Schindler's List* [1993], it was about dinosaurs. Therefore, those effects and what they bring to the film are extremely important. Where film-makers or directors without vision, or studio heads without vision, go wrong is they see a movie with fantastic special effects, which turns out to be extremely successful because the audiences go in droves, but they don't realise that the movie was successful not because of the effects, but because it had at its core a good script, good performances and good direction. So, then they think, I am going to make a big film with a lot of effects. But they don't know what they're doing and the priorities are out of wack. There is nothing wrong with spectacle, I embrace it. I've embraced it for years, since *Ben-Hur* [1959] and *Spartacus* [1960], *The Planet of the Apes* [1968], when it came out, and the first *Alien* movie [1979], all of them. They're wonderful, big movies that are spectacular because it's the only way to tell that story, visually in film. Film as a tool is a wonderful tool.

I get the question a lot – are we getting too effects-heavy? People have been saying that for thirty years. For me, bad filmmakers will always make bad films, whether there are effects in them or not. Bad filmmakers who don't understand what a good story is or how to tell it will put a lot of effects in something and it will still be a bad movie.

C: Given that you think of your creations in terms of characterisation – I interviewed the novel writer, Brian Aldiss, in connection with *AI* [2001] and he spoke about how Kubrick originally hoped that the central character could be played by an actual robot. When Spielberg took over the project, I wondered whether there had been any consideration of whether or not you could produce an animatronic boy for the film?

W: I tried to talk Steven into it. I tried – not necessarily to replace Haley Joel Osment, who was so wonderful – brilliant performance and a wonderful actor.

But I really wanted to make a robotic child, to look as close to real as possible and to, in fact, have a springboard for Haley Joel Osment to react to. So if I'd made the robot and there were glitches in it and it didn't act perfectly, it would be OK, because it was a robot. It was something that I wanted to be able to do, but I don't think he made a bad choice because Haley was brilliant. But it's definitely something that I would have liked to have done.

We do have the ability to create robotic characters that can act. We have been doing it. It depends on how real you want those characters to be. We cannot yet really duplicate, with actual robotics, all of the nuances of life, of reality. We can come close. We can make something look extremely real. There are times when I will replace an actor with an artificial version of that actor in a film and you won't know the difference, but it's limited in its range of performance. A long form of answering your question 'have I ever thought about it' – yes, I wanted to do it.

C: Several of the effects you've created deal with a mixing of the mechanical and the organic. I'd like to know more about your thinking in the design of these kinds of characters and how you think these visualisations have developed over the years.

W: If we're talking about cyborgs, we're talking about *The Terminator* films or you're talking about *AI*. *The Terminator* was ground-breaking as far as bringing to life a robotic character – a virtually humanoid robot from the future, an artificial intelligence – and doing it in a completely realistic way, in a way that we had never seen in motion-picture history. In fact, from a technical standpoint, I ripped off the technology from Jim Henson and used puppetry to create that character. At first we tried to do all of the endoskeleton, that's the metal robot under the skin, with stop-motion animation. I said I felt we could do much of it live and create an animatronic, a puppet, and actually move into the arena of actually seeing this robot live. So in *The Terminator* we pretended to build robots, in *Terminator 2* we actually broke ground again and, for the first time in motion picture history, seamlessly blended technologies of live action, animatronic, puppetry and CGI from ILM. And with those technologies we continued to pretend to create robots, AIs of the future. The fact of the matter is that [in] creating the robotic characters under the skins of the dinosaurs in *Jurassic Park,* we have advanced robotic technology, with more points of motion in organic movement, to make something look real. Through the years, because we are first and foremost artists, we have also created the look of our characters to be the most realistic and organic looking characters. We started by pretending to build cyborgs and artificial intelligence with *The Terminator.* We continued that with *Terminator 2* and advanced this melding of effects, of technologies – CGI and animatronics, seamlessly blended. Then, in an organic way, those technologies were blended and advanced with *Jurassic Park*. With that film the robotics were much more advanced than ever before, because we used a computer to design them, to control them, to operate them – along with human operators. So it wasn't just computer-generated animation, we also had computer-generated robotics and animatronics.

Now I have come to *AI*, which is Steven's movie, all about the robots of the future. Now we need to design an entire world of robotic characters of artificial intelligences – ranging from human, to kind-of-human, to not-so-human – using all of our different techniques. Using make-up effects when it came to things like Haley Joel Osment's and Jude Law's characters, to more extensive prosthetic make-up effects, to complete robots, to kind of populate this world of *AI*. In terms of how art advances science and science advances art – after the movie *AI* came out, I was approached by a professor called Cynthia Brazeal from MIT, where they really are doing artificial intelligence. She was interested in the line between science fiction and science fact: what about *AI* was real, what is possible and what is not. She was very enamoured by Teddy.

C: Was there anyone who wasn't?

W: By the way, Teddy was the most extensive robot we had ever created – fifty points of articulation – more than any of the dinosaurs we had ever done. This character had to act and perform and it was a robot. There were some CGI shots; long running shots, which we can't do with a robot, but virtually all of its close-up action and performance, the character that you fall in love with is a robot. The reason that you fall in love with him is because he acts organically and looks real. Well, Cynthia Brazeal came to me and said, you know what we're lacking at MIT is the advancement in organic and robotic technology that you have and your ability to make your robots look organic and real – would we consider collaborating with MIT to create an artificial intelligence? Over the last two years, since the release of the movie *AI*, I have been a sponsor of MIT and have collaborated with them and we are building an AI. Now we share technology with technology at MIT. The concept of AI means that robots, in order to truly learn in a human interactive way, must interact with human beings. The biggest chance to get a human being to actually interact with a robot is if it looks real – if it looks organic, acts organic – all of the things that we think of as science fiction. And, since the AI aspect of robotics is in its infancy right now, the best chance that this AI has to learn will be interacting with children. Therefore, we have designed a child-friendly character, like Teddy. That's what we've done. The character's name is Leonardo. We are in fact doing what we've only pretended to do for years.

Also, In *Terminator 3* [2003] there are huge robots called the T1s. Well, the T1s which we built were robots. In *The Terminator* we pretended to build robots. In *Terminator 2* we pretended to build robots. In *Terminator 3* we built robots. We built them because the art of movies has forced us to advance the technology that has allowed us to actually do the things that we've only imagined in the past. That has always been the case. If we imagine it, we will do it. When Jules Verne wrote *Twenty Thousand Leagues under the Sea* [1869] there were no such things as submarines. When Jules Verne wrote *From the Earth to the Moon* [1864] there were no such things as rocket ships. Creative minds imagine these fantastic stories and then human beings' creative minds make it happen. If we imagine it, some day it will happen.

C: I know you work with all these mediums in creating your characters, but it might be possible to imagine something like *Jurassic Park* as a film that relies solely on say CGI. What do you think your own models and animatronics bring to a film in that respect?

W: Everything that I'm about. Let's go back to what I said I feel is at the core of every good film. Let's go back to the very first things that I said are important: the script, the story, and the characters, the actors. In any movie, historically, the performances of the actors are important – right. If you buy into that, if you agree with me – as an audience, as a writer, as a person – if you agree that one of the important things about *Dog Day Afternoon* [1975] is Al Pacino's performance, if that is important to you – talk to any fine actor, and they will tell you that 50 per cent of acting is reacting. The greatest actors in the world will tell you that they will give their best performance when they are acting with another good actor. It raises the bar of the actor, it raises the bar of performance – you with me? Now, imagine an actor having to act a scene and the other actor in the scene is a dinosaur. If you care about the performance of that actor, are you going to have it there or you are going to pretend it's there? It raises the bar of the performance by the human actor. Not having it there is disregarding the actor, is telling him that his performance is not important, so we will just do it all by CG. It's fine to do that if you are doing an animated movie, but if you are in a movie where actors have to act and react, it is a disservice to them for the other actor not to be there. It has been proven over and over again. In the *Jurassic Park* movies – in the last one where the dinosaur is jamming its head into that aeroplane fuselage and Téa Leoni and Sam Neill are all inside, they didn't have to act afraid – they were terrified, because it was happening. There was this huge dinosaur that weighed twenty-five pounds that could kill them, that was jamming its head into that fuselage and they could have gotten hurt.

A perfect example is – did you ever see a movie called *Dragon Heart* [1998] with Dennis Quaid? Well, I didn't dislike it, but I thought that Dennis Quaid was probably the weakest I'd ever seen him. I think that he's such a brilliant actor and I thought then that his performance was so flat and you know why?

Because he was acting against something that was never there. It was a brilliantly conceived creature that was created and designed, but it was all digital. And this actor who was playing against it was flat. I thought if that thing had been sitting there, if that really was there, he couldn't have been that flat – there's no way. It's the same thing with one of the *Star Wars* movies – I mean everybody made all this fuss about Jar Jar Binks when it came out. Well, Liam Neeson – brilliant actor, wonderful actor, done some wonderful things – was flat. Well, yeah, because that character, Jar Jar Binks, who is bouncing around, isn't there. There's no way Liam Neeson would be acting the way he is if he was actually dealing with the characters that he's meant to be dealing with. People don't always respect the need for the performance of the actor to be as great as it can be.

On the other side of that is the necessity to raise the bar on the performance of the artificial actor – the dinosaur or the alien or whatever. Now, we can't do everything live. In order to get the best performance, some shots are going to have to be CG because we can't make a robotic dinosaur run and jump and leap and do all of those things, be that dynamic. So, not to use CG ever is a disservice to that actor. CG must be used to raise the bar of the performance for that artificial actor. But if you can do it live, do it live. It's the best thing for the director to be able to see his scene there, to see his actors working together – whether it be human actor and dinosaur, they're actors – and to know exactly how they are interacting and to shoot it any way he wants to. Then if that artificial actor needs to do something to tell that story that we're not capable of doing in the live world, do it CG. Let the human actor have to find it within himself to pretend.

C: Do you think that the use of CG then is a stop-gap until you can do all those things?

W: No – you mean where there's no CG? Nothing will ever replace any new tool or new art form. Just like CG will not replace robotics or animatronics or live action, live action won't replace CG. It's a technique and it's a tool. Every director who is a storyteller likes to use different tools. Take three brilliant artists – one of them draws, one of them paints, one of them sculpts. They are all brilliant artists, but each one likes to use a different tool, likes to express themselves with a different tool. The director is the artist, the director is the storyteller, the director is going to choose what tools he wants to use to tell that story. If it's a cel animated film, it is directed by an animation director. Even today there is cel animation. Everybody said that CG animation would put an end to cel animation. *The Lion King* (1994) was one of the great movies of that year, right in the middle of CG animation, because it's an art form. Stop-motion animation is an art form. *Chicken Run* [2000] was one of the most successful movies of that year. *Chicken Run* was old-time technology using stop-motion animation, but it worked because it was a great story, told by wonderful characters, directed by a terrific director, but it was stop-motion animation. Just like nothing will replace the pencil – even though some people like to draw on a computer now, that's fine, it's a new tool – the pencil will not replace the computer, but the computer will not replace the pencil either. No, CG will never replace live action and, no, live action will never replace CG. It's here to stay, it's a new technology.

C: It's just another medium that can be used artistically?

S: Exactly, it's just another tool. That's all it is. They're all tools. For me special effects are a tool. It helps me paint a picture, or create a character, or tell a story. I'm not *about* special effects, I'm about telling stories or creating characters.

INTERVIEW: DIRECTOR ROLAND EMMERICH

C: I understand that you've been a science fiction fan from childhood; I wondered what it is about this genre in particular that continues to fascinate you?

E: Well I think every kid wants to escape into another world and I think it's that escape into another world that's mainly attracted me. It's like a boundless world out there and I think every kid dreams of other worlds.

C: Of course, most of us would know you as the director of very spectacular blockbuster films like *Stargate* [1994] and *Independence Day* [1996], both of which featured desert terrain – quite bleak landscapes.

E: I'm European, so I'm terribly fascinated by desert terrain. Coming from Germany where everything is green – you come for the first time to America and you see these amazing, expansive landscapes.

C: So, it's that sense of wonder that you're expressing?

E: I think so, because when you start making movies in America you realise that you can put them wherever you want. That's a big part of being a director – finding locations. Because I'm a writer/director I think, oh well that would be cool, because I know it's there.

C: Of course, science fiction film generally relies very heavily on special effects, which often operate to display the very latest in cinematic technology . . .

E: Well, it's traditional to use special effects in science fiction movies. I mean right back to Méliès, when he made *A Trip to the Moon [Le Voyage dans la Lune, 1902]*. I think this is inherent in movies – it's always make-believe. Whatever you do is make-believe. Science fiction movies, the genre movies, are in that sense more classical than any other movies because they really use the magic of make-believe. I like an example from the early days of film – they filmed a locomotive coming right at you. It was like a camera on the track and the locomotive was far in the distance and it comes closer and closer and closer – until it goes right over you. The people ran screaming out of the theatre, but they went back in because it's a thrill you cannot have in real life. A lot of block-busters produce this kind of effect. You can experience something that in normal everyday life you wouldn't experience and the movie can show you things you have never seen before. Science fiction movies, in the way of fantasy movies, inherently have that element. That's why they are so successful.

C: Reviewers have often associated you with 'big, splashy effects' – would you agree that this is your directorial stamp?

E: Well, that's a big part of what I do. I try to come up with images that people haven't seen yet. Actually my movies are always set in real life and counter or opposite to that are these fantastic elements – things which happen.

C: So, are you clashing those two elements together?

E: Exactly. For instance, *Independence Day* was very simple, with very regular people, but facing aliens, which is very, very fantastic. This clash, that's the drama of the film. Right now I'm making a movie about the coming of the next ice age – with very regular people in extraordinary situations. That's probably what sets me apart from a director like Lucas – although Spielberg did two of these kinds of movies too – *E.T.* and *Close Encounters* – with regular people finding themselves in the middle of a very extraordinary event.

C: I find your films are a little more ironic in style than, perhaps, Spielberg's films.

E: But I'm European! Right now, I'm doing the biggest disaster movie ever attempted. I love disaster movies. Actually my attempt with *Independence Day* was to make a disaster movie in the sky – the disaster was the aliens. The studio never wanted me to say that it was a disaster movie, because they were pan-icking – they said oh, disaster movies are a thing of the past. The moment *Independence Day* was a huge hit they went on to make straight disaster movies, about a volcano, about a flood. But this kind of disaster movie is too small for people now . . .

C: So now an audience wants a more extraordinary, more fantastical kind of disaster?

E: Exactly, they can see the other kind on TV.

C: The most talked-about effect in *Independence Day* is the blowing up of the White House. When I saw the film in Britain there was a cheer from the audience when this happened.

E: At that time it was a different situation. People were very frustrated with Washington and we expressed that.

C: Is that kind of effect something you could not do now – given the events of 11 September, 2001?

E: No, it couldn't be filmed now. A big building exploding is a no-no for years to come. When the planes flew into the World Trade Center, I was in Mexico in my house and somebody woke me up and I saw it happening live. It immediately reminded me *Independence Day,* and all these friends of mine called me and said it looks just like a movie. I said well it's the first time that a live disaster has been filmed in this way – it's never happened before on this magnitude, with the different camera angles and with helicopter shots etc. The style was very similar to the way movies are filmed. Then we heard that the news editors did exactly what Hollywood would have done – they cut out all the people jumping out of the building because that was too gruesome. All of a sudden it became like this little movie almost. Every newscaster used the same four or five images over and over again. It was like a trailer. It was very interesting to watch. On the one hand I was shocked, but it was very interesting to see how the media always criticised us for doing certain things and then they used the same method. They went for the montage of victims at the fence, you know, and they used really, really emotional music – like in the movies, always like in the movies. That has changed something for movies. Now people say, can we do this, can we do that; is it right, is it wrong, and everybody has to ask themselves this question now.

C: If I could go back to *Stargate* for a moment – that had a multi-national cast. I wondered whether there was a sense in which this casting was bound up with an attempt to reach a world market?

E: I'm like a foreigner in America myself, so I would always try to have a multi-national cast. I think that it's an important message that you have to get – I mean this world has lots of different races, not just white people. With *Independence Day,* at least I tried – I had Jewish people, a black man, an Italian guy etc. save the world. They were fighting me on the casting of Will Smith as the pilot – they were totally against it – and I said, well he's more American to me than many other actors and he represents America. I fought them for so long that they had no other choice because they wanted to start shooting.

C: So multi-racial, multi-national casting is definitely something you bear in mind then?

E: Oh yes, I mean I'm doing that on purpose. The fact that it might work better in a world market – you know what, I don't think about that.

C: Coming back to *Independence Day* one critic has said – and I quote – 'It serves American power in the name of attacking it'.[30] I wondered what your response would be to this statement?

E: That's really weird. I mean when you look carefully at *Independence Day*, the message is that the world is one nation and the whole world has to unite. National divides should be a thing of the past and world patriotism should be a thing of the future. There's the speech that the president gives, which clearly states that. Because it's based on Independence Day you see a lot of national flags. But then the president says, let's make this Independence Day our Independence Day for the world – to free the world. Everywhere we went people said that it promoted American patriotism, but it was not intended that way. Because people saw all the flags they thought that it was saying, oh Americans save the world again. Nobody saw the message that it was actually a Jewish guy, a black guy and a white guy that saved the world – that got totally lost. What people also forget is that it's an American-financed movie and all the main characters have to be American – there's no way around that, you know what I mean. With my new movie, now that I am in a position in my career where I can do what I like – now I'm doing much more subversive things.

C: From what I've read your next film is about an ice age – people are calling it an eco-science fiction. I've also read that there are scenes of an iced-over New York setting and I wondered what your thinking was behind that kind of image.

E: It's a very, very simple idea. One day I read this article about a book which is called *The Coming of the Global Superstorm*. Then I saw it in the bookstores and I bought it and I didn't read it for about a year or so. Then one day I started reading it. It's a very simple theory. I guess at the very beginning I thought it was pure science fiction – the idea that in one big storm the climate will switch and we will get a new ice age. I thought, what a great scenario for a movie, but I also thought it was totally fantastic. Anyway, I bought the rights and while I was working on the script I researched more. More and more it seemed less fantastic. Everywhere in the newspapers there were signs for what they were talking about in the book – the storms get stronger, the climate is warming up, the ice caps are melting, the ocean currents are changing and one day there will a catastrophe. I don't know if this will happen, but I kind of state in my movie that this will happen and the consequences are so massive and so staggering that the Western world, as we know it, will be a thing of the past. In my films, everybody has to go south. All the Americans end up in Mexico. There will be scenes of thousands and thousands of people climbing over the fence to get to Mexico. As I was saying, I'm being subversive now. It's financed by Rupert Murdoch and they cannot change anything about it because I have final cut.

C: How closely do you work with the people who produce these kinds of effects – say the set designers, the CGI people?

E: Very closely. Most of the time, I come up with the images. Then I hire people firstly to draw these images, then somebody to help me create them. This time it's Karen Goulekas, who worked on *Fifth Element,* and this time I'm working with Digital Domain, who will do all the visual effects.

C: You did have a special-effects company . . .

E: Yes, but I sold it. I'm a filmmaker, not a business man.

C: What's it like working with Digital Domain – do you still have control over the 'look'?

E: Oh yeah, it's pretty hands on, you still have the control. You can do whatever you want. You are trying to get people to create the way it looks in your head, you know. It's sometimes a painful process.

C: Is this easier to do now with CGI, do you think? I mean, you have used a mixture of effects in the past.

E: In this movie we've had to go pretty much all CGI on a lot of things. There's no model work any more, apart from one little scene. With this movie everything has to be, in a way, very realistic – so we imitate helicopter shots by moving the camera constantly, and you cannot do that with models. We have these people who do texture maps, who survey New York for months and months – it's called LIDAR – they kind of laser scan buildings.

C: Do you think you will continue to work within the genre, and where do you see it going in coming years?

E: Well . . . I don't know. My next movie's about the Mayans. It can be hard to find anything new, to find something that excites you. I was really interested in Artificial Intelligence, but there were so many movies made and they were all, in a way, not to my liking – for me, as an audience member.

C: So, do you think that science fiction is a bit stale at the moment?

E: Well it's kind of weird for me to say this, but science fiction at its best is about ideas – it's more an intellectual pleasure than a visual pleasure. So you always have to find something which combines an idea with the visual.

NOTES

1. Not all of this film survives, although the train section can be seen in full. However, Paul's catalogue details the rest of the content of the film.
2. In Elsaesser and Barker (eds) 1990.
3. Ibid., p. 58.

4. Ibid., p. 59.
5. Ibid., p. 61.
6. Wireframe is a way to display a 3-D outline of an object using computer software. The edges and lines of the object are drawn as a series of lines, so that the object looks like a transparent model made out of wire. In other words, the model is not shaded in any way, the surfaces between lines remain clear.
7. Blue-screen and green-screen photography involves filming a subject in front of a colour-lit backing screen so that the subject can be placed against a separately filmed or computer generated background during the compositing of a complete shot.
8. The following definition of 'motion blur' is taken from Goulekas 2001, pp. 321 488: 'The blurring or smearing of an image caused by the distance an object moves relative to the amount of camera motion. For film, the natural blurring of the captured images that occurs when the camera shoots a moving object . . . For computer graphics, this effect needs to be added artificially, either by 3D motion blur that is calculated during rendering or with a 2D motion blur that is applied as a post process on the already rendered images. Moving objects rendered without motion blur can create strobing.' Strobing is 'the jerky motion of a subject due to a lack of or insufficient amount of motion blur'.
9. The budget for this film was approximately $10 million.
10. The weekend gross figure was obtained from boxofficemojo.com and the world-wide gross from IMDB.com.
11. Harrington 1992.
12. Arnold 1992, Edition 2, p. c2
13. Review written in 1992, *The SF, Horror and Fantasy Film Review*, http://www.moria.co.nz/sf/Lawnmower.htm
14. I have borrowed this phrase from Thomas Elsaesser and Warren Buckland. See 's/Z, the "readerly" film, and video game logic', in Elsaesser and Buckland 2002, pp. 146–67.
15. Ibid., p. 165.
16. Ibid., p. 164.
17. See Chapter 3, 'The Wonder Years and Beyond: 1989–1995', in Pierson 2002, pp. 93–136.
18. 'The Boys in the Hoods: A Song of the Urban Superhero', in Bukatman 2003, p. 191.
19. By this I am purely referring to those films based upon pre-existing games, which also becomes a major selling point in their marketing. I do not mean to suggest that other films have not gone on to become games and acknowledge that many films have been designed with 'remediation' into game format in mind.
20. Pierson 2002, p. 141.
21. 'The Imagination of Disaster', in Sontag 1967, pp. 209–62.
22. Keane 2001, pp. 7–8.
23. Examples include: the immediately pulled trailer for *Spider-Man* (dir. Sam Raimi, 2002) (consisting of a shot of a helicopter caught in a giant web suspended between the Twin Towers), the rewriting of the ending for *Men in Black II* (dir. Barry Sonnerfold, 2002) (originally intended to take place in the World Trade Center) and the cutting of a scene from *The Time Machine* (dir. Simon Wells, 2002) (featuring a meteor shower raining down on New York).
24. A Jackie Chan vehicle called *Nosebleed* was scrapped because its narrative revolved around a terrorist attack on the World Trade Center and the Arnold Schwarzenegger vehicle, *Collateral Damage,* was held back until 2002.
25. Žižek 2002, p. 16.

26. See Chapter 1, 'Why Trauma Now?', in Kaplan 2005, pp. 24–41.
27. Ibid., p. 39.
28. Dixon 2003, p. 68.
29. Thompson 2003, pp. 45–63.
30. Rogin 1998, p. 40.

BIBLIOGRAPHY

Adler, Renata (1968), ' "2001" Is Up, Up and Away', *New York Times*, 4 April.

Aldiss, Brian (2001), *Barefoot in the Head*, London: House of Stratus (first published 1969).

Aldiss, Brian (2002), *Super-State: A Novel of the Future Europe*, London: Orbit Books.

Aldiss, Brian (2004), *Non-Stop*, London: Orion/Gollancz (first published 1958).

Aldiss, Brian, and Roger Penrose (2000), *White Mars*, New York: St Martin's Press.

Altman, Rick (1999), *Film/Genre*, London: BFI Publishing.

Anderson, Craig W. (1985), *Science Fiction Films of the Seventies*, Jefferson, NC/London: McFarland & Company, Inc.

Arnold, Gary (1992), 'The Lawnmower Man', *Washington Times*, 7 March.

Ashcroft, Bill, Gareth Griffiths and Helen Tiffin (1999), *The Post-Colonial Studies Reader*, London/New York: Routledge.

Asimov, Isaac (1983), *Asimov on Science Fiction*, London: Granada.

Auslander, Philip (1997), *From Acting to Performance: Essays in Modernism and Postmodernism*, London/New York: Routledge.

Ballard, J. G. (2001), *Crash*, New York: Picador (first published 1973).

Barker, Martin, Jane Arthurs and Ramaswari Harindranath (2001), *The Crash Controversy: Censorship Campaigns and Film Reception*, London: Wallflower Press.

Barnett, Chad P. (2000), 'Reviving Cyberpunk: (Re)Constructing the Subject and Mapping Cyberspace in the Wachowski Brothers' Film *The Matrix*', *Extrapolations*, 41: 4, 359–74.

Battock, Gregory (ed.) (1984), *Art of Performance: A Critical Anthology*, New York: E. P. Dutton, Inc.

Bell, Art, and Whitley Strieber (1999), *The Coming Global Superstorm*, New York: Pocket Books.

Bellamy, Edward (2000), *Looking Backward: 2000–1887*, Harmondsworth, Middlesex: Penguin (Signet Classic) (first published 1888).

Bernstein, Matthew, and Gaylyn Studlar (eds) (1997), *Visions of the East: Orientalism in Film*, London/New York: I. B. Tauris Publishers.

Bhabha, Homi K. (1988), 'The Commitment to Theory', *New Formations* 5, 5–23.

Bhabha, Homi K. (1990), *Nation and Narration*, London/New York: Routledge.

Biskind, Peter (1983), *Seeing Is Believing: How Hollywood Taught Us to Stop Worrying and Love the Fifties*, London: Pluto Press.

Booker M., Keith (2001), *Monsters, Mushroom Clouds, and the Cold War: American Science Fiction and the Roots of Postmodernism, 1946–1964*, London/Westport, CT: Greenwood Press.

Bordwell, David, and Kristin Thompson (1993), *Film Art* (4th edn), Boston, MA: McGraw-Hill Education.

Brosnan, John (1978), *The Cinema of Science Fiction: Future Tense*, New York: St Martin's Press.

Brosnan, John (1979), 'Illustrated review of *Alien*', *Starburst* 14, 4–8.

Brosnan, John (1991), *The Primal Screen: A History of Science Fiction Film*, London: Orbit Books.

Bukatman, Scott (1993), *Terminal Identity: The Virtual Subject in Postmodern Science Fiction*, Durham, NC: Duke University Press.

Bukatman, Scott (2003), *Matters of Gravity: Special Effects and Supermen in the 20th Century*, London/Durham, NC: Duke University Press.

Burgin, Victor (1990), 'Paranoiac Space', *New Formations*, 12, 62–73.

Butler, Jeremy G. (ed.) (1991), *Star Texts: Image and Performance in Film and Television*, Detroit, MI: Wayne State University Press.

Butler, Judith (1990), *Gender Trouble: Feminism and the Subversion of Identity*, London/New York: Routledge.

Cadigan, Pal (1991), *Synners*, London: Grafton.

Carroll, Lewis (2002), *Alice's Adventures in Wonderland and Through the Looking-Glass*, New York: Random House (Modern Library edition) (first published 1869).

Carroll, Noel (1990), *The Philosophy of Horror: Or, Paradoxes of the Heart*, London/New York: Routledge.

Chayefsky, Paddy (1978), *Altered States*, New York: HarperCollins.

Chion, Michel (2001), *Kubrick's Cinema Odyssey*, trans. Claudia Gorbman, London: BFI Publishing.

Clover, Carol (1992), *Men, Women, and Chainsaws: The Modern Horror Film*, London: BFI Publishing.

Clynes, Manfred E., and Nathan S. Kline (1960), 'Cyborgs and Space', *Astronautics*, September.

Collins, Jim, Hilary Radner and Ava Preacher Collins (eds) (1993), *Film Theory Goes to the Movies*, London/New York: Routledge.

Conrad, Joseph (2000), *Heart of Darkness*, Cheswold, DE: Prestwick House, Literary Touchstone Press (first published 1902).

Conroy, Mariannne (1993), 'Acting Out: Method Acting, the National Culture, and the Middlebrow Disposition in Cold War America', *Criticism – A Quarterly for Literature and the Arts*, 35:2, 239–64.

Creed, Barbara (1993), *The Monstrous Feminine: Film, Feminism, Psychoanalysis*, London/New York: Routledge.

Darwin, Charles (2003), *The Origin of Species by Means of Natural Selection, or The Preservation of Favoured Races in the Struggle for Life*, New York: Penguin (Signet Classic) (first published 1859).

Davis, Darrell William (2001), 'Reigniting Japanese Tradition with *Hana-Bi*', *Cinema Journal*, 40: 4, 55–80.

Delany, Samuel R. (1989), 'Neither the Beginning, Nor the End of Structuralism, Post-Structualism, Seminotics, or Deconstruction for SF Readers: An Introduction', *New York Review of Science Fiction*, 6–8 (in three parts).

Devlin, Rachel (2005a), ' "Acting Out the Oedipal Wish": Father–Daughter Incest and the Sexuality of Adolescent Girls in the United States, 1941–1965', *Journal of Social History*, Spring, 609–33.

Devlin, Rachel (2005b), *Relative Intimacy: Fathers, Adolescent Daughters, and Postwar American Culture*, London/Chapel Hill, NC: University of North Carolina Press.

Dixon, Wheeler Winston (2003), *Visions of the Apocalypse: Spectacles of Destruction in American Cinema*, London/New York: Wallflower Press.

Doe, Richard L. (1968), ' "2001" Flings Man into Space', *Washington Post*, 14 April.

Dyer, Richard (1997), *White*, London/New York: Routledge.

Ellison, Harlan (1984), 'A Boy and His Dog', in *The Beast that Shouted Love at the Heart of the World*, New York: St Martin's Press (first published 1969).

Elsaesser, Thomas, and Adam Barker (eds) (1990), *Early Cinema: Space, Frame, Narrative*, London: BFI.

Elsaesser, Thomas, and Warren Buckland (eds) (2002), *Studying Contemporary American Movies: A Guide to Film Analysis*, London: Hodder Arnold.

Elsaesser, Thomas, Noel King 2nd Alexander Horwath (eds) (2004), *The Last Great American Picture Show: New Hollywood Cinema in the 1970s*, Amsterdam: Amsterdam University Press.

Ezra, Elizabeth (2000), *George Méliès: The Birth of the Auteur*, Manchester/New York: Manchester University Press.

Fanon, Frantz (1970), *Black Skin, White Mask*, London: Paladin.

Fehrenback, Heide, and Uta G. Poiger (eds) (2000), *Transactions, Transgressions, Transformations: American Culture in Western Europe and Japan*, Oxford/New York: Berghahn Books.

Foster, Hal (ed.) (1983), *The Anti-Aesthetic: Essays on Postmodern Culture*, Seattle, WA: Bay Press.

Frum, David (2000), *How We Got Here – The 70's: The Decade That Brought You Modern Life – For Better Or Worse*, New York: Basic Books.

Gay, Peter (ed.) (1995), *The Freud Reader*, trans. James Strachey, London: Vintage.

Gelmis, Joseph (1968a), 'Space Odyssey Fails Most Gloriously', *Newsday*, 4 April.

Gelmis, Joseph (1968b), 'Another Look at Space Odyssey', *Newsday*, 20 April.

Geraghty, Christine (2000), *British Cinema in the Fifties: Gender, Genre and the 'New Look'*, London/New York: Routledge.

Gibson, William (1994), *Virtual Light*, Harmondsworth, Middlesex: Penguin.

Gibson, William (1995), *Johnny Mnemonic: The Screenplay and the Story*, New York: Ace Books.

Gibson, William (2000), *Neuromancer*, New York: Ace Books (first published 1984).

Goulekas, Karen E. (2001), *Visual Effects in a Digital World: A Comprehensive Glossary of over 7,000 Visual Effects Terms*, San Diego/San Francisco/New York/Boston/London/Sydney/Tokyo: Morgan Kaufmann.

Greene, Eric (ed.) (1998), *Planet of the Apes as American Myth: Race, Politics, and Popular Culture*, NH/London: Wesleyan University Press.

Harper, Sue, and Vincent Porter (2003), *British Cinema of the 1950s: The Decline of Deference*, Oxford/New York: Oxford University Press.

Harrington, Richard (1992), ' "Mower" cuts swathe of diabolical silliness', *Washington Post*, 7 March, http://www.washingtonpost.com/wp-srv/style/longterm/movies/videos/thelawnmowermanrharrington_a0ab25.

Hendershot, Cyndy (1999), *Paranoia, the Bomb, and 1950s Science Fiction Films*, Bowling Green, OH: Bowling Green State University Popular Press.

Hendershot, Cyndy (2001), *I Was a Cold War Monster: Horror Films, Eroticism, and the Cold War Imagination*, Bowling Green, OH: Bowling Green State University Popular Press.

Hill, John (1999), *British Cinema in the 1980s*, Oxford: Clarendon Press.

Hill, John, and Pamela Church Gibson (eds) (1998), *The Oxford Guide to Film Studies*, Oxford: Oxford University Press.

Hjort, Mette, and Scott MacKenzie (eds) (2000), *Cinema and Nation*, London/New York: Routledge.

Howells, Christina (ed.) (1992), *The Cambridge Companion to Sartre*, Cambridge: Cambridge University Press.

Huxley, Aldous (1998), *Brave New World*, New York: HarperCollins (first published 1932).

Huxley, Aldous (2002), *Island*, New York: HarperCollins (Harper Perennial Modern Classics) (first published 1962).

Huxley, Aldous (2004), *The Doors of Perception and Heaven and Hell*, New York: HarperCollins (Harper Perennial Modern Classics) (first published 1954).

Ing, Dean and Robert A. Heinlein (1991), *Silent Thunder/Universe*, New York: Tor Books (first published in 1941).

Jackson, Rosemary (1981), *Fantasy: The Literature of Subversion*, New York: Methuen.

Jacobus, Mary, Evelyn Fox Keller and Sally Shuttleworth (eds) (1990), *Body/Politics: Women and the Discourses of Science*, London/New York: Routledge.

James, Edward (1994), *Science Fiction in the 20th Century*, Oxford: Oxford University Press.

Jameson, Fredric (1991), *Postmodernism: or, The Cultural Logic of Late Capitalism*, London/New York: Verso.

Jancovich, Mark (1996), *Rational Fears: American Horror in the 1950s*, Manchester/New York: Manchester University Press.

Jeffords, Susan (1994), *Hard Bodies: Hollywood Masculinity in the Reagan Era*, New Brunswick, NJ: Rutgers University Press.

Jenkins, Henry (1992), *Textual Poachers: Television Fans and Participatory Culture*, New York: Routledge, Chapman and Hall.

Jezewski, Mary Ann (1984), 'Traits of the Female Hero', *New York Folklore*, 10: 1–2.

Jones, Alan (1990), 'Hardcore Hardware: An Interview by Alan Jones', *Starburst*, 145, September.

Kaplan, E. Ann (1980), *Women in Film Noir*, London: BFI Publishing.

Kaplan, E. Ann (2005), *Trauma Culture: The Politics of Terror and Loss in Media and Literature*, New Brunswick, NJ/London: Rutgers University Press.

Kaysing, Bill, and Randy Reid (1976), *We Never Went to the Moon: America's Thirty Billion Dollar Swindle*, Pomeroy, WA: Health Research.

Keane, Stephen (2001), *Disaster Movies: The Cinema of Catastrophe*, London/New York: Wallflower.

Kelly, Kevin (1995), *Out of Control*, London: Fourth Estate.

Kloman, William (1968), ' "2001"and "Hair" – Are They the Groove of the Future?', *New York Times*, 12 May.

Kolker, Robert Phillip (1988), *A Cinema of Loneliness: Penn, Kubrick, Scorsese, Spielberg, Altman*, Oxford/New York: Oxford University Press.

Kuhn, Annette (ed.) (1990), *Alien Zone: Cultural Theory and Contemporary Science Fiction*, London/New York: Verso.

Kuhn, Annette (ed.) (1999), *Alien Zone II: The Spaces of Science Fiction*, London/New York: Verso.

Kroker, Arthur, and Marilouise Kroker (eds) (1997), *Digital Delirium*, New York: St Martin's Press.

Landon, Brooks (1992), *The Aesthetics of Ambivalence: Rethinking Science Fiction Film in the Age of Electronic (Re)production*, Westport, CT/London: Greenwood Press.

LaValley, Al (ed.) (1989), *Invasion of the Body Snatchers*, New Brunswick, NJ, and London: Rutgers University Press.

Levy, David (1966), *Maternal Overprotection*, New York: W. W. Norton and Company (first published 1943).

McKee Charnas, Suzy (1978), *Motherlines*, New York: Berkley Publishing.

Masters, Robert E. L., and Jean Houston (1968), *Psychedelic Art*, London: Weidenfeld and Nicolson.

Merril, Judith (1971), 'What do you Mean: Science? Fiction?', in *SF: The Other Side of Realism*, ed. Thomas D. Clareson, Bowling Green, OH: Bowling Green State University Popular Press.

Morley, David, and Kevin Robins (1995), *Spaces of Identity: Global Media, Electronic Landscapes and Cultural Boundaries*, London/New York: Routledge.

Morris, William (1993), *News from Nowhere*, Harmondsworth, Middlesex: Penguin (first published 1890).

Mulvey, Laura (1989), *Visual and Other Pleasures*, Bloomington, IN: Indiana University Press.

Myers, Robert E. (ed.) (1983), *The Intersection of Science Fiction and Philosophy*, Westport, CT: Greenwood Press.

Napier, Susan Jolliffe (2001), *Anime: From Akira to Princess Mononoke: Experiencing Contemporary Japanese Animation*, New York: Palgrave.

Neale, Steve (2000), *Genre and Hollywood*, London/New York: Routledge.

Neale, Steve (1983), 'Masculinity as Spectacle', *Screen*, 24: 6, 11–16.

Nichols, Bill (ed.) (1985), *Movies and Methods: Volume II*, Berkeley, CA: University of California Press.

Penley, Constance (1997), *NASA/TREK: Popular Science and Sex in America*, London/New York: Verso.

Penley, Constance, Elizabeth Lyon, Lynn Spigel and Janet Bergstrom (eds) (1991), *Close Encounters: Film, Feminism, and Science Fiction*, Minneapolis: University of Minnesota Press.

Piercy, Marge (1992), *Body of Glass* (aka *He, She and It*), London: Michael Joseph.

Pierson, Michele (2002), *Special Effects: Still in Search of Wonder*, New York: Columbia University Press.

Rayner, Jonathan (2000), *Contemporary Australian Cinema*, Manchester: Manchester University Press.

Rheingold, Howard (1994), *The Virtual Community: Surfing the Internet*, London: Secker and Warburg.

Rodley, Chris (1996), 'Crash: David Cronenberg talks about his new film "Crash" based on J. G. Ballard's disturbing techno-sex novel', *Sight and Sound*, 6, 6–11.

Rogin, Michael (1998), *Independence Day, or How I Learned to Stop Worrying and Love Enola Gay*, London: BFI.

Rushkoff, Douglas (1995), *Cyberia: Life in the Trenches of Hyperspace*, New York: HarperCollins.

Russ, Joanna (1975), *The Female Man*, New York: Bantam Books.

Russell, Ken (2001), *Ken Russell: Directing Film: The Director's Art from Script to Cutting Room*, Washington, DC: Brassey's Inc.

Ryan, Michael, and Douglas Kellner (1988), *Camera Politica: The Politics and Ideology of Contemporary Hollywood Film*, Bloomington, IN: Indiana University Press.

Said, Edward W. (2003), *Orientalism,* London: Penguin Modern Classics (first published by Routledge & Kogan Paul, 1978).

Sardar, Ziauddin, and Sean Cubitt (eds) (2002), *Aliens R Us: The Other in Science Fiction Cinema*, London/Sterling, VA: Pluto Press.

Sarris, Andrew (1968), *The American Cinema: Directors and Directions, 1929–1968*, New York: Dutton.

Sartre, Jean-Paul (2000), *Being and Nothingness: An essay on phenomenological ontology*, trans, Hazel E. Barnes, London/New York: Routledge (first published in 1943).

Sartre, Jean-Paul (1974), *Existentialism and Humanism*, trans. Philip Mairet, London: Methuen (first published in 1948).

Schechner, Richard (1982), *The End of Humanism: Writings on Performance*, New York: Performing Arts Journal Publications.

Scheib, Richard (1992), *The SF, Horror and Fantasy Film Review*, http://www.moria.co.nz/sf/lawnmower.htm, accessed May 2006.

Schneider, Rebecca (1997), *The Explicit Body in Performance*, London/New York: Routledge.

Schulman, Bruce J. (2001), *The Seventies: The Great Shift in American Culture, Society, and Politics*, Cambridge, MA: Da Capo Press.

Seed, David (1995), *Anticipations: Essays on Early Science Fiction and Its Precursors*, Syracuse, NY: Syracuse University Press.

Segal, Lynne (1990), *Slow Motion: Changing Masculinities, Changing Men*, London: Virago.

Shapiro, Jerome F. (2002), *Atomic Bomb Cinema: The Apocalyptic Imagination on Film*, London/New York: Routledge.

Shelley, Mary (2004), *Frankenstein*, New York: Pocket Books (first published 1818).

Shilling, Chris (1993), *The Body and Social Theory*, London/Thousand Oaks, CA/New Delhi: Sage Publications.

Silverman, Kaja (1988), *The Acoustic Mirror: The Female Voice in Psychoanalysis and Cinema*, Bloomington, IN: Indiana University Press.

Silverman, Kaja (1991), 'Back to the Future', *Camera Obscura*, 27, 108–32.

Smith, Gavin (1997), 'Mind Over Matter', *Film Comment*, 33: 2, 14–29.

Sobchack, Vivian (1993), *Screening Space: The American Science Fiction Film*, New York: Ungar.

Sontag, Susan (1967), *Against Interpretation and Other Essays*, London: Eyre & Spottiswoode.

Springer, Claudia (1991), 'The Pleasure of the Interface', *Screen*, 32: 3, 303–23.

Stanislavski, Konstantin (1989), 'An Actor Prepares', trans. Elizabeth Reynolds Hapgood, New York: Routledge (first published 1936).

Stevenson, Robert, Louis (2003), *The Strange Case of Dr. Jekyll and Mr. Hyde*, New York: Barnes and Noble (first published 1886).

Suvin, Darko (1979), *Metamorphoses of Science Fiction: On the Poetics and History of a Literary Genre*, New Haven, CT: Yale University Press.

Tart, Charles T. (ed.) (1969), *Altered States of Consciousness*, New York: John Wiley and Sons.

Tasker, Yvonne (1993), *Spectacular Bodies: Gender, Genre and the Action Cinema*, London/New York: Routledge.

Telotte, J. P. (2001), *Science Fiction Film*, Cambridge: Cambridge University Press, 2001.

Terranova, Tiziana (1996), 'Digital Darwin: Nature, Evolution, and Control in the Rhetoric of Electronic Communication', *New Formations*, 29, 69–83.

Thompson, Kristin (2003), 'Fantasy, Franchises, and Frodo Baggins: "The Lord of the Rings" and Modern Hollywood', *Velvet Light Trap: A Critical Journal of Film and Television*, 52, 45–63.

Todorov, Tzvetan (1975), *The Fantastic: A Structural Approach to a Literary Genre*, New York: Cornell University Press.

Toepfer, Karl (1996), 'Nudity and Textuality in Postmodern Performance', *Performing Arts Journal*, 54, 76–91.

Tolkien, J. R. R. (2005), *The Lord of the Rings*, New York: Houghton Miffin (first published 1954–5).

Tomlinson, John (1999), *Globalization and Culture*, Cambridge: Polity Press.

Tullock, John, and Henry Jenkins (eds) (1995), *Science Fiction Audiences: Watching Doctor Who and Star Trek*, London/New York: Routledge.

Turkle, Sherry (1997), *Life on the Screen: Identity in the Age of the Internet*, Guernsey: Phoenix.

Turner, Bryan S. (1996), *The Body and Society* (2nd edn), London/Thousand Oaks, CA/New Delhi: Sage Publications.

Verne, Jules (1993), *Twenty Thousand Leagues under the Sea*, London: Puffin Books (first published 1869).

Verne, Jules (2006), *From the Earth to the Moon*, New York: Barnes and Noble/Aegypan Books (first published 1864).

Walker, Alexander (1996), 'A Movie Beyond the Bounds of Depravity', *London Evening Standard*, 6 June.

Watson, Sophie, and Katherine Gibson (eds) (1994), *Postmodern Cities and Spaces*, Malden, MA/Oxford/Victoria: Blackwell Publishing.

Werbner, Phina, and Tariq Modood (eds) (1997), *Debating Cultural Hybridity: Multi-Cultural Identities and the Politics of Anti-Racism*, London: Zed Books.

Wexman, V. W. (1993), *Creating the Couple: Love, Marriage, and Hollywood Performance*, Pinceton, NJ: Princeton University Press.

Wiener, Norbert (1965), *Cybernetics: or Control and Communication in the Animal and Machine*, Cambridge, MA: MIT Press (first published in 1948).

Wells, H. G. (2002), *The Invisible Man*, Harmondsworth, Middlesex: Penguin (Signet Classic) (first published 1897).

Wells, H. G. (2002), *The Time Machine*, Harmondsworth, Middlesex: Penguin (Signet Classic) (first published 1895).

Wells, H. G. (2002), *The War of the Worlds*, Cutchogue, NY: Modern Library Classics (first published 1898).

Wells, H. G. (2003), *The First Men in the Moon*, Cutchogue, NY: Modern Library Classics (first published 1901).

Wells, H. G. (2006a), *The Island of Doctor Moreau*, Boston, MA: Adamant Media Corporation (Elibron Classic) (first published 1896).

Wells, H. G. (2006b), *The Shape of Things to Come*, Harmondsworth, Middlesex: Penguin (first published 1933).

Wood, Robin (1986), *Hollywood from Vietnam to Reagan*, New York: Columbia University Press.

Wylie, Philip (1996), *Generation of the Vipers*, Normal, IL: Dalkey Archive Press (first published 1942).

Young, Robert J. C. (1995), *Colonial Desire: Hybridity in Theory, Culture and Race*, London/New York: Routledge.

Žižek, Slavoj (2002), *Welcome to the Desert of the Real*, London/New York: Verso.

FILMS CITED

The Abyss (dir. James Cameron, 1989)
The Adventures of Superman (dir. Spencer Gordon Bennet and Thomas Carr, 1948)
Aelita (dir. Yacov Protazanov, 1924)
Akira (dir. Katsuhiro Ôtomo, 1988)
Alexander (dir. Olivor Stone, 2004)
Alien (dir. Ridley Scott, 1979)
Alien: Resurrection (dir. Jean-Pierre Jeunet, 1997)
Alien 3 (dir. David Fincher, 1992)
Alien Nation (dir. Graham Blaker, 1988)
Alien Vs Predator (dir. Paul W. S. Anderson, 2004)
Aliens (dir. James Cameron, 1986)
Alphaville (dir. Jean-Luc Godard, 1965)
Altered States (dir. Ken Russell, 1980)
The Andromeda Strain (dir. Robert Wise, 1971)
The Angry Red Planet (dir. Ib Melchior, 1960)
Apocalypse Now (dir. Francis Ford Coppola, 1979)
Armageddon (dir. Michael Bay, 1998)
L'Arrivee d'un Train à la Ciotat (dir. Auguste and Louis Lumière, 1895)
Artificial Intelligence: AI (dir. Steven Spielberg, 2001)
Attack of the Puppet People (dir. Bert I. Gordon, 1958)
Back to the Future (dir. Robert Zemeckis, 1985)
Barbarella (dir. Roger Vadim, 1967)
The Batman (dir. Lambert Hillyer, 1943)
Ben Hur (dir. William Wyler, 1959)
Black Hawk Down (dir. Ridley Scott, 2001)
The Black Hole (dir. Gary Nelson, 1979)
Blade Runner (dir. Ridley Scott, 1982)
Bonnie and Clyde (dir. Arthur Penn, 1967)
A Boy and His Dog (dir. L. Q. Jones, 1975)

The Brain Eaters (dir. Bruno VeSota, 1958)
Brazil (dir. Torry Gilliam, 1985)
The Brother from Another Planet (dir. John Sayles, 1984)
Buck Rogers Conquers the Universe (dir. Ford Beebe and Saul A. Goodkind, 1939)
The Cabinet of Dr. Caligari (dir. Robert Wiene, 1920)
Capricom One (dir. Peter Hyams, 1977)
Cars (dir. John Lasseter, 2006)
Chicken Run (dir. Nick Park, Peter Lord, 2000)
Children of the Damned (dir. Anton Leader, 1963)
Citizen Kane (dir. Orson Welles, 1941)
Close Encounters of the Third Kind (dir. Steven Spielberg, 1977)
The Countryman and the Cinematograph (Robert Paul, 1901)
Crash (dir. David Cronenberg, 1996)
The Creature from the Black Lagoon (dir. Jack Arnold, 1954)
The Crying Game (dir. Neil Jordan, 1992)
Daleks' Invasion Earth: 2150 A.D. (dir. Gordon Flemyng, 1966)
Dark City (dir. Alex Proyas, 1998)
The Dark Mirror (dir. Robert Siodmak, 1946)
Dark Star (dir. John Carpenter, 1974)
The Day after Tomorrow (dir. Roland Emmerich, 2004)
The Day of the Triffids (dir. Steve Sekely, 1963)
The Day the Earth Stood Still (dir. Robert Wise, 1951)
Death Wish (dir. Michael Winner, 1974)
Death Wish II (dir. Michael Winner, 1982)
Death Wish 3 (dir. Michael Winner, 1985)
Death Wish 4 (dir. J. Lee Thompson, 1987)
Death Wish V (dir. Allan A. Goldstein, 1994)
Delicatessen (dir. Marc Caro and Jean-Pierre Jeunet, 1991)
Demon Seed (dir. Donald Cammell, 1977)
Destination Moon (dir. Irving Pichel, 1950)
Devil Girl from Mars (dir. David McDonald, 1954)
The Devil (dir. Ken Russell, 1971)
Die Hard (dir. John McTiernan, 1988)
Die Hard 2 (dir. Renny Harlin, 1990)
Die Hard: With a Vengeance (dir. John McTiernan, 1995)
Dirty Harry (dir. Don Siegel, 1971)
Diva (dir. Jean-Jacques Beineix, 1980)
The Doctor's Experiment: or, Reversing Darwin's Theory (dir. unknown, 1908)
Doom (dir. Andrzej Bartkowiak, 2005)
DragonHeart (dir. Rob Cohen, 1998)
Dr. Jekyll and Mr. Hyde (dir. Victor Fleming, 1941)
Dr. Strangelove, or How I Learned to Stop Worrying and Love the Bomb (dir. Stanley Kubrick, 1964)
Dr. Who and the Daleks (dir. Gordon Flemyng, 1965)
Dog Day Afternoon (dir. Sidney Lumet, 1975)
The Duality of Man (dir. unknown, 1910)
Duel in the Sun (dir. King Vidor, 1946)
Earth vs. the Flying Saucers (dir. Fred F. Sears, 1956)
Earth Versus the Spider (dir. Bert I. Gordon, 1958)
Easy Rider (dir. Donnis Hopper, 1969)
L'Eclipse du soleil en pleine lune (Georges Méliès, 1907)
Enemy Mine (dir. Wolfgang Peterson, 1985)

Enter the Dragon (dir. Robert Clouse, 1973)
E.T. the Extra-Terrestrial (dir. Steven Spielberg, 1982)
Eve of Destruction (dir. Duncan Gibbins, 1991)
Event Horizon (dir. Paul W. S. Anderson, 1997)
eXistenZ (dir. David Cronenberg, 1999)
Fahrenheit 451 (dir. Francois Truffaut, 1967)
Fail Safe (dir. Sidney Lumet, 1964)
Fantastic Voyage (dir. Richard Fleischer, 1966)
The Far Country (dir. Anthony Mann, 1954)
The Fifth Element (dir. Luc Besson, 1997)
The Final Programme (dir. Robert Fuest, 1974)
First Blood (dir. Ted Kotcheff, 1982)
Flash Gordon: Space Soldiers (dir. Frederick Stephani, 1936)
The Flying Saucer (dir. Mikel Conrad, 1950)
Forbidden Planet (dir. Fred M. Wilcox, 1956)
Frankenstein (dir. J. Searle Dawley, 1910)
Frankenstein (dir. James Whale, 1931)
Firday the 13th (dir. Sear S. Cunningham, 1980)
Ghost in the Shell (dir. Mamoru Oshii, 1995)
Godzilla, King of the Monsters! (dir. Ishirô Honda Terry O. Morse, 1956)
Gojira (dir. Ishirô Honda, 1954)
The Graduate (dir. Mike Nichols, 1967)
The Greatest Show on Earth (dir. Cecil B. DeMille, 1952)
Grid Dunners (aka *Virtual Combal*, US; dir. Andrew Stevens, 1996)
Guess Who's Coming to Dinner (dir. Stanley Kramer, 1967)
Guyver: Out of Control (dir. Hiroshi Watamable, 1986)
Halloween (dir. John Carpenter, 1976)
Hana-Bi (dir. Takeshi, 1997)
Hardware (dir. Richard Stanley, 1990)
Harry Potter and the Philosopher's Stone (dir. Chris Columbus, 2001)
Hart's War (dir. Gregory Hablit, 2002)
Heal and Dust (dir. James Ivory, 1981)
High Noon (dir. Fred Zinnemann, 1952)
The Hundrback of Notre Dame (dir. William Dieterle, 1939)
Illusions Funambulesques (aka *Extraordinary Illusions*, dir. George Méliès, 1903)
The Incredibles (dir. Brad Bird, 2004)
Independence Day (dir. Roland Emmerich, 1996)
Indiana Jones and the Last Causade (dir. Steven Spielberg, 1989)
Indiana Jones and the Temple of Doom (dir. Steven Spielberg, 1984)
Invaders from Mars (dir. William Cameron Menzies, 1953)
Invasion (dir. Alan Bridges, 1966)
Invasion of the Body Snatchers (dir. Don Siegel, 1956)
Invasion of the Saucer Men (dir. Edward Cahn, 1957)
Invasion USA (dir. Alfred E. Green, 1952)
It Came from beneath the Sea (dir. Robert Gordon, 1955)
It Came from outer Space (dir. Jack Arnold, 1953)
It Conquered the World (dir. Roger Corman, 1956)
It! The Terror from Beyond Space (dir. Edward L. Kahn, 1958)
It's Always Fair Weather (dir. Gene Kelly and Stanley Donen, 1955)
Jaws (dir. Steven Spielberg, 1975)
Johnny Mnemonic (dir. Robert Longo, 1995)
Jurassic Park (dir. Steven Spielberg, 1993)

Just Imagine (dir. David Butler, 1930)
Kingdom of Heaven (dir. Ridley Scott, 2005)
King Kong (dir. Merian C. Cooper Ernest B. Schoedsack, 1933)
A Kiss Before Dying (dir. James Dearden, 1991)
Lara Croft: Tomb Raider (dir. Simon West, 2001)
The Last Starfighter (dir. Nick Castle, 1984)
The Lawnmower Man (dir. Brett Leonard, 1992)
The Lion King (dir. Roger Allers, 1994)
Logan's Run (dir. Michael Anderson, 1976)
The Lonely Shore (dir. Ken Russell, 1964)
The Lord of the Rings: The Fellowship of the Ring (dir. Peter Jackson, 2001)
The Lost City (dir. Harry Revier, 1933)
Lost in Space (dir. Stephen Hopkins, 1998)
The Love Pill (dir. Kenneth Turner, 1971)
Luxor Jr. (dir. John Lasseter, 1986)
Mad Max (dir. George Millor, 1979)
Mahlor (dir. Ken Russell, 1974)
(The Man Who Fell to Earth (dir. Nicholas Roeg, 1976)
(Mars Attacks! (dir. Tim Burton, 1996)
Marty (dir. Delbert Mann, 1955)
The Matrix (dir. Larry and Andy Wachowski, 1999)
The Matrix Reloaded (dir. Larry and Andy Wachowski, 2003)
The Matrix Revolutions (dir. Larry and Andy Wachowski, 2003)
Men in Black (dir. Barry Sonnenfeld, 1997)
Men in Black II (dir. Barry Sonnenfeld, 2002)
Metropolis (dir. Fritz Lang, 1927)
Minority Report (dir. Steven Spielberg, 2002)
Miss Evers' Boys (dir. Joseph Sargent, 1997)
Monsters Inc. (dir. Pete Docter, 2001)
Mortal Kombat (dir. Paul Anderson, 1995)
The '?' Motorist (dir. Walter R. Booth, 1906)
My Beautiful Laundrette (dir. Stephen Frears, 1985)
Nemesis (dir. Albert Pyun, 1993)
Nemesis 2: Nebula (dir. Albert Pyun, 1995)
Nemesis III: Prey Hardor (dir. Albert Pyun, 1996)
Nemesis 4: Death Angel (dir. Albert Pyun, 1997)
The Net (dir. Irwin Winkler, 1995)
The Night Caller (dir. John Gilling, 1965)
The One (dir. James Wong, 2001)
Panic in the Year Zero (dir. Ray Milland, 1962)
The Passion of the Christ (dir. Mel Gibson, 2004)
Peeping Tom (dir. Michael Powell, 1960)
The Phantom of the Air (dir. Ray Taylor, 1933)
Pirates of the Caribbean (dir. Gore Verbinski, 2003)
Plan 9 from Outer Space (dir. Ed Wood Jr, 1959)
Planet of the Apes (dir. Franklin J. Schaffner, 1968)
Predator (dir. John McTiernan, 1987)
Psycho (dir. Alfred Hitchcock, 1960)
The Quatermass Conclusion (dir. Piers Haggard, 1978)
The Quatermass Experiment (dir. Val Guest, 1955)
Quatermass and the Pit (dir. Roy Ward Baker, 1967)
Quatermass II (dir. Val Guest, 1957)

Quest for Love (dir. Ralph Thomas, 1971)
Raiders of the Lost Ark (dir. Steven Spielberg, 1981)
Rebel without a Cause (dir. Nicholas Ray, 1955)
Red Planet Mars (dir. Harry Horner, 1952)
Red's Dream (dir. John Lasseter, 1987)
Repo Man (dir. Alex Cox, 1984)
Resident Evil (dir. Paul Anderson, 2002)
Robocop (dir. Paul Verhoeven, 1987)
Robocop 2 (dir. Irvin Kershner, 1990)
Robocop 3 (dir. Fred Dekkor, 1993)
Roman Holiday (dir. William Wyler, 1953)
A Room with a View (dir. James Ivory, 1985)
Samson and Delilah (dir. Cecil B. DeMille, 1949)
Savage Messiah (dir. Ken Russell, 1972)
Schindler's List (dir. Steven Spielberg, 1993)
The Shadow of the Eagle (dir. Ford Beebe, 1932)
Singin' in the Rain (dir. Gene Kelly, Stanley Donen, 1952)
Den Skaebnesvangre (dir. Ford Beebe, 1910)
Solaris (dir. Andei Tarkovsky, 1972)
Soylent Green (dir. Richard Fleischer, 1973)
Spartacus (dir. Stanley Kubrick, 1960)
Spider-Man (dir. Sam Raimi, 2002)
Stalag 17 (dir. Billy Wilder, 1953)
Stargate (dir. Roland Emmerich, 1994)
Starship Troopers (dir. Paul Verhoeven, 1997)
Star Trek: First Contact (dir. Jonathan Frakes, 1996)
Star Trek: The Motion Picture (dir. Robert Wise, 1979)
Star Trek: The Wrath of Khan (dir. Nicholas Meyer, 1982)
Star Wars (dir. George Lucas, 1977)
The Stepford Wives (dir. Bryan Forbes, 1975)
Strange Days (dir. Kathryn Bigelow, 1995)
Stranger from Venus (dir. Burt Balaban, 1954)
A Streetcar Named Desire (dir. Elia Kazan, 1951)
Street-fighter (dir. Steven E. De Souza, 1994)
Subway (dir. Luc Besson, 1985)
The Ten Commandments (dir. Cecil B. DeMille, 1956)
The Terminal Man (dir. Michael Hodges, 1974)
The Terminator (dir. James Cameron, 1984)
Terminator 2: Judgment Day (dir. James Cameron, 1991)
Terminator 3: Rise of the Madines (dir. Jonathan Mostow, 2003)
Le Thaumaturge Chinois (aka *Tchin-Chao: The Chinese Conjurer*, dir. George Méliès, 1904)
Them! (dir. Gordon Douglas, 1954)
The Thing (dir. Howard Hawks, 1951)
Things to Come (dir. William Cameron Menzies, 1936)
This Island Earth (dir. Joseph M. Newman, 1955)
The Time Machine (dir. George Pal, 1960)
The Time Machine (dir. Simon Wells, 2002)
The Time Travelers (dir. Ib Melchior, 1964)
Tin Toy (dir. John Lasseter, 1988)
Total Recall (dir. Paul Verhoeven, 1990)
The Trip (dir. Roger Corman, 1967)

Triumph of the Will (dir. Leni Riefenstahl, 1935)
Tron (dir. Steven Lisberger, 1982)
2001: A Space Odyssey (dir. Stanley Kubrick, 1968)
Unearthly Stranger (dir. John Crish, 1963)
United 93 (dir. Paul Greengrass, 2006)
Universal Soldier (dir. Roland Emmerich, 1992)
Until the End of the World (dir. Wim Wenders, 1991)
Vertigo (dir. Alfred Hitchcock, 1958)
Village of the Damned (dir. Wolf Rilla, 1960)
Virtual Combat (aka *Grid Runners*, UK; dir. Andrew Stevens, 1996)
Virtuosity (dir. Brett Leonard, 1995)
Virus (dir. John Bruno, 1999)
Les Visiteurs (dir. Joan-Marie Poiré, 1993)
Le Voyage dans la lune (dir. Georges Méliès, 1902)
Le Voyage à travers l'impossible (dir. Georges Méliès, 1904)
The War of the Worlds (dir. Byron Haskin, 1953)
War of the Worlds (dir. Steven Spielberg, 2005)
Westworld (dir. Michael Crichton, 1973)
We Were Soldiers (dir. Randall Wallace, 2002)
The Wild Angels (dir. Roger Corman, 1966)
The Wild One (dir. László Benedek, 1953)
Willow (dir. Ron Howard, 1988)
The Wizard of Oz (dir. Victor Fleming, 1939)
The World Trade Center (dir. Oliver Stone, 2006)
X the Unknown (dir. Leslie Norman, 1956)
Zardoz (dir. John Boorman, 1974)

INDEX

Note: page numbers in italics denote illustrations